CULTURE, POWER, PLACE

CULTURE

POWER

PLACE

EXPLORATIONS IN CRITICAL ANTHROPOLOGY

EDITED BY AKHIL GUPTA AND JAMES FERGUSON

DUKE UNIVERSITY PRESS   DURHAM AND LONDON 1997

Third Printing, 2001
© 1997 Duke University Press
All rights reserved
Printed in the United States of America on acid-free paper ∞
Typeset in Baskerville by Keystone Typesetting, Inc.
Library of Congress Cataloging-in-Publication Data appear
on the last printed page of this book.

CONTENTS

PART II: CULTURE, POWER, RESISTANCE

ACKNOWLEDGMENTS

This collection of essays originally grew out of three organized sessions presented some years ago at meetings of the American Anthropological Association (AAA). One, organized by Akhil Gupta and Lisa Rofel, dealt with "The Culture and Politics of Space"; another, organized by Liisa Malkki and James Ferguson, concerned "Themes of Place and Locality in the Collective Identity of Mobile and Displaced Populations"; while a third, organized by Roger Rouse, was titled "Transformers: The Cultural Politics of Bricolage." Early versions of all essays in this collection were originally presented in these sessions, with the exception of Gupta's "The Song of the Nonaligned World" and Gupta and Ferguson's "Culture, Power, Place: Ethnography at the End of an Era," which were written later.

The papers by Malkki, Borneman, Ferguson, Rofel, Gupta, and Gupta and Ferguson ("Beyond 'Culture' ") all appeared in a special 1992 issue of *Cultural Anthropology* (7 [1]) devoted to the theme of space and place in anthropology. They are reprinted here (in substantially revised form) with the kind permission of the AAA. We also thank Michael Watts for contributing a thoughtful commentary to the *Cultural Anthropology* volume, which we have found stimulating in the continuing development of our own thinking about space and place.

It was Arjun Appadurai who first suggested that the themes we had originally developed as AAA sessions might be brought together and who first put us in touch with one another. For that, he has our thanks and appreciation. Akhil Gupta would also like to thank Lisa Rofel for co-organizing the original panel, and Purnima Mankekar, whose critical reading and commentary throughout has contributed much to the project. James Ferguson would like to acknowledge the influence of Liisa Malkki's thinking in shaping his ideas about space, place, and identity. Her acute comments and imaginative discussion contributed greatly to this project. He also thanks Roger Rouse for a long, thoughtful conversation about the themes integrating the volume. We are both grateful to John Peters for a helpful critical reading of both the introductory essay and "Beyond 'Culture' " at a late stage. We thank Ken Wissoker at Duke University Press for his unflagging support and confidence in the project, through what has been a sometimes difficult process. Finally, we are grateful to the two anonymous reviewers for Duke University Press for a host of unusually valuable and constructive suggestions that have helped to make this a better book.

AKHIL GUPTA AND JAMES FERGUSON

AFTER "PEOPLES AND CULTURES"

It has become usual to assert that the theoretical thread linking twentieth-century American cultural anthropology through its various moods and manifestations has been the concept of culture. In a sense, this is true. Certainly, the Boasian success in establishing the autonomy of the cultural from biological-cum-racial determination set the stage for the most important theoretical developments to follow. But perhaps just as central as the concept of "culture" has been what we might call the concept of "cultures": the idea that a world of human differences is to be conceptualized as a diversity of separate societies, each with its own culture. It was this key conceptual move that made it possible, in the early years of the century, to begin speaking not only of culture but also of "a culture" — a separate, individuated cultural entity, typically associated with "a people," "a tribe," "a nation," and so forth (Stocking 1982:202–3).[1] It was this entity ("a culture") that provided the theoretical basis for cross-cultural comparison, as well as the normal frame for ethnographic description (hence accounts of "Hopi culture," fieldwork "among the Ndembu," and so on). This often implicit conceptualization of the world as a mosaic of separate cultures is what made it possible to bound the ethnographic object and to seek generalization from a multiplicity of separate cases.[2]

The later development of the idea of "a culture" as forming a system of meaning only reinforced this vision of the world.[3] A culture, whether pictured as a semiotic system to be deciphered (Marshall Sahlins) or as a text to be read (Clifford Geertz), required description and analysis as an integrated totality. As a universe of shared meaning, each culture was radically set apart from other cultures, which had, of course, "their own" meanings, their own holistic logic.

Today, it would be widely agreed that it has become increasingly difficult to conduct anthropological research in these terms. In ethnographic practice, as in theoretical debate, the dominant "peoples and cultures" ideal carries ever less conviction. Ethnographically, much of the best work today no longer fits within the model of a study of "a culture," while the most challenging contemporary fieldwork cannot be contained within the stereotypical "among the so-and-so" mold. What would once have appeared as a logical impossibility — ethnography without the ethnos — has come to appear, to many, perfectly sensible, even necessary (Appadurai 1991). Theoretically, too, a move away from the "peoples and cultures" vision of the world, always a live concern for a small section of anthropologists, appears to have become a leading position within the discipline.

Two otherwise quite different lines of anthropological critique have converged on this point. First, scholars employing political economic approaches have for some time insisted on foregrounding regional and global forms of connectedness, while denying the ideas of separateness and isolation implicit in anthropological ideas of "cultures" (Gunder Frank 1967; Mintz 1985; Wallerstein 1974; Wolf 1982). In Eric Wolf's memorable image, the division of "a totality of interconnected processes" into a set of discrete, homogeneous "billiard balls" (whether cultures, societies, or nations) threatens "to turn names into things" (1982:3, 6). In place of such a world of separate, integrated cultural systems, then, political economy turned the anthropological gaze in the direction of social and economic processes that connected even the most isolated of local settings with a wider world.[4]

More recently, a far-reaching critique of representation has undermined in a rather different way the traditional anthropological confidence in the solidity of its analytic objects, its "cultures" (Marcus and Fischer 1986; Clifford and Marcus 1986; Clifford 1988). Studies of ethnographic writing have revealed the apparent boundedness and coherence of "a culture" as something made rather than found; the "wholeness" of the holistically understood object appears more as a narrative device than as an objectively present empirical truth (Fabian 1990; Marcus 1989a; Thornton 1988). The "polyphony" of ethnographic fieldwork — the many different "voices" present in the actual discussions and dialogues through which ethnographic understandings are constructed — is contrasted with the monophonic authorial voice of the conventional ethnographic monograph. Such critiques have implied that anthropology's "cultures" must be seen as less uni- *obs!* tary and more fragmented, their boundedness more of a literary fiction — albeit a "serious fiction" (Clifford 1988:10) — than as some sort of natural fact. If anthropologists working in this vein continue to speak of "culture," in spite of such concerns, it is with a clear awareness of just how problematic a concept this has become. "Culture," as James Clifford laments, remains "a deeply compromised idea I cannot yet do without" (1988:10).[5]

At the level of anthropological theory, then, the turn away from ideas of whole, separate "cultures" would appear to be fairly well established. Yet what such a shift might mean for ethnographic practice, we suggest, is still very much in the process of being worked out.[6] As a way of clarifying the issues at stake and indicating some useful ways in which an ethnography beyond "cultures" might proceed, we will begin by discussing two broad sets of issues that seem especially important to us. The first of these centers on questions of place and the way *place!* that culture is spatialized, whereas the second deals with issues raised by relationships between culture and power. These two overarching themes provide the basic organizational structure for the volume, with *culture & place* the first half concentrating on issues of culture and place and the second half highlighting questions of culture and power.

The authors of essays in part 1 aim to raise questions about anthropology's implicit mapping of the world as a series of discrete, territorialized cultures. The idea that "a culture" is naturally the property of a spatially localized people and that the way to study such a culture is to go "there" ("among the so-and-so") has long been part of the unremarked common sense of anthropological practice. Yet, once questioned, this anthropological convention dissolves into a series of challenging and important issues about the contested relations between difference, identity, and place.

At a time when cultural difference is increasingly becoming deterritorialized because of the mass migrations and transnational culture flows of a late capitalist, postcolonial world (as Arjun Appadurai, Ulf Hannerz, and others have pointed out), there is obviously a special interest in understanding the way that questions of identity and cultural difference are spatialized in new ways. The circumstances of an accelerating "global cultural ecumene" (Hannerz 1989; Appadurai and Breckenridge 1988a:3; Appadurai 1990; Foster 1991), of a "world in creolization" (Hannerz 1987), make the project of exploring the intertwined processes of place making and people making in the complex cultural politics of the nation-state an especially vital part of the contemporary anthropological agenda. Certainly, such real-world developments do much to account for the increased academic visibility of these theoretical issues.

But the larger point is not simply the claim that cultures are no longer (were they ever?) fixed in place. Rather, the point, well acknowledged but worth restating, is that all associations of place, people, and culture are social and historical creations to be explained, not given natural facts. This is as true for the classical style of "peoples and cultures" ethnography as it is for the perhaps more culturally chaotic present. And the implication, animating an enormous amount of more recent work in anthropology and elsewhere,[7] is that whatever associations of place and culture may exist must be taken as problems for anthropological research rather than the given ground that one takes as a point of departure; cultural territorializations (like ethnic and national ones) must be understood as complex and contingent results of ongoing historical and political processes. It is these processes, rather than pregiven cultural-territorial entities, that require anthropological study.

A second sort of critique that has helped to move discussions of difference beyond the idea of "cultures" is highlighted in part 2. This line of criticism raises questions over the classical idea of culture as "order," emphasizing instead questions of partiality, perspective, and — above all — power. The idea of culture as order — standing, like a Hobbesian Leviathan, against the ever present threat of chaos and anomie — is, of course, a very well established one in Western thought. Whether styled as the functionalist glue making social cohesion possible (the Durkheimian reading); the abstract code enabling societal communication (the structuralist one); or the domain of shared, intersubjective meanings that alone make sense of symbolic social action (the Weberian/Geertzian interpretation), concepts of culture have consistently emphasized the shared, the agreed on, and the orderly.

Marxist and feminist revisions in the 1960s and 1970s only partly displaced these earlier visions.[8] By centering questions of domination, both approaches made it possible to ask searching questions about how the cultural "rules of the game" got made, by whom, and for whom. But the idea of culture (and of ideology) as order remained mostly intact, even as that order was politicized.[9]

More recent developments, sometimes (if misleadingly) lumped together under the label "poststructuralism," have implied a more complicated conception. From Foucault (1978, 1980) ethnographers
have borrowed the idea that power relations permeate all levels of
society, with a field of resistances that is coextensive with them. From
such writers as Bourdieu (1977) and de Certeau (1984), they have
taken a stress on the active practices of social agents, who never simply
enact culture but reinterpret and reappropriate it in their own ways.
And from Gramsci (1971) and his more recent interpreters (Raymond Williams [1977] and Stuart Hall [1986] chief among them),
they have taken a focus on the partiality, the eternally incomplete
nature of hegemony, with its implication of the cultural as a contested, contingent political field, the battlefield in an ongoing "war of
position."

For those who seek to make sense of contemporary processes of
cultural globalization and transnational culture flows, these theoretical developments raise a rich set of ethnographic possibilities. Rather
than opposing autonomous local cultures to a homogenizing movement of cultural globalization, the authors in this volume seek to trace
the ways in which dominant cultural forms may be picked up and
used — and significantly transformed — in the midst of the field of
power relations that links localities to a wider world. The emphasis is
on the complex and sometimes ironic political processes through
which cultural forms are imposed, invented, reworked, and transformed. The sense of culture as a space of order and agreed-on meanings, meanwhile, undergoes a transformation of its own in the process.
Rather than simply a domain of sharing and commonality, culture
figures here more as a site of difference and contestation, simultaneously ground and stake of a rich field of cultural-political practices.

Such approaches in anthropology link up at this point, of course,
with a large body of more recent work in cultural studies.[10] This area
has been one of the most exciting within more current interdisciplinary activity, and the essays in part 2 reveal how much is to be gained
from such cross-fertilizations at the interstices of disciplines. It is clear,
at the same time, though, that even as they refer to issues raised in
cultural studies, the pieces in this volume continue to stress the value
of an ethnographic approach. The attention to "reading" cultural
products and public representations here does not displace but com-
plements the characteristically anthropological emphasis on daily rou-
tines and lived experience.

These two lines of critical thinking about culture that we have sketched here — the line through space and the line through power — are intimately intertwined. In the essays to follow, it is possible to identify three major themes that crosscut the two-part organization of the volume and bring together a set of crucial issues about the interrelations of culture, power, and place: place making, identity, and resistance.

PLACE MAKING

The challenge to spatially territorialized notions of culture leads the contributors of this volume to emphasize processes and practices of place making. Anthropologists have long studied spatial units larger than the "local," and a well-established anthropological tradition exists that has emphasized interrelations and linkages between local settings and larger regional or global structures and processes. Such studies have led to rich and informative accounts that have deepened the collective disciplinary understanding of particular regions or "peoples," enlivening the methods and techniques of fieldwork as traditionally conceived. Too often, however, anthropological approaches to the relation between "the local" and something that lies beyond it (regional, national, international, global) have taken the local as given, without asking how perceptions of locality and community are discursively and historically constructed. In place of the question, How is the local linked to the global or the regional? then, we prefer to start with another question that enables a quite different perspective on the topic: How are understandings of locality, community, and region formed and lived? To answer this question, we must turn away from the commonsense idea that such things as locality and community are simply given or natural and turn toward a focus on social and political processes of place making, conceived less as a matter of "ideas" than of embodied practices that shape identities and enable resistances (see also Bird et al. 1993; Friedland and Boden 1994; Harvey 1993; Massey 1994; Morley and Robins 1995; Probyn 1990; Pratt 1984; and Pred and Watts 1992).

The contributions to this volume suggest just how complicated commonsensical notions of "locality" or "community" actually turn out to be. Liisa Malkki's essay elegantly demonstrates that concepts of locality or community can appear natural and unproblematic because of what she calls "a metaphysics of sedentarism," in which the rootedness of peoples and cultures in "their own" territories is taken as the normal state in the taken-for-granted "national order of things." This pervasive, implicit vision of a natural world of "peoples" unproblematically rooted in their proper soils, Malkki argues, has powerfully shaped the ways in which such things as displacement and mobility have been conceptualized by anthropologists and others.

Rather than begin with the premise that locality and community are obvious, that their recognition and affective power flow automatically out of direct sensory experience and face-to-face encounters, our contributors argue that the apparently immediate experience of community is in fact inevitably constituted by a wider set of social and spatial relations. Thus we suggest that it is fundamentally mistaken to conceptualize different kinds of non- or supralocal identities (diasporic, refugee, migrant, national, and so forth) as spatial and temporal extensions of a prior, natural identity rooted in locality and community. Such thinking, we find, often haunts contemporary anthropological approaches to local communities, where "the local" is understood as the original, the centered, the natural, the authentic, and opposed to "the global," understood as new, external, artificially imposed, and inauthentic (Probyn 1990; Young 1990).[11] Such conventional oppositions of local and global often entail, as Doreen Massey (1994) has pointed out, a gendered association of the local with women and with a feminized private, domestic, or natural space. Through such associations, a feminized "local" may come to seem the "natural" basis of home and community, whereas an implicitly masculine "global" is cast as an artificial intrusion on it (Massey 1994:9–10). Only by challenging such deeply entrenched thinking does it become possible for an anthropological exploration of "the local" to proceed without succumbing to a nostalgia for origins.

Mary Crain's essay is a fine example of such a critical approach to "the local." The identity of a new, democratic Spain, she argues, involves a nostalgia for rurality in which the reinvention of regional traditions plays a critical role. One such "local" religious pilgrimage, to the Virgin of El Rocío, has been radically transformed by its incorporation as a nostalgic point of reference in a new "regional-national" narrative. No longer of only "local" interest, the pilgrimage today forms a spectacle in which hundreds of tourists, representatives of the media broadcasting the event live to a worldwide audience, and trendy urban elites all participate. Faced with the transformation of "their" pilgrimage by diverse regional, national, and transnational reconstructions of locality, villagers in the region have reconfigured the event by shifting the emphasis from the shrine of the Virgin itself to the locations traversed in undergoing the pilgrimage. In so doing, a particularly brazen subgroup of these villagers further distinguish their experience of the pilgrimage from that of the visiting urban *yupeez* who would join them by referring to themselves as "Indians" and to the *yupeez* as "cowboys." To be a "local" in this Andalusian *romería* (pilgrimage) is thus to possess an identity shaped by contestations within the nationalist recuperation of the colorful and diverse regional traditions that make up Spain, transnational representations of the exotic cult of the Virgin of El Rocío, the desire of urbanites to experience a vanishing authentic rurality characterized by knowable communities, and the reappropriation of a frontier narrative imported from Hollywood in which the more rebellious, youthful villagers cast themselves as "Indians" in opposition to "cowboys." This case is an excellent ethnographic demonstration of just how far the meanings of "locality" and "community" are from being self-evident.

In her fascinating and provocative essay, Kristin Koptiuch provides an example of how a neighborhood, a Puerto Rican barrio in North Philadelphia, has been remade as a "third world" imperial frontier by transnational and global forces. The urban ghetto, depopulated by an exodus of the middle class, disciplined by the forces of state repression, saddled by cutbacks in federal monies, and facing increasing unemployment as a result of post-Fordist globalization of production, is transformed into a unique "locality," a "third world at home." Koptiuch points out that the "third world" is "a *name,* a representation, not a place" that can be geographically mapped as distinct from the "first world." The irony is that this place, made by struggles waged by forces of transnational capital, the state, and the residents of the barrio, then becomes a site for ethnographic constructions of "authentic" ways of life, to be recorded by folklorists. By pointing to anthropologists' and reporters' complicity in constructing representations of authentic localities (which thereby become suitable places to do "fieldwork"), Koptiuch highlights the fact that the establishment of spatial meanings — the making of spaces into places — is always implicated in hegemonic configurations of power. Even when displaying continuity with older patterns of urban poverty, the sweatshops, racism, homelessness, gang warfare, unemployment, and so forth of the present are inserted into a new series of global transformations that have altered their relationship with the structures and discourses of domination and exploitation. Thus, Koptiuch's essay forces us to be vigilant about the historicity of constructions of locality and community, a theme to which other articles in this volume have much to contribute as well.

Like Crain and Koptiuch, John Durham Peters focuses on the spatially dispersed forces—regional, national, and transnational—that mediate the experience of "knowable communities." Drawing imaginatively on his field of media studies and communication theory, Peters argues that one way to characterize modernity is to see it as the condition of "bifocality," in which social actors simultaneously experience the local and the global, possessing both "near-sight" and "far-sight." Bifocality is made possible by processes of social representation that first became widespread in the eighteenth century: newspapers, novels, statistics, encyclopedias, dictionaries, and panoramas. Peters points out that both novels and statistics represent invisible social totalities, the one by narrative, the other by aggregation. The irony is that these techniques of social representation in the mass media portray the "global" as a coherent and graspable vision, whereas the "local" environment is experienced fleetingly and incoherently through the senses: our perception of fair weather as indicated by blue skies is undercut by the knowledge disseminated on television that the weather satellite "sees" a storm. In this way, the global circulation of capital, signs, bodies, and commodities actively configures the experience of locality itself rather than imposing itself from the "outside" as a source of confinement or constraint. Like Koptiuch, Peters criticizes the penchant in ethnographic work to prize "the local," suggesting that the romance of spatial confinement was that it contrasted "the native's" supposed enchantment, tradition, culture, and simplicity with the ethnographer's spatial mobility, which stood for enlightenment, modernity, science, and development.

It is not surprising, then, that there is so little ethnographic work on the mass media. The mass media violate the notion that places are containers of integrated cultures: the words and images of mass media travel to you rather than you having to travel to them; they are commonly understood to be alienated discourse, not the expression of the consciousness and worldview of a collective "people" seen as originating authors; and they are mediated by the market, not rooted in place, tradition, or locality. Peters's essay profoundly upsets the commonsensical notions that "nearsightedness" characterizes "the local" and that the way to understand the relation of "local" to "global" is one of linkage, mediation, or articulation. He instead suggests such concepts as configuration, constitution, construction, and perhaps even emanation: the person who interprets blue skies through the satellite map represented on the television screen reverses the commonsensical reliance on sensory perception and the ontological imperative of presence. The "native's point of view" on even the most local of happenings may be as much formed by the mass media as by immediate sensory perception, because the mass media may form an integral or, better still, constitutive part of the lived experience of face-to-face communities.[12]

While Crain, Koptiuch, and Peters destabilize the spatial certainties inherent in notions of "locality" and "community," George Bisharat, Karen Leonard, and Malkki underscore the contingent historicity of the imagining of place by migrants and refugees. Bisharat demonstrates how the longing for "home" has changed for Palestinian refugees living in camps in the West Bank. Whereas return was previously conceived concretely in terms of a return to specific villages and particular dwellings, the rhetoric of Palestinian refugees has shifted over time toward an emphasis on a collective national return to "the homeland" conceived more abstractly. The society they had to leave behind was one in which attachment to land and to villages of origin, identified by distinctive patterns of speech and intonation, was unusually strong. People continued to be identified into the next generation by "their" villages, and even today many families retain keys to homes that have long since been destroyed by the occupation. As the chances of return became more remote, memories of particular homes were displaced by the memory of the "homeland," an intensely romanticized place sometimes likened to a lost lover. The imagery of exile portrayed the alliance of Palestinian life with the land, with earth and the elements, while seeing the occupation as a perversion of nature and a deviation from history. Bisharat focuses not merely on the connections between enforced displacement and place making in the form of imagining "home" and "homeland" but also poignantly shows how memory itself is exiled and shaken loose as its physical embodiments are erased: when children of refugees are finally allowed to visit the villages that have been enshrined in their parents' memories, they see just shrubs and trees, the villages and homes that once stood there having been systematically removed. In exile, there thus occurs a displacement of community, once understood as being rooted in particular localities, to the level of the nation. The connection of the idea of "community" to that of "locality" — a link that was once so strong — has now been sundered by the dual forces of memory and displacement.

Some of the same processes linking memory and refuge are found in Malkki's discussion of Hutu refugees from Burundi who now live in exile in Tanzania. She shows how two very different strategies of place making are employed by refugees living in two different contexts. Those living in refugee camps continued to see their displacement as a temporary condition, longing for a return to the "homeland" conceived as a moral as well as a geographical location. In contrast, those who lived in the town had made a new home in Kigoma and no longer saw themselves as a "community in exile." Memory and history played very different roles for these two groups. For the dwellers of the refugee camp, the "homeland" as a location was tied to their identity as a community of displaced people, a nation in exile; for the town dwellers, Burundi was a geographical location but not one that organized their sense of community in Tanzania. Where the camp refugees countered the "sedentarist metaphysics" that dominates Western scholarship with a nationalist metaphysics of their own, locating "the real homeland" in the moral trajectory of a displaced nation, the town refugees subverted "rooting" assumptions even more profoundly by cannily evading or manipulating every national, ethnic, or religious identity that might presume to capture them.

In her article on the superimposition of "Asian" landscapes on rural California by immigrant Japanese and Indian agricultural workers, Leonard provides a vivid demonstration of how the imaginative uses of memory enable people to construct localities and communities. Showing how some of these immigrants remade the geography of California's agricultural regions by faithfully overlaying the image of colonial Punjab on the Sacramento Valley, or that of the three kingdoms of third-century China on the Imperial Valley, paradoxically serves to highlight less the continuity of "community" and more its invention. What is striking about this seemingly wholesale "imposition" of an alien landscape is not its lack of inventiveness but rather the sheer audacity — one might even say, the excessiveness — of its ingenuity. How else could one account for a group of Punjabi men, mostly Sikh and Muslim, who married Catholic Mexican or Mexican American women because both partners could enter "Brown" where the form for obtaining the marriage license asked about "race" and thus not violate California's miscegenation laws; whose descendants spoke Span-

ish and English, practiced Catholicism, and referred to themselves as
"Hindu"; whose ashes, if Sikh, were scattered into either the "holy
waters" of the Salton Sea or the Pacific Ocean and who, if Muslim, lie
buried in "Hindu plots" in rural California cemeteries; who looked
out over the Sacramento Valley and saw a landscape *identical* to their
beloved Punjabi homeland? Prevented from owning land by California's Alien Land Laws of 1913 and 1920, these men created representations of their locales and communities that were entirely devoid of
the powerful Anglos who owned the land on which they farmed as well
as the industries that supplied most of the input to and absorbed the
output from agriculture. Imagining their new surroundings through
the memories of their homelands was not merely a means to wrap a
cloak of familiarity around a new landscape and thereby to reattain an
aura of mastery over the land but also a means to construct hybridized,
rhizomatic identities for their community of Indian–Mexican American families. Whereas earlier authors had destabilized "locality" by
drawing attention to the role of farsightedness, or transnational and
global forces, Leonard does so by focusing on the artful instabilities of
memory and invention (see also essays in Boyarin 1994).

IDENTITY

Leonard's essay leads us to the second important theme of this collection, namely, the relationship between constructions of "locality" and
"community," on the one hand, and identity, on the other. One of the
reasons for the multidisciplinary explosion of writing on the subject of
"identity" in the last few years (Schiller 1994) is that very different
kinds of political and analytic projects can be advanced under this
rubric. Although the interest in identity is often assumed to emanate
from a poststructuralist emphasis on the multiple, crosscutting, and
shifting basis of self-representation, the idea of identity itself is perfectly compatible with theoretical projects that move in a quite different direction. Indeed, discussions of identity, it seems to us, all too
easily fall into the model of possession and ownership embodied in
discourses about the sovereign subject: an identity is something that
one "has" and can manipulate, that one can "choose"; or, inversely, it
is something that acts as a source of "constraint" on the individual, as
an ascribed rather than a chosen feature of life. In both cases, the
individual subject is taken as a pregiven entity, identities as so many
masks or cages it may inhabit. Such positions are perfectly compatible

with the observation that identities (like the contents of "cultures" themselves) are historically contingent. But what is missing from such a conception is the crucial insight that the subject is not simply affected by changing schemes of categorization and discourses of difference but is actually constituted or interpellated by them. As Stuart Hall has suggested (cited in Watts 1992), rather than posit an essential temporal stability and continuity of the subject, we might better conceive of identity as a "meeting point" — a point of suture or temporary identification — that constitutes and re-forms the subject so as to enable that subject to act (see also Diprose and Ferrell 1991). It is in this way that we bring together identity and subject formation with the question of agency.

Our goal here is not to offer an introduction to the voluminous literature on the politics of identity but to highlight the contribution of this volume to understanding the specific relationship between place making and identity (Keith and Pile 1993). There is a tension between commonsensical notions of "rooted" localities and communities that imply a primordial and essential group identity and notions of identity which rely on the sovereign individual subject and which imply that it is something nonessential, an instrumental and strategic choice made by preconstituted (often styled "rational") social actors. This division has proved to be an enduring and central debate in the discussion of ethnicity. Perhaps the very terms within which this discussion proceeds needs to be abandoned. By stressing that place making always involves a construction, rather than merely a discovery, of difference, the authors of the essays here emphasize that identity neither "grows out" of rooted communities nor is a thing that can be possessed or owned by individual or collective social actors. It is, instead, a mobile, often unstable relation of difference.

Identity and alterity are therefore produced simultaneously in the formation of "locality" and "community." "Community" is never simply the recognition of cultural similarity or social contiguity but a categorical identity that is premised on various forms of exclusion and constructions of otherness. This fact is absolutely central to the question of who or what it is that "has" such identities (a group? an individual?), for it is precisely through processes of exclusion and othering that both collective and individual subjects are formed. With respect to locality as well, at issue is not simply that one is located in a certain place but that the particular place is set apart from and opposed to other places. The "global" relations that we have argued are constitutive of locality are therefore centrally involved in the production of "local" identities too. As the essays in this volume demonstrate, the construction of difference is neither a matter of recognizing an already present commonality nor of inventing an "identity" out of whole cloth but an effect of structural relations of power and inequality. Questions of identity therefore demonstrate with special clarity the intertwining of place and power in the conceptualization of "culture." Rather than following straightforwardly from sharing the "same" culture, community, or place, identity emerges as a continually contested domain.

Furthermore, as Michael Watts (1992) reminds us, efforts to forge identities are not always successful. Because of the widespread tendency to take identities as self-evident or automatic, not enough scholarly attention has been paid to the frequent failure of projects that seek to map the construction of selves onto the creation of territorial or other sorts of "communities." In other words, the question of identity has often been approached in a manner that tends to diminish the role of processes of legitimation and authentication. Restoring these concerns to the heart of the discussion of identity would enable us to ask not only why certain kinds of identities become salient at particular historical moments but also why some marks of distinction and difference do not form the basis of an identity.

Although all the essays in this volume speak to the various relations of difference and inequality that shape the construction of identities, those most centrally concerned with it are by John Borneman, James Ferguson, and Akhil Gupta. In his essay, Borneman skillfully demonstrates that the same historical event may have very different outcomes for the construction of national identities by comparing what were formerly East Berlin and West Berlin. The two German states formed after the Second World War not only had to distance themselves from the Nazi regime but each also had to construct itself as being different from and superior to the other. The West German state, while periodizing Fascism narrowly as the time between 1933 and 1945, adopted all the norms of citizenship of the Nazi regime. "Belonging" came to be defined through blood ties encoded in the notion of "German descent." Thus immigrants who had become culturally or linguistically "German" found themselves legally excluded from citizenship, even when, as with Turkish workers, they obtained rights of permanent residence, whereas people of "German descent" who had settled anywhere in the world in the past two hundred years were eligible to join the national "community." By contrast, official East German historiography traced Nazism to the emergence of capitalism after the German defeat of 1918. Citizenship was open to anyone who came from a socialist state: membership in the national community was defined in terms of class identity and socialist pedigree. The West German state constructed a new national identity for its citizens not by emphasizing descent (which could not serve to distinguish West German nationality from East German) but by emplotting the currency reform of 1948 and postwar prosperity as a clean break with the Nazi past. This national narrative found resonance in individual lives through automobile ownership and foreign travel, two symbols that gave concrete form to national prosperity for millions of citizens. By contrast, the East German state was unable, through its rhetoric of people, state, and party, to offer a national narrative that linked up with individual lives. Women in East Germany found socially valued employment outside the home in large numbers, but no parallel domain existed in which men could construct an identity that compared favorably with their counterparts in West Germany. Instead of a close fit, there was an ironic distancing, a dislocation, between individual identities and state narratives. Here, then, is an example of what Watts (1992:124) has termed an "identity failure," as the efforts of the nation-state to construct a national community by emphasizing its difference (and superiority) from West Germany ended up being subverted by citizens' ironic interpretations that emphasized the difference between their inferior Trabants ("sounds like a lawnmower, moves like a racing pasteboard") and the Mazdas, Volkswagens, and Volvos of their capitalist neighbors.

Like Borneman, Ferguson too conceptualizes identity as a relation of difference. In the Zambian case that he examines, however, the identity issues concern not two national communities but the mutually determining and antagonistic relations between "town" and "country." The "country" was employed first by nationalists and later by postcolonial regimes as an imagined locus of purity, cooperation, sharing, and neighborliness. The purported opposition of the values of the countryside with those of the city served both to inspire urban workers to act in the "national interest" and to discipline them. These urban workers included people who displayed a "cosmopolitan" style which asserted distance from rural kin and which indicated a desire to remain in the city after retirement and others who adhered to a "localist" style in which workers invested heavily, both financially and emotionally, in maintaining links with the "home" village, with the intention of moving back after retirement. Thus, discourses about rurality in the urban political arena found echoes in the lives of workers in the Copperbelt. But the enormous economic decline of the 1980s changed the significance and meaning of the opposition between rural and urban. In public discourse, the decline came to be explained by an inwardly directed moral critique that did not spare even the village as a sanctified place. The country lost its moral character and came to be seen as an increasingly corrupt place. "Cosmopolitan" workers who never dreamt of going back to their "home" villages found they were forced to do so by economic pressures. On their return, they were confronted by hostile kin whom they had long ignored. More localist workers, those who had all along kept an eye on the village "home," might have been expected to benefit from this turn of events. But they too found themselves in a difficult spot. For as these localist workers were being squeezed between the expectations of their rural kin (themselves suffering through economic hard times) and their own shrinking real wages, rural villagers in general (previously idealized by such rurally oriented urbanites for their generosity and humanity) came to be perceived as increasingly grasping and demanding. Both sorts of urban workers, therefore, though for different reasons, began to resent the village as a selfish and sinister place. The country, long an imagined locus of goodness and purity ("the real Zambia"), became increasingly the site of a decidedly unromantic social antagonism. Ferguson demonstrates how transformations in global political economy work their way into changing conceptions of place, which are, in turn, fundamental to the construction of identities. In the period before the economic collapse, different sets of workers — cosmopolitans and localists — maintained contrasting urban identities that depended on constructions of community in which the villagers "at home" played roles of other and ally, respectively. These positions of disengagement and affiliation were made possible by a buoyant economy. When conditions changed significantly during the eighties, the particular binary of cosmopolitanism and localism was reconfigured, as both sets of workers, for different reasons, found their relationships with "the village" to be fundamentally transformed. National narratives and individual identities that were both anchored in a common vision of the countryside collapsed, and the meaning of "the village" as a place changed dramatically.

In a manner analogous to Ferguson's historicization of images of the countryside, Gupta's contribution to this volume situates the formation of national identities within the macrologies of decolonization and late capitalism. By comparing the formation of national identities with those provided by such forms of transnational community as the Nonaligned Movement and the European Community, Gupta focuses on the role of forms of legitimation and forces of spatial organization that make certain identities viable in the contemporary world. Discussions of nationalism often proceed by focusing almost entirely on the historical and cultural practices of place making within a given territory. Yet, in so doing, they leave open the larger question of why nation-states have become the dominant form of organizing space in the contemporary world as well as what challenges other forms of imagining community and constructing identity — transnational, international, or subnational — might offer nationalism at the present time. Gupta emphasizes not only that processes of place making are always contested and unstable but also that relations between places are continuously shifting as a result of the political and economic reorganization of space in the world system. The legitimation and authentication of national identities, therefore, can be understood by opposing it both to other national identities and to commitments and affiliations with other communities that have an altogether different basis of spatial organization. In other words, national identities need to be understood against subnational ones and against supranational identities — and perhaps even against forms of imagining community that are not territorially based.

RESISTANCE

The relation between identity and place illuminates processes of subject construction, which brings us to the third major theme of this collection, namely, resistance. So far, we have emphasized how place making involves a play of differences. The structures of feeling that enable meaningful relationships with particular locales, constituted and experienced in a particular manner, necessarily include the marking of "self" and "other" through identification with larger collectivities. To be part of a community is to be positioned as a particular kind of subject, similar to others within the community in some crucial respects and different from those who are excluded from it. In insisting that these identities are not "freely" chosen but overdetermined by structural location and that their durability and stability are not to be taken for granted but open to contestation and reformulation, we wish to draw attention to the crucial role played by resistance.

Few concepts in the recent past have proved to be as popular — and as elusive — as has "resistance" (see especially the thoughtful essays by Sherry Ortner [1995], Lila Abu-Lughod [1990], and Martha Kaplan and John Kelly [1994]), and it is certainly not our intention here to rehearse the multitudinous ways in which the term has been overused. We propose to stick closely to the Foucauldian sense of the term in two essential regards.

First, we do not propose to make resistance the property of a sovereign subject who is either transcendental with respect to the course of history or evolving within it (Foucault 1980:117). Rather, the task is to understand that form of power "which categorizes the individual, marks him by his own individuality, attaches him to his own identity . . . a form of power which makes individuals subjects. There are two meanings of the word subject: subject to someone else by control and dependence, and tied to his own identity by a conscience or self-knowledge" (Foucault 1983a:212; see also Althusser 1971). These themes of being attached or fastened to identity will be particularly crucial for our purposes.

Second, we wish to underline the conjunctural and strategic aspects of resistance: affixed or indexed not to particular acts, events, or results — or even to the attainment, development, or secure occupancy of a state of consciousness — but to an ongoing struggle with the ever changing deployment of strategies of power.[13] Power, for Foucault, was not a substance one might have or an essential force one might resist but "the name that one attributes to a complex strategical situation in a particular society" (1978:93). Resistance, in this conception, can have meaning only in relation to such a strategic assessment. One cannot decide whether something is or is not resistance in absolute terms; resistance can exist only in relation to a "strategy of power," and such strategies are shifting, mobile, and multiple. Thus, as Foucault insisted of discourses (1978:101–2): "There is not, on the one side, a discourse of power, and opposite it, another discourse that runs counter to it. Discourses are tactical elements or blocks operating in the field of force relations; there can exist different and even contradictory discourses within the same strategy; they can, on the contrary, circulate without changing their form from one strategy to another, opposing strategy." Practices that are resistant to a particular strategy of power are thus never innocent of or outside power, for they are always capable of being tactically appropriated and redeployed within another strategy of power, always at risk of slipping from resistance against one strategy of power into complicity with another. It is a theoretical necessity, then, and not only an unfortunate empirical tendency, that resistance should time and again be linked with processes of co-optation, complicity, and the ironic recycling of former points of resistance within new strategies of power.[14]

Rather than conceptualize resistance in a disembodied duel with power, we would like to emphasize a little-noted aspect of it, which clarifies the connection with place making and identity. That is, we find it useful to think of resistance as an experience that constructs and reconstructs the identity of subjects.[15] As a form of experience, resistance's effects on the identity of subjects may be profoundly transformative. But it may equally result in reconfirming or strengthening existing identities, ironically contributing to maintaining the status quo. In both cases, however, resistance produces not simply tactical success or failure but a formative effect on the resisting subject. Of experience, Foucault once said: "An experience is something you come out of changed" (1991:27), and, "An experience is neither true nor false: it is always a fiction, something constructed, which exists only after it has been made, not before; it isn't something that is 'true' but it has been a reality" (36).

Reading "resistance" for "experience" in the quote above helps one to see how resistance may shape the identity of subjects despite its conjunctural character: it is that which changes subjects, which defines the way in which they are subject to someone else and the manner in which they come to be tied to their own identities through self-knowledge. However, the reconstruction of subjects in each of the two senses requires the retrospective recovery of "experience" — and this brings us to processes and modes of representation. Bisharat's contribution to this volume is a fine example of how the experience of exile, as represented in the longing for a national homeland, profoundly altered the specific relationship that Palestinian refugees had with "their" villages. Resistance to occupation thus reconfirmed and maintained national identity, deepening and naturalizing that identity but simultaneously transforming it.

As Foucault emphasized, it is important that experience, at least to some extent, be connectable to a "collective practice" so that others can "cross paths with it or retrace it" (1991:38–40). So much is implicit in the notion that experience transforms identities, for, as we have seen, identities can be understood only as relations of difference with others who are seen as categorical entities. For the experience of resistance to alter the identity of subjects, therefore, it has to be connectable to some form of collective practice. It is here that the role of representation looms large. Representations of resistance play a crucial part in the legitimation struggles that take place around the authentication of identities. If one of the modes of operation of power is to attach identities to subjects, to tie subjects to their own identities through self-knowledge, then resistance serves to reshape subjects by untying or untidying that relationship. Resistances, as Foucault insisted, "produce cleavages in a society that shift about, fracturing unities and effecting regroupings, furrowing across individuals themselves, cutting them up and remolding them, marking off irreducible regions in them, in their bodies and minds. Just as the network of power relations ends by forming a dense web that passes through apparatuses and institutions, without being exactly localized in them, so too the swarm of points of resistance traverses social stratifications and individual unities" (1978:96).

This conception of resistance as "fracturing unities and effecting regroupings," "furrowing across individuals themselves," and "travers[ing] . . . individual unities" allows us to see how it is possible for resistance, conceived as an experience, to be so transformative. Indeed, it allows us to understand the possibility of very radical forms of experience, which may break apart the subject, reconfiguring it so fundamentally that what emerges from it cannot even be spoken of as "the same" subject (Foucault 1991:46–49).[16] Here we see that experience, like identity, is not something that the sovereign subject "has"; rather, the subject itself must be conceived as the unstable and often unpredictable outcome of experience.[17] Parallel to the notion of "identity failures," therefore, lies the concept of the discontinuity of the subject, its "explosion" through transformative experience into something radically other. Such "limit experiences," moments of revolutionary upheaval and reconstitution of the subject, enable us to see the limitations of attempts to historicize the subject that, even while succeeding in undermining notions of the transcendental or preconfigured subject, nevertheless fail to break with a continuist narrative of identity.[18] In such cases, resistance does not merely reconfigure the relationship of subjects to their identities but may sunder that relationship entirely. The strategic struggle between resistance and power then "shifts ground," happens in a different place, in a new configuration of "community" and "identity."

Of course, such fundamental upheavals of subject constitution are relatively rare; nonetheless, they enable us to problematize what is usually taken for granted, namely, that subjects "naturally" have continuous histories and biographies whose narrativization poses analytical problems but whose constitution is largely self-evident. The possibility of the "explosion" of the subject thus underlines the contingency of continuity in identity. Just as strong and "successful" identities exist within a field of possible and actual "identity failures," so do radical transformations of the subject exist in a field of possible and actual failed transformations. And it is these "transformation failures" that make possible the continuous, apparently "given" identities that social actors are able to take for granted (most of the time).[19]

The contributions of Rosemary Coombe, Lisa Rofel, and Richard Maddox illustrate this intertwining of place making, identity, and resistance especially well. Coombe demonstrates the dialectics of struggle between tactics of power and tactics of appropriation within regimes of signification, considering demonic rumors spread by marginalized populations about the trademarks of transnational corporations. Reinvesting faceless and placeless corporate powers with narratives of origin, demonic rumors situate such powers in the local specificities of relations of hegemony and exploitation. It is significant that these struggles take place around the meaning and consumption of signs, an increasingly important site of resistance in late capitalism. Coombe demonstrates the point with a series of telling examples. For instance, she shows how Procter & Gamble was forced to abandon its 134-year-old man-in-the-moon logo when the company found itself unable, despite a multimillion-dollar campaign, to counter the rumor that the man was actually the figure of the devil. The most fascinating examples of rumor as resistance, however, are those that circulate in African American communities with regard to the role of the Ku Klux Klan in products marketed to African Americans. The rumor that Church's Fried Chicken had tainted their chicken recipe to sterilize black men is one such instance. Coombe offers a historically sensitive reading of this rumor, showing how the entire history of southern race relations is "condensed" in the fear that black men's sexuality should be so targeted. In a similar manner, a Korean American company called Troop Sport, which marketed military clothing to young black

men, also found itself out of business when a rumor began to circulate
that it was secretly operated by the Ku Klux Klan. Coombe suggests
that the reason rumor, in particular, flourishes in the hyperreal world
of late capitalism is that it deploys the same tactics of anonymity,
dearth of meaning, excess of fascination, fleetingness, and placelessness as the commercial powers that it attacks. Placelessness and pervasiveness may be key properties of corporate capital, but they become
features of cultural subversion as well. Coombe's essay is another fine
demonstration of how one might conduct an analysis of the conjunctural and tactical nature of resistance, its mobility and imbrication
in strategies of power, and its place in an era in which signs increasingly replace products as sites of fetishism.

In her essay Rofel cautions against universalizing the experience of
modernity (and, by extension, that of postmodernity) by extrapolat-
ing from the presence of certain modernist spatial practices and styles
of architecture and from the fact of incorporation in a global political
economy. In the silk factories of Hangzhou, the dictates of scientific
management and efficiency led to a spatial layout and design that
closely matches those found in other "global" factories. Intended to
produce a certain kind of subjectivity, modes of spatial dispersion and
discipline are resisted by workers who draw on their memory of previous spatial arrangements. Rofel shows subtle but significant differences in the techniques of resistance used by older workers, who remember what it meant to be a skilled silk worker in the days after
liberation; by "radical" workers who came of age during the Cultural
Revolution, when leaving one's work site was an indication of revolutionary fervor; and by younger workers, mostly women from the countryside, who make "mistakes" that cause them to be labeled "slow"
and "dull witted" by management. Layers of memories across generations thus mediate the microtechniques of power implicit in the spatial positionings of the "modern" factory. As new dominant cultural
narratives attempt to reshape subjectivities, from the extremes of the
Cultural Revolution to the China that will assume a leadership role in
the global economy, quite radical redefinitions of "community" and
"identity" have taken place. Rofel's achievement is to interpret these
changes initiated by state projects, while being sensitive to the manner
in which they have been altered or "consumed" by resisting subjects.

Maddox deals with a similar question. The "consumption" of hegemonic projects, he shows, takes a variety of forms. Maddox makes a
well-articulated plea not to equate crudely different kinds of actions

under the rubric of "resistance" but to search for a variety of terms that would do justice to the diversity of acts that are usually labeled "resistance." His essay is especially valuable in that it brings the location of the author into the foreground of the analysis. Maddox argues that those of us who are most interested in analyzing other people's modes of resistance often fail to situate ourselves more fully within multinationalized academic institutions that largely function to reproduce relations of inequality in advanced capitalist societies. Identifying with other people's struggles may be a "symptom of an alienating and repressive sublimation" that "tend[s] to locate the truly critical sites of struggle elsewhere." Maddox therefore raises some politically and ethically disturbing questions that undermine a particular mode of claiming identity that is often employed by anthropologists — that is, by affirming or asserting solidarity with subaltern others. The representation of resistance may make that experience available for other people to "cross paths with it or retrace it," as Foucault claims (1991:40), but quite apart from the question of who those other people are among whom anthropological representations circulate is the larger question of the relationship such representations may have with the structural inequalities that shape the identities of anthropologists and their subjects.

Maddox touches on the final issue we wish to treat here: the question of the social and political location of anthropologists in relation to questions of culture, power, and place. Anthropologists have become increasingly aware that ethnographic representations are not simply "about" such social processes as place making and people making but are at the same time actively involved in such constructions. As a great deal of anthropological work has been concerned to show, ethnographies participate, willy-nilly, in the politics of representation and social construction that they also aim to describe.[20] When this observation is combined with a recognition of the situatedness of all knowledge — a readiness to acknowledge that no "god's-eye view" exists and that every view is a view "from somewhere" (Haraway 1991b) — it becomes clear that the question of the location from which anthropological knowledge is constructed must be a central one.

We are wary, however, of an anthropological tendency (which we have observed both in some of the scholarly literature and, perhaps more often, in informal discussions) to generalize too easily about the location of "the" anthropologist. We have become used to a kind of anguished self-consciousness surrounding this issue. How can "we" anthropologists presume to speak for "them," our informants? Is not "our" knowledge of "them" inevitably shaped by colonial and neo-colonial power relations that render the whole enterprise suspect? How can "our" anthropological mission of understanding "others" proceed without falling into the familiar traps of exoticization, primitivism, and orientalism? What disturbs us in this line of thinking is not so much that it is misplaced as that it is insufficiently specific. For the whole discussion proceeds as if all anthropologists occupy the same social location — implicitly that of a white, middle-class, Western (often North American) academic — and as if all are equally preoccupied with the liberal political project of sympathetically presenting otherness to "our own" Western society. What this ignores are the significant internal differences that fracture such a complacent anthropological "we." We have in mind here two sorts of differences, which are closely related to each other but analytically separable.

First, and most obvious, by no means all anthropologists today occupy the white, Western "we" position that this discourse ascribes to them. As we argue in the following essay, the "we" versus "they" that frames much contemporary debate on the location of "the" anthropologist ignores this fact and rests on an unproblematized assumption of a Western "we," located "here," and a Third World "they," located "there." Such assumptions fail to consider not only the ambiguous position of Third World anthropologists but also the position of anthropologists who are located within "the West" but are nevertheless in various ways left out of, or marginalized by, the idea of a unitary Western "we" (for example, minorities, women, people of working-class background, and anthropologists in the West's internal periphery, such as Eastern and Southern Europe).

Second, if ethnographic practice inevitably participates in the politics of representation, as has often been suggested, then the location of "the" anthropologist must be specified in relation to practical political commitments as well. Taking this point seriously further fragments the fiction of a single, undifferentiated location for "the" anthropologist, because anthropologists do not share a unitary political project. Indeed, different anthropologists occupy quite different political locations and seek to advance diverse and often conflicting political agendas. Taking ethnographic practice as a form of political practice means recognizing a variety of different ways in which anthropological representations may be engaged with questions of culture and power, place making and people making, resistance and subjectivity. Such considerations do not mean that discussions of reflexivity and anthropological positioning are unnecessary but on the contrary that they must be pursued much more seriously and less abstractly, in relation to concrete anthropological practices and specific forms of political engagement.

ETHNOGRAPHY AND ITS POSSIBILITIES

We suggested at the start of this essay that a widespread sense of crisis in the discipline of anthropology was linked to fundamental challenges raised in more recent years to dominant conceptions of culture, power, and place. We also observed that the demise of a certain "peoples and cultures" paradigm had left in its wake a host of thorny and unresolved problems for ethnographic practice, which contemporary anthropologists are dealing with in various ways. If one thing seems clear in the present disorderly theoretical moment, it is that there will be no single successor paradigm to "peoples and cultures"; ethnographic work will continue to proceed as it has, along a number of different methodological lines and in diverse theoretical directions. In this context, a collection such as this may contribute the most simply by making available concrete illustrations of some of the existing theoretical directions that ethnographic work has been exploring and some of the useful methodological lines along which it has been possible for an anthropology "after peoples and cultures" to proceed. Such an anthropology cannot confine itself to the conventional ethnographic method of participant observation, as it comes to grips with transnational institutions and processes (Borneman, Gupta, Koptiuch), with such "placeless" phenomena as the mass media (Peters, Coombe), with displaced people such as refugees and immigrants (Bisharat, Leonard, Malkki), with regional or spatial identities (Ferguson, Rofel, Crain), and with self-reflective concerns and questions (Maddox). But neither can it afford to give up anthropology's traditional attention to the close observation of particular lives in particular places. Rather, these essays suggest that it is not necessary to choose between an unreconstructed commitment to traditional fieldwork, on the one hand, and more macroscopic or textual approaches, on the other. Creatively eclectic methodological strategies can allow anthropological tools originally developed for the study of "local communities" to contribute to the project of critically interrogating the very meaning of "locality" and "community" (Gupta and Ferguson in press and Hastrup and Olwig in press).

We have spoken of these essays as examples of "critical anthropology," but we emphasize that we do not conceive of a critical anthropology as a negative or reactive project. On the contrary, questioning assumptions and deeply entrenched habits of thought is important, for us, not as an end in itself but because doing so enables different kinds of ethnographic work to go forward. The essays in this volume are presented, then, in a positive spirit, one that seeks to explore some of the possibilities for ethnographic work that have sprung up in the wake of two decades of critique.

A time of great uncertainty for anthropology, we suggest that this time is also one of enormous possibilities. The contours of ethnography's emerging landscape are perhaps only beginning to be discernible. But politically important and theoretically challenging opportunities for ethnographic work are surely all around us. The issues that we have discussed here — issues of space and its social construction, of collective identity and its contestations, of subject formation and practices of resistance, of the location of anthropologists and anthropology in the politics of place and culture — all require studying in an ethnographic spirit, and there is much to be done. If we are working in a time when the ground seems to be shifting beneath our feet (as Foucault once suggested), the challenge remains to make creative and usable mappings of the changed terrain and to do what ethnographers have always done: try to find our feet in a strange new world.

NOTES

1   The identification and valorization of distinct "peoples," "tribes," and "nations" are, of course, linked to celebrations of the "folk" that have emerged from nineteenth-century European romanticism, as well as to various projects of building and legitimating European nation-states, all of which undoubtedly predate the anthropological turn to "cultures" (which George Stocking Jr. [1982:202–3] traces to Franz Boas). But while the historical links between the idea of "a culture" and the hegemonic form of the nation-state are strong and important (as Roger Rouse [personal communication] has pointed out), the causal links and temporal sequences are complex and not easily summarized. A proper treatment of this issue would require a major digression into nine-

teenth- and early-twentieth-century intellectual history, which we will not pursue in this brief introduction.

2 The idea of culture is, of course, much less elaborated in British social anthropology. Ideas of "society" and "social structure" in the British tradition, however, do much of the same work as the American idea of "a culture," effectively segmenting the world into an array of discrete and comparable "societies" or "social systems."

3 Indeed, earlier conceptions of culture were often a good deal less committed to the idea of separate, bounded entities than are more recent ones. As Wolf (1982:13) points out, the early-twentieth-century diffusionists, for all their faults, were quite attentive to the connectedness and nonboundedness of cultures. The idea of cultures as so many separate "cases," each with its own internal logic, however, seems to have been well established by the time Ruth Benedict penned her authoritative synthesis *Patterns of Culture* (1934). Later "symbolic anthropology" conceptions of culture as a semiotic system gave only more sophisticated theoretical elaboration to a "peoples and cultures" vision that was already quite firmly in place.

4 It has been justly observed (Ortner 1984:142–43; Marcus and Fischer 1986:85; Hannerz 1987; Clifford 1986a) that political economy approaches such as Wolf's have generally slighted questions of meaning and of cultural difference, tending to give central place to social and economic processes without providing an adequate account of the cultural. Wolf himself noted that in the wake of political economic critique, "we . . . stand in need of a new theory of cultural forms" (1982:19), yet he failed to do much to develop such a new theory. It should be noted, though, that other work in the political economy tradition has been more explicitly concerned with culture, producing impressive analyses that bring together questions of meaning, identity, and cultural difference with questions of political-economic structures and processes (cf., for instance, O'Brien and Roseberry 1991; Wilmsen 1989; Donham 1990; Mintz 1985; Roseberry 1989; and, in a rather different way, Taussig 1980, 1987).

5 Certain lines of the critique that we have referred to here do not, in our view, go nearly far enough in challenging conventional territorializations of "peoples and cultures." George Marcus and Michael Fischer (1986), for instance, while challenging key aspects of the epistemology and methodology of classical anthropology, largely remained satisfied with the vision of the world as a mosaic of separate, different cultures. Our objections to this position are developed more fully in "Beyond 'Culture': Space, Identity, and the Politics of Difference" in this volume.

6 The extent to which our thinking about cultural difference remains haunted by ideas of bounded, separate entities should not be underestimated. Paul Gilroy (1992) and Joan Scott (1992) have both shown how fundamental such conceptions are to contemporary debates around ethnicity and multiculturalism. And such ideas may also remain implicit, as we have shown elsewhere

(Gupta and Ferguson in press), in anthropology's own disciplinary practices (from conventions of "the field" and fieldwork to modes of conducting job searches) long after they cease to be seriously defended in the theoretical arena.

7   Here, we think of the now immense literatures following upon Benedict Anderson's (1983) exploration of nations as "imagined communities" and of Eric Hobsbawm and Terence Ranger's (1983) opening of the discussion on "the invention of tradition."

8   Works that review this literature include Bloch 1985; O'Laughlin 1975; Ortner 1984; Rosaldo and Lamphere 1974; Ortner and Whitehead 1981; and Collier and Yanagisako 1987.

9   We would like to thank Roger Rouse for a stimulating discussion of this point.

10   For a sampling of work in this vein, see Grossberg, Nelson, and Treichler 1992.

11   We are struck by the extent to which ideas of "the local" and "the global" in practice tend to replicate existing dualisms opposing tradition to modernity, cold societies to hot ones, or *Gemeinschaft* to *Gesellschaft*. In this way, "the local" can take the place of the traditional, "globalization" can take the place of modernization, and a new "transnational anthropology" can wind up bearing a disturbing resemblance to a sort of recycled modernization theory.

12   The decentering of direct sensory experience and the implications of an increasing reliance on machine-mediated perception are explored (in quite different ways) by Jean Baudrillard (1983b) and Donna Haraway (1991a).

13   This is how Foucault puts the matter in his discussion of the body: "Mastery and awareness of one's own body can be acquired only through the effect of an investment of power in the body: gymnastics, exercises, muscle-building, nudism, glorification of the body beautiful. All of this belongs to the pathway leading to the desire of one's own body. . . . But once power produces this effect, there inevitably emerge the responding claims and affirmations, those of one's own body against power, of health against the economic system, of pleasure against the moral norms of sexuality, marriage, decency. Suddenly, what had made power strong becomes used to attack it. Power, after investing itself in the body, finds itself exposed to a counter-attack in that same body. . . . But the impression that power weakens and vacillates here is in fact mistaken; power can retreat here, re-organize its forces, invest itself elsewhere . . . and so the battle continues. . . . What's taking place is the usual strategic development of a struggle. . . . One has to recognise the indefiniteness of the struggle — though this is not to say it won't some day have an end" (1980:56–57).

14   It is this, too, that accounts for Foucault's often criticized refusal to "side with" this or that political struggle unequivocally or to accept at face value the claims of organizations and ideologies that would lead or speak for those who would resist power. For Foucault, all struggles, even those expressions of resistance with which one is most sympathetic, are inherently dangerous, capable of mutations, reversals, and redeployments that may produce the most ironic of results. What such an approach demands, politically, is neither a naïve celebration of resistance for its own sake (a temptation to which anthropologists in

particular have too often succumbed) nor a cold analytic detachment from the compromised ground of real-world political struggles (the curse of American academia in general) but a combination of real political engagement with a skeptical strategic analysis. As Foucault insisted: "My point is not that everything is bad, but that everything is dangerous, which is not exactly the same as bad. If everything is dangerous, then we always have something to do. So my position leads not to apathy but to a hyper- and pessimistic activism" (1983b:231–32).

15   In *Remarks on Marx* (1991), Foucault discusses "experience" in a manner that immediately takes one beyond debates of whether experience is discursively constituted or whether it produces discursive formations.

16   Foucault says: "To call the subject into question had to mean to live it in an experience that might be its real destruction or dissociation, its explosion or upheaval into something radically 'other.' . . . Can't there be experiences in which the subject, in its constitutive relations, in its self-identity, isn't given any more? And thus wouldn't experiences be given in which the subject would dissociate itself, break its relationship with itself, lose its identity?" (1991:46, 49).

17   We can understand Joan Scott's view (1992:37) that "it is tempting, given its usage to essentialize identity and reify the subject," to abandon the concept of experience altogether. But there is a compelling reason to resist this temptation, which Scott seems not to appreciate fully — namely, it is only by attending to the question of experience that one may "escape the twin dangers of naïve essentialism (which Scott rightly opposes) and of mechanical understandings of processes of subject constitution (which Scott unfortunately tends to slip into). By decoupling the idea of experience from the vision of an ontologically prior subject who is "having" it, it is possible to see in experience neither the adventures and expression of a subject nor the mechanical product of discourses of power but the workshop in which subjectivity is continually challenged and refashioned.

18   We do not agree with those, such as James Miller (1993), who seem to conceive of Foucault's idea of the "limit experience" as a kind of heroic individual quest for transcendence. We agree with Gary Gutting (1994:24) that in Foucault's later work "transgression and intensity remain fundamental ethical categories, but they are now increasingly rooted more in lived social and political experiences than in refined aesthetic sensitivity."

19   We are indebted to John Peters (e-mail letter to Ferguson and Gupta, 9 November 1994) for having pointed out to us the importance of "transformation failures" and their relation to "identity failures."

20   This issue is treated with great sensitivity in Clifford 1988, and in such feminist writings on location and representation as Mohanty 1987 and Mani 1989.

PART ONE

SPACE, CULTURE, IDENTITY

AKHIL GUPTA AND JAMES FERGUSON

For a subject whose central rite of passage is fieldwork, whose romance has rested on its exploration of the remote ("the *most* other of others" [Hannerz 1986]), whose critical function is seen to lie in its juxtaposition of radically different ways of being (located "elsewhere") with that of the anthropologists' own, usually Western culture, there has been surprisingly little self-consciousness about the issue of space in anthropological theory. (Some notable exceptions are Appadurai 1986, 1988b; Hannerz 1987; Rosaldo 1988, 1989a). This essay aims at a critical exploration of the way received ideas about space and place have shaped and continue to shape anthropological common sense. In particular, we wish to explore how the renewed interest in theorizing space in postmodernist and feminist theory (for example, in Foucault 1980; Jameson 1984; Baudrillard 1988c; Deleuze and Guattari 1987; Anzaldúa 1987; Kaplan 1987; Martin and Mohanty 1986) — embodied in such notions as surveillance, panopticism, simulacra, deterritorialization, postmodern hyperspace, borderlands, and marginality — forces us to reevaluate such central analytic concepts in anthropology as that of "culture" and, by extension, the idea of "cultural difference."

Representations of space in the social sciences are remarkably dependent on images of break, rupture, and disjunction. The distinctiveness of societies, nations, and cultures is predicated on a seemingly unproblematic division of space, on the fact that they occupy "naturally" discontinuous spaces. The premise of discontinuity forms the starting point from which to theorize contact, conflict, and contradiction between cultures and societies. For example, the representation of the world as a collection of "countries," as on most world maps, sees it as an inherently fragmented space, divided by different colors into diverse national societies, each "rooted" in its proper place (compare Malkki, this volume). It is so taken for granted that each country embodies its own distinctive culture and society that the terms "society" and "culture" are routinely simply appended to the names of nation-states, as when a tourist visits India to understand "Indian culture" and "Indian society" or Thailand to experience "Thai culture" or the United States to get a whiff of "American culture."

Of course, the geographical territories that cultures and societies are believed to map onto do not have to be nations. We do, for example, have ideas about culture areas that overlap several nation-states, or of multicultural nations. On a smaller scale perhaps are our disciplinary assumptions about the association of culturally unitary groups (tribes or peoples) with "their" territories: thus "the Nuer" live in "Nuerland" and so forth. The clearest illustration of this kind of thinking are the classic "ethnographic maps" that purported to display the spatial distribution of peoples, tribes, and cultures. But in all these cases, space itself becomes a kind of neutral grid on which cultural difference, historical memory, and societal organization is inscribed. It is in this way that space functions as a central organizing principle in the social sciences at the same time that it disappears from analytical purview.

This assumed isomorphism of space, place, and culture results in some significant problems. First, there is the issue of those who inhabit the border, that "narrow strip along steep edges" (Anzaldúa 1987:3) of national boundaries. The fiction of cultures as discrete, objectlike phenomena occupying discrete spaces becomes implausible for those who inhabit the borderlands. Related to border inhabitants are those who live a life of border crossings—migrant workers, nomads, and members of the transnational business and professional elite. What is "the culture" of farm workers who spend half a year in Mexico and half in the United States? Finally, there are those who cross borders more or less permanently—immigrants, refugees, exiles, and expatriates. In their case, the disjuncture of place and culture is especially clear: Khmer refugees in the United States take "Khmer culture" with them in the same complicated way that Indian immigrants in England transport "Indian culture" to their new homeland.

A second set of problems raised by the implicit mapping of cultures onto places is to account for cultural differences *within* a locality. "Multiculturalism" is both a feeble recognition of the fact that cultures have lost their moorings in definite places and an attempt to subsume this plurality of cultures within the framework of a national identity. Similarly, the idea of "subcultures" attempts to preserve the idea of distinct "cultures" while acknowledging the relation of different cultures to a dominant culture within the same geographical and territorial space. Conventional accounts of ethnicity, even when used to describe cultural differences in settings where people from different regions live side by side, rely on an unproblematic link between identity and place.[1] While such concepts are suggestive because they endeavor to stretch the naturalized association of culture with place, they fail to interrogate this assumption in a truly fundamental manner. We need to ask how to deal with cultural difference, while abandoning received ideas of (localized) culture.

Third, there is the important question of postcoloniality. To which places do the hybrid cultures of postcoloniality belong? Does the colonial encounter create a "new culture" in both the colonized and colonizing country, or does it destabilize the notion that nations and cultures are isomorphic? As discussed below, postcoloniality further problematizes the relationship between space and culture.

Last and most important, challenging the ruptured landscape of independent nations and autonomous cultures raises the question of understanding social change and cultural transformation as situated within interconnected spaces. The presumption that spaces are autonomous has enabled the power of topography successfully to conceal the topography of power. The inherently fragmented space assumed in the definition of anthropology as the study of cultures (in the plural) may have been one of the reasons behind the long-standing failure to write anthropology's history as the biography of imperialism. For if one begins with the premise that spaces have *always* been hierarchically interconnected, instead of naturally disconnected, then cultural and social change becomes not a matter of cultural contact and articulation but one of rethinking difference *through* connection.

To illustrate, let us examine one powerful model of cultural change that attempts to relate dialectically the local to larger spatial arenas: articulation. Articulation models, whether they come from marxist structuralism or "moral economy," posit a primeval state of autonomy (usually labeled "precapitalist") that is then violated by global capitalism. The result is that both local and larger spatial arenas are transformed, the local more than the global to be sure, but not necessarily in a predetermined direction. This notion of articulation allows one to explore the richly unintended consequences of, say, colonial capitalism, with which loss occurs alongside invention. Yet, by taking a preexisting, localized "community" as a given starting point, it fails to examine sufficiently the processes (such as the structures of feeling that pervade the imagining of community) that go into the construction of space as place or locality in the first instance. In other words, instead of assuming the autonomy of the primeval community, we need to examine how it was formed *as a community* out of the interconnected space that always already existed. Colonialism then represents the displacement of one form of interconnection by another. This is not to deny that colonialism or an expanding capitalism does indeed have profoundly dislocating effects on existing societies. But by always foregrounding the spatial distribution of hierarchical power relations, we can better understand the processes whereby a space achieves a distinctive *identity* as a place. Keeping in mind that notions of locality or community refer both to a demarcated physical space and to clusters of interaction, we can see that the identity of a place emerges by the intersection of its specific involvement in a system of hierarchically organized spaces with its cultural construction as a community or locality.

It is for this reason that what Fredric Jameson (1984) has dubbed "postmodern hyperspace" has so fundamentally challenged the convenient fiction that mapped cultures onto places and peoples. In the capitalist West, a Fordist regime of accumulation, emphasizing extremely large production facilities, a relatively stable work force, and the welfare state combined to create urban "communities" whose outlines were most clearly visible in company towns (Harvey 1989; Mike Davis 1986; Mandel 1975). The counterpart of this in the international arena was that multinational corporations, under the leadership of the United States, steadily exploited the raw materials, primary goods, and cheap labor of the independent nation-states of the postcolonial "Third World." Multilateral agencies and powerful Western states preached and, where necessary, militarily enforced the "laws" of the market to encourage the international flow of capital, whereas national immigration policies ensured that there would be no free (that is, anarchic, disruptive) flow of labor to the high-wage islands in the capitalist core. Fordist patterns of accumulation have now been replaced by a regime of flexible accumulation — characterized by small-batch production, rapid shifts in product lines, extremely fast movements of capital to exploit the smallest differentials in labor and raw material costs—built on a more sophisticated communications and information network and better means of transporting goods and people. At the same time, the industrial production of culture, entertainment, and leisure that first achieved something approaching global distribution during the Fordist era led, paradoxically, to the invention of new forms of cultural difference and new forms of imagining community. Something like a transnational public sphere has certainly rendered any strictly bounded sense of community or locality obsolete. At the same time, it has enabled the creation of forms of solidarity and identity that do not rest on an appropriation of space where contiguity and face-to-face contact are paramount. In the pulverized space of postmodernity, space has not become irrelevant: it has been *re*territorialized in a way that does not conform to the experience of space that characterized the era of high modernity. It is this reterritorialization of space that forces us to reconceptualize fundamentally the politics of community, solidarity, identity, and cultural difference.

IMAGINED COMMUNITIES, IMAGINED PLACES

People have undoubtedly always been more mobile and identities less fixed than the static and typologizing approaches of classical anthropology would suggest. But today, the rapidly expanding and quickening mobility of people combines with the refusal of cultural products and practices to "stay put" to give a profound sense of a loss of territorial roots, of an erosion of the cultural distinctiveness of places, and of ferment in anthropological theory. The apparent deterritorialization of identity that accompanies such processes has made James Clifford's question (1988:275) a key one for recent anthropological inquiry: "What does it mean, at the end of the twentieth century, to speak . . . of a 'native land'? What processes rather than essences are involved in present experiences of cultural identity?"

Such questions are, of course, not completely new, but issues of collective identity do seem to take on a special character today, when more and more of us live in what Edward Said (1979:18) has called "a generalized condition of homelessness," a world where identities are increasingly coming to be, if not wholly deterritorialized, at least differently territorialized. Refugees, migrants, displaced and stateless peoples—these are perhaps the first to live out these realities in their

most complete form, but the problem is more general. In a world of
diaspora, transnational culture flows, and mass movements of populations, old-fashioned attempts to map the globe as a set of culture
regions or homelands are bewildered by a dazzling array of postcolonial simulacra, doublings and redoublings, as India and Pakistan seem
to reappear in postcolonial simulation in London, prerevolution Te-
heran rises from the ashes in Los Angeles, and a thousand similar
cultural dramas are played out in urban and rural settings all across
the globe. In this culture-play of diaspora, familiar lines between
"here" and "there," center and periphery, colony and metropole become blurred.

Where "here" and "there" become blurred in this way, the cultural
certainties and fixities of the metropole are upset as surely, if not in the
same way, as are those of the colonized periphery. In this sense, it is not
only the displaced who experience a displacement (compare Bhabha
1989:66). For even people remaining in familiar and ancestral places
find the nature of their relation to place ineluctably changed and the
illusion of a natural and essential connection between the place and
the culture broken. "Englishness," for instance, in contemporary, in-
ternationalized England is just as complicated and nearly as deterritorialized a notion as Palestinian-ness or Armenian-ness, for "England" ("the real England") refers less to a bounded place than to an
imagined state of being or a moral location. Consider, for instance, the
following quote from a young white reggae fan in the ethnically chaotic neighborhood of Balsall Heath in Birmingham:

There's no such thing as "England" any more . . . welcome to India brothers! This is
the Caribbean! . . . Nigeria! . . . There is no England, man. This is what is coming.
Balsall Heath is the center of the melting pot, 'cos all I ever see when I go out is half-
Arab, half-Pakistani, half-Jamaican, half-Scottish, half-Irish. I know 'cos I am [half-
Scottish/half-Irish] . . . who am I? . . . Tell me who I belong to? They criticize me,
the good old England. Alright, where do I belong? You know, I was brought up with
blacks, Pakistanis, Africans, Asians, everything, you name it . . . who do I belong
to? . . . I'm just a broad person. The earth is mine . . . you know we was not born in
Jamaica . . . we was not born in "England." We were born here, man. It's our right.
That's the way I see it. That's the way I deal with it. (In Hebdige 1987:158–59)

The broad-minded acceptance of cosmopolitanism that seems to be
implied here is perhaps more the exception than the rule, but there

can be little doubt that the explosion of a culturally stable and unitary "England" into the cut-and-mix "here" of contemporary Balsall Heath is an example of a phenomenon that is real and spreading. It is clear that the erosion of such supposedly natural connections between peoples and places has not led to the modernist specter of global cultural homogenization (Clifford 1988). But "cultures" and "peoples," however persistent they may be, cease to be plausibly identifiable as spots on the map.

But the irony of these times is that as actual places and localities become ever more blurred and indeterminate, *ideas* of culturally and ethnically distinct places become perhaps even more salient. It is here that it becomes most visible how imagined communities (Anderson 1983) come to be attached to imagined places, as displaced peoples cluster around remembered or imagined homelands, places, or communities in a world that seems increasingly to deny such firm territorialized anchors in their actuality. In such a world, it becomes ever more important to train an anthropological eye on processes of construction of place and homeland by mobile and displaced people.

Remembered places have, of course, often served as symbolic anchors of community for dispersed people. This has long been true of immigrants, who use memory of place to construct their new lived world imaginatively. "Homeland" in this way remains one of the most powerful unifying symbols for mobile and displaced peoples, though the relation to homeland may be very differently constructed in different settings. Moreover, even in more completely deterritorialized times and settings — settings not only where "home" is distant but also where the very notion of "home" as a durably fixed place is in doubt — aspects of our lives remain highly "localized" in a social sense. We need to give up naïve ideas of communities as literal entities (compare Anthony Cohen 1985) but remain sensitive to the profound "bifocality" that characterizes locally lived existences in a globally interconnected world and to the powerful role of place in the "near view" of lived experience (Peters, this volume).

The partial erosion of spatially bounded social worlds and the growing role of the imagination of places from a distance, however, themselves must be situated within the highly spatialized terms of a global capitalist economy. The special challenge here is to use a focus on the way space is imagined (but not *imaginary*) as a way to explore the mechanisms through which such conceptual processes of place making meet the changing global economic and political conditions of lived spaces — the relation, we could say, between place and space. For important tensions may arise when places that have been imagined at a distance must become lived spaces. Places, after all, are always imagined in the context of political-economic determinations that have a logic of their own. Territoriality is thus reinscribed at just the point it threatens to be erased.

The idea that space is made meaningful is, of course, a familiar one to anthropologists; indeed, there is hardly an older or better established anthropological truth. East or west, inside or outside, left or right, mound or floodplain — from at least the time of Durkheim, anthropologists have known that the experience of space is always socially constructed. The more urgent task would seem to be to politicize this uncontestable observation. With meaning-making understood as a practice, how are spatial meanings established? Who has the power to make places of spaces? Who contests this? What is at stake?

Such questions are particularly important where the meaningful association of places and peoples is concerned. As Malkki (this volume) shows, two naturalisms must be challenged here. The first is what we will call the ethnological habit of taking the association of a culturally unitary group (the "tribe" or "people") and "its" territory as natural, which we discussed in the previous section. A second and closely related naturalism is what we will call the national habit of taking the association of citizens of states and their territories as natural. Here the exemplary image is of the conventional world map of nation-states, through which schoolchildren are taught such deceptively simple-sounding beliefs as that France is where the French live, America is where the Americans live, and so on. Even a casual observer knows that not only Americans live in America, and it is clear that the very question of what is a "real American" is largely up for grabs. But even anthropologists still talk of "American culture" with no clear understanding of what such a phrase might mean, because we assume a natural association of a culture ("American culture"), a people ("Americans"), and a place ("the United States of America"). Both the ethnological and the national naturalisms present associations of people and place as solid, commonsensical, and agreed on, when they are in fact contested, uncertain, and in flux.

Much more-recent work in anthropology and related fields has focused on the process through which such reified and naturalized national representations are constructed and maintained by states and national elites (see, for instance, Anderson 1983; Kapferer 1988; Handler 1988; Herzfeld 1987; Hobsbawm and Ranger 1983; and Wright 1985). Such analyses of nationalism leave no doubt that states play a crucial role in the popular politics of place making and in the creation of naturalized links between places and peoples. But it is important to note that state ideologies are far from being the only point at which the imagination of place is politicized. Oppositional images of place have, of course, been extremely important in anticolonial nationalist movements, as well as in campaigns for self-determination and sovereignty on the part of contested nations such as the Hutu (Malkki, this volume), the Eritreans, the Armenians, or the Palestinians (Bisharat, this volume). Such instances may serve as a useful reminder, in the light of nationalism's often reactionary connotations in the Western world, of how often notions of home and "own place" have been empowering in anti-imperial contexts.

Indeed, future observers of twentieth-century revolutions will probably be struck by the difficulty of formulating large-scale political movements *without* reference to national homelands. Whether we are speaking of the nonaligned movement (Gupta, this volume) or the proletarian internationalist movement, what stands out is the extraordinary difficulty in attempting to rally people around such nonnational collectivities. Indeed, class-based internationalism's tendencies to nationalism (as in the history of the Second International or that of the USSR) and to utopianism imagined in local rather than universal terms (as in William Morris's *News from Nowhere* [1970/1890], where "nowhere" [*utopia*] turns out to be a specifically English "somewhere") show with special clarity the importance of attaching causes to places and the ubiquity of place making in collective political mobilization.

Such place making, however, need not be national in scale. One example of this is the way idealized notions of "the country" have been used in urban settings to construct critiques of industrial capitalism (compare, for Britain, Raymond Williams 1973, with, for Zambia, Ferguson, this volume). Another case is the reworking of ideas of "home" and "community" by such feminists as Biddy Martin and Chandra Talpade Mohanty (1986) and Caren Kaplan (1987). Yet it must be noted that such popular politics of place can as easily be conservative as progressive. Often enough, as in the contemporary United States, the association of place with memory, loss, and nostalgia plays directly into the hands of reactionary popular movements. This is true not only of explicitly national images long associated with the right but also of imagined locales and nostalgic settings such as "small-town America" or "the frontier," which often play into and complement antifeminist idealizations of "the home" and "family."[2]

SPACE, POLITICS, AND ANTHROPOLOGICAL REPRESENTATION

Changing our conceptions of the relation between space and cultural difference offers a new perspective on recent debates surrounding issues of anthropological representation and writing. The new attention to representational practices has already led to more sophisticated understandings of processes of objectification and the construction of otherness in anthropological writing. With this said, however, it also seems to us that more recent notions of "cultural critique" (Marcus and Fischer 1986) depend on a spatialized understanding of cultural difference that needs to be problematized.

The foundation of cultural critique — a dialogic relation with an "other" culture that yields a critical viewpoint on "our own culture" — assumes an already existing world of many different, distinct "cultures" and an unproblematic distinction between "our own society" and an "other" society. As George E. Marcus and Michael M. J. Fischer put it, the purpose of cultural critique is "to generate critical questions from one society to probe the other"; the goal is "to apply both the substantive results and the epistemological lessons learned from ethnography abroad to a renewal of the critical function of anthropology as it is pursued in ethnographic projects at home" (1986:117, 112).

Marcus and Fischer are sensitive to the fact that cultural difference is present "here at home" too and that "the other" need not be exotic or far away to be other. But the fundamental conception of cultural critique as a relation between "different societies" ends up, perhaps against the authors' intentions, spatializing cultural difference in familiar ways, as ethnography becomes a link between an unproblematized "home" and "abroad." The anthropological relation is not simply with people who are different but with "a different society," "a different culture," and thus, inevitably, a relation between "here" and "there." In all this, the terms of the opposition ("here" and "there," "us" and "them," "our own" and "other" societies) are taken as received: the problem for anthropologists is to use our encounter with "them," "there," to construct a critique of "our own society," "here."

A number of problems exist with this way of conceptualizing the anthropological project. Perhaps the most obvious is the question of the identity of the "we" that keeps coming up in phrases such as "ourselves" and "our own society." Who is this "we"? If the answer is, as we fear, "the West," then we must ask precisely who is to be included and who excluded from this club. Nor is the problem solved simply by substituting "the ethnographer's own society" for "our own society." For ethnographers as for other natives, the postcolonial world is an interconnected social space; for many anthropologists — and perhaps especially for displaced Third World scholars — the identity of "one's own society" is an open question.

A second problem with the way cultural difference has been conceptualized within the "cultural critique" project is that, once excluded from that privileged domain "our own society," "the other" is subtly nativized — placed in a separate frame of analysis and "spatially incarcerated" (Appadurai 1988b) in that "other place" that is proper to an "other culture." Cultural critique assumes an original separation, bridged at the initiation of the anthropological field-worker. The problematic is one of "contact," communication not within a shared social and economic world but "across cultures" and "between societies."

As an alternative to this way of thinking about cultural difference, we want to problematize the unity of the "us" and the otherness of the "other" and question the radical separation between the two that makes the opposition possible in the first place. We are interested less in establishing a dialogic relation between geographically distinct societies than in exploring the processes of *production* of difference in a world of culturally, socially, and economically interconnected and interdependent spaces. The difference is fundamental and can be illustrated by a brief examination of one text that has been highly praised within the "cultural critique" movement.

Marjorie Shostak's *Nisa: The Life and Words of a !Kung Woman* (1981) has been very widely admired for its innovative use of life history and has been hailed as a noteworthy example of polyphonic experimentation in ethnographic writing (Marcus and Fischer 1986:58–59; Mary Louise Pratt 1986a; Clifford 1986b; Clifford 1988:42). But with respect to the issues we have discussed here, *Nisa* is a very conventional and deeply flawed work. The individual, Nisa, is granted a degree of singularity, but she is used principally as the token of a type: "the !Kung." The San-speaking !Kung of Botswana (the "Bushmen" of old) are presented as a distinct, "other," and apparently primordial "people." Shostak treats the Dobe !Kung as essentially survivals of a prior evolutionary age: they are "one of the last remaining traditional gatherer-hunter societies," racially distinct, traditional, and isolated (1981:4). Their experience of "culture change" is "still quite recent and subtle" and their traditional value system "mostly intact" (6). "Contact" with "other groups" of agricultural and pastoral peoples has occurred, according to Shostak, only since the 1920s, and only since the 1960s has the isolation of the !Kung really broken down, raising for the first time the issue of "change," "adaptation," and "culture contact" (346).

The space the !Kung inhabit, the Kalahari Desert, is clearly radically different and separate from our own. Again and again the narrative returns to the theme of isolation: in a harsh ecological setting, a way of life thousands of years old has been preserved only through its extraordinary spatial separateness. The anthropological task, as Shostak conceives it, is to cross this spatial divide, to enter into this land that time forgot, a land (as Edwin Wilmsen [1989:10] notes) with antiquity but no history, to listen to the voices of women which might reveal "what their lives had been like for generations, possibly even for thousands of years" (Shostak 1981:6).

The exoticization implicit in this portrait, in which the !Kung appear almost as living on another planet, has drawn surprisingly little criticism from theorists of ethnography. Mary Louise Pratt has rightly pointed out the "blazing contradiction" between the portrait of primal beings untouched by history and the genocidal history of the white "Bushman conquest" (1986a:48). As she says, "What picture of the !Kung would one draw if instead of defining them as survivors of the stone age and a delicate and complex adaptation to the Kalahari desert, one looked at them as survivors of capitalist expansion, and a delicate and complex adaptation to three centuries of violence and intimidation?" (1986a:49). But even Pratt retains the notion of "the !Kung" as a preexisting ontological entity — "survivors," not products (still less, producers) of history. "They" are victims, having suffered the deadly process of "contact" with "us."

A very different and much more illuminating way of conceptualizing cultural difference in the region may be found in Wilmsen's devastating critique of the anthropological cult of the "Bushman" (1989). Wilmsen shows how, in constant interaction with a wider network of social relations, the difference that Shostak takes as a starting point came to be produced in the first place — how, one might say, "the Bushmen" came to be Bushmen. He demonstrates that San-speaking people have been in continuous interaction with other groups for as long as we have evidence for; that political and economic relations linked the supposedly isolated Kalahari with a regional political economy both in the colonial and precolonial eras; that San-speaking people have often held cattle and that no strict separation of pastoralists and foragers can be maintained. He argues powerfully that the Zhu (!Kung) have never been a classless society and that if they give such an impression, "it is because they are incorporated as an underclass in a wider social formation that includes Batswana, Ovaherero, and others" (1989:270). Moreover, he shows that the "Bushman/San" label has been in existence for barely half a century, the category having been produced through the "retribalization" of the colonial period (280), and that "the cultural conservatism uniformly attributed to these people by almost all anthropologists who have worked with them until recently, is a consequence — not a cause — of the way they have been integrated into the modern capitalist economies of Botswana and Namibia" (12).

With respect to space, Wilmsen is unequivocal: "It is not possible to speak of the Kalahari's isolation, protected by its own vast distances. To those inside, the outside — whatever 'outside' there may have been at any moment — was always present. The appearance of isolation and its reality of dispossessed poverty are recent products of a process that unfolded over two centuries and culminated in the last moments of the colonial era" (157). The process of the production of cultural difference, Wilmsen demonstrates, occurs in continuous, connected space, traversed by economic and political relations of inequality. Where Shostak takes difference as given and concentrates on listening "across cultures," Wilmsen performs the more radical operation of interrogating the "otherness" of the other, situating the production of cultural difference within the historical processes of a socially and spatially interconnected world.

What is needed, then, is more than a ready ear and a deft editorial hand to capture and orchestrate the voices of "others"; what is needed is a willingness to interrogate, politically and historically, the apparent "given" of a world in the first place divided into "ourselves" and "others." A first step on this road is to move beyond naturalized conceptions of spatialized "cultures" and to explore instead the production of difference within common, shared, and connected spaces — "the San," for instance, not as "a people," "native" to the desert, but as a historically constituted and depropertied category systematically relegated to the desert.

The move we are calling for, most generally, is away from seeing cultural difference as the correlate of a world of "peoples" whose separate histories wait to be bridged by the anthropologist and toward seeing it as a product of a shared historical process that differentiates the world as it connects it. For the proponents of "cultural critique," difference is taken as starting point, not as end product. Given a world of "different societies," they ask, how can we use experience in one to comment on another? But if we question a pregiven world of separate and discrete "peoples and cultures" and see instead a difference-producing set of relations, we turn from a project of juxtaposing pre-existing differences to one of exploring the construction of differences in historical process.

In this perspective, power does not enter the anthropological picture only at the moment of representation, for the cultural distinctiveness that the anthropologist attempts to represent has always already been produced within a field of power relations. Thus a politics of otherness exists that is not reducible to a politics of representation. Textual strategies can call attention to the politics of representation, but the issue of otherness itself is not really addressed by the devices of polyphonic textual construction or collaboration with informant-writers, as such writers as Clifford and Vincent Crapanzano (1980) sometimes seem to suggest.

In addition to (not instead of!) textual experimentation, then, there is a need to address the issue of "the West" and its "others" in a way that acknowledges the extratextual roots of the problem. For example, the area of immigration and immigration law is one practical area where the politics of space and the politics of otherness link up very directly. Indeed, if the separateness of separate places is not a natural given but an anthropological problem, it is remarkable how little anthropologists have had to say about the contemporary political issues connected with immigration in the United States.[3] If we accept a world of originally separate and culturally distinct places, then the question of immigration policy is just a question of how hard we should try to maintain this original order. In this perspective, immigration prohibitions are a relatively minor matter. Indeed, operating with a spatially naturalized understanding of cultural difference, uncontrolled immigration may even appear as a danger to anthropology, threatening to blur or erase the cultural distinctiveness of places that is our stock-in-trade. If, on the other hand, it is acknowledged that cultural difference is produced and maintained in a field of power relations in a world always already spatially interconnected, then the restriction of immigration becomes visible as one of the main means through which the disempowered are kept that way.

The enforced "difference" of places becomes, in this perspective, part and parcel of a global system of domination. The anthropological task of denaturalizing cultural and spatial divisions at this point links up with the political task of combating a very literal "spatial incarceration of the native" (Appadurai 1988b) within economic spaces zoned, as it were, for poverty. In this sense, changing the way we think about the relations of culture, power, and space opens the possibility of changing more than our texts. There is room, for instance, for a great deal more anthropological involvement, both theoretical and practical, with the politics of the United States/Mexico border, with the political and organizing rights of immigrant workers, and with the appropriation of anthropological concepts of "culture" and "difference" into the repressive ideological apparatus of immigration law and the popular perceptions of "foreigners" and "aliens."

A certain unity of place and people has long been assumed in the anthropological concept of culture. But anthropological representations and immigration laws notwithstanding, "the native" is "spatially incarcerated" only in part. The ability of people to confound the established spatial orders, either through physical movement or through their own conceptual and political acts of reimagination, means that space and place can never be "given" and that the process of their sociopolitical construction must always be considered. An anthropology whose objects are no longer conceived as automatically and naturally anchored in space will need to pay particular attention to the way spaces and places are made, imagined, contested, and enforced. In this sense, it is no paradox to say that questions of space and place are, in this deterritorialized age, more central to anthropological representation than ever.

In suggesting the requestioning of the spatial assumptions implicit in the most fundamental and seemingly innocuous concepts in the social sciences such as "culture," "society," "community," and "nation," we do not presume to lay out a detailed blueprint for an alternative conceptual apparatus. We do, however, wish to point out some promising directions for the future.

One extremely rich vein has been tapped by those attempting to theorize interstitiality and hybridity: in the postcolonial situation (Bhabha

1989; Rushdie 1989; Hannerz 1987); for people living on cultural and national borders (Anzaldúa 1987; Rosaldo 1987, 1988, 1989a); for refugees and displaced peoples (Malkki this volume, 1995a, 1995b; Ghosh 1989); and in the case of migrants and workers (Leonard this volume, 1992). The "syncretic, adaptive politics and culture" of hybridity, Homi K. Bhabha points out (1989:64), raises questions about "the imperialist and colonialist notions of purity as much as it question[s] the nationalist notions." It remains to be seen what kinds of politics are enabled by such a theorization of hybridity and to what extent it can do away with all claims to authenticity, to all forms of essentialism, strategic or otherwise (see especially Radhakrishnan 1987). Bhabha points to the troublesome connection between claims to purity and utopian teleology in describing how he came to the realization that . . . "the only place in the world to speak from was at a point whereby contradiction, antagonism, the hybridities of cultural influence, the boundaries of nations, were not sublated into some utopian sense of liberation or return. The place to speak from was through those incommensurable contradictions within which people survive, are politically active, and change" (1989:67). The borderlands make up just such a place of incommensurable contradictions. The term does not indicate a fixed topographical site between two other fixed locales (nations, societies, cultures) but an interstitial zone of displacement and deterritorialization that shapes the identity of the hybridized subject. Rather than dismissing them as insignificant, as marginal zones, thin slivers of land between stable places, we want to contend that the notion of borderlands is a more adequate conceptualization of the "normal" locale of the postmodern subject.

Another promising direction that takes us beyond culture as a spatially localized phenomenon is provided by the analysis of what is variously called "mass media," "public culture," and the "culture industry." (Especially influential here has been the journal *Public Culture*.) Existing symbiotically with the commodity form, profoundly influencing even the remotest people that anthropologists have made such a fetish of studying, mass media pose the clearest challenge to orthodox notions of culture. National, regional, and village boundaries have, of course, never contained culture in the way that the anthropological representations have often implied. But the existence of a transnational public sphere means that the fiction that such boundaries enclose cultures and regulate cultural exchange can no longer be sustained.

The production and the distribution of mass culture—films, television and radio programs, newspapers and wire services, recorded music, books, live concerts—are largely controlled by those notoriously placeless organizations: multinational corporations. The "public sphere" is therefore hardly "public" with respect to control over the representations that are circulated in it. Recent work in cultural studies has emphasized the dangers of reducing the reception of multinational cultural production to the passive act of consumption, leaving no room for the active creation by agents of disjunctures and dislocations between the flow of industrial commodities and cultural products. We worry at least as much, however, about the opposite danger of *celebrating* the inventiveness of those "consumers" of the culture industry (especially on the periphery) who fashion something quite different out of products marketed to them, reinterpreting and remaking them, sometimes quite radically and sometimes in a direction that promotes resistance rather than conformity. The danger here is the temptation to use scattered examples of the cultural flows dribbling from the "periphery" to the chief centers of the culture industry as a way of dismissing the "grand narrative" of capitalism (especially the "totalizing" narrative of late capitalism) and thus of evading the powerful political issues associated with Western global hegemony.

The reconceptualization of space implicit in theories of interstitiality and public culture has led to efforts to conceptualize cultural difference without invoking the orthodox idea of "culture." This is as yet a largely unexplored and underdeveloped area. We do, clearly, find the clustering of cultural practices that do not "belong" to a particular "people" or to a definite place. Jameson (1984) has attempted to capture the distinctiveness of these practices in the notion of a "cultural dominant," whereas Ferguson (forthcoming) proposes an idea of "cultural style" that searches for a logic of surface practices without necessarily mapping such practices onto a "total way of life" encompassing values, beliefs, attitudes, and so on, as in the usual concept of culture. We need to explore what Bhabha calls "the uncanny of cultural difference": "Cultural difference becomes a problem not when you can point to the Hottentot Venus, or to the punk whose hair is six feet up in the air; it does not have that kind of fixable visibility. It is as the strangeness of the familiar that it becomes more problematic, both politically and conceptually . . . when the problem of cultural difference is ourselves-as-others, others-as-ourselves, that borderline" (1989:72).

Why focus on that borderline? We have argued that deterritorialization has destabilized the fixity of "ourselves" and "others." But it has not thereby created subjects who are free-floating monads, despite what is sometimes implied by those eager to celebrate the freedom and playfulness of the postmodern condition. As Martin and Mohanty (1986:194) point out, indeterminacy too has its political limits, which follow from the denial of the critic's own location in multiple fields of power. Instead of stopping with the notion of deterritorialization, the pulverization of the space of high modernity, we need to theorize how space is being *re*territorialized in the contemporary world. We need to account sociologically for the fact that the "distance" between the rich in Bombay and those in London may be much shorter than that between different classes in "the same" city. Physical location and physical territory, for so long the *only* grid on which cultural difference could be mapped, need to be replaced by multiple grids that enable us to see that connection and contiguity — more general, the representation of territory — vary considerably by factors such as class, gender, race, and sexuality and are differentially available to those in different locations in the field of power.

NOTES

This paper was originally published in *Cultural Anthropology* 7 (1): 6–23. Because our most recent thoughts on questions of space, place, and identity have been laid out in the above essay, we have not revised the present paper but have reprinted it (apart from a few corrections and updatings) as it appeared in 1992.

1   This is obviously not true of the "new ethnicity" literature, texts such as Anzaldúa 1987 and Radhakrishnan 1987.

2   See also Jennifer Robertson (1988, 1991) on the politics of nostalgia and "native place making" in Japan.

3   We are, of course, aware that a considerable amount of more recent work in anthropology has centered on immigration. But we think that too much of this work remains at the level of describing and documenting patterns and trends of migration, often with a policy science focus. Such work is undoubtedly important, and often strategically effective in the formal political arena. Yet there remains the challenge of taking up the specifically *cultural* issues surrounding the mapping of otherness onto space, as we have suggested is necessary. One area where at least some anthropologists have taken such issues seriously is that of Mexican immigration to the United States; see, for instance, Rouse 1991;

Chavez 1991; Kearney 1986, 1990; Kearney and Nagengast 1989; Alvarez 1987; and Bustamente 1987. Another example is Borneman 1986, which is noteworthy for showing the specific links between immigration law and homophobia — between nationalism and sexuality — in the case of the Cuban "Marielito" immigrants to the United States.

National Geographic: The Rooting of Peoples and the Territorialization of National Identity among Scholars and Refugees

LIISA H. MALKKI

"To be rooted is perhaps the most important and least recognized need of the human soul," wrote Simone Weil (1987:41) in wartime England in 1942. In our day, new conjunctures of theoretical inquiry in anthropology and other fields are making it possible and necessary to rethink the question of roots in relation — if not to the soul — to identity and to the forms of its territorialization. The metaphorical concept of having roots involves intimate linkages between people and place — linkages that are increasingly recognized in anthropology as areas to be denatured and explored afresh.

As many have suggested (Appadurai 1988b, 1990, 1992; Said 1979; Clifford 1988:10–11, 275, and 1994; Rosaldo 1989a:196; Hannerz 1987; Hebdige 1987; Löfgren 1989; Malkki 1994, 1995a, 1995b; Balibar 1991a; Gilroy 1993; Hall 1990; Gupta and Ferguson 1992; Massey 1992; Rouse 1991), notions of nativeness and native places become very complex as more and more people identify themselves or are categorized in reference to deterritorialized "homelands," "cultures," and "origins." There has emerged a new awareness of the global social fact that, now more than perhaps ever before, people are chronically mobile and routinely displaced, inventing homes and homelands in the absence of territorial, national bases — not in situ but through memories of and claims on places that they can or will no longer corporeally inhabit.

Exile and other forms of territorial displacement are not, of course, exclusively "postmodern" phenomena. People have always moved — whether through desire or through violence. Scholars have also written about these movements for a long time and from diverse perspectives (Arendt 1973; Heller and Feher 1988:90; Fustel de Coulanges 1980:190–93; Mauss 1969:573–639; Sally Falk Moore 1989; Zolberg 1983; Marrus 1985). What is interesting is that now particular theoretical shifts have arranged themselves into new conjunctures that give these phenomena greater analytic visibility than perhaps ever before. Thus, we (anthropologists) have old questions, but also something very new.

The recognition that people are increasingly "moving targets" (Breckenridge and Appadurai 1989:i) of anthropological inquiry is associated with the placing of boundaries and borderlands at the center of our analytic frameworks, as opposed to relegating them to invisible peripheries or anomalous danger zones (compare Gupta and Ferguson, "Beyond Culture," this volume; Comaroff and Comaroff 1987; van Binsbergen 1981; Balibar 1991a:10). Often, the concern with boundaries and their transgression reflects not so much corporeal movements of specific groups of people but rather a broad concern with the "cultural displacement" of people, things, and cultural products (for example, Clifford 1988; Hannerz 1987; Torgovnick 1990; Goytisolo 1987). Thus, what Edward Said, for instance, calls a "generalized condition of homelessness" is seen to characterize contemporary life everywhere.[1]

In this new theoretical crossroads, examining the place of refugees in the national order of things becomes a clarifying exercise. On the one hand, trying to understand the circumstances of particular groups of refugees illuminates the complexity of the ways in which people construct, remember, and lay claim to particular places as "homelands" or "nations." On the other, examining how refugees become an object of knowledge and management suggests that the displacement of refugees is constituted differently from other kinds of deterritorialization by those states, organizations, and scholars who are concerned with refugees. Here, the contemporary category of refugees is a particularly informative one in the study of the sociopolitical construction of space and place.

The major part of this essay is a schematic exploration of taken-for-granted ways of thinking about identity and territory that are reflected in ordinary language, in nationalist discourses, and in scholarly studies of nations, nationalism, and refugees. The purpose here is to draw attention to the analytic consequences of such deeply territorializing concepts of identity for those categories of people classified as "displaced" and "uprooted." These scholarly views will then be juxtaposed very briefly with two other cases. The first of these derives from ethnographic research among Hutu refugees who have lived in a refugee camp in rural Western Tanzania since fleeing the massacres of 1972 in Burundi. It will trace how the camp refugees' narrative construction of homeland, "refugeeness," and exile challenges scholarly constructions and common sense. In the second case, the ethnography moves among these Hutu refugees in Tanzania who have lived (also since 1972) outside a refugee camp, in and around the township of Kigoma on Lake Tanganyika. These "town refugees" present a third, different conceptual constellation of links between people, place, and displacement—one that stands in antagonistic opposition to views from the camp and challenges, from yet another direction, scholarly maps of the national order of things. I will also mention the way that conceiving of "peoples" as properly "rooted" in national soils may have played a role in the waves of genocidal killings that have swept across Rwanda and Burundi in more recent years.

MAPS AND SOILS

To begin to understand the meanings commonly attached to displacement and "uprootedness" in the contemporary national order of things, it is necessary to lay down some groundwork. This means exploring widely shared, commonsense ideas about countries and roots, nations and national identities. It means asking, in other words, what it means to be rooted in a place (compare Appadurai 1988b:37). Such commonsense ideas of soils, roots, and territory are built into everyday language and often also into scholarly work, but their very obviousness makes them elusive as objects of study. Common sense, as Clifford Geertz has said (1983:92), "lies so artlessly before our eyes it is almost impossible to see."

That the world should be composed of sovereign, spatially discontinuous units is a sometimes implicit, sometimes stated premise in much of the literature on nations and nationalism (for example, Giddens 1987:116, 119; Hobsbawm 1990:9–10; Gellner 1983).[2] To take one example, Ernest Gellner sees nations as recent phenomena, functional for industrial capitalism,[3] but he also conceptualizes them as discrete ethnological units unambiguously segmented on the ground, thereby naturalizing them along a spatial axis. He invites us to examine two kinds of world maps:

Consider the history of the national principle; or consider two ethnographic maps, one drawn up before the age of nationalism, and the other after the principle of nationalism has done much of its work. The first map resembles a painting by Kokoschka. The riot of diverse points of colour is such that no clear pattern can be discerned in any detail.... Look now instead at the ethnographic and political map of an area of the modern world. It resembles not Kokoschka, but, say, Modigliani. There is very little shading; neat flat surfaces are clearly separated from each other, it is generally plain where one begins and another ends, and there is little if any ambiguity or overlap. (1983:139–40)

The Modigliani described by Gellner (*pace* Modigliani) is much like any school atlas with yellow, green, pink, orange, and blue countries composing a truly global map with no vague or "fuzzy spaces" and no bleeding boundaries (Tambiah 1985:4; Trinh 1989:94). The national order of things, as presented by Gellner, usually also passes as the normal or natural order of things. For it is self-evident that "real" nations are fixed in space and "recognizable" on a map (Anthony Smith 1986:1).[4] One country cannot at the same time be another country. The world of nations is thus conceived as a discrete spatial partitioning of territory; it is territorialized in the segmentary fashion of the multicolored school atlas.

The territorialization expressed in the conceptual, visual device of the map is also (and perhaps especially) evident on the level of ordinary language. The term, "the nation," is commonly referred to in English (and many other languages) by such metaphoric synonyms as "the country," "the land," and "the soil." For example, the phrase "the whole country" could denote all the citizens of the country or its entire territorial expanse. And "land" is a frequent suffix, not only in "homeland" but also in the names of countries (Thailand, Switzerland, England) and in the old colonial designations of "peoples and cultures" (Nuerland, Basutoland, Nyasaland). One dictionary definition for "land" is "the people of a country," as in "the land rose in rebellion."[5] Similarly, soil is often "national soil."[6] Here, the territory itself is made more human (compare Handler 1988:34).

This naturalized identity between people and place is also reflected and created in the course of other, nondiscursive practices. It is not uncommon for a person going into exile to take along a handful of the soil (or a sapling or seeds) from his or her country, just as it is not unheard of for a returning national hero or other politician to kiss the ground upon setting foot once again on the "national soil."

Demonstrations of emotional ties to the soil act as evidence of loyalty to the nation. Likewise, the ashes or bodies of persons who have
died on foreign soil are routinely transported back to their "homelands," to the land where the genealogical tree of their ancestors
grows. Ashes to ashes, dust to dust: in death, too, native / national soils
are important.

The powerful metaphoric practices that so commonly link people to
place are also deployed to understand and act upon the categorically
aberrant condition of people whose claims on and ties to national soils
are regarded as tenuous, spurious, or nonexistent. It is in this context, perhaps, that the recent events in Carpentras, Southern France,
should be placed (Dahlburg 1990:H1; Plenel 1990:16; compare Balibar 1990:286). On the night of 9 May 1990, thirty-seven graves
in an old Jewish cemetery were desecrated, and the body of a man
newly buried was disinterred and impaled with an umbrella (Dahlburg
1990:H1). One is compelled to see in this abhorrent act of violence a
connection to "love of country" in the ugliest sense of the term. The
old man's membership in the French nation was denied because he
was of the category "Jew." He was a person in the "wrong" soil and was
therefore taken out of the soil (compare Balibar 1990:285). Reports
of a similar logic have surfaced in Europe since Carpentras, most
recently in the case of Serbs moving the bodies of their dead out of
territory that is to become "Bosnia"—apparently so that their enemies will not exhume or desecrate them.

ROOTS AND ARBORESCENT CULTURE

The foregoing examples already suggest that the widely held commonsense assumptions linking people to place, nation to territory, are not
simply territorializing but deeply metaphysical. To begin to understand the meaning of displacement in this order of things, however, it
is necessary to explore further aspects of the metaphysic. The intent in
this section is to show that the naturalizing of the links between people
and place is routinely conceived in specifically botanical metaphors.[7]
That is, people are often thought of, and think of themselves, as being
rooted in place and as deriving their identity from that rootedness.
The roots in question here are not just any kind of roots; very often
they are specifically arborescent in form.

Even a brief excursion into nationalist discourses and imagery
shows them to be a particularly rich field for the exploration of such

arborescent root metaphors. Examples are easy to find: Keith Thomas has traced the history of the British oak as "an emblem of the British people" (1983:220, 223; compare Daniels 1988:47; Graves 1966). Edmund Burke combined "the great oaks that shade a country" with metaphors of "roots" and "stock" (cited in Thomas 1983:218). A Quebecois nationalist likened the consequences of tampering with the national heritage to the withering of a tree (Handler 1988:44–45). An old Basque nationalist document links nation, race, blood, and tree (Heiberg 1989:51).

Put more broadly, metaphors of kinship (motherland, fatherland, *Vaterland, patria, isänmaa*) and of home (homeland, *Heimat, kotimaa*) are also territorializing in this same sense, for these metaphors are thought to "denote something to which one is naturally tied" (Anderson 1983:131). Motherland and fatherland, aside from their other historical connotations, suggest that each nation is a grand genealogical tree, rooted in the soil that nourishes it. By implication, it is not possible to be a part of more than one tree. Such a tree evokes both temporal continuity of essence and territorial rootedness.

Thinking in terms of arborescent roots is, of course, in no way the exclusive province of nationalists. Scholars, too, often conceptualize identity and nationness in precisely such terms. Anthony Smith's *The Ethnic Origins of Nations* (1986) provides one example of the centrality of root metaphors in this intellectual domain. In an effort to find constructive middle ground between "primordialist" and "modernist" versions of the emergence of nations,[8] Smith sets out "to trace the ethnic foundations and roots of modern nations" (1986:15), stating, "No enduring world order can be created which ignores the ubiquitous yearnings of nations in search of roots in an ethnic past, and no study of nations and nationalism that completely ignores the past can bear fruit" (5).[9]

Thinking about nations and national identities may take the form of roots, trees, origins, ancestries, racial lines, autochthonism, evolutions, developments, or any number of other familiar, essentializing images; what they share is a genealogical form of thought that, as Gilles Deleuze and Felix Guattari (1987:18) have pointed out, is peculiarly arborescent: "It is odd how the tree has dominated Western reality and all of Western thought, from botany to biology and anatomy, but also gnosiology, theology, ontology, all of philosophy . . . : the root-foundation, *Grund, racine, fondement*. The West has a special relation to the forest, and deforestation."

THE NEED FOR ROOTS AND THE SPATIAL INCARCERATION
OF THE NATIVE

Two kinds of connection between the concept of the nation and the anthropological concept of culture are relevant here. First, the conceptual order of the "national geographic" map (elucidated above by Gellner) is comparable with the manner in which anthropologists have often conceptualized the spatial arrangement of "peoples and cultures." This similarity has to do with the ways in which we tend to conceptualize space in general. As Akhil Gupta (1988:1–2) points out: "Our concepts of space have always fundamentally rested on . . . images of break, rupture, and disjunction. The recognition of cultures, societies, nations, all in the *plural,* is unproblematic exactly because there appears an unquestionable division, an intrinsic discontinuity, *between* cultures, *between* societies, etc." This spatial segmentation is also built into "the lens of cultural relativity that, as Johannes Fabian points out, made the world appear as culture gardens separated by boundary-maintaining values — as posited essences" (Prakash 1990:394). The conceptual practice of spatial segmentation is reflected not only in the narratives of "cultural diversity" but also in the internationalist celebration of diversity in the "family of nations" (Malkki 1994).

A second, related set of connections between nation and culture is more overtly metaphysical. It has to do with the fact that, like the nation, culture has for long been conceived as something existing in "soil." Terms like "native," "indigenous," and "autochthonous" have all served to root cultures in soils; and it is, of course, a well-worn observation that the concept of "culture" derives from the Latin for "cultivation" (see, for example, Wagner 1981:21). "The idea of culture carries with it an expectation of roots, of a stable, territorialized existence," notes James Clifford (1988:338). Here, culture and nation are kindred concepts: they are not only spatializing but also territorializing; they both depend on a cultural essentialism that readily takes on arborescent forms.[10]

A powerful means of understanding how "cultures" are territorialized can be found in Arjun Appadurai's (1988b:37) account of the ways in which anthropologists have tended to tie people to places through ascriptions of native status: "Natives are not only persons who are from certain places, and belong to those places, but they are also those who are somehow *incarcerated,* or confined, in those places." The spatial incarceration of the native operates, he argues, through the attribution not only of physical immobility but also of a distinctly eco- logical immobility (37). Natives are thought to be ideally adapted to their environments — admirable scientists of the concrete mutely and deftly unfolding the hidden innards of their particular ecosystems, PBS-style (38). As Appadurai observes, these ways of confining people to places have deeply metaphysical and moral dimensions (37).

The ecological immobility of the native, so convincingly argued by Appadurai, can be considered in the context of a broader conflation of culture and people, nation and nature — a conflation that is in- carcerating but also heroizing and extremely romantic. Two ethno- graphic examples will perhaps suffice here.[11]

On a certain North American university campus, anthropology fac- ulty were requested by the Rainforest Action Movement (R.A.M.) Com- mittee on Indigenous Peoples to announce in their classes that "Octo- ber 21st through the 28th is World Rainforest Week. The Rainforest Action Movement will be kicking the week off with a candlelight vigil for Indigenous Peoples." (The flyer also lists other activities: a march through downtown, a lecture "on Indigenous Peoples," and a film.) One is, of course, sympathetic with the project of defending the rain forests and the people who live in them, in the face of tremendous threats. The intent is not to belittle or deny the necessity of suprana- tional political organizing around these issues. But these activities on behalf of "the Indigenous," in the *specific* cultural forms that they take, raise a number of questions: Why should the rights of "Indigenous People" be seen as an "environmental" issue? Are people "rooted" in their native soil somehow more natural, their rights somehow more sacred, than those of other exploited and oppressed people? And, one wonders, if an "Indigenous Person" wanted to move away to a city, would her or his candle be extinguished?

But something more is going on with the "Indigenous Peoples Day." That people would gather in a small town in North America to hold a vigil by candlelight for other people known only by the name of "In- digenous" suggests that being indigenous, native, autochthonous, or otherwise rooted in place is, indeed, powerfully heroized.[12] At the same time, it is hard not to see that this very heroization — fusing the faraway people with their forest — may have the effect of subtly ani- malizing while it spiritualizes. Like "the wildlife," the indigenous are an object of inquiry and imagination not only for the anthropologist but also for the naturalist, the environmentalist, and the tourist.[13]

The romantic vision of the rooting of peoples has recently been amplified in new strands of "green politics" that literally sacralize the fusion of people, culture, and soil on "Mother Earth." An article in the *Nation*, "How Paradise Was Lost: What Columbus Discovered" (1990), by Kirkpatrick Sale, is a case in point. Starting from the worthwhile observation that the history of the discovery of the Americas needs to be rewritten, Sale proceeds to lay out a political program that might be described as magical naturalism. The discovery, he writes, "began the process by which the culture of Europe, aptly represented by this captain [Columbus], implanted its diseased and dangerous seeds in the soils of the continents" (445). The captain, we are told, is best thought of as "a man *without place* . . . always rootless and restless" (445). By contrast, "the cultures" discovered and destroyed are best thought of as originally "*rooted in place*" (445). For they had "an exquisite sense of . . . the bioregions." Sale is not content with mere nostalgia; he distills moral lessons and a new form of devotional politics from this history: "The only political vision that offers any hope of salvation is one based on an understanding of, a rootedness in, a deep commitment to, and a resacralization of, *place.* . . . It is the only way we can build a politics that can spread the message that Western civilization itself, *shot through with the denial of place* and a utilitarian concept of nature, must be transformed" (446; emphasis added).

Such a politics, based, as the original peoples of the Americas had it, upon love of place, also implies the place of love. For ultimately love is the true cradle of politics, the love of the earth and its systems, the love of the particular bioregion we inhabit, the love of those who share it with us in our communities, and the love of that unnameable essence that binds us together with the earth, and provides the water for the roots we sink. (446)

The "natives" are indeed incarcerated in primordial bioregions and thereby retrospectively recolonized in Sale's argument. But a moral lesson is drawn from this: the restless, rootless "civilization" of the colonizing "West," too, urgently needs to root itself. In sum, the spatial incarceration of the native is conceived as a highly valued rooting of "peoples" and "cultures" — a rooting that is simultaneously moral and literally botanical, or ecological.

It is when the native is a national native that the metaphysical and moral valuation of roots in the soil becomes especially apparent. In the national order of things, the rooting of peoples is not only normal but also perceived as a moral and spiritual need. As Weil wrote in *The Need for Roots,* "Just as there are certain culture-beds for certain microscopic animals, certain types of soil for certain plants, so there is a certain part of the soul in every one and certain ways of thought and action communicated from one person to another which can only exist in a national setting, and disappear when a country is destroyed" (1987: 151–52).

A SEDENTARIST METAPHYSICS

The territorializing, often arborescent conceptions of nation and culture explored here are associated with a powerful sedentarism in our thinking. Were we to imagine an otherworldly ethnographer studying us, we might well hear that scholar observe, in Yi-Fu Tuan's (1977:156) words, "Rootedness in the soil and the growth of pious feeling toward it seem natural to sedentary agricultural peoples." This is a sedentarism that is peculiarly enabling of the elaboration and consolidation of a national geography that reaffirms the segmentation of the world into prismatic, mutually exclusive units of "world order" (Anthony Smith 1986:5). This is also a sedentarism that is taken for granted to such an extent that it is nearly invisible. And, finally, this is a sedentarism that is deeply metaphysical and deeply moral, sinking "peoples" and "cultures" into "national soils" and the "family of nations" into Mother Earth. It is this transnational cultural context that makes intelligible the linkages between contemporary celebratory internationalisms and environmentalisms.

The effects of this sedentarism are the focus of the following section on refugees. Refugees are not nomads, but Deleuze and Guattari's (1987:23) comments on allegorical nomads are relevant to them: "History is always written from a sedentary point of view and in the name of a unitary State apparatus, at least a possible one, even when the topic is nomads. What is lacking is a Nomadology, the opposite of a history."

UPROOTEDNESS: SOME IMPLICATIONS OF SEDENTARISM FOR CONCEPTUALIZING DISPLACEMENT

Conceiving the relationships that people have to places in the naturalizing and botanical terms described above leads, then, to a peculiar sedentarism that is reflected in language and in social practice.

Territorial displacement as pathological

transplantism
uprootedness
& up

62   LIISA H. MALKKI

This sedentarism is not inert. It actively territorializes our identities, whether cultural or national. And as I will attempt to show, it also directly enables a vision of territorial displacement as pathological. The broader intent here is to suggest that in confronting displacement, the sedentarist metaphysic embedded in the national order of things is at its most visible.

That displacement is subject to botanical thought is evident from the contrast between two everyday terms for it: transplantation and uprootedness. The notion of transplantation is less specific a term than the latter, but it may be agreed that it generally evokes live, viable roots. It strongly suggests, for example, the colonial and postcolonial, usually privileged category of "expatriates" who pick up their roots in an orderly manner from the "mother country," the originative culture-bed, and set about their "acclimatization"[14] in the "foreign environment" or on "foreign soil" — again, in an orderly manner. Uprootedness is another matter. Even a brief overview of the literature on refugees as uprooted people shows that in uprooting, the orderliness of the transplantation disappears. Instead, broken and dangling roots predominate — roots that threaten to wither, along with the ordinary loyalties of citizenship in a homeland (Malkki 1985:24–25; Heller and Feher 1988:89).

The pathologization of uprootedness in the national order of things can take several different (but often conflated) forms, among them political, medical, and moral. After the Second World War and also in the interwar period, the loss of a national homeland embodied by refugees was often defined by policymakers and scholars of the time as a politico-moral problem. For example, a prominent 1939 historical survey of refugees states, "Politically uprooted, he [the refugee] may sink into the underworld of terrorism and political crime; and in any case he is suspected of political irresponsibility that endangers national security" (Simpson 1939:9).[15]

It is, however, the moral axis that has proven to command the greatest longevity in the problematization of refugees. A particularly clear, if extreme, statement of the perceived moral consequences of loss of homeland is to be found in the following passage from a postwar study of the mental and moral characteristics of the "typical refugee":

Homelessness is a serious threat to moral behavior. . . . At the moment the refugee crosses the frontiers of his own world, his whole moral outlook, his attitude toward

what is why it becomes uprooted? If transplantation in other soils were possible, it would not be uprooting, it would be relocation. But under the current conditions refugees once uprooted are kept in a liminality — neither here nor there. Where is the order in displacement prompted by violent displacement?

the divine order of life changes. . . . [The refugees'] conduct makes it obvious that we are dealing with individuals who are basically amoral, without any sense of personal or social responsibility. . . . They no longer feel themselves bound by ethical precepts which every honest citizen . . . respects. They become a menace, dangerous characters who will stop at nothing. (Cirtautas 1957:70, 73)

The particular historical circumstances under which the pathologization of the World War II refugees occurred has been discussed elsewhere (Malkki 1985). The point to be underscored here is that these refugees' loss of bodily connection to their national homelands came to be treated as a loss of moral bearings. Rootless, they were no longer trustworthy as "honest citizens."

obsolete

moral breakdown

The theme of moral breakdown has not disappeared from the study of exile and displacement (Tabori 1972; Kristeva 1991). Francesco Pellizzi (1988:170), for instance, speaks of the "inner destruction" visited upon the exile "by the full awareness of his condition." Suggesting that most of us are today "in varying degrees of exile, removed from our roots," he warns: "1984 is near" (168). Another observer likens the therapeutic treatment of refugees to military surgery; in both cases, time is of the essence: "Unless treated quickly, the refugee almost inevitably develops either apathy or a reckless attitude that 'the world owes me a living', which later proves almost ineradicable. There is a slow, prostrating and agonising death — of the hopes, the idealism and the feeling of solidarity with which the refugees began" (Aall 1967:26).[16]

Apathy! All old sources!

The more contemporary field of "refugee studies" is quite different in spirit from the postwar literature. But it shares with earlier texts the premise that refugees are necessarily "a problem." They are not ordinary people but represent, rather, an anomaly requiring specialized correctives and therapeutic interventions. It is striking how often the abundant literature claiming refugees as its object of study locates "the problem" not in the political conditions or processes that produce massive territorial displacements of people but within the bodies and minds (and even souls) of people categorized as refugees.

contemporary field different

refugees are not a problem

The internalization of the problem within "the refugee" in the more contemporary study of refugees now occurs most often along a medicalizing, psychological axis. Barbara Harrell-Bond, for instance, cites evidence of the breakdown of families and the erosion of "normative social behaviour" (1986:150), of mental illness (152, 283),

In this case you are right!

"psychological stress" (286), and "clinical levels of depression and anxiety" (287).[17] The point here is obviously not to deny that displacement can be a shattering experience. It is rather this: our sedentarist assumptions about attachment to place lead us to define displacement not as a fact about sociopolitical context but as an inner, pathological condition of the displaced.

THE "FAMILY OF NATIONS" AND THE EXTERNALITY OF "THE REFUGEE"

These different texts on the mental and moral characteristics of refugees create first of all the effect of a generalized, even generic, figure: "the refugee."[18] But the generalization and problematization of "the refugee" may be linked to a third process, that of the discursive externalization of the refugee from the national (read "natural") order of things. Three examples may clarify this process.

In a study of the post–World War II refugees, John Stoessinger (1956:189) notes the importance of studying "the peculiar psychological effects arising from prolonged refugee status," and he stresses that "such psychological probings constitute an excursion into what is still largely *terra incognita*." The title of a more recent article reflects a comparable perception of the strangeness and unfamiliarity of the world peopled by refugees: "A tourist in the refugee world" (Shawcross 1989:28–30). The latter is a commentary in a photographic essay on refugees around the world, *Forced Out: The Agony of the Refugee in Our Time* (Kismaric 1989). Excursions into terra incognita, guided tours in "the refugee world," and the last image of being "forced out": all three point to the externality of "the refugee" in the national order of things.

Hannah Arendt outlined these relations of strangeness and externality very clearly when writing about the post–World War II refugees and other displaced peoples in Europe. The world map she saw was very different from the school atlas considered earlier: "Mankind, for so long a time considered under the image of a family of nations, had reached the stage where whoever was thrown out of one of these tightly organized closed communities found himself thrown out of the family of nations altogether. . . . [T]he abstract nakedness of being nothing but human was their greatest danger."[19]

Refugees, liminal in the categorical order of nation-states, thus fit Victor Turner's famous characterization of liminal personae as "naked unaccommodated man" or "undifferentiated raw material"

(1967:98–99). The objectification to which Arendt's and Turner's observations refer is very evident in the scholarly and policy discourse on refugees. The term "refugees" denotes an objectified, undifferentiated mass that is meaningful primarily as an aberration of categories and an object of "therapeutic interventions" (compare Foucault 1979). One of the social and analytic consequences of the school atlas, then, is the political sensitivity and symbolic danger of people who do not fit, who represent "matter out of place" (Douglas 1966).

These relations of order and aberration also raise questions for anthropological practice: if "the refugee" is "naked unaccommodated man," naked and not clothed in culture, why should the anthropologist study him? The heroizing concept of the "family of nations" can be likened to another naturalistic term, the "family of man" (see Haraway 1986:9, 11). Thus does the nakedness of the ideal-typical refugee suggest another link: that between nationlessness and culturelessness. That is, territorially "uprooted" people are easily seen as "torn loose from their culture" because culture is itself a territorialized (and even a botanical and quasi-ecological) concept in so many contexts.[20] As Clifford (1988:338) observes, "Common notions of culture" are biased "toward rooting rather than travel." Violated, broken roots signal an ailing cultural identity and a damaged nationality. The ideal-typical refugee is like a native gone amok (compare Arendt 1973:302). It is not illogical in this cultural context that one of the first therapies routinely directed at refugees is a spatial one. The refugee camp is a technology of "care and control" (Proudfoot 1957; Malkki 1985:51) — a technology of power entailing the management of space and movement — for "peoples out of place."

In the foregoing, I have tried to unfold into clear view these four points: First, the world of nations tends to be conceived as discrete spatial partitionings of territory. Second, the relations of people to place tend to be naturalized in discursive and other practices. This naturalization is often specifically conceived in plant metaphors. Third, the concept of culture has many points of connection with that of the nation and is likewise thought to be rooted in concrete localities. These botanical conceptions reflect a metaphysical sedentarism in scholarly and other contexts. And, finally, the naturalization of the links between people and place lead to a vision of displacement as pathological, and this, too, is conceived in botanical terms, as uprootedness. Uprootedness comes to signal a loss of moral and, later, emotional bearings. Since both cultural and national identities are

conceived in territorialized terms, uprootedness also threatens to de-
nature and spoil these.

NATIONALS AND COSMOPOLITANS IN EXILE

The following two ethnographic examples of conceptions of links between people and place are drawn from detailed accounts presented
elsewhere (Malkki 1990, 1995a). Based on one year of anthropological field research in rural, western Tanzania, among Hutu refugees
who fled the genocidal massacres of 1972 in Burundi, this work ex-
plores how the lived experiences of exile shape the construction of
national identity and historicity among two groups of Hutu refugees
inhabiting two very different settings in Tanzania. One group was
settled in a rigorously organized, isolated refugee camp, whereas the
other lived in the more fluid setting of Kigoma Township on Lake
Tanganyika. Living outside any camp context, these "town refugees"
were dispersed in nonrefugee neighborhoods. Comparison of the
camp and town settings revealed radical differences in the meanings
ascribed by the refugees to national identity and homeland and to
exile and displacement.

The most striking social fact about the camp was that its inhabitants
were continually engaged in an impassioned construction and reconstruction of their history as "a people." Ranging from the "autochthonous" origins of Burundi as a "nation" to the coming of the pastoral
Tutsi "foreigners from the North," to the Tutsi capture of power from
the autochthons by ruse, and, finally, to the culminating massacres
of Hutu by Tutsi in 1972, which have been termed a "selective genocide" (Lemarchand and Martin 1974), the Hutu refugees' narratives
formed an overarching historical trajectory that was fundamentally
also a national trajectory of the "rightful natives" of Burundi. The
camp refugees saw themselves as a nation in exile, defining exile in
turn as a moral trajectory of trials and tribulations that would ultimately empower them to reclaim (or create anew) the "homeland"
in Burundi.

Refugeeness had a central place in these narrative processes. Far
from being a "spoiled identity," refugee status was valued and protected as a sign of the ultimate temporariness of exile and of the
refusal to become naturalized, to put down roots in a place to which
one did not belong. Insisting on one's liminality and displacement as a
refugee was also to have a legitimate claim to the attention of "interna-

tional opinion" and to international assistance. Displacement is usually defined by those who study refugees as a subversion of (national) categories, as an international problem (Malkki 1985, 1994). Here, in contrast, displacement had become a form of categorical purity. Being a refugee, a person was no longer a citizen of Burundi and not yet an immigrant in Tanzania. One's purity as a refugee had become a way of becoming purer and more powerful as a Hutu.

The "true nation" was imagined as a "moral community" being formed centrally by the "natives" in exile (Malkki 1990:34; compare Anderson 1983:15). The territorial expanse named Burundi was a mere state. The camp refugees' narratives agree with Ernest Renan: "A nation is a soul, a spiritual principle" (1990:19). Here, then, would seem to be a deterritorialized nation without roots sunk directly into the national soil. Indeed, the territory is not yet a national soil because the nation has not yet been reclaimed by its "true members" and is instead governed by "impostors" (Malkki 1995a). If "[a]nything can serve as a reterritorialization, in other words, 'stand for' the lost territory," then the Hutu nation has reterritorialized itself precisely in displacement, in a refugee camp (Deleuze and Guattari 1987:508). The homeland here is not so much a territorial or topographic entity as a moral destination. And the collective, idealized return to the homeland is not a mere matter of traveling. The real return can come only at the culmination of the trials and tribulations in exile.

These visions of nation, identity, and displacement challenge the common sense and scholarly views discussed in the first section of this paper not by refuting the national order of things but by constructing an alternative, competing nationalist metaphysic. It is being claimed that state and territory are not sufficient to make a nation and that citizenship does not amount to a true nativeness. Thus, present-day Burundi is an "impostor" in the "family of nations."

In contrast, the town refugees had not constructed such a categorically distinct, collective identity. Rather than defining themselves collectively as "the Hutu refugees," they tended to seek ways of assimilating and of manipulating multiple identities — identities derived or "borrowed" from the social context of the township. The town refugees were not *essentially* "Hutu" or "refugees" or "Tanzanians" or "Burundians" but rather just "broad persons" (Hebdige 1987:159). Theirs were creolized, rhizomatic identities — changing and situational rather than essential and moral (Hannerz 1987; Deleuze and

Guattari 1987:6, 21). In the process of managing these "rootless" identities in township life, they were creating not a heroized national identity but a lively cosmopolitanism — a worldliness that caused the camp refugees to see them as an "impure," problematic element in the "total community" of the Hutu refugees as "a people" in exile.

For many in town, returning to the homeland meant literally traveling to Burundi, to a spatially demarcated place. Exile was not a moral trajectory, and homeland was not a moral destination but simply a place. Indeed, it often seemed inappropriate to think of the town refugees as being in exile at all. Many among them were unsure about whether they would ever return to Burundi even if political changes were to permit it in future. But, more important, they had created lives that were located in the present circumstances of Kigoma, not in the past in Burundi.

The town refugees' constructions of their lived circumstances and their pasts were different from *both* the national metaphysic of the camp refugees and that of scholarly common sense. Indeed, they dismantled the national metaphysics by refusing a mapping and spurning queries over origin altogether. They mounted instead a robust challenge to cultural and national essentialisms; they denaturalized those scholarly, touristic, and other quests for "authenticity" that imply a mass traffic in "fake" and "adulterated" identities; and finally, they trivialized the necessity of living by radical nationalisms. They might well agree with Deleuze and Guattari (1987:15): "To be rhizomorphous is to produce stems and filaments that seem to be roots, or better yet connect with them by penetrating the trunk, but put them to strange new uses. We're tired of trees. We should stop believing in trees, roots, and radicles. They've made us suffer too much."

Just how much it is possible to suffer from root-thinking is illustrated in a particularly terrifying way by developments in Burundi and Rwanda since I completed fieldwork there. I have reviewed this recent history of violence elsewhere (Malkki 1995b:495–523), and many careful, detailed studies have since been published by scholars of the region (for example, Reyntjens 1994; Lemarchand 1994; Guichaoua 1995; Prunier 1995; Newbury and Newbury 1995; Mbonimpa 1993; Jefremovas n.d.; and Destexhe 1994). To give the barest chronological account: 1987 in Burundi saw a coup that brought Major Pierre Buyoya to power. Buyoya's regime first opened a broad discussion of national unity and reconciliation, initiating programs of liberalization. These changes in policy heightened political tensions in the country. In 1990, in Rwanda, a civil war began as the Rwandan Patriotic Front (RPF) (a mainly Tutsi fighting force trained in exile) moved from Uganda into Rwanda to challenge the Hutu-dominated regime of President Juvenal Habyalimana. In 1993, the first democratic elections in the history of independent Burundi resulted in the elections of the first Hutu president, Melchior Ndadaye. After only one hundred days in office, Ndadaye was assassinated in a coup attempt apparently planned by high officers of the Burundi army. The assassination touched off massive political unrest and culminated in the killings of untold numbers of Tutsi before the army stepped in and in turn killed massive numbers of Hutu. It is thought that some one hundred thousand people were killed then and another million forced into exile in neighboring countries. The democratically elected government was reinstalled, but it was clear that the army held the real power. Since that time, continual political repression and fighting have been reported from Burundi. In April 1994, the presidents of both Rwanda and Burundi were killed in a plane crash as they were returning together from a meeting of heads of state in Tanzania. These deaths precipitated a terrible genocide in Rwanda, with systematic mass killing that primarily targeted people of the Tutsi category, as well as politically moderate Hutu. It is estimated that the 1994 Rwanda genocide had a death toll of perhaps 500,000–800,000 (although some estimates are higher) and caused the mass displacement of over two million people after the RPF gained power. In the meantime, the United Nations and other organizations are warning that the ongoing political violence in Burundi is likely to culminate in further genocidal violence. Even a cursory study of the forms of violence and repression in Rwanda and Burundi suggests that it is useful to try to trace or identify larger regional histories, patterns, and commonalities of forms of thought, which may not respect the boundaries of the nation-state (compare Reyntjens 1994; Lemarchand 1994; Guichaoua 1995).

One must be careful, of course, not to assume that the structures of thought about the Tutsi "enemy" that lay behind the Rwandan genocide are isomorphic with those that I observed in Mishamo refugee camp. There is evidence that some Hutu refugees from Burundi have been involved in political violence in both Rwanda and Burundi in recent years, and that some men from Mishamo have returned to Burundi to fight in the ongoing civil war there. But Mishamo is not Rwanda, and it would be irresponsible to make too close a connection between the nationalist metaphysic of purity that grew in Mishamo and the genocidal thinking that motivated the Rwandan massacres. It is also important to remember that tracing commonalities in forms of thought is not to imply common authorship of a crime.

That said, it must also be observed that the extremist Hutu national-ist rhetoric that led up to the Rwandan genocide invoked ideas of indigenous, rooted Hutu and Tutsi "invaders" out of place in the Rwandan national soil, ideas that are disturbingly reminiscent both of the material from Mishamo and of extreme national-categorical think-ing more generally. An African Rights study entitled *Rwanda: Death, Despair, and Defiance* (a hotly debated, controversial document that is nevertheless valuable as a compilation of eyewitness testimony on the genocide) states that propaganda appeals were reportedly made, in the months preceding the genocide, to Hutu as "Sons of the Cultiva-tors" in order to incite people to violence (African Rights 1994:69). The same report states: "Other phrases with important cultural and historical resonances have been given currency by extremist poets and ideologues. Some of these play on the theme of communal work: the word 'interahamwe' itself was previously used for communal work par-ties; 'clearing the bush' originally referred to clearing land for cultiva-tion and has subsequently been used for killing Tutsi (African Rights 1994:70)." One radio broadcast told the Tutsi: "I'd like to tell you that your home is in Ethiopia and we will dump you in the Nyabarongo [river] for you to arrive quickly" (African Rights 1994:73). Like the Jews in the French cemetery at Carpentras, the alien elements were to be removed from the national soil. In May of 1994, some forty thousand such alien elements were retrieved from Lake Victoria in Uganda, carried there by a river reportedly choked with corpses (Pru-nier 1995:255).

Anderson (1983:19) proposes that "nationalism has to be understood by aligning it, not with self-consciously held political ideologies, but with the large cultural systems that preceded it, out of which — as well as against which — it came into being" (compare Orwell 1968:362; Bhabha 1990:1; Kapferer 1988; Balibar and Wallerstein 1991; Gilroy 1990; Yanagisako and Delaney 1995; and Guillaumin 1995). It is in this spirit that the phrase "the national order of things" has been used here (in preference to "nationalism"). Its intent has been to de-scribe a class of phenomena that is deeply cultural and yet global in its significance. That is, the nation — having powerful associations with particular localities and territories — is simultaneously a supralocal, transnational cultural form (Appadurai and Breckenridge 1988b:5–9). (Compare Löfgren 1989; Reé 1992; Gupta 1992; Malkki 1994, 1995a.)

In this order of things, conceptualizations of the relations between people and place readily take on aspects of the metaphysical sedentarism described here. It is these naturalized relations that this paper has tried to illuminate and decompose through the three-way comparison of sedentarist common sense, of the Hutu in the refugee camp, and of the cosmopolitan refugees in Kigoma. These ethnographic examples underscore what a troubled conceptual vehicle "identity" still is, even when the more obvious essentialisms have been leached out of it. Time and again, it reappears as a "root essence," as that "pure product" (Clifford 1988:1) of the cultural, and the national, soil from which it is thought to draw its nature and its sustenance. That many people (scholars included) see identity through this lens of essentialism is a cultural and political fact to be recognized, perhaps especially in the wake of recent events in Rwanda and Burundi. But this does not mean that our analytic tools must take this form. The two main oppositions in this paper — that between sedentarism and displacement in general and that between "the nationals" and "the cosmopolitans" in exile in Tanzania — suggest alternative conceptualizations.

They suggest that identity is always mobile and processual, partly self-construction, partly categorization by others, partly a condition, a status, a label, a weapon, a shield, a fund of memories, and so on. It is a creolized aggregate composed through bricolage. The camp refugees celebrated a categorical "purity," and the town refugees, a cosmopolitan "impurity." But both kinds of identity were rhizomatic, as is any identity, and it would not be ethnographically accurate to study these as mere approximations or distortions of some ideal "true roots."[21]

What Deleuze and Guattari (1987:3) somewhat abstractly describe as rhizomatic is very succinctly stated by Dick Hebdige in his study of Caribbean music and cultural identity. Defining the terms of his project, he says: "Rather than tracing back the roots . . . to their source, I've tried to show how the roots themselves are in a state of constant flux and change. *The roots don't stay in one place.* They change shape. They change colour. And they grow. There is *no such thing as a pure point of origin* . . . but *that doesn't mean there isn't history*" (1987:10; emphasis added).

Observing that more and more of the world lives in a "generalized condition of homelessness" — or that there is truly an intellectual need for a new "sociology of displacement," a new "nomadology" — is not to deny the importance of place in the construction of identities.[22] On the contrary, as I have attempted to show and as Hebdige suggests above, deterritorialization and identity are intimately linked: "Diasporas always leave a trail of collective memory about another place and time and create new maps of desire and of attachment" (Breckenridge and Appadurai 1989:i).[23] To plot only "places of birth" and degrees of nativeness is to blind oneself to the multiplicity of attachments that people form to places through living in, remembering, and imagining them.

NOTES

I would like to thank the following friends and colleagues for their valued comments on this paper: Jim Ferguson, Laurie Kain Hart, Ann Stoler, Karen Leonard, Jane Guyer, Fernando Coronil, David Scobey, Mihalis Fotiadis, and the faculty and students at the Departments of Anthropology at Stanford, Princeton, and Columbia and at the Department of Ethnic Studies at the University of California, San Diego. My colleagues at the Michigan Society of Fellows, the University of Michigan, Ann Arbor, provided an exciting intellectual environment during the writing of this paper. The Society of Fellows and a Grant for Advanced Area Research from the Social Science Research Council provided funding that made this work possible. This essay originally appeared in 1992 under the same title in *Cultural Anthropology* 7 (1): 24–44. The present version has been updated to take account of recent events in Burundi and Rwanda.

1   Said 1979:18, cited by Gupta and Ferguson, "Beyond 'Culture,' " this volume. Julia Kristeva (1991) arrives at similar observations along quite different theoretical trajectories.

2   A more detailed discussion of the literature on nations and nationalism can be located in Malkki 1989:11 and of nations as "citizens of humanity" in Malkki 1994.

3   A critique of Gellner's position has been done by Sally Falk Moore (1989).

4   The "real" nation is implied in such terms as Anthony Giddens's "classical form" (1987:269) and Anthony Smith's "standard or 'classic' European 'nation' " (1986:8). See also Smith 1986:17 on "dubious" forms.

5   *Webster's New Collegiate Dictionary* 1980:640.

6   "Heimat is first of all the mother earth who has given birth to our folk and race, who is the holy soil, and who gulps down God's clouds, sun, and storms. . . . But more than all this, our Heimat is the land which has become fruitful through the sweat of our ancestors. For this Heimat our ancestors have fought and suffered, for this Heimat our fathers have died." Extracted and translated from a 1950s South Tyrolean almanac by Doob (1952:196) and cited in Tuan 1977:156.

7   Clearly, the other great metaphor for community is blood, or stock. But the
    tree more closely reveals the territorialization of identity and is thus given
    primacy here. Frequently these dominating metaphors are also combined, of
    course, as in the family tree. My understanding of the politico-symbolic signifi-
    cance of blood has been enriched by conversations with Ann Stoler.

8   One variety of primordialism is to be found in Mazzini's view that God "di-
    vided Humanity into distinct groups upon the face of our globe, and thus
    planted the seeds of nations" (cited in Emerson 1960:91).

9   Compare Kapferer 1988:1 on culture as the "root essence" of nations and
    national identities in discourses of nationalism.

10 How Durkheimian views of the nation seem to rest on metaphors of the organ-
    ism and the body (the female body, in particular) has been examined else-
    where (Malkki 1989:16).

11 The first example raises the issue of rain forests and the people who live in
    them. Here it is necessary to emphasize that it is not being suggested that the
    political efforts converging on these forests are futile or trivial. Similarly, in the
    case of the second example of environmentalism and green politics, the intent
    is not to advocate a cynically agnostic stance toward environmental politics or
    to echo the unfortunate relativism of a book like Douglas and Wildavsky's *Risk
    and Culture* (1982). The purpose is to sharpen the focus of these phenomena
    so as to better study their place and effects in the contemporary transnational
    context.

12 Thierry Verhelst's study *No Life without Roots* (1990) is an example of such
    heroization. Looking to Third World "grass-roots communities" (4) for a
    "spiritual message" (87) for the West, he states, "Indigenous cultures contain
    within them the seeds necessary to give birth to societies which differ from the
    standardized and devitalized model that has spread over the world" (24).

13 This postcolonial relationship was powerfully portrayed in the fine ethno-
    graphic film *Cannibal Tours*.

14 Notably not "acculturation."

15 A more detailed study of European refugees at the end of the Second World
    War has been done by Malkki (1985, 1995b).

16 Compare Jacques Vernant (1953:17) on "the refugee complex" and also
    Robert Neumann on "émigré life" as a "highly contagious," "corrosive dis-
    ease" (cited in Tabori 1972:398–99).

17 See also Harrell-Bond 1989:63. Compare further Godkin 1980:73–85, a study
    of "rootedness" and "uprootedness" among alcoholics, which finds that be-
    longing to a place fosters psychological well-being.

18 Many of the themes discussed in this section are also treated in Malkki
    1994:41–68.

19 Arendt 1973:294, 300, discussed in Malkki 1989:57–58. ⟨

20 Marrus 1985:8. William Shawcross (1989) echoes this sense of the loss of
    culture: "The poignant voices of refugees recall their lost homes, their pre-
    cious rituals forcibly abandoned" (29).

21 Deleuze and Guattari (1987) state: "Unlike trees or their roots, the rhizome

connects any point to any other point, and its traits are not necessarily linked to traits of the same nature; it brings into play very different regimes of signs, and even nonsign states. . . . It is composed not of units but of dimensions, or rather directions in motion. It has neither beginning nor end, but always a middle (*milieu*) from which it grows and which it overspills" (21). And, "The tree is filiation but the rhizome is alliance . . . the fabric of the rhizome is the conjunction, 'and . . . and . . . and' " (25).

22   On the question of a new sociology of displacement, see Breckenridge and Appadurai 1989:iv. On the concept of a new nomadology, see Deleuze and Guattari 1987:23.

23   It is also worth considering why "to some people the very 'state of movement' is being 'at home' " (Marianne Forro, cited in Tabori 1972:399).

J O H N   D U R H A M   P E T E R S

BIFOCALITY

Bothered by dimming eyesight in his later years, Benjamin Franklin had to use, he wrote, "two pairs of spectacles which I shifted occasionally, as in travelling I sometimes read and often wanted to regard the prospects." To avoid the trouble of switching them, he had lenses cut so that both sorts would fit in one frame. "This I find more particularly convenient since my being in France, the glasses that serve me best at table to see what I eat not being the best to see the face of those on the other side of the table who speak to me; and when one's ears are not well accustomed to the sounds of a language, a sight of the movements in the features of him that speaks helps to explain; so that I understand French better by the help of my spectacles" (Franklin, quoted in Van Doren 1968:637).

Benjamin Franklin knew already in 1784 that a dual vision to the near and far helps in the understanding of a foreign culture. Bifocals were invented in a set of strikingly ethnographic circumstances: blurred vision, traveling, reading, novel food and language. As a rider in coaches, Franklin wanted both to read the texts he had brought with him and to observe the novelties on the horizon. As a stranger, he wanted to check unfamiliar food and understand unfamiliar words. Franklin's bifocals addressed for him what are the more general anthropological dilemmas of near-sight and far-sight, interpretation of detail and orientation to outline, pre-text and new text; they allowed him to switch his gaze rapidly between close-up signs and distant prospects.

An astute and wealthy businessman, Franklin had good reason to want to keep his eyes on both the local and the global. Perhaps capitalism itself (whose spirit Franklin typified for Max Weber) requires such a double surveillance of space: local profits (private property), remote markets (freedom of exchange). Throughout Franklin's century, new kinds of bifocal vision of the social world arise; the eighteenth century is the seedbed of what we have since learned to call "mass media."

Two dominant narratives in recent social thought treat this period as axial for the rise of nonlocalized forms of action and vision. In his *Structural Transformation of the Public Sphere,* Jürgen Habermas (1989) describes the appearance of a new principle of political organization in the eighteenth century: "publicity." Whereas the feudal order consisted of secret deliberations by the rulers and public spectacles for the ruled, the modern state is supposed to make its deliberations visible to the public and legitimate through reason so that the rulers and the ruled are one. The public face of feudal power had been processions, public executions, and the court's pomp-filled, personality-laden fanfare; the constitutional state, in contrast, reveals itself to the public's gaze through organs of sober publicity, particularly but not only journalism, which are supposed to nourish the public sphere and make intelligent discussion possible. Publicity, as the principle of public access to state decisions and of glasnost within social intercourse, is the legitimating idea of modern democracy and signifies, according to Habermas, a shift in the nature of political power: instead of the fiat of the king's arbitrary power comes the reason of the public's opinions. The remaining danger, as Habermas notes, is that the public sphere may be "refeudalized" by the market and the state: that is, the organs of publicity that are supposed to dispense enlightenment to the public may revert to being the stage managers of spectacles that keep the citizens in awe rather than in discussion. In Habermas's panorama of mid- to late-twentieth-century public culture, feudal spectacle is always threatening to take over democratic information, and the mass media, as the Janus-faced agents of both news (which is supposed to instruct the citizenry) and advertising (which is supposed to sell commodities to consumers), find themselves pawns in larger political and cultural battles.

Michel Foucault's story in *Discipline and Punish* (1979) about the rise of new kinds of politics and vision in the eighteenth century is strikingly similar, though with a gloomier spin. Habermas's publicity becomes Foucault's panopticism. "Royal power" showed itself via flamboyant torture of the criminal's body; modern (or "carceral" or disciplinary) power, in contrast, is based on the (self-)surveillance of the citizen's soul. The aim of royal power was to make one body (the king's) visible to all people; the aim of modern power is to make all bodies visible to one person, as typified in Jeremy Bentham's architectural designs for a penitentiary (or hospital, school, or barracks) called the Panopticon. A guard, hidden in a central tower, can peer into each cell of a concentric prison. The inmates, never knowing whether they are being watched at a given moment, internalize this gaze and become guardians over their own behavior. Every citizen becomes a prisonmaster and every soul a panoptic gallery. For Foucault, citizens who think they are acting before the public gaze are only implementing a new kind of subtle discipline of themselves and of the social body. The Panopticon is the nightmare of, to speak with Habermas, systematically distorted communication: the inmates, says Foucault, are objects of information, not subjects in communication.

Whereas Habermas takes the increasing visibility ("publicity") of the social body as a step toward a more enlightened polity, Foucault sees it as a trap. However one positions oneself with regard to the Enlightenment and its attending notions of emancipation and visibility — and it is not an easy question to sort through — both Habermas and Foucault can be read as narrating the rise of modern mass media, those representational modes that promise to depict otherwise unseeable totalities to ordinary citizens. The institutions of conversation in Habermas's bourgeois public sphere (coffeehouses, salons, table societies) would not exist without the press, which he calls "the preeminent institution of the public sphere" (1989:181); and it doesn't take much squinting to see in Foucault's panopticism an allegory of invasive media. Emergent eighteenth-century forms such as newspapers, novels, maps, encyclopedias, dictionaries, statistics and demography, scatterplots and pie charts, zoos, museums, the census, and visual panoramas all fabricate representable totalities beyond the direct acquaintance of any mortal — such as human knowledge (*l'encyclopédie*), the English language (Samuel Johnson's dictionary), or national birth or death rates. Such media begin to democratize the sovereign gaze. Though it is quite plausible to take the twentieth century as the critical moment when the range of the visible outstrips the unaided eye for large portions of the population (Ludes 1992), practices of graphically representing large numbers have a longer ancestry reaching at least to the eighteenth century (Tufte 1983).

It is no accident that the novel and statistics both decisively arise in the eighteenth century. More ancient lineages of these practices can, of course, be traced, but the moment of cultural efficacy for both begins in the Enlightenment, with the rise of a middle-class reading public and rationalized state bureaucracy. The novel and statistics are each a narrative mode answering the problem of how to display a cross section of a quantitative complexity. One uses narrative, the other aggregation. Both enact—and depend on—a new apprehension of space and time: the possibility of envisioning spatially dispersed events at a single moment in time. (Naturally, this conquest of simultaneity in representations is loosely coupled to the integration of regional and world systems.) A novel weaves between several strands of plot with the device of "meanwhile," whereas statistics does so with a "cross section." A newspaper, likewise, aggregates the diversity of its material first and foremost by date (Anderson 1983). The newspaper, whose current form also arises in many respects in the eighteenth century, falls between novels and statistics as modes of social reportage (Lennard Davis 1983). The tension between story and fact, as Michael Schudson, borrowing a page from Walter Benjamin, has argued, structures classic twentieth-century journalistic genres: human interest stories and stock market reports, narrations of sporting feats and box scores (Schudson 1978). The polarity of narrative and data marks the twin limits of modern social description, with many hybrid forms between. Academic battles between number crunchers and tale-spinners are only a local variant on this larger theme.

Given a sufficiently broad definition, it is easy to see mass media in a wide variety of social formations, not only modern, electrified ones (for example, Menache 1990). All social orders in history have probably conjured grand pictures that outstripped anyone's powers of experience or sensation, but modernity is distinguished by the graphic portrayal of actualities. We generally do not suppose the stock market report belongs to the same order of truth as older stories about the antics of Zeus or the wrath of Huitzilopochtli: we imagine that the one sort of totality is endowed with a density of empirical reference that the other lacks. Moderns have figured out how to make their gods empirical. The forces that shape our world may be portrayed in story, image, or statistic, but modernity claims that they can be cashed in for the hard currency of observation. What is uniquely modern is the claim of indexical verifiability embedded in our representations of social totalities. This claim informs the diverse practices of the mass media, which we should not conceive only as television, cinema, radio, newspapers, and magazines, or as the even more various apparatuses of information and entertainment, but as all practices of social envisioning, reporting, and documentation, including statistics, accounting, insurance, census taking, polling, and the work of social services and of the social sciences. Part of what it means to live in a modern society is to depend on representations of that society. Modern men and women see proximate fragments with their own eyes and global totalities through the diverse media of social description. Our vision of the social world is bifocal. Institutions of the global constitute totalities that we could otherwise experience only in pieces, such as populations, the weather, employment, inflation, the gross national product, or public opinion. The irony is that the general becomes clear through representation, whereas the immediate is subject to the fragmenting effects of our limited experience. Our sense organs, having evolved over the ages to capture immediate experience of the local, find themselves cheated of their prey.

Modern media pose the question of the continuing relevance of place as a marker of intelligibility in social description. Habermas's bourgeois public sphere in eighteenth-century London is already a diasporic assembly; a virtual public may be the only kind of public there has ever been. But received images of political action (the Athenian Pnyx, the Roman forum, the London coffeehouse, the New England town meeting) presuppose the appointment of places for face-to-face conversation. Media and mass communication seem to threaten the existence of local sites of talk. In this essay, I am interested in the waning of place as a container of experience. Clearly, nomadic cultures are ancient, and signs have long been dispersed, but electronic media do present new challenges or at least exacerbate old ones. Recent debates in anthropology about the practice of ethnography reflect the dilemma of lost semiotic homelands. The issue of power and complicity in the dialogic encounter and the subsequent crafting and circulation of the ethnographic text is implicitly undergirded by the loss of faith in place as an epistemological ordering principle. Recent internal critiques of ethnography have attacked its myopic attention to the local and the dispersion of cultures into the crisscrossing flows of capital, people, technology, ideas, and media narratives across the globe (Appadurai 1990). Reading glasses, it is argued, are not enough; ethnography must survey the global circulation of capital, signs, bodies, and commodities, seeing that circulation

as fundamental, not extraneous to the local worlds traditionally fa-
vored by ethnography. The art of writing cultures must "break with the
trope of community" and the dream of immediate presence (Marcus
1989b).

In its beginnings, ethnography focused on local worlds that were
seen, sometimes conveniently so, as dangerously delicate in contrast
to the scale and power of engulfing cosmopolitan orders: the Aztec
language and culture chronicled by Father Bernardino de Sahagún,
the Scottish ballads collected/invented by James Macpherson under
the name of "Ossian," the "Indo-Germanic" language and lore of the
brothers Grimm, the Magyar music of Béla Bartók, the coastal Indians
of Franz Boas, and so on. An implicit doctrine about the relation of
culture and place prevailed: spatial confinement stood for the native's
enchantment, tradition, culture, and primitive economy, as opposed
to the anthropologists' enlightenment, modernity, science, and developed economy. Spatial mobility stood for the ethnographer's privilege, and territorial restriction became the symbol of ethnographic
intelligibility. Ethnography became, in part, the task of finding pockets of knowability within a dizzy world system.

One of the traditional appeals of ethnography, then, is that it claims
to offer the anthropologist an apparent escape from the bifocality of
the social world of origin, an epistemologically unencumbered eye for
things social. It offers a social world whose scale is commensurate with
face-to-face inquiry. Eric Leed (1980) argues that much academic
discourse on folk and preliterate cultures has been conditioned historically by an implicit longing for an alternative to the industrial-
capitalist homeland of academics. One goes abroad to find what one
lacks at home. In the Mato Grosso of Brazil or the Sepik River region of
New Guinea, it was supposed, one may find a pristine culture, undis-
turbed by the worldwide circulation of matter and mentalities of the
last five centuries, a world ultimately knowable even if initially be-
wildering. The commitment to the local is part of the dream of finding
a "knowable community" (Raymond Williams 1973), legible and visible in its entirety. Strangeness is dialectically related to the familiar,
and anthropology, as the study of the strange, has long had the underlying moral and political project of critique on the homefront (Marcus
and Fischer 1986). Every frontier, as James Carey (1989) has quipped,
has its "backtier."

Shifting the burden of autobiography from self to other has long
been one of anthropology's sublimated dramas, from Malinowski on-

ward. The other tells our tales in alienated form. If we are to heed the call to be more frank about the effects and commitments of our discourse and interests, then we might try to explore the nature of our "own" culture, trying not to overlook whether (1) the proprietary "our" is possible, (2) the implied unity of the "we" is defensible, and (3) the name "culture" fits the strange suspension between what we academics, de facto members of a worldwide professional and cosmopolitan class whatever our political sympathies, can experience for ourselves close-up and what we experience via the globalizing discourses and images of the media. If ethnographers once assumed that the local is both autonomous and readable, neither assumption quite holds in the privileged environments in which most people who write and read such essays as this one live. Thanks to various media of social representation, the local environment is often seen fleetingly, whereas global events — war in Iraq, pollution in Eastern Europe, famine in Africa, or strife in the Middle East — are portrayed as coherent, if often violently foreshortened, visions for our gaze. (Here I bracket the crucial questions of the accuracy and ideology of those representations: my concern is the pretense of presenting those images as knowable wholes.)

The authority of the local, in contrast, is often undercut by image totalities, just as it is by economic ones: I may see blue skies, but the satellite picture on the TV news tells me a huge storm is on its way; in 1988, almost everyone with whom I talked face-to-face in Iowa City, a Democratic stronghold, said she or he was voting for Dukakis, whereas the national polls — much more accurately — foretold Bush's election; I may know many people moving east, but the demographic data show the slow west-southwestward drift of the U.S. population. Local knowledge, the erstwhile prize of ethnographic inquiry, is constantly discredited as a guide to living in the modern world for being too concrete, too mired in immediacy. My embodied experience belongs to a smaller orbit than that of the "information" I receive from various media of social representation: in fact, transcendence of our bodies may be the peculiar hallmark of "information" (Benjamin 1968a). Immediate experience of the local, long prized by common sense as the only experience worth having, is, for people in certain class positions, no longer a trustworthy guide to practical life in the modern world. Close reading can no longer claim to be an authoritative interpretive method of a social world whose shape is discernible only through general visions offered by agencies of social reporting. The irony is that one's own eyes provide fragments of "society," whereas media representations are panoramic and total.

In contrast to most of our fellow humans in history, the global has become a graphic part of our local experience. People have always had the wildest things in their heads, but modern media of social reportage claim to provide an actuality and realism of social imagination, as above, that is quite unprecedented. The representation of a social totality that transcends the circumference of an individual's possible experience is always potentially a political act, an act of constitution or revelation: for many social critics in the nineteenth century, to document society was already to protest it (Engels, Dickens, Zola, Riis, Tarbell, and so forth). But in the late twentieth century, few believe they can describe current social conditions armed with nothing but camera and pencil: the gap between what we can know face-to-face and what we have to know via the big picture makes any foray into social portraiture an exercise fraught with epistemological, existential, and political difficulties. And yet we can "see" arctic air masses on the evening news or national taste in breakfast cereals in *USA Today* graphics. We need to understand media (again, in the broad sense as machines for the representation of social life as a knowable whole) as the court painters of the global, as providers of a kind of sight that lifts our gaze beyond immediate experience to distant, concurrent events, as key factors in the confused local-global cultures in which we students of culture find (or lose) ourselves. We must examine how the age-old link of locality and truth has been made strange for us, if not topsy-turvy.

CULTURE AND MASS CULTURE

A central intuition informing two centuries of mass culture criticism is that mass culture does not respect the bounds of locality. Cultures in diaspora have been ignored or disdained. Notions of culture and place have long been intertwined. Connected with both is a third term, "authenticity," which helps give the concept of culture a polemical edge that excludes certain candidates from its status — the mass media foremost among them. Raymond Williams (1983, 1985b; also Hall 1980) has, of course, helped us parse this term. One branch of *culture*'s meaning refers to the totality of practices and lived experiences of a people — culture as "a whole way of life." The other refers to those imaginative and intellectual achievements canonized as somehow great or immortal — culture as "high art." In both the democratic-anthropological and the elitist-artistic senses of the term, culture is remote, elusive, a scarce resource. Whether as "the expression of a people's experience" or "culchah," both definitions exclude the culture of the mass media (soap operas, sports, westerns, music videos, comics, parades, T-shirts) or of the middle range (collegiate sports, parades, picnics, Airstream trailers, fireworks) more generally. The middle is taken as either inadequately serious or inadequately sincere. The top and bottom are authentic, but the middle is banal.

What is it precisely about the middle that makes it wanting in the department of "real" culture? First, mass-mediated symbols violate the notion that place collects an integrated culture. They travel to you electronically or by other space-collapsing means and via rationalized systems of marketing and distribution; you needn't do fieldwork in exotic places to find them. They testify less to the global variety of human practices than to the worldwide reach of economic, political, or religious empires. Traveling, goes the plaint, is no longer a guarantee of encountering densely textured symbolic differences in everyday life. Mass culture, one might say, is spread too thin to invite thick description. Second, mass culture obscures authorship. It cannot be seen as an uncomplicated expression of a people's consciousness or worldview. Whereas a folklorist could once assume that folk songs and house decorations are conscious creations people make in the context of their imaginative and material conditions, no such strong link between soul and symbol can be assumed for the products of culture industries. Mass culture is thus taken as a kind of alienated discourse, mediated and filtered, not pure. Notions of uprootedness explicitly invoke a romantic image of nourishing bondage to place. Third, mass culture is mediated by the market, which, as Marx noted, is governed by the fetishism created by the movement of a commodity from one place to another. The commodity fetish appears in the jump-cut of spatial displacement. It is produced with the audience/buyer in mind, rather than as immediate unconstrained labor. Again, its integrity is tarnished: the Nielsen ratings and the New Guinean's sense of a market for primitive sculpture are both symptoms of the same disease: loss of authentic self-expression. Mass(-mediated) culture, in short, violates all the tenets of pop romanticism — place, soul, and expression — and replaces them with dispersion, artifice, and the market.

The concept of mass culture forces certain commitments out of the woodwork, because both ethnographers and curators have been able to dismiss it as always on the wrong side of such dualisms as creativity versus commerce, original versus copy, face-to-face as opposed to mass communication, end versus means, and self-expression as opposed to market orientation. Eric Rothenbuhler's comments (1990) on the way that the classic distinction between *Gemeinschaft* and *Gesellschaft* informs judgments about the degraded character of mass communication are apposite: "Interpersonal communication appears a primordial expression of the self and other mutually reaching out to share each other's experience. Mass communication appears to be a manufactured stimulus based on the rational calculations of those who run the media to take advantage of the attention of strangers, and, from the audience's point of view, a matter of spectatorship rather than participation, of the entertainment value of differences rather than the nutrient value of commonalities" (5). Culture is a body's voice; mass culture is mediated artifice. Culture as conceived in its romanticist vein is the fantasy of a pure disclosure of soul (whether a nonliterate artisan or a Beethoven), the product of a laboring body (rather than rationalized mechanism), with origins within an identifiable place and time (rather than the spaceless center of a dream factory).

Culture, then, in Walter Benjamin's terms, is marked by an "aura" (1968b:220–24). This notoriously elusive concept is itself about elusiveness: an aura is "the unique perception of a distance, however close it may be." The aura of a work of art derives from its unique localization in space and time. The aura tracks the singular mortal body of the work through space and time. The true *Mona Lisa* is in the Louvre; the image of the *Mona Lisa* on a T-shirt, in contrast, inhabits a very different practical universe (it can be washed, worn, sweat in) and hence is unprotected by the prohibitions and "microadjustments" (Lévi-Strauss 1966:10) that surround sacred things. If some miraculous technical process could reproduce the *Mona Lisa* exactly, molecule for molecule, so that no analysis could distinguish the two, down to the historical effects of aging and deterioration, the copy would still lack the history connecting the "true" *Mona Lisa* to its originary authority as a relic carrying Leonardo's contagious magic across the centuries. The copy would be only a spectacle of technical ingenuity, not a moving or perplexing work of art. It would be a simulation, not an expression. We would wonder how it was done, not what it meant. It would be fit for Disneyland, not the Louvre.

That hardly anyone would dispute the very different institutional destinies of the two objects reveals what metaphysicians we seem to be in dealing with culture — in any sense of the term. Culture is evidently more than matter in motion; Benjamin alerts us to its delicate ontology. Artworks are not only texts; they include their site of origin, afterlife, and discursive and historical complex of valuation and reception. Identical objects can invite radically different hermeneutic stances from their audiences/readers. The Louvre painting could sustain questioning about possible reasons for the famous smile, whereas the Disneyland copy would be admired mainly for its amazing technical skill. The one has an author whose intent may be probed, if only in imagination, and the other is the result of a technical process. The origins of the two works are part of their possible interpretations, even of their essence. The one work is haunted by a whole texture of historical ghosts and legends; the other needs to have that supplied. Each one offers its viewers a radically different hermeneutic invitation. Indiscernible objects, pace Gottfried Wilhelm Leibniz, are not identical in the realm of signs.

In Jorge Luis Borges's story "Pierre Menard, Author of the Quixote" (1964), a similar point is made. A twentieth-century French symbolist poet, Pierre Menard, learns the rules of chivalry, converts to Catholicism, and learns early-seventeenth-century Spanish in an effort that can only be described as quixotic: to rewrite the Quixote without consulting the original. After Herculean efforts, Menard reproduces a few pieces of the text (that he can write only parts of the text is a comment on the "availability" of texts in different historical moments). After doing all the classic acts of historicism (immersion in source materials, mentalities, language, and so on), only to a logically absurd extreme, Menard is still unable to write the past "as it really was." Historicism stands refuted: Menard produces a new text eccentric to the original. As the tale's narrator notes, though both texts are "verbally identical," Menard's fragments "are almost infinitely richer" than those of Cervantes. What were literary flourishes in 1609 ("Truth, whose mother is history") resound in the age of Marxism and pragmatism. The setting of a sentence in history endows it with references and resonances. Whether a copy is richer (Menard's Quixote) or poorer (Disney's Mona Lisa) than the original, things cultural derive meaning not solely from formal patterning, semiotic suggestiveness, or power of statement but also from a tissue of relationships with history, time, and place.

The apparent attenuation of such a tissue is what characterizes mass culture, not the supposedly lousy quality of Hollywood movies, soap operas, comic strips, or romance novels. Scale, commerce, and mass reproduction do not affect the quality of texts (though the question of "quality" is intimately involved in the entire apparatus); they produce aura-free texts that invite people to supply their own frame of interpretation. The products of mass culture seem to come without hermeneutic "directions for use," though not without obvious ideological weightings. Benjamin, for one, found the loss of aura to be politically progressive because it opened up art, he thought, to public and collective modes of reception. Others argue that the impoverishment of interpretive resources in much mainstream media fare is debilitating politically, for it offers nothing to keep mass culture from being lazily digested into prevailing opinion. Whether TV viewers, for instance, are poets of the screen, able to rewrite narratives that speak to their own condition, or are dupes who are overwhelmingly constrained by extant ideologies and reading formations — or sometimes both or neither or something else — is hotly debated. What a booming industry of research into audience decodings of television programming has revealed is not the sweeping away of local consciousness and identity through a media-imperialist deluge, as was widely feared in the 1970s, but the flourishing of localized meaning-makings, in turn shaped by a wide variety of proximate constraints, such as gender, control over TV technology, access to critical counterdiscourses, education, and religious and ethnic identity (Liebes and Katz 1990; Morley 1992; Purnima Mankekar 1993; Livingstone 1994). Audiences, we have learned, resist ideologies, snooze, argue, eat, make love, party, weep, laugh, channel-surf (men more so than women), debate, and tune out in front of the television set. Audience research is, in part, the revenge of the local, the reassertion of the small scale in the midst of space-transcending media systems. That much of this research is done in the name of ethnography suggests the perseverance of near-sight as a mode of human experience of the world, even when the objects of vision are transported from afar. Audience research suggests that localization and globalization are not just matters of physical availability and access but of attachment and affection, interpretation and ideology, power and privilege. The romantic longing for a rooted place is often belated; only the uprooted cry for roots; the innocent know not to lament their fall. Localization and globalization are cultural processes like any other ones (Friedman 1990).

"Mass culture," in sum, consists of what "culture" is supposed to consist of — symbols — and yet those symbols behave in ways that violate much of the work "culture" was originally supposed to do as a concept. Mass culture no longer stands for diversity of practices; for rootedness in space, place, and tradition; for the local. It defies the equation of cultural integrity and geographical finitude. We metropolitan souls living among ethno-pop, sound bytes, McDonalds, e-mail, and global circulation of patterns, people, and products easily see ourselves as "people without culture," as Renato Rosaldo (1988) observes. Like Raymond Williams, Rosaldo notes the contradictory meanings of culture in the discourse of anthropology: officially, it is supposed to be an aspect of all human activity, and yet cultures that are spatially localized, homogeneous, and immediate are preferred. Lowland Filipinos or North Americans, for example, are branded "people without culture." Our mobility, rationality, markets, differentiation, and multiplicity of options make our culture invisible. "Evidently, the concept of culture [can] barely describe, let alone analyze, flux, improvisation, heterogeneity" (1988:77). For Rosaldo, the creation or effacement of cultural differences is a charged gesture in a zone of conflict, not an innocent census of varieties. The cultureless are often that way as a luxury; those with cultures are often marked as such and not given the privilege of being culture-free. Hence the apparent lack of integrated cultural spaces is just as worthy of anthropological interrogation and analysis: "Border zones, pockets, and eruptions, along with our supposedly transparent cultural selves, are as profoundly cultural as anything else" (Rosaldo 1988:87).

As students of culture, then, we should recognize the self in the other and the other in the self, be explicit when we blend the autobiographical and the ethnographic, and explore our spatially mobile, culturally translucent, and informationally saturated status. The rediscovery of audience interpretations revives ethnography's relevance and suggests the inevitability of localized forms of life. Bifocality may be not just a stance we should adopt as social analysts but also precisely the thing we already possess that makes our status as cultural animals problematic — and deserving of inquiry.

THE WALL AND THE CASTLE

Franz Kafka can be read as an anatomist of the paradoxes of making an animal whose body and senses are fitted for finitude into a global being. His writings suggest that the effort to transcend a local vision is more perilous than might be expected. His stories simulate the vertigo one can feel, suspended between the range of our bodies and the totality of systems.

His "The Great Wall of China" is an extraordinary tale about imagining the state, as befits a story about the most enduring state and (with the pyramids of Egypt) the most famous state edifice in human history. In building the wall, Kafka recounts, a "principle of piecemeal construction" was used. Two gangs of laborers would work on a small stretch, working toward each other. When the piece was completed, the laborers would not build additions on its two outer ends but would be transferred to a completely different locale to repeat the same activity there. "Naturally in this way many great gaps were left, which were only filled in gradually and bit by bit, some, indeed, not till after the official announcement that the wall was finished. In fact it is said that there are gaps which have never been filled in at all, an assertion, however, that is probably merely one of the legends to which the building of the wall gave rise, and which cannot be verified, at least by any single man with his own eyes and judgment, on account of the extent of the structure" (Kafka 1971:235). But why this method of building, so obviously inadequate to the professed aim of keeping out the barbarians? Kafka exploits the truism that the wall served more to keep the Chinese in than the barbarians out. "The legends to which the building of the wall" gives rise are its most important product. The Great Wall for Kafka is a work of spiritual social control—in other words, of nationalizing civic consciousness. The grandiosity of the project forces citizens to ponder its purpose; the impossibility of ever seeing the wall as a whole stimulated the circulation of official discourse and counterdiscourses; the curious method of building made villagers into Chinese. The enforced need to interpret an enigma, Kafka knew, generates both faith and wavering. The state creates enigmas as a matter of policy to secure the good faith of its citizens and to secure for itself monopoly rights in the representation of unseeable totalities.

Because the wall exists as complete only in the discourse of state edicts, it must constantly be imagined and reimagined. The need to build the wall with thoughts as well as stones, Kafka suggests, keeps up the morale of the supervisors, who have received exacting training in architecture and yet are wearied by the dullness of the actual work. The movement of supervisors and laborers across the land takes them on a *tour d'horizon* in which they may recognize themselves as belonging to something—China—that could command such an infinite ex-

ertion as the building of the wall. In pilgrimages across the provinces
the supervisors and laborers confront the enigma of their common
lot. Reflection on such we-ness, as Benedict Anderson (1983) argues,
is a key moment in the formation of nationalism. (Though Anderson's
book is often taken as the voice of a soft cultural Marxism — perhaps
thanks to its publication by Verso and his brother Perry Anderson's
preeminent status in the British left — its central narrative of nationalism as an answer to the search for meaning in a disenchanted world is
fundamentally Weberian.) As in our love lives, so in our national histories: accidents become destinies. Something as magnificently unverifiable and manifestly absurd as the Great Wall with huge gaps in it
created the spiritual need for constant national puzzlement and allegiance. With Leon Festinger, the discoverer of "cognitive dissonance,"
Kafka knew that absurd assignments generate their own rationales.
Kafka is the analyst of the ways that absurdity recruits allegiances, that
the state, among other institutions, dangles images of unverifiable
totalities before its populace to keep them in a constant condition of
loyal wonderment. Kafka's China has found a way to exploit the finitude of human sense perception for political ends. It sponsored a
public work that could be completed only in the heart and mind of
each citizen.

In the beginning of Kafka's *The Castle* ([1926] 1974), "K" enters a
village inn and finds himself accosted by a representative of the Castle,
a vaporous entity whose identity remains permanently veiled in the
book and thus functions as an allegory of infinity and bureaucracy.
Haughtily K claims to be "the surveyor," summoned by the Castle, and
the representative checks twice with the Castle by telephone. On being
recognized by the Castle the second time, K reflects that this is pro-
pitious (since it gets him off the hook from the representative, who
wants to banish him from the country) but unpropitious because it
means the Castle is on to him and is giving him the chance to make his
next move. K does not know, cannot know, if he has been recognized
or is only fabricating it.

This interpretive wavering before an enigmatic answer is a fundamental experience in the modern world: carrying on a fencing match
with a partner who seems to be responding but whose motives are
inscrutable or whose responses can never be verified as responses.
Modern men and women stand before bureaucracies and their representations in the same way that sinners stood before the God who
hides his face: anxiously sifting the chaos of events for signs and mes-

sages. The *deus absconditus* (hidden god) of theology no longer hides in the farthest corners of the universe; his successor has moved into the infernal machines of administration. Dante's vision of the place beyond the heavens was a kaleidoscopic reflection of spheres against spheres, a multifoliate rose of infinitely refracted light. K, like the rest of us, peers into a place in which the reverberations are not optical but informational. (Game theory is the scientized form of this experience.) He does not know whether the permission given him to stay in the village is a mandate from the Castle itself, from some sleepy bureaucrat on the other end of the telephone trying to cover a possible failure to note K's arrival, or from the representative himself, fascinated by K's haughty certitudes. K must interpret the gestures from the Castle (if they are indeed from the Castle) with the same attentiveness that augurs once monitored the sky above the *templum* for the flight of birds or the fall of stars; equally, he must follow them with the same falsificationist rationality of the modern scientist, carefully peeling away alternate hypotheses, checking the data for clerical errors, wondering if the instrument was flawed or tapped the right information. To survive in the modern world, men and women must become the diviners of inscrutable others, interpret the moods of secretaries, the words of department heads, the decisions of deans and CEO's, and shake-ups in the organization of the Kremlin as if they were the language of some hidden, murky, remote god, content only to speak in darkness and in dreams.

K, as a surveyor, one who must read not only local but global signs as well, never knows if such signs are a coherent language expressing an overall design or if whatever design exists is only a paranoid projection of the overactive interpreter. Are there dark secrets hidden in the government's statistical tables, or is there simply the accumulation of lots of noise and little data? The signs that we read with our farsighted lenses are all around us; they refuse to tell us how to read them. We hesitate, caught between the fear of being paranoid ("everything's a message") and the fear of missing a revelation if we act as if nothing is a message. The inability to verify for certain whether a sign is a projection of self or an utterance of other, an interpretive artifact or an objective pattern in the world, confronts a variety of social types: wizards who read tea leaves or entrails, believers who receive answers to prayers, takers of the Turing test who wager if the conversant is a human or a smart machine, or the Ks, the students of culture and society, who read the structures on the horizon as well as the texts that are up close (or *in* the texts that are up close).

The space that we have to discern and portray as bifocal readers of culture — as scholars and citizens — is thoroughly Kafkaesque. The world beyond the local exists as a visible totality only in discourse and image, though its fragmentary and scattered effects are all too evident in the lives of flesh-and-blood people. If we are to criticize it or falsify it, our only tools are more representations. We are, once and for all, bound to our bodies and their thresholds, and yet our heads swim with visions of things that we claim are real facts, not just one more item in the list of historical delusions that people have killed and died for. Kafka points to an incommensurability between the finite capacity for experience our mortal bodies possess and the infinitude that infests the reigning representational institutions of our time. Corporate financial reports, government documents, actuarial tables, omniscient narration, or the TV news might seem unlikely candidates for out-of-body experiences, but our experience is rife with objects that could be experienced only by gods; and gods, alas, we are not.

Ethnography, as the description of palpable human experience, may seem old-fashioned in a time when locality no longer guarantees the link between symbol and soul as it once seemed to. But there is the danger of breaking through to the other side of the sound barrier if we overcelebrate the contingent bricolage of cultural and personal identity in a delirious dance with "Mr. In-Between" (Bhabha 1994). The improvisation of identity is wonderful if you have the cultural and finance capital to cushion you against the traumas of postmodernity, but most of the human species still lives out its days in localized spaces, dependent in various ways on people they have known for years. The means for making one's identity a poetic work are inequitably distributed. Distance from the local is often a luxury. Localities — chosen or fated — still govern the lives of most humans, even the rapidly increasing numbers with access to global, regional, national, and local media. The Anglo-Muslim immigrant opposition to Salman Rushdie's *Satanic Verses* (1989), for instance, suggests not just that some people are insufficiently enlightened (as some commentators would have it) but also that global flows may follow weird circuits, not merely center to periphery, and in-betweenness can be a profoundly painful — not just playful — condition. That popular resistance to cultural artifacts may not take the form we might approve of is a necessary reminder to laborers in the vineyard of cultural studies. We should neither drain the concept of culture of its ties to place and matter nor freeze it into absolute identity. On the need for analytic (but not existential) in-betweenness, Bhabha is right.

Though we cultural analysts must shake off a debilitating preference for the culturally contained over the mobile, the effort to gain some kind of narrative sense of our species' desperate and magnificent condition as mortal and embodied beings, to find discourses that make links to other people in other worlds, cannot be pushed aside. We need to continue to develop arts of reading the global as it pushes its way into the local, which is the age-old task of humane self-understanding. As the practice of creating social theory dialogically (Marcus 1989b), ethnography will necessarily remain a constitutive tool in our kits, as long as the necessary faith continues that we can learn something by talking to people whose experience is other than ours. We must take a gamble on the ongoing relevance of the lifeworld, however perforated it may be by the system.

NOTE

I thank Katie Trumpener, Carl Couch, Eric Rothenbuhler, Ken Cmiel, and especially Akhil Gupta for criticism, useful references, encouragement, and patience. An earlier version of this essay was presented at the Annenberg Scholars Conference on Public Space, University of Pennsylvania, 1–4 March 1995.

State, Territory, and National Identity Formation
in the Two Berlins, 1945–1995

JOHN BORNEMAN

For Germans and Germany, the novel way in which the nation form of collective belonging connects polity, territory, and cultural identity has been a riddle. This form, as Ernest Gellner (1983) has noted, presupposes that territory and people are coterminous. Without both territory and culture, a "people" can make no legitimate claim to a national polity, and conversely, such a polity can make no legitimate claim to a people unless it circumscribes itself territorially and delineates its people culturally. At least since the Treaty of Westphalia in 1648, the external form of the polity has been defined as a state, whereas the internal form has been defined as the nation — codified as a culturally homogeneous people (Borneman 1994). Hence we can observe everywhere a dual movement since the signing of this peace treaty ending the Thirty Years War: of peoples calling themselves a nation and then demanding their own territorial states, and states legitimating their claims to a people by turning them into nationals. To create the nation-state, territorial sovereignty and cultural distinctiveness become necessary accomplices (compare Anderson 1983; Balibar 1991b; and Hobsbawm 1990).

Particularly troublesome for this century's Berlin residents has been the notion of cultural distinctiveness — Who is German? — perhaps best expressed by the untranslatable concept *Heimat*. Conventionally translated as "home," Heimat is semantically much broader and emotionally more evocative than the English term; it denotes habitat, locality, birthplace, homeland, and native place. In other words, to lose one's Heimat is to lose not only one's home but also some of the central referents of German personhood that define familiarity and the conditions in which one feels secure. In this essay I will explicate the relation of Heimat to shifts in territorial sovereignty since the end of World War II. Key to this explication is an acknowledgment of the instability of the meanings of "place" and "people" in Germany.

Both world wars resulted in shifts in physical boundaries and massive population movements of German-speaking peoples known for their regional loyalties. The retreat of the German army from the eastern front in 1944 was followed by a massive territorial displacement of German-speaking peoples. From 1944 to 1961, more than twelve million people were displaced from East Prussia and former German territories, either forcibly expelled or driven into exile by fear of revenge, in the largest "ethnic cleanup," as it was called, known in history (Korte 1985:14–15; Meinicke 1988). The events that caused and were used to justify this forced exodus — the Holocaust and the search for a "final solution" — can be understood as a radicalization and mixture of two "failed" programs: first, the euthanasia program designed to eliminate "sick people" or *Untermenschen* (subhumans), and, second, resettlement policies carried out by Germans in the eastern regions of the Reich that were intended to create *Lebensraum* (living space) for Germans by removing Slavs, primarily Poles, from productive land (Aly 1995). These policies of resettlement and internal cleansing were then applied as tools in the genocide against the Jews, resulting in the gruesome medical experiments, forced labor, concentration camps, and ovens of Auschwitz (on the popular appeal of these policies, see Lüdke 1993:S46–S67).

The peculiar solution of the Allies to the Holocaust and the Second World War was the 1945 Potsdam Accord, which sought to deconstruct any semblance of the unity of culture, territory, nation, and state. The Allies divided the nation territorially and ideologically, displaced large parts of the population, and through occupation policies installed new regimes that left open for contestation the physical boundaries of Heimat. After the war, German identity could no longer be linked to a finite, secure territory precisely because of continued claims to land forcibly surrendered and because large numbers of displaced persons refused to give up the dream of returning home. The new metaphorical *Heimatlose* (literally, homeless and stateless people) made up between 20 and 25 percent of all people in the two postwar German states. Many refused to submit to the appellation *Fluchtling* (refugee), instead calling themselves *Vertriebene* (expellee) and forming political organizations to reobtain their land and return to their former homes. The dual structure of Berlin became the focal site and symbol of occupation policies — the Allied "answer" — which were then reinscribed in varied form by the two new German states after they were founded in 1949. By contrast, Austria, which had also belonged to the Third Reich, was left alone to determine its own history after the war; its territorial sovereignty was left relatively intact.

For the city of Berlin specifically and the country of Germany generally, the nation form way of connecting culture and territory has not proven adequate to organize the people's collective belonging patterns. With respect to territoriality, the international community revoked German territorial sovereignty following this century's two world wars, both of which were begun by German states (Geyer 1992:75–100). With respect to national-cultural identity, the various states on German soil have also had limited success. Collective belonging in Germany has always been characterized by an extreme provincialism, with Germans cultivating regional folk differences (*Volkstümlichkeit*) in language and customs. Although many scholars note that Bismarck united Germans in one state (*Reich*) in 1871, this unity was merely a formal governmental one; it resulted in neither cultural delineation in the nation form nor clear territorial circumscription. Rather, the founding of the Reich, as I shall discuss below, was inspired by a scientific analogy of competition between species and competition between states, wherein the new state was in a geopolitical fight with its neighbors for more territory.

The discontinuity in German history between official ideology and state form, territoriality, and cultural identity is by no means unique to Germany, but one finds it there in an extreme form. In this century alone, German-speaking peoples have lived in six different kinds of regimes — the Wilhelmine German empire, democratic Weimar Republic, fascist Third Reich, Allied occupation, and either socialist authoritarian German Democratic Republic (GDR) or liberal-democratic capitalist Federal Republic of Germany (FRG) — not counting the regimes in East-Central Europe under which large irredentist populations have been living for several hundred years. Each of these regimes has made different territorial claims. Each has deployed a different program for constructing cultural identity.

During the cold war, the two new German states competed for legitimacy in resignifying and representing the nation, in creating a new sense of peoplehood and a new sense of Heimat. Asymmetrical mirror images of each other, these states were involved in what Hegel (1953) called a "struggle to the death": seeking recognition (*Anerkennung*) of self without having to recognize the other in turn. They were involved in a mutual project of demarcation, in the production of oppositional cultures for the nation form, which in turn was necessary to claim legitimate statehood. This struggle to the death meant publicly denouncing and threatening to overcome the social and territorial other. It was nowhere more transparent than in the divided Berlin, where over forty years a "dual organization" took shape: two asymmetrical moieties constructed in opposition yet making up a whole. This struggle for recognition took place in an atmosphere in which territorial boundaries and peoplehood were constantly disputed and shifting.

The four-decade effort in state-orchestrated production of difference abruptly ended with the opening of the Berlin Wall on 9 November 1989, a currency union on 1 July 1990, and a political union on 3 October 1990. The common assumption that cultural unity had never been seriously disrupted and therefore that economic and political unity would quickly lead to a new national-cultural unity has proven false (Borneman 1993a, 1993c, 1991). In fact, five years after unity, it appears that the processes of differentiation have taken on a new life, independent of the dual state structure that provided the initial structures of division. Although most East Germans consistently indicate in opinion surveys that they are better off today than they were before 1990, an increasing number characterize unity as a form of colonization. That unification of the two halves should entail forms of occupation should not surprise us, for as Elman Service (1985:182) remarked after reviewing anthropological research on the origins of government, "We still do not know of a single case of the conquest of one society by another that resulted in the *creation* of governmental institutions which incorporated the conquerors and conquered. Whenever a conquest was successfully consolidated, it was because such institutions already existed among one or both of the societies."

In my conclusion I will return briefly to the terms of unification. First, I want to take us back to forms of cold war identity and to its antecedent forms to examine the consequences of the deterritorialization of Heimat that has been true for this century's Berliners. I will focus on what this has meant for the national identity, the Germanness, of the specific generation of German residents in the two Berlins who reached adulthood during the Third Reich and who were the architects of the two postwar Germanys.

STATE AND NATIONAL NARRATIVES

Contemporary state narratives about a national identity are constructed in a long conversation between states and their residents, most of whom are citizens.[1] In its laws and policy statements, the state proposes for its citizens a model life course using tools including educational institutions, housing regulations, fiscal and monetary policy, and marital laws.[2] The citizen reflects on and responds to this model life course in everyday experiences and ritual encounters. In these interactions with the state's narrative, the citizen formulates his or her own variant autobiographical account of the life course. Both state and individual commentary on this life course take narrative form; in other words, the life course is understood as having a sequence with a beginning, middle, and end and with a subject or narrator, namely, the citizen as a member of the nation. There is necessarily a discrepancy between individual experiences and their narration either by the individual or the state and its proto-agents. The long-term legitimation of a nation-state is dependent on the extent to which the state can claim to represent a specific national identity unique to it, which means that it creates people with characteristics it can call its own.

The legitimacy of the state narrative is established when citizens can be said to validate its official codes for belonging — in other words, when the narrative implicit in official texts (state models embedded in laws and policy) is affirmed by individual (national) interpretations or "readings" revealed in autobiographical accounts. A comparison of the narrativity of legal and autobiographical texts confronts official (state) significations with their appropriation by individual (national) actors and thereby reveals the relative efficacy of different legitimation strategies. The legitimacy of state policies, then, can be analyzed as a series of historical interactions or generation-specific readings about the nature, coherence, and validity of national identity.

Individuals and states do not include all experience or every event in narrative constructions. Rather, they select specific nodes that are for them most significant in the construction of a coherent story. Periods and categories are the devices necessary to figure narratives. Taken together, they constitute what I shall call "experiential tropes." Because the tropes are themselves of indeterminate meaning, their potential polyvocality allows for different individuals with dissimilar experiences to use the same trope to figure autobiographical accounts. Yet, only in relation to the totality of a life — that is, in the emplotment of experience over time into coherent form — do tropes become meaningful through regular appeals to master narratives. I define "master narratives" as public matrices for the creation of collective belonging — ordering devices for defining the political semantics of Germanness.

PRE-1945 HISTORY OF CODES FOR GROUP MEMBERSHIP

A history of the political semantics of Germanness should take into consideration the tremendous regional variation in codes for group membership among German-speaking peoples, especially since a sense of Heimat is always about regional identity. These regional codes also vary over time, as David Sabean writes in his study of the village of Neckerhausen (1990:432): "The nature of alliance, the forms of reciprocity, the structure of social divisions, and the systemic character of conflict all changed continuously." To describe regional variation (the subject of German *Volkskunde* [folklore]) and pay attention to the instability of social categories is, unfortunately, beyond my competence. Also, I am omitting a discussion of variation at the level of individual practices. Here I would merely like to give the reader a very general sense of what a history of pre-1945 transformations in official codes for group membership in the German polity would look like. My goal is a preliminary one: to position us to consider postwar transformations.

Until the rise of National Socialists to power in the 1930s, German self-identity, meaning the categories for membership in the community, had been bound in different combinations to the concepts of household, work, residence, and religion. Language, custom, and behavior were, of course, important indicators of village membership, but such formal cultural traits were not part of any coherent religion or ideology. Efforts by elites to construct a national ideology in terms of a *Kulturnation* (cultural nation) is a different history than the one I am outlining here. Throughout the nineteenth century, German intellectual elites did formulate a Kulturnation version of national identity independent of, above, and prior to any political entity (which they called the *Staatsnation*). This version of the nation was in explicit opposition to the French model, being antidemocratic, antipolitical, and equated with a set of inborn cultural traits. Rather than describe this intellectual project, the following account will focus on the everyday codes for membership as they relate to transformations in the polity.

A membership code centered around the *Haus,* or *ganzes Haus* (entire house), was the generative category for German membership well into the eighteenth century. During the territorial consolidation of German *Länder* (provinces) in the seventeenth century, the terms used to organize collective belonging were *Stammbaum* (clan) and *Hausgenossenschaft* (household), the former based on the residential unit, the latter on the place of work. Although *Geschlecht* (lineage) was not foreign to German thought, it was also never primarily associated with *Erbgut* (inheritance through shared blood) as it was during the Third Reich. Whether the "descent was real or fictitious," write Michael Mitterauer and Reinhard Sieder, "seems to have made no difference to the lineage as a social unit" (1983:10). The term used in the late fifteenth century by Martin Luther, for example, in the first chapter of the Gospel of Matthew was *Geschlechtsregister* (genealogy), referring to inheritance through the paterfamilias (authority of the male); it had nothing to do with biological parenthood — women were in fact not even listed in the register.

In sum, neither the Geschlechtsregister nor the Hausgenossenschaft was organized around principles of consanguinity and affinity, though German-speaking peoples also utilized such kinship principles. Rather, a Geschlechtsregister was generated by tracing dependency relationships based on male authority, and a Hausgenossenschaft, by relations to residence and work. Also, unlike France or other Latin countries, the *Familie* (family) as a widely shared social and legal unit came very late to Germany (Flandrin 1979; Mitterauer and Sieder 1983:5–13). Such a distinction between family as a discrete group of blood relatives and the Hausgemeinschaft entered German legal codes in 1791–94 with the passage of the Prussian Land Rights Act. At that time the family unit became increasingly important because of the growth of private property and the need to regulate its inheritance.

Until 1875, the confessions regulated entry into one of the provincial communities of the German Reich. Anyone could theoretically become a member of the *Gemeinde* (community) by changing faith, either to the Catholic or Protestant or, in some places, the Jewish faith. The power of the confessions to control the terms of immigration can in turn be traced back to the Reformation, which some scholars argue resulted in a coerced confessionalization of most of Europe. For adults, the change of faith was most often accompanied by marriage to a member of the community. Only after political unity in 1871 was it possible for the state to introduce uniform rules or pan-national standards for membership. One of the new state's early acts was to introduce the civil marriage in 1875. Thereafter, the state and church shared control over rules for membership in the Reich, rules that no longer centered around dependency through work or in a household but around affinal ties and ascribed marriage and increasingly around consanguinity and inheritance.

In 1896, with the enactment of the *Bürgerliches Gesetzbuch* (comprehensive civil law), the state codified the complex set of marital and property relations that centered around patrilineal inheritance. By the late nineteenth century, anthropologists were increasingly involved in research that biologized the generative categories for membership, eventually resulting in a racialization of culture traits. The disciplinary division between Volkskunde (studying traditional German customs) and *Völkerkunde* (studying dark-skinned *Volk*, or "races") was important to legitimate this direction of study. With research focused on natives in the African colonies or on Eastern European Slavs, folklorists, physical anthropologists, and biologists began linking physiological differences with cultural ones, producing typologies of cultures based on the newly discovered blood types (Ploetz 1895; Rehse 1969). The concept *Blutsverwandtschaft* (blood relative), whose validity the German-Jewish-American anthropologist Franz Boas so vehemently questioned, was conveniently deployed as a scientific category for laws demanding different treatment of northern European Aryans from other so-called racial types (Pommerin 1979). This research shifted the redefinition of male input into reproduction from the authority of the father to semen and blood, which ironically also permitted the conceptualization of females as capable of passing on their traits through their blood. Laws establishing bilateral inheritance soon followed.

Emerging alongside the discourse about race was one about territoriality and state legitimacy. The research of the political geographer Friedrich Ratzel (1844–1904), which is experiencing a renaissance in Germany and elsewhere, was particularly important in drawing links between culture and territory. Applying Darwin's organicist conception of order and progress of species to the growth of states, Ratzel's major work *Der Lebensraum* (1900) searched for the "laws of the spatial growth of states" in what was even then understood as a justification for future German territorial expansion. He borrowed the concept "Lebensraum" from an 1860 review by Oscar Peschel of Darwin's *Origin of the Species* (1848). For Ratzel, the essence of states was to enter into fights with their neighbors, where the victor's reward was usually a piece of the loser's territory.

A large corpus of academic work on culture, race, and territory formed the basis for the Nazi racialization of the diffuse ethnic concept of *Volk* and later for a biologization of race concepts through eugenic theory. The National Socialists based their marital laws (demanding separation of races) in the 1930s on "scientifically proven" correlations between the distribution of blood types among groups and of cultural traits (Stolting 1987:129–33). Initially more concerned with male rather than female blood ties (extending the principle of paterfamilias), the Nazis stubbornly showed a structural preference for male over female blood in their hierarchy of *Mischehen* (mixed marriages), even though according to Jewish custom (and it was primarily Jews who were the object of these laws) it is the blood of the woman that is crucial for classification.

Other possible codes of belonging, such as a territorial one (jus soli, or "place of birth"), a voluntaristic one (by choice or learning), or one of historical fate (*Schicksalsgemeinschaft*) remained essentially outside the purview of German law through 1945. During the Nazi period, administrators and politicians used marital and blood categories to make further distinctions between Germanness and non-Germanness, forcing, for example, a large number of their female citizens to abort but criminalizing abortion for others, who were then coerced into producing more children. Male and female sterilization programs and the extermination policies directed toward Jews and Slavs were built on these pre-Nazi kinship distinctions (Bock 1986; Kaufmann 1988:34–43; Koonz 1993:S8–S31; Mühlfeld and Schönweiss 1989).

Among the Nazi "innovations" was the particular way in which they used scientific research on blood types as a principle to distinguish *Menschen* (humans) from *Untermenschen* (subhumans). They then linked this distinction to the concepts of Heimat and Lebensraum (Koselleck 1985:159–97). Nazi policies of internal purification and external expansion were justified scientifically—politics in the language of evolutionary biology. A secure Heimat was possible only when the *Volk-ohne-Raum* (people without space) was cleansed internally so that the nation of Blutsverwandschaften (blood relatives) could be given sufficient Lebensraum in which to grow. In realizing this policy each family unit was "asked" to compile a family genealogy—and it is rare to find a German family that did not comply—for no other purpose than to aid in the Final Solution: to ascertain if there were any Jews in the family. This act of banal everyday compliance is seldom spoken about today, and it remains an extreme embarrassment to Germans of all ages. After the war, the two new German states had the difficult tasks of distancing themselves from the concept of Lebensraum and constructing new semantic referents for the concepts of Volk, Nation, Heimat, and *Land* (country). Natives often referred to 1945 as *Stunde Null* (zero hour) and to the German territory as *Niemandsland* (nobody's land), referring to the desire to see time and space as a tabula rasa.

Citizenship rules — who deserves the protection and rights guaranteed by the state — were also formulated and changed according to these models. The jus sanguinis, or blood-based, principle of the citizenship law of the Federal Republic of Germany can be traced back to a 1913 amendment to the 1870 *Reichs- und Staatsangehörigkeitsgesetzes*. The 1870 law basically limited citizenship to those with at least one German parent, but not all German people were citizens of the Reich: thus the distinction mentioned earlier between *Kulturnation* (member of the cultural nation) and *Staatsnation* (citizenship in the state). Being a member of the "German Volk" was already, in 1870, a category broader than the citizen, for it included the large German irredentist population. "Volk" emerged as a central legal concept only with the 1913 revision, which defined a German as a person who either already had citizenship in one of the federal states (*Länder*) or was a German living in the Reich. The Allies nullified the National Socialist racializations of this citizenship law in 1945. West Germany reinstated the 1913 statute with the passing of the Basic Law in 1949, and East Germany formulated a new "socialist" citizenship law.

POSTWAR STATE STRATEGIES, 1945–1989

Differences in postwar state strategies for reconstituting and recategorizing Germanness might best be illustrated by two examples: first, of distancing from the past — the comparative periodization of fascism; and second, of recategorizing — the comparative reconstruction of kinship codes and rules for membership in the group. Although citizenship laws are perhaps the major source establishing rules for inclusion and exclusion, they are but the formal expression of state strategies. Other strategies also inform the definition of Germanness, making the application of citizenship laws much less uniform in practice than the written law would seem to indicate.

One informal expression of state strategies concerns the periods and explanations for the origin and end of Nazism. In its official historiographical tracts periodizing fascism, the West German state dated the origin of fascism to 1933, when Hitler "took over power" (in preference to the idea that he was given or "assumed power" through an election). The end of fascism was dated to the unconditional German surrender in 1945. This periodization, 1933–45, because it made fascism coterminous with a particular German political event, the Third Reich, led to an internalization of the Third Reich, meaning that Nazism had to be explained as a German problem (on West German historiography, see Mommsen 1983:168–90; Wehler 1984:221–62).

The West German state also claimed to be the only legitimate successor state to the Third Reich, and in this respect it had more problems than did East Germany in distancing itself from the past. American/French/British denazification policies were contradictory and halfheartedly carried out, with much successful resistance at the local level. The American denazification, for example, focused on Nazi Party membership alone; in most cases the major penalty was temporary disqualification from public service. Even in the field of government, no great stigma was attached to a Nazi background. For example, the former minister-president of Baden-Würtemberg, Hans Filbinger, a military judge during the Nazi period who had not been reluctant to sentence deserters or others accused of political crimes to death, had appealed to positivist legal theory in his defense. Many German adults of his generation accused of complicity with the Nazis cited the popular dictum, "What was *Recht* (law/right) yesterday cannot be *Unrecht* (illegal/wrong) today." By restricting the definition of fascism to a narrowly political periodization, the Federal Republic was relieved of having to account for Nazism in economic or cultural terms. Subsequently, even though this periodization tends to reduce fascism to a problem of political leadership (in other words, to "Hitlerism"), its dating within German history still resulted in an internalization of the problem and forced some sort of reckoning, albeit intermittent and narrowly defined, with fascism.[3]

By contrast, official historiography in East Germany categorized fascism as a child of capitalism; it emerged after the German defeat in 1918 and resulted in the Nazi government some fifteen years later.[4] This periodization is both economic and political, though; like the West German example, it is not a cultural one. By claiming that fascism is a problem of capitalism and not necessarily of German history alone, the GDR universalized and abstracted the Third Reich. Fascism became a universal problem of an abstract, nonlocal nature, attributable to a virulent form of capitalism and class conflict that could, theoretically, exist anywhere in the world. The GDR insisted that the reforms introduced between 1945 and 1949 during the Russian occupation marked an absolute break with fascism and that the post-1949 state (because it was socialist and antifascist) eliminated the preconditions for fascism, which still lived on in capitalist West Germany. Responsibility for the Nazi period, GDR leaders said, was not theirs, for many of those who sat in the leadership had themselves been incarcerated in concentration camps or had worked in the resistance. In contrast to most West German leaders, they had been among the victims of fascism. They also pointed to the "131 Law" in West Germany, which took effect on 11 May 1951, amnestying all former Nazi Party members. Their own more thorough reeducation program, more complete demonopolization, and initial demilitarization more strictly conformed to the stipulations of the Potsdam Accord.

The strategies of internalization by West Germany and universalization and abstraction by the GDR were also formative for reconstructing kinship or codes for group membership. Seen from this light, West Germany had to struggle against the internalization of the concepts of "blood relatives" and "Lebensraum." Although both concepts had been thoroughly delegitimated, they lived on in different form. The West German state always claimed to represent all German people — *deutschstämmig* (of German descent) — including those who had since become citizens of the GDR or those who had emigrated to the Soviet Union or East Europe in the previous two hundred years and were citizens of Warsaw Pact countries. Article 116 of the Basic Law guarantees that all *Aussiedler* (Germans who had settled out) and *Volksdeutsche* (ethnic Germans) have the right to resettle in the Federal Republic at any time if they can prove "affinity to Germanness." GDR citizens had a special right (having to prove nothing but GDR citizenship) to resettle to the FRG as either *Zuwanderer* (literally, wandered over) or *Übersiedler* (literally, settled over). Even in its domestic policies, the FRG resisted kinship reform until a partial reform in 1965, with more major reforms in 1977 (Glendon 1989). Despite these reforms, the central category of belonging remained Deutschstammigkeit, which could best be proved through shared blood, although state authorities also recognized such other "ethnic" indicators of "affinity to Germanness" as linguistic competence or continuous cultivation of German customs and traditions (see Forsythe 1989).

West Germany also never relinquished claims to land ceded by the Allies to Poland, the USSR, and Czechoslovakia until six months after the Berlin Wall came down, when it formally signed peace treaties that the GDR had signed shortly after its founding. During the cold war, powerful organizations of expellees successfully lobbied the government to keep open the issue of retaining lost land and property, as well as of reuniting with kin left behind. Moreover, with the formal accession (*Beitritt*) of the GDR into the FRG on 3 October 1990, the FRG was able to make good on its claim to the GDR as *Inland* (homeland) and not *Ausland* (foreign land).

In general, one should keep in mind that GDR codes for belonging were much more restrictive in practice than in theory, in contrast to FRG codes, which were more restrictive in theory than practice. Theoretically, kinship codes in East Germany were radically reconstructed in 1949, organized around a universal and abstract concept of socialist brotherhood: anyone claiming shared ideology could apply for membership. Belonging to the East German community was always defined officially in terms of shifting definitions of class and socialist ideology along with a Volk element. Unlike West Germany, the GDR no longer granted automatic membership to individuals of German descent or with affinity to Germanness living outside its territories. This Volk was territorially circumscribed, for the GDR had signed peace treaties with all East European states, recognizing their right to land ceded by the Allies. East Germany also did not have a generous asylum right or an open immigration policy for the Volksdeutsche, as did West Germany. Much as in the Federal Republic, affinity through marriage was also a mechanism for entering East Germany. But the GDR was more likely to approve a marriage to a citizen from another socialist country than from a capitalist one, although it made little difference as to the race or place of birth of that individual — whether from Poland or Angola did not matter. What did count, though, was prior citizenship in a socialist state (Hacker 1974:48–60; Ludz 1973:9–24).

AUTOBIOGRAPHICAL ACCOUNTS

How did these two state strategies of coming to terms with the past and of incorporating members — internalization by West Germany, universalization and abstraction by East Germany — relate to the way in which their respective citizens reconstructed personal histories? In autobiographical accounts of citizens in West Berlin born between approximately 1915 and 1935, women commonly began their postwar history with rape or the threat of rape by the invading Russian soldiers. This event was followed by the great hunger of the winters of 1946 and 1947, by the currency reform of 1948 introducing the deutsche mark, and by themes related to domestic purchases of basic consumer goods, to child care, and to the fate of kin. Men began their postwar experience as prisoners of war, followed by the currency reform and by economic or labor themes (such as the purchase of a new automobile or changes in status on the job).

For both men and women in West Berlin, the one commonly related event, the currency reform, functioned as an experiential trope because it signified a clean break with the Nazi past and a distancing from the Communist East. Moreover, it was an event with no clear agency, with no necessary implication of Germans themselves in the planning (in fact, the plan originated with the Americans and was forced on reluctant Germans). Finally, this event was appealing because it signified the possibility for a new future through the introduction of the Marshall Plan, which eventually contributed to the *Wirtschaftswunder* (economic miracle).

At another level, the symbol that West Berliners most often used in their narratives to periodize the economic miracle in the late 1950s and 1960s was the private automobile. In nearly all the accounts of domestic life related to me, the purchase of the first automobile was used as a rhetorical device, a trope, to figure a larger narrative about group identity. The personal automobile was a reason to be proud to be German again. This pride at the ritual level was first proclaimed in 1954 after the West Germans won the World Soccer Championship. After this victory, the slogan "Wir sind wieder wer" ("We're somebody again!") resonated among West Germans as a symbol of recovery, paralleling the signs of economic prosperity achieved through hard work.

Automobile ownership became the private symbol of this public prosperity. It increased steadily, from 1 percent in 1950 to 50 percent in 1969 and to 83 percent in 1985. During this period, the number of cars increased from eight to thirty-six million, and the building of freeways and the reconstruction of cities for automobile traffic became major public enterprises. In an incredibly brutal fashion, public authorities chopped down old trees, destroyed private gardens, and built parking garages in the middle of medieval city centers to make room for the automobile (see Monheim and Monheim-Dandorfer 1991). Not only the number of owners but also the type of autos consumed dramatically changed. Deluxe German cars such as the Mercedes-Benz, Porsche, and BMW slowly replaced the standard Volkswagen (Maase 1985:219; *Zahlenspiegel* 1988:79). Also crucial for the enjoyment of these automobiles is the lack of a speed limit on the freeways. Although West Germany enjoys the strictest environmental laws on the European continent and the most developed environmental consciousness, it remains the only country in Europe without a speed limit on its freeways.

A second symbol appeared in accounts of the 1970s: the once- or twice-a-year vacation — traveling as a tourist, most often to a foreign country. Vacations bring together important aspects of time, space, and memory. *Arbeit* (work) is opposed to *Freizeit* (free time), with the goal of maximizing the latter. By the late 1970s, vacations became a quantifiable measure of free time. The space in which this free time should be spent is outside rather than inside, meaning literally a trip abroad, outside German space. In 1954 only 5 percent of all Germans traveled abroad on vacations; in 1982 some 58 percent did so, with 67 percent of those traveling to a foreign country (Maase 1985:214–19). Length of vacations also increased: in 1975 only 30 percent of all West Germans vacationed for five to six weeks, and 0 percent did so for six or more weeks; by 1985, 25 percent vacationed for five to six weeks, with 72 percent doing so for six or more weeks (Süssmuth 1988:225). Rather than learning a new culture (a *Bildungsreise*), most current tourists express a desire to escape home (hectic, the stress of work, bad German weather), even though well-established tourist sites that cater to Germans (such as Greece, Majorca, or Croatia) reestablish forms of the German everyday abroad.

Despite differences in the way men and women trope their autobiographies, these differences are in and of themselves unimportant at the group level. These tropes are significant only when they are metonymically linked at the group or national level through appeals for meaning to common master narratives. The two focal symbols of the car and the vacation, along with the experiential tropes of rape for women, flight for expellees and refugees, and confinement in a POW camp for men, obtain coherence by relying on the state's master narrative of prosperity. This master narrative reterritorializes space, reemploting the different experiential tropes of rape, confinement, and flight. Prosperity provides an answer to the loss of faith in cultural particularities (due to Nazi delegitimation, territorial loss, and allied occupation) mentioned earlier. This answer is often expressed as a *Selbstverflüchtigung,* a flight or evaporation/sublimation of the self caught between debasement and adaptation (a term I take from Heinz Bude [1987]). The state-directed prosperity of the Wirtschaftswunder, troped in individual narratives as the currency reform of 1948 and work that enables free time, provides a mechanism enabling flight. It, along with the automobile, provide a "way out" of not only Germany but Germanness as well.

The trope of flight and the master narrative of prosperity are intimately related to the state strategy of internalization of the Nazi past. Many scholars have documented how the West German state absorbed Nazism and how prosperity served as a panacea for a people shocked by the defeat and by the gravity of Nazi crimes committed in their name, often with their help. One need not, as is usually done, list the large number of political and economic leaders whose careers were relatively seamless following the end of the Third Reich (Dux 1988:174–86; Korte 1985:17). Many ordinary citizens joke about having obtained a *Persilschein* (Tide certificate of denazification), which the Western Allies issued without thorough scrutiny. The currency reform and the automobile and the master narrative used to emplot these tropes, prosperity, were provided by the state. The symbols of wealth resulting from this economic reform — consumer goods, cars, free time, vacations — are today sacrosanct items, often used by other Europeans to caricature West Germans even though they themselves also share an attachment to these symbols.

In the autobiographies of East Berliners, women began their postwar narratives with the same events as their West Berlin counterparts: rape, hunger, and child care. But when they began talking about life in the 1950s, most of them also made reference to their work accomplishments during what was officially called *Aufbau,* the reconstruction period. Though often experienced as coercion at the time, today they selected integration into the economy as a meaningful node for emplotment into their life story. In this they differ radically from West Berlin women, most of whom did not hold steady employment in the 1950s. By 1965, 75 percent of all East German women were employed, and by 1985, 91 percent. In contrast, by 1965, 47.5 percent of all West German women were employed, and by 1985, 51 percent (Obertreis 1985). Another difference in life stories is that East German women did not tend to return to the experiential tropes of rape and hunger, as did women in the West; instead they either dwelled on the hardships and obstacles encountered in the decade after the war or emphasized their own distinct contributions to society. Insofar as they felt their work was important, they related it to increased self-esteem (see Niethammer 1988).

Most East Berlin men with whom I talked began their narratives much like West Berlin men, with experiences as POWs, followed by the currency reform. But for them, both events were experiences of victimization. The currency reform functioned to exclude them from West German prosperity; what followed from this was the Marshall Plan for West Berliners/West Germans, whereas they continued paying reparations to the Soviet Union. Hence their own accomplishments of the Aufbau were counterbalanced by other experiences of separation and victimization. For example, some mourned the loss of kin who moved to the West, bemoaned their lost time as Nazi soldiers, or resented their powerlessness in the realm of politics in East Germany. Conversely, a very few, mostly members of the ruling Socialist Unity Party whom I knew, defended their satisfaction with socialism in an exaggerated manner — "Ich fühle mich wohl!" (I feel good!). How are these experiential tropes connected? With difficulty, to say the least. If anything connects them as a coherent narrative, it is not the state's strategies of abstraction and universalization but the citizen's own experiential trope of victimization. Whereas GDR women often had one experience — socially valued work — that distinguished them from their West German counterparts, GDR men had no domain of experience with which to construct an identity that might positively compare with that of their West German counterparts.

Despite the East German state's inability to provide a convincing master narrative to organize and make coherent the experiences of individual citizens, it nonetheless had a significant influence on their identity construction. Indeed, it set the ideational and aesthetic framework in which individual citizen experiences could be related to the larger group narrative of Germanness. The way in which this framework interacts with experience can again be best illustrated with an example of a key symbol, one that appeared in nearly all the autobiographies of GDR citizens and was also manufactured by the East German state: the automobile. But this car is not the efficient, powerful West German type — not the Mercedes or the BMW — but the state-produced Trabant, a small, powerless, heavy-polluting, two-cylinder model made purely for domestic consumption. My thoughts about this were provoked by a friend who had waited for her Trabant for thirteen years — the average wait in the GDR — who exclaimed, "I don't have a car, I have a Trabant!" The word "Trabant" comes from astronomy and means "neighboring planet"; like the moon, it follows and accompanies but does not lead. For whatever reason, GDR leaders chose this name for the mass-produced people's car. In hindsight, it appears as a premonition of the problems they would have in keeping pace economically with the West Germans. Not only did most East Germans drive the pathetic Trabants, but most citizens were also limited to traveling in their own country and in Czechoslovakia (with occasional approval for Hungary and Poland) until after the opening of the wall in November 1989. Even if they did receive permission to leave the GDR, they were not permitted to travel with these cars in Western Europe. Hence the kind of "flight abroad" characteristic of the West Berliners/Germans was not available to those in the East.

The importance of the Trabant as a symbol of East German identity is captured well in the text of a song entitled "Mein Trabbi" (My Trabbi) by Reinhold Andert (1989), a GDR singer-songwriter.

> My Trabbi fits me like a glove,
> a car of the people, for citizens, comrades.
> A vehicle of the people, for you and me,
> something we can afford, but certainly nothing more.
> Small and narrow, something you feel close to,
> it loudly warns everyone it's coming,
> slowly, then I begin to notice how large my homeland is,
> My Trabbi guzzles a bit much, but in that we're like relatives.
> Mazda, Peugot, Golf, Volvo, Citröen,
> products of alienated labor — obscene.
> My little motor, sometimes it sputters
> was built according to the book, with a hammer,
> Sounds like a lawnmower, moves like a racing pasteboard.

Andert's lyrics contain many of the symbols and themes that index experiences widely shared by East Germans. In the second line he links the car to people, state, and party — a holy trinity in the GDR. He then presents this car as synecdoche for the self-image of the East German: "small and narrow" — a petty bourgeois, or *Kleinbürger*, spatially incarcerated in a Heimat. But this description is more parody and rejection of the state's conception of self than use of state emplotment forms to bring disparate experiences into coherent form. No metonymical work of incorporation is being performed here. The conclusion I wish to draw about East Berliners is not that they had fewer experiential tropes with which to periodize their life stories than did West Berliners but that the GDR's master narrative of state socialism, which was meant to link these tropes, was not widely accepted or employed by citizens — except in parody.

Of most significance is the lack of fit between the state's strategies and the citizen's narrations. The "fit me like a glove" about which Andert sings in the second line acknowledges a fit between state-produced automobile and citizen only to undermine its legitimacy. East Germans knew rather well what the state expected from them, and they responded appropriately — either by accommodating themselves to these expectations (often through parody) or by becoming a cold war "dissident" (Borneman 1993b). Neither response necessarily resulted in a legitimation of the state's emplotment form, though both responses were necessarily complicitous, part of ongoing conversations with the state's authority. Citizen refusal, or inability, to reemplot experience with the Trabant in terms of the state's master narrative of the universal and abstract values of socialist nationhood and progress indicates reservations about the kind of "society" that the GDR was constructing. With no agreed-upon integrative stories, people told their lives in chronicle as opposed to narrative form, as a series of unconnected experiential tropes, with no metonym to link the experiences into a coherent whole and close the narrative. To the extent that people's experiences did cohere, as in stories about the Trabant, they did so around a trope of victimization. Victimization, in turn, united people by acting as a metaphor — borrowing a phrase from James Fernandez (1986:25) — to "cross-reference domains."

Yet, feeling "the aptness of each other's metaphors" (Fernandez 1986:25), although perhaps a distinguishing feature of ritual action, was not sufficient to unite East Germans into a collective "nation." At most, the Trabant operated as metaphor to distinguish GDR citizens from their wealthier, well-traveled counterparts in the West. Whatever "sensation of wholeness" that GDR citizens experienced was contrasted with a more complete wholeness in the Federal Republic. So long as East Germans remained spatially confined and culturally *heimatlos* (without a home and without a state), they defined their experience in contradistinction to the master narratives of the state. Ultimately this incongruence between state project and citizen identity worked to the detriment of both state legitimation and citizen cohesion.

It was often said that the East Germans suffered from an inferiority complex, which, as the story of the Trabant indicates, has much truth to it. Certainly, the West Germans were by far more confident and aggressive in asserting their identities. This inferiority alone, however, was incapable of being used by the East German state in its utopian project of building socialism. Martyrdom and passion for sacrifice may be Polish and Israeli master narratives, but they are not mythological tropes that permeate German culture. Over time, the resolve to sacrifice that had been so apparent among both East and West Germans for several decades after the war weakened. With all the superior symbolic value attached to "made in Germany," the West German economy proved more powerful in fulfilling the dream of prosperity held in common by both capitalist and socialist believers. East German products never attained the same status on the world market or among the East Germans themselves. Moreover, world market products such as Ikea furniture, which was manufactured by East Germans and sold under the label of a Swedish firm, were unavailable to East German consumers. Pricing mechanisms required that they pay in convertible currency, but the effect of that initial currency reform in 1948 was to make GDR currency (the "mark" as opposed to the West German "deutsche mark") convertible only within East bloc states. The effect of the increasing economic and cultural asymmetry between the two cold war blocs was to enhance East German idealization of the symbols of West Germanness (see Borneman 1991).

In sum, the East German state strategy of universalization and abstraction was not able to generate the kind of master narratives capable of integrating its citizens in the form of durable social cohesion we call the nation form. At best, its utopian project provoked parodies of itself that indeed united the group to some extent, but against rather than with the state. By contrast, the West German strategy of internalization was embraced by the majority of West Germans, 25 percent of whom (similar to those in the GDR) were highly skilled and motivated expellees living on "foreign" soil. This strategy facilitated the generation of a master narrative of prosperity that proved superior to the GDR's alternative. Further, although most West Germans have an extremely problematic relationship to their collective, ergo national, past—fleeing from it when given the chance, bonding around prosperity and consumption, reducing the Nazi period to a political aberration—they did, in fact, develop a relationship to themselves and their history that enabled them to reform (prompted by the 1968 student rebellion) their government rather than merely oppose it.

HEIMAT IN POSTUNITY GERMANY

Another flight in late summer 1989 precipitated the opening of the Berlin Wall on 9 November 1989, the dissolution of the GDR, and the integration of East German people and territory into the West German state on 3 October 1990. This time, however, the flight was by several hundred thousand members of a largely postwar generation of East Germans to West Germany, the "children" and "grandchildren" of those who fled at the end of World War II. Only after the resolution of the questions of "territoriality" (absorbing the GDR's territory, recognizing international boundaries with Poland and Russia, resolving the claims of ethnic Germans expelled from Czechoslovakia after the war) and of the "people" (incorporating East Germans into the Federal Republic) by making the two terms congruent did the issue of "culture" take center stage—though, as I have been arguing, cultural distinctiveness, or defining Heimat, has been the central issue all along. Cultural distinctiveness in the international order means the nation form, and it is this particular order of identity that has been a predicament for Germans. According to some highly disputed theories, there is a normal historical development of nationness among European peoples, but Germans have never followed it, instead always creating a *Sonderweg*, a "special path."

Initially, national unity proceeded as one might expect, with East German appropriation of the symbols of West German prosperity, with West Germans refusing to change except to expand markets in the East. Foremost among these appropriated symbols is the automobile. Within a year of unity, more than half of all Trabbis had been scrapped—crushed and reportedly eaten by a "worm" devised for those purposes—and replaced by West German brands. By 1995, a Trabbi was a rare sight on the streets of Berlin. And, whereas 59 percent of all East German households owned automobiles in 1989, by the end of 1994, 97 percent did (German Information Center [GIC] 1995:3). Money obtained from a favorable exchange in the second postwar currency reform on 1 July 1989 (a 1 : 1 exchange rate for salaries, wages, and certain categories of personal savings, and a 2 : 1 rate for most personal and commercial accounts) was initially used for new cars and, not surprisingly, for vacations abroad, primarily to Western Europe and the United States. Those East Germans who had established the first car dealerships after the opening of the Berlin Wall quickly became one of the first publicly identifiable classes of the nouveaux riches.

Following unity, the periodic West German debate about introducing speed limits on the freeways erupted again. Among the first improvements in "infrastructure," new freeways were immediately built or renovated and telecommunications expanded. By contrast, the services offered by trains and other forms of public transportation seemed either to stand still or to get worse, this deterioration, then, used to justify a partial privatization of such public works. A much disputed compromise to the speed limit debate was found in a so-called ozone law, which went into effect in July 1995 — environmental protection being the one issue on which all Germans seem to agree. This confusing law attempts to regulate the level of damage to the ozone layer by forcing drivers to pay for the amount of pollution they create and thus hopefully restricting the number of autos and drivers on the road. The point of the compromise was to avoid a speed limit on the freeway, something still being demanded by several West German parties. People will continue to drive as fast as possible: the hope is for fewer drivers.

The newly secured territorial borders have provided security, but only for some. For many East Germans, the new legal securities guaranteed by the Rechtsstaat have been counterbalanced by the new insecurities of unemployment, the extension of market logic into all domains and the experience of its unpredictable vacillations, and an increase in everyday criminality. Politicians have been so preoccupied with internal problems that as yet there has been little exercise of "sovereignty" externally. Rather, the major preoccupation has been to establish sovereignty within the new borders, and there the effects of unity on legitimacy and security have been significant, though not uniform. For now, one might say that most West Germans gained something from unity: many got professional jobs in the East, especially in law, management, and at the universities; many inherited or reclaimed property in the East; most gained generally from the competitive advantage obtained from the collapse of East German and Ostblock markets and the privatization of East German firms. All told, the average West German household has DM 64,000 in financial assets and DM 215,000 in property, whereas the average East German household has DM 23,000 in financial assets and DM 59,000 in property. As "it takes money to make money" is one of the rules of capitalism, this discrepancy is likely to grow. Yet, to talk to most West Germans, one gets the impression that they are uniformly victimized by unity, because they have to pay a 7.5 percent "solidarity surcharge," automatically deducted from each individual paycheck. Enacted in 1991, this surcharge was to be temporary but was extended in 1993 and again in 1995. And they complain that East Germans are not thankful for what the West has done for them. Of the total DM 70 billion of subvention for eastern Germany, DM 21 billion comes from the West German investment assistance, another DM 6.7 billion from federal tax breaks (GIC 1995:2). Moreover, the further west one gets from the Polish border, the less noticeably influenced West Germans appear to be by unification. By contrast, West Berliners, like all East Germans, are most directly confronted with the effects of unification, becoming more like the East over time.

One of the most dramatic experiences of East Germans following unification was the introduction of West German insurance companies, putatively to "secure" them from various threats that accompany capitalism and freedom. Expecting crime waves of all sorts, many East Germans insured everything they owned, from the few pieces of Meissen porcelain they had in their china cabinets to their new West German automobiles. Insurance companies apparently recruited former workers for the State Security (Stasi) because it was thought that they knew best the insecurities of East Germans. Rumor has it that the three fields where most former Stasi employees found work were in border areas as guards, in public transportation, and in insurance companies. Five years since unification, most former East Germans have dropped all but the minimal amount of insurance. But the effects of this early experience are still visible. A friend told me of having seen bars on the windows of private homes in East German small towns and villages. She asked them why. The response: to protect ourselves from West German salespeople. No longer is it crime that creates insecurity but the protection from the protection of crime. In capitalism, one needs protections from the propagators of insecurity.

These examples, which I could multiply endlessly, are indications of the fields in which "cultural distinctiveness" is being played out. Though experienced as dramatic and often violent conflicts over the nation form in the new Germany, these new practices appear relatively innocuous when compared with past forms of German nationalism. Indeed the very noticeable increase in xenophobia and right-wing violence in Germany pales when compared with the genocide in Bosnia and with the violence in other East-Central European states that has accompanied the end of the cold war. These developments are part of a worldwide restructuring of political authority, a response to the collapse of the cold war structures and not the enactment of a repetition compulsion (Borneman 1995). The territorial sovereignty that Germany now enjoys has not yet been used to dominate its neighbors or to purify itself of marginal groups but instead, as the "Unity Chancellor" Helmut Kohl has insisted, is a sovereignty to be used to unite Europeans and to become active in the United Nations. Further, Germany has acknowledged its historical responsibilities to aiding the transformations in Eastern Europe and Russia, and it has acknowledged what it has gained from being integrated into Western European legal and political traditions. Whether this Germany moves in the direction of an abstract "postnational" identity, as Jürgen Habermas argues for, or works within its own national-cultural traditions while transforming them, remains to be seen. In either case, the fact that Germans today are divided internally into an East and a West and are still working through the meaning of several generations of territorial displacement means that cultural distinctiveness, or the feeling of Heimat, will remain an unsettling and elusive quest well into the twenty-first century.

NOTES

This article is a substantially revised version of "State, Territory, and Identity Formation in the Postwar Berlins" (1992), *Cultural Anthropology* 7 (1): 44–61. Research from 1986 to 1989 was supported by grants from International Research Exchange, Harvard Krupp Fellowship, Social Science Research Council–Berlin Program for Advanced German and European Study, and Fulbright Hays. Subsequent research has been supported by grants from the MacArthur Peace Studies Program and the National Council for Soviet and East European Research. I thank them for their generous support.

1   This framework, as well as the analysis of state policy and summary of auto-biographical accounts, is developed more completely in Borneman 1992.

2   I am following Hegel in my definition of the state as a system of legality and

legitimacy, a specific kind of politically organized moral community. The other dimension of the state, as a bureaucratic system of norms and commands, of organizations and regulations, is more visible and perhaps easier to grasp but not necessarily a key to its legitimacy. To pursue the state's legitimacy, one must consider it as a "temporal totality," which both takes form and authority from the cultural order and in turn tries to shape that order (see Hegel 1953:49–62, 75–77).

3   For a superb ethnographic study of how a particular West German village dealt with its role in eliminating its large Jewish population, see Becker 1994.

4   Much GDR historiography was written, or "authorized," by East German leaders themselves, including Politburo members (see Axen 1973; Norden et al. 1967).

Finding One's Own Place:

Asian Landscapes Re-visioned in Rural California

K A R E N   L E O N A R D

Most immigrants from Japan and India's Punjab province to California in the early twentieth century ended up working in agriculture, settling in small towns in the state's agricultural valleys. It is probably safe to say that specific conditions of climate, soil, and topography in their new settings did not strongly resemble those in the agrarian regions from which they came in Japan and India's northwestern Punjabi-speaking region. Yet in several striking instances, these immigrants' representations of their new homes stressed similarities — resemblances — to their homelands. These similarities may have been invented (Hobsbawm and Ranger 1983) and their elaboration can be seen to fulfill needs, although a functionalist explanation does not capture the complexity of the process. Clearly, these representations helped shape collective identities in the new country, delineating new communities (Okihiro 1988) grounded in California and based on categories broader than those in the homeland. Some of them defended against stereotypes imposed by the dominant culture, yet I will argue that they were not simply "externally instigated, articulating and confirming a position of subordination" (Ang 1994:14). Other representations obscured or bridged differences between the newcomers and others in the new context, suggesting that immigrants do not just develop new or revalorized identifications but can elude easy identification by "mobilizing quite different visions of social and political practice" (Rouse 1994:4). Or, like Salman Rushdie speaking of migrants as "translated men," while it is "normally supposed that something always gets lost in translation; . . . something can also be gained"

(1991:17). I will try to show, briefly for the Japanese and more fully for the Punjabis, what has been gained.

Geography has been thought of as dividing cultures, societies, and nations (Gupta 1988), and immigrants have been seen as experiencing dramatic ruptures from their native places, their own contextual cultures. Renato Rosaldo conceptualized a zone of immigration as a zone of "zero degree" culture, "where individuals move between two national spaces" (1988:81). There may be some truth to these notions, particularly when thinking of the past. In the early twentieth century, journeys across oceans and continents were difficult, lengthy undertakings; even communication with those left behind was slow and uncertain. And in the case of immigrants from Asia to the United States, legal barriers made it impossible to move freely between Asia and America, preventing the bringing of relatives from the old place to the new.

Early restraints on Asian immigration to America were forthrightly based on race or national origin, but later, more sophisticated immigration laws were based on notions correlating spatial and cultural distance. The Chinese Exclusion Act of 1882 was proclaimed unilaterally by the United States, and the Gentlemen's Agreement of 1907 was concluded between the United States and Japan. Subsequently, both the Canadian and United States governments turned to concepts of space to demarcate categories of unwanted Asian immigrants.

The Pacific Ocean was becoming an important commercial route, but most Americans and Canadians thought any kind of intermixture of Oriental and Occidental peoples undesirable, so laws were devised to stop Asian immigration. California's governor voiced the uncomfortable sense that, although geography imposed wide spaces between the western coast of America and Asia, immigrants from Asia were too easily arriving and settling "within her [California's] midst." He saw California as "an outpost on the western edge of Occidental civilization," saying that "the mind's eye takes its gaze and sees on the other shores of that great ocean the teeming millions of the Orient, with its institutions running their roots into the most venerable antiquity, its own inherited philosophy and standards of life, its own peculiar races and colors" (California, State Board of Control 1920:10). Canadians had the same ideas. In 1908, Canada required a direct or "continuous" journey for those coming by ship to Canada: the dramatic refusal to let the *Komagata Maru,* filled with Sikhs and others from India who had embarked in Hong Kong and Shanghai, dock in Vancouver in 1914 created an international incident (Dhillon 1981). In 1917, the United States created a "barred zone" for the continent of Asia west of the 110th meridian and east of the 50th meridian, thus denying entry to immigrants from Japan and China to Saudi Arabia and effectively ending Asian immigration to the United States until the 1940s (Jacoby 1982; United States Statutes at Large 1915–1917:876).

There is a case, then, for viewing those immigrants from Japan and India who came and settled in California in the early twentieth century as separated more or less completely from their countries and cultures. The problems posed by space and law were great. Sometimes, disappointed expectations in the new environment made immigrants reluctant to maintain connections with relatives and contributed to the sense of discontinuity between their old and new lives (Kikumura 1981:33).

The situation of these early Asian immigrants seems quite unlike that which pertains today, when families and communities can have transnational, global networks (Appadurai and Breckenridge 1986; Basch, Schiller, and Blanc-Szanton 1992). Now, people can be dispersed but not alienated from their homes, and space and the "otherness" of the host society can be bridged by a continuing connection with and sense of one's own society (Rutherford 1984:298–307). It is even thought that "postmodern" identities can be construed as fragmented, shifting, contextually and constantly reformulated, far more so than in the past (Hall 1992). But earlier, too, I contend that people were not bounded by "culture" (Gupta and Ferguson, "Beyond 'Culture,' " this volume) but worked inventively and interactively, creating identities that were hybrid (Rushdie 1991:394), based on consent not descent (Sollors 1986), and that implicated the mainstream as much as the margins (Okihiro 1994; Hall 1993).

It is certainly true that in the early twentieth century, immigrants from Asia were rigidly stereotyped by the dominant society. The Japanese and Punjabis were categorized as Orientals by both popular and academic publications: *Oriental Crime in California, California and the Oriental, Resident Orientals. . . ,* and so forth (Beach [1932] 1971; California, State Board of Control 1920; Mears [ca. 1928] 1978). They were also viewed as "alien" and an "immigration problem," and their activities were investigated as un-American (United States Statutes at Large 1915–1917; California State Commission of Immigration and Housing 1918; California Legislature, Senate 1953). At a time when intermarriage between Scandinavian and German immigrants was thought to be causing a decline in the caliber of the midwestern farming population (Brunner 1929), miscegenation between racial groups in California was feared and made illegal. In studies of intermarriage done in the 1930s and 1940s, the "yellow-brown" category was created to include Orientals and Mexicans (Leonard 1993:149). Thus members of both groups were largely seen as Asian, noncitizens, nonmarriageable — as overwhelmingly "other."

Differences between them were also recognized: the Japanese were called "Japs" and "blanket boys," the latter a reference to the bedding carried on the migratory labor circuit, whereas the Punjabis were called "Hindoos," East Indians, and "Rag-heads," the last a reference to the turbans worn by the Sikh majority among them (Allen 1945; Johnson 1922). And the Punjabis and Japanese did not draw on each other in their reformulations of identity, although the Japanese did draw on Chinese history. I am grouping them together here because they made similar use of Asian landscapes and political representations in their new lives in California; the comparison is useful and suggests further research to be done in Asian American and cultural studies.

Both groups of immigrants formulated new identities in rural California. The Japanese immigrants first constituted associations in California based on their *kens,* or prefectures of origin back in Japan, but associations based on their localities in California quickly became more important and were organized up to the state and national level (Chan 1991:68; Ichihashi 1932). In the case of the Punjabis, they accepted the term "Hindu" but constituted under that label a new (and now controversial) American ethnic identity. The Punjabi language proved more important than religious or regional differences, as the "Hindu" label brought together Sikhs, Muslims, and Hindus and also bridged regional differences important back in the Punjab (the Doab, Majha, and Malwa regions demarcated by rivers). "Hindu" also incorporated, ultimately, the men's wives of Mexican heritage and the biethnic children born to the couples (Leonard 1994; Leonard forthcoming).

Too little is known, still, about the process of construction of new Asian, hybrid, and pan-Asian communities and identities in the context of American society. Sources are fragmentary.[1] There are no autobiographies or historical narratives by the Punjabi pioneers themselves; there are a few interviews and accounts by others, and I have interviewed several surviving first-generation Punjabi men and many wives and children of the Punjabi pioneers. Of the Japanese-language materials, I have been able to use only one, *Traces of a Journey* (1957), by Shiro Fujioka (for which there is a typescript English translation), about people and places he knew.[2]

Fujioka shows the inscription of Asian landscapes on their new homeland by Japanese farmers in California's Imperial Valley. To appreciate his account better and because the Imperial Valley is also the main location for my analysis of the Punjabi immigrants, some background on this area is needed. Located along California's Mexican border inland from San Diego, the Imperial Valley was a desert until the first decade of the twentieth century. In 1907, engineers tamed the Colorado River, and in 1911 the Imperial Irrigation District took over and began consolidating the water management and delivery companies. In its early days, the valley was a raw, rough place, inhabited by mostly male immigrants who farmed with horses and crude implements. Slowly these men developed the system of capital-intensive, labor-intensive, predominantly large-scale agriculture that characterizes the valley today.

Asians were among the earliest settlers in the Imperial Valley. In 1901, the first and only house in the frontier town of Imperial was a tent hotel run by "a Chinaman."[3] The Japanese were among those who grew the first melon and vegetable crops in the valley, moving from tenancy to ownership rapidly. Yet from the beginning they encountered prejudice. The economic standards of the Japanese farmers were termed "impossible to our white ideals" (insecure tenants, many lived in poor housing and had few possessions). The Japanese birth rate and importation of spouses were closely scrutinized and viewed as strategies to evade immigration restrictions (California, State Board of Control 1920:9–11). The practice of bringing picture brides from Japan was labeled an immoral social custom, foreign and un-Christian (Gee 1976:361). After 1913, the right of Japanese farmers to lease and own agricultural land was curtailed by California's Alien Land Law. Aimed especially at California's successful Japanese farmers, this law barred aliens ineligible for U.S. citizenship from owning agricultural land or leasing it for longer than three years; another Alien Land Law in 1920 prohibited leasing altogether and added other loophole-closing provisions. Thus despite their early successes and their ability to get around the law by putting land in the names of their U.S.-born (and therefore citizen) children, the valley was in many ways a hostile environment for the Japanese farmers.

About the Imperial Valley Fujioka (1957) writes, "You may be able to imagine the warlike sight of the pioneer days" (465), by which he means rivalry among Japanese farmers in the 1920s. He continues:

After overcoming such stage of hardships, each engaged in the farming they [sic] liked. Needless to say some of them failed in spite of their hard work, and some were blessed by god of luck and dashed forward [on] the road to success. Success or not they were trained by hardship, and there was so to speak the rivalry of powerful warlords.

If we follow the example of China's history of three kingdoms and divide the Imperial Valley in three parts leaving out the cotton growers on the border, there was Mr. Kikutaro Nishimoto in the southern area, Mr. Shonan Kimura in the central part around Holtville and El Centro, and in the northern area around Brawley was Mr. Rika Takahashi. They were, so to speak, Wu Ti, Shu Han and Wei of the three kingdoms. (465–66)

Here, an Asian political geography has been relocated in the Imperial Valley, with the three regions around the towns of Calexico, Holtville/El Centro, and Brawley likened to the historical three kingdoms of China in the third century A.D. But why did Fujioka locate his kingdoms in China rather than Japan? Probably he did so because Japanese history features several periods of *two*, but not three, kingdoms feuding and also because the Japanese immigrants were a relatively well-educated group, conversant with Chinese history as well as their own.[4] Still, it is interesting to speculate about the easy appropriation and use of Chinese history here, which indicates a consciousness of the larger "Asian" category being used by the dominant society and an acceptance of that usage. But the way in which the Chinese kingdoms analogy is used empowers its enunciators, helping them to view themselves as lords of the land. The Japanese immigrants showed a keen awareness of Chinese history in the United States too, trying to avoid arousing prejudice by adopting Western dress, especially for their women — the Chinese had been criticized for not doing this (Gee 1976:362). The self-conscious "we" in Fujioka's text above could be Japanese or could mean all Asians, but there is no "other" indicated, no mention of the non-Asian growers, shippers, and bankers who dominated the political economy. The leading Japanese farmer in each region is called a king, reigning over his own territory and contending with the others much like the three royal houses following the decline of the Han dynasty in A.D. 220. (The period from A.D. 220 to A.D. 317, one of political disunion in Chinese history, has inspired many works of fiction centered on the internecine wars of the three kingdoms — particularly the famous *San Kuo shih yen i,* a long historical story attributed to the late fourteenth century; see Moss Roberts 1991.)

Objectively, the Imperial Valley was another place, another time, but Fujioka represented it in a way that made it familiar, beloved, and Asian — peopled by warlords, powerful Japanese to whom others owed allegiance. This imagery helped create a collective identity and an attachment to the new land. Never mind that the Japanese were *doing* things very differently in California. For example, when the first Japanese man in the valley brought his picture bride home, the first thing he taught her was to ride a horse so that she could escape from the many woman-hungry Japanese bachelors! (The story is reproduced in Leonard 1992:40–41.) But they were *seeing* similarities to an Asian landscape and imagining themselves free to farm and fight on it. Perhaps the Japanese were accepting a redrawn Asian category — as Sara Suleri says, one can "situate the language of the colonizer within the precarious discourse of the immigrant" (1992:5) — but they were using that broader identification to contest subordination, to assert a different vision of the political landscape.

The Punjabi accounts of the California landscape evoke similar visions. The accounts are several and come from two time periods. Punjabi men from landowning and martial castes in India's Punjab Province came to California, most from 1907 to 1917. Many had served overseas in the British Indian army or police service. They came on to California for the better wages in railroad, lumbering, and agricultural work. In the northern Sacramento Valley, Punjabis tended to work in gangs, the so-called Hindu crews. Most of the Punjabi men there remained bachelors in the United States, at least partly because of California's antimiscegnation laws, which made marriage with women of other "races" difficult. In the Imperial Valley, however, there were Mexican or Mexican American women whom the Punjabis married, for both men and women could fill in the blank for race with "brown" on the marriage license (I will discuss these biethnic families later). In the San Joaquin Valley, around Fresno in the middle of the state, bachelors and Punjabi Mexican families were mixed.

Only one written account by an early Punjabi immigrant survives — that by Puna Singh, who moved to northern California from Utah in

1924 and who comments on the California landscape in his account. Here too Asian farmers had helped develop new crops after 1911: Japanese, Koreans, and Punjabis grew rice in the Gridley/Colusa area. Agriculture was longer established in the Sacramento Valley than in the Imperial Valley, but the socioeconomic structure was similar. Anglo growers, shippers, and bankers dominated the rural economy, and Asian farm laborers had a hard time working their way up the agricultural ladder. Compared with the Japanese immigrants, the Punjabis had initial disadvantages because they were largely illiterate and faced stronger initial prejudice as a result of their distinctive turbans and beards. Also, their religious and social values were thought "so entirely repugnant to American principles," according to the State Board of Control, that they were "the most undesirable" of Asians (California, State Board of Control 1920:115–16). Being of the Caucasian "race," however, they had an initial advantage over the Japanese in their access to American citizenship. Access by naturalization to United States citizenship was based on race, and only "free whites" and (after 1870) people of African descent were eligible. This circumstance changed, however, with the 1923 Supreme Court decision which opined that South Asian Indians were not "white" in the popular meaning of the term (Jacoby 1958). So the Punjabis also became "aliens ineligible to citizenship" and subject to the Alien Land Law (Leonard 1985). (Puna Singh had become a United States citizen before 1923 and later had his citizenship revoked.)

Puna Singh (1972) recalled his impression of northern California in 1924: "On arriving in the Sacramento Valley, one could not help but be reminded of the Punjab. Fertile fields stretched across the flat valley to the foothills lying far in the distance. Most of the jobs available were agricultural and I found many Punjabis already working throughout the area" (109–10). Descendants of the early Punjabi immigrants repeated similar statements. Many told me that their fathers and others claimed that the Imperial Valley — or the San Joaquin Valley or the Sacramento Valley — was "like the Punjab"; the fields, the crops, and the early farming methods were "just like the Punjab."

Later Punjabi immigrants have left fuller, written accounts. One described the Punjabi farmers: "Since a good many of them worked in groups with other Sikh friends, they could continue in their own *Little Punjab*. The land of California valleys is very much like that of Punjab" (Sidhu 1972:102). A particularly nostalgic account comes from a man who joined the older immigrant community in the Yuba City/Marysville region in northern California. Hari Singh Everest came to the United States after South Asian citizenship and immigration rights were won through the Luce-Cellar Bill in 1946, and he submitted the story "Land of Five Rivers" to a northern California Sikh journal. This was a deliberate, elaborate representation of the Sacramento Valley as the Punjabi homeland; "punjab" means "five rivers" in Persian and Punjabi. He explained his story (which was never printed) in a follow-up letter to the editor (which was printed):

I agree that almost all the details . . . match the description of the city of Rupar, in the Punjab. However, the name of the city I tried to describe, was Yuba City. . . . I should not have been so poetic. I left too much to the imagination of the reader.

For example: In my story the Land of Five Rivers was Sacramento Valley. The river Sutlej was Feather River. The rest of the four rivers—American, Bear, Yuba, and Sacramento. My Bhakhra [Dam], the Oroville Dam. My Govind Sagar, the Oroville Lake. The city of Anandpur Sahib, the nearby town of Paradise. The Shivaliks, the Sierra foothills. There was Naina Devi, our Mount Shasta. And yes, the Jawalamukhi, the Lassen Volcanic Park. Obviously, I was carried away by my imagination. Yet, the reality was not left far behind. The water, like the water in the Punjab, had the same urge to run downward. The distant hills had the same charm. The fire in Jawalamukhi and in the Lassen Volcano has the same way to burn things!

I assure you, chief, the Sikh Temple in Yuba City, is much like any Gurdwara in Rupar. In the city bazar, here, a Sikh shopkeeper wears the same black turban. A liquor store (*sharab da theka*) is run by a Sikh. . . . Like in Rupar, Sikh lawyers, Sikh doctors, Sikh engineers and Sikh nurses live and work in Yuba City. . . .

Out of the city, on the farm, the Sikh farmers have brought the "green revolution." . . . And the man with the flowing beard whom we stopped to ask our way to the Sikh Temple, was an American Sikh.

Did you say, chief, my riding with the Sikh taxi driver looked like a fiction? Not really, sir. I did not make it clear that the capital of the state was Sacramento, not Chandi Garh [*sic*]. . . . The taxicab I hired to go to Yuba City, belonged to the Greyhound Taxi Company, owned by a Sikh. (Everest 1972)

Everest's title explicitly bestows the very name of the homeland on the new environment. His original story must have been carefully crafted, and he himself refers to it as poetic. Notice that Everest relocates Punjabi regional sacred landmarks, both Sikh and Hindu, in California, and he is not the only one among the new Punjabi immigrants to claim the Yuba City area for Sikhism. The secretary of one of the three Yuba City Sikh temples (in 1988) talked about the annual parade for Guru Granth Sahib week: "Most Sikh people come to Yuba City like Muslims would go to Mecca. Yuba City gives us the feeling of being back home, in the Punjab."[5]

So the men from Japan and India re-visioned landscapes from Asia as they viewed the California landscape. As with the Japanese, the Punjabi immigrants were certainly doing things differently. Most strikingly, many were marrying out of caste, language, and religion; they stood as godparents to one anothers' children in the Catholic Church (a Muslim godfather to a Sikh's child, and so forth). But they too visualized their new locality in terms of the old, using familiar landmarks to ground their new identity. The two longer written accounts (Fujioka and Everest), addressed to their compatriots, are quite romanticized and metaphorical, consciously re-creating familiar images in California. This framing of the new landscape appears to have been an important feature of accounts by members of both communities; reality was made meaningful through representation (a distinction made by W. J. T. Mitchell [1986] and cited by Comaroff and Comaroff 1987:193).

It is significant that the Asian men are part of the landscape in all these accounts. The land is not unpeopled but is being farmed by countrymen — men taking physical possession of the land and making a livelihood from it. And, significantly, given that both Asian groups began as agricultural laborers and were deprived of citizenship and political power, in these accounts there are no other actors on the land. The Japanese and Punjabi farmers are depicted as kings and landowners in the Imperial and Sacramento Valleys, with kingdoms and capital cities of their own. The whites who in reality blocked them have magically disappeared from the scene. If one believes, with John Comaroff (1987), that collective social identity entails some form of self-definition founded on a marked opposition between "we" and "other/s," it is striking that the pioneers in these written accounts situated themselves alone and in charge of the physical landscape.

A remembered landscape and an orientation to one's own people also underlie the burial and cremation practices of these early Asian immigrants. The Japanese and the Punjabi Muslims buried their dead, and both groups purchased cemetery plots as collectivities. Burial associations were often organized along lines of ethnicity or national origin, and American cemeteries customarily set aside plots for racial and ethnic groups in any case. The Japanese sections of California's rural cemeteries featured the Japanese language on the tombstones, and the flowers and other grave offerings were distinctive. The "Japanese plot" contrasted visually with the plots of Mexicans, Swiss, and other groups.[6]

The Punjabi Sikhs were unable to reproduce India's outdoor funeral pyres. In 1918 some Sikhs tried to cremate a dead compatriot in a field in the Imperial Valley, but they were prevented from doing so by officers of the law.[7] A deceased Sikh was always photographed in the coffin with a turban on his head so that those at home could confirm his death and his orthodoxy with their own eyes (although the Sikhs in California had stopped wearing turbans almost immediately on their arrival there and none standing around the coffin wore them; see Leonard 1992:photo 14). The Sikh men's ashes were often scattered in the Salton Sea or the Pacific Ocean, possibly because of a feeling that these bodies of water were analogous to the Ganges or other sacred rivers of India. (In today's Britain, the Thames is receiving ashes, as Hindu immigrants there have made it their sacred river.)[8]

It is the so-called Hindu plots in rural California cemeteries, however, that convey the strongest sense of a re-created landscape — a final resting place and community of meaning transferred from the homeland. These plots contain the graves of the male Punjabi Muslims (women and children were buried in the Mexican Catholic plot). The graves are oriented toward Mecca, and the small gravestones characteristically have the men's names written only in Urdu (the script derived from Arabic), the language of education for their generation. Little additional information is given: the decedent's father's name, the home village in the Punjab, the death date, and sometimes the birth date. Even the name of the district in the Punjab is not always given, much less that of the province or country of origin. This final resting place speaks meaningfully only to the members of the small, face-to-face community of first-generation Punjabi immigrants.[9]

Turning to matters of daily life and livelihood, how did the Japanese and Punjabi farmers place themselves in the sociopolitical landscape in California? How did they think about the dominant groups — the powerful, predominantly Anglo growers, shippers, and bankers whom they omitted from their visions of the physical landscape? Their conceptions here are likely to have been different. The Japanese immigrants were able to form families through the legal immigration of brides and picture brides from Japan. The Japanese farming community was large and concentrated enough in particular crops to develop both horizontal and vertical marketing structures. These immigrants had a strong political relationship to the Japanese Consul in San Francisco, and Japan tried hard to protect its overseas citizens. Yet despite a body of good research on the Japanese immigrants, studies focusing on their perceptions of their place in rural California are still needed.[10]

In contrast to the more favorable sex ratio for Japanese men and women, there were hardly any Punjabi women in California before 1947, so that almost all Punjabis who married had non-Punjabi spouses. The Punjabi men were few in number (under two thousand at any one census), not numerous enough to develop an "ethnic enclave" in agriculture. And by forming the Ghadar Party in California which worked for freedom from British rule in India and which used violent means to do so, they set themselves at odds with British officials in the United States and India. I was able to interview elderly Punjabis and/or their wives and children to see how they constructed their social place through stories and conversations ("experience narratives"; Schrager 1983) that did mention "others" in the new homeland.

The Punjabi farmers had many points of connection to others in rural California. They depended on Anglo growers, shippers, lawyers, and bankers to help them continue farming despite the Alien Land Law (Leonard 1985). Furthermore, the systematically biethnic marriages of Punjabi men and Mexican women in the first decades of this century produced a so-called Mexican-Hindu community in California (Leonard 1992). Thus the pioneers and their descendants told stories that reflected their thoughts not only about their place in local society but about their ethnicity.

The names used by the Punjabis and their families for themselves stressed an identification with the Punjab and India. Most of the older men referred to themselves as "Hindu," by which they meant simply that they were from India or (in Persian, Urdu, and Hindi) Hindustan, and most descendants continue to call themselves Hindus (Leonard 1989). When they talk about being Hindu, these descendants do not mean objective criteria that link them to India or the Punjab, attributes such as an anthropologist might list. They are fundamentally ignorant of Punjabi and Indian culture, of which they have little or no direct experience. For example, most of the men who founded these families were actually Sikhs, not Hindus, but their descendants (and even some descendants of Muslim Punjabis) proudly claim to be Hindu. Almost all are nonspeakers of Punjabi; they speak Spanish and English, and most are Catholic. Bereft of a South Asian language or religion, two of the most common attributes shared by those claiming membership in an ethnic group, the descendants nonetheless have a sense of place and history that is distinctively Hindu in their eyes.

One of the reasons Punjabi Mexican descendants claim to be Hindu rather than Mexican is a negative one — to be Mexican in California's agricultural towns is to affiliate with the laborer, not the landowner, class — but there are other, positive reasons for claiming to be Hindu. Here I want to move beyond place and locality in the spatial sense and talk about the perception or creation of other similarities with which the men framed their new lives. They perceived similarities between their place in the political system in the Punjab and in California, between Punjabi and Mexican material culture, between the Punjabi and Spanish languages, and between Indian religions and Christianity. These are the ways in which the descendants feel themselves to be Hindu in California today.

Not only the physical landscape but also the political landscape and their place in it struck the Punjabi men as decidedly similar to that in British India. The men's resentment at being colonial subjects, their resentment at being deprived of legal rights in the United States as well, comes through strongly in all interviews (see also Jensen 1988). The Punjabi men organized the militant Ghadar Party in California to fight against the British in India; they contributed money, and some returned to India to participate in Ghadar Party activities there. After United States citizenship was denied them in 1923, they fought hard for political rights in the United States too, organizing groups and supporting lobbyists to gain citizenship and overturn the Alien Land Laws. They interpreted both their past and present as a struggle for one's rightful place in society and particularly on the land, a very important component of Punjabi identity (Pettigrew 1975:55–59).

Mola Singh, in his life history, which I tape-recorded, explained the intersection of race, citizenship, and political power this way (1983):

Only a few people, Hindustani, were here and they had no right to anything then. See, these countrymen, 1000, maybe 2000 Hindus here, they should have had rights together. Rights to live, hold a job, work. Most of our people lived by labor, you know. We were just farmers, common labor people. Some people, educated ones, they used to live in other places, they knew about the national movement, our country. They came here, made a corporation, made it with white men [to front for Punjabi farmers after 1923 when the Alien Land Law was applied to them]. The white men said, "I'll keep the records, let the Hindu people work and suffer." Who got the pistol, he got the law. Who got the power, he got the law. No power, no law.

There are records about the 1933 case [when an Imperial County grand jury indicted Mola, his father, and two other Punjabis and five Anglos for conspiracy to evade the Alien Land Law by forming a corporation], they're in the big book, they kept them. They kept records in India too, and when India got free the records showed what they did. The Government always keeps records, when the time comes, they'll need them. Even Guru Gobind Singh [the tenth and last Sikh guru, who formed a political community] kept records, he knew that someday they'd be needed. Always the Government keeps records.

This interpretation, with its central theme of deprivation of political rights, still has meaning to the children of the Punjabis. Most descendants still live and work in agricultural valleys in California. They too feel strong resentment: for being looked down on as "half-and-halfs," for being pushed into the Mexican and black schools in rural California's until recently segregated school systems, and most of all for not having the land today that their fathers "really earned" but were unable to acquire easily because of the Alien Land Law. Passionate resistance to the British and American political authorities that had subordinated them had linked the fathers to one another in the past, and memories of that resistance link their descendants to one another today.

I can only briefly indicate the social place occupied by their Punjabi Mexican families in the minds of the Punjabi men (but see Leonard 1992). How did they think about their marriages with non-Punjabi women, women perceived today by new immigrants from India as markedly different? Rather than emphasize or even mention the antimiscegenation laws that played a major role in determining their choice of spouses, the men and their descendants talked about commonalities between the Punjabi men and Mexican women.[11] They did not argue that they occupied the same space in the social landscape; that would go against the strong Punjabi feelings of superiority to Mexicans. They did argue that there were similarities of physical appearance and even of language ("Spanish is just like Punjabi, really").

They also argued that Mexicans and Punjabis shared the same material culture. As Mola Singh, who had thirteen children from three marriages with Mexican women, put it:

I never have to explain anything India [sic] to my Mexican family. Cooking the same, only talk is different. I explain them, customs in India same as in Mexico. Everything same, only language different. They make roti over there, sit on the floor — all customs India the same Mexico, the way of living. I went to Mexico two, three times, you know, not too far; just like India, just like it. Adobe houses in Mexico, they sit on floor there, make tortillas (*roti,* you know). All kinds of food the same, eat from plates sometimes, some places tables and benches. India the same, used to eat on the floor, or cutting two boards, made benches. (1983)

Thus the men viewed the women as coming from a similar material culture, but what about the religious difference? Essentially, the Punjabi men argued that all religions are one, a view again in sharp contrast to that expressed by more recent immigrants from India. The men were Sikh, Muslim, and Hindu; they married mostly Catholics, although a few of the wives were Protestants. Yet the men and their descendants said repeatedly that all religions are the same. The statement took different forms: the Sikh religion is just like the Catholic one; Sikhism is a composite of Islam, Hinduism, and Christianity; the Granth Sahib is just like the Bible; all Gods are the same but they are called different names because languages are different; Sikhism has the ten *cruz,* or ten crosses, which are the ten gurus; the founding Sikh guru preached just what is in the Old Testament; Sikhs have all the commandments Catholics have; one can be Muslim and Catholic, or Sikh and Catholic, at the same time.[12]

These statements ignore religious differences now significant in India,[13] stressing similarities between Indian religions and Christianity and frequently using metaphors and analogies to erase distinctions. While there were many vigorously contested matters between Punjabi husbands and Mexican wives, the children's religious training was not one of them. Rather, the men wanted to inculcate respect for Sikhism, Hinduism, or Islam, while they encouraged their children to practice Catholicism (or whatever form of Christianity their wives practiced). Thus when talking to their wives and children about religion, the husbands reconceptualized differences as similarities at a higher analytic level.

In the early twentieth century, the Punjabi immigrant men talked about similarities between their homeland and California,[14] similarities on which they based their continuing collective identity — geography and landscape, the struggle for one's rightful social and political place, wives whom they viewed as similar to themselves in important ways. Today, their descendants face different socioeconomic conditions, different sets of social actors. The descendants' perceptions of recent immigrants from India — perceptions not of the many educated professional people coming from India (people obviously very different from their Punjabi ancestors) but of people very similar to the original immigrants — sharpen awareness of the historically changing configurations of "we" and "other."[15]

Large numbers of Punjabi farmers from the same villages of origin are now coming to California's rural areas where descendants of the older Punjabis reside. The descendants' claim to be Hindu is contested by these new immigrants. Just as some descendants who have actually traveled to the Punjab, untroubled by a need to claim India as a homeland, may not acknowledge similarities of landscape,[16] they see few similarities between their fathers and the new Punjabi immigrants. These differences begin with physical appearance and manner of self-presentation: they say their fathers were big men, light-skinned, commanding, and proud, whereas the newcomers are small, dark-skinned, obsequious, and deferential.[17] Other attitudinal and behavioral differences are stressed as well — the willingness of the original Punjabi immigrants to relinquish beliefs and practices inappropriate to the new setting, the ways in which the Punjabi newcomers are *not* becoming American as did the older Punjabis. Significantly, the Punjabi Mexican descendants defend their claim to be Hindu by claiming also to be more American, by emphasizing those characteristics which bridged differences of national origin, which helped win acceptance for their fathers in the dominant culture. These perceptions lend historical depth to the discussion of changing landscapes and remind one sharply of the Japanese as well.

The Japanese and the Punjabis, citizens of a modernizing nation-state and subjects of a British colony, respectively, were drawn to California by the global political economy developing at the turn of the century. Both groups came voluntarily. The relatively well-educated Japanese had to apply to and be approved by their own government. The Punjabis, less educated but cosmopolitan, often had already worked overseas in British imperial service or had relatives who had done so. The Punjabi immigrants were peasants, and many of the Japanese also came from farming backgrounds; both groups of Asian immigrants worked in California agriculture.

Akhil Gupta has argued that some anthropologists regard peasants as the archetypal natives, primarily because of their occupation of "sedentary space that is distinguished by its boundedness," boundedness as a result of "its purported economic self-sufficiency or the enclosure of its moral universe" (1988:5). And natives, Arjun Appadurai argues (1988b:37–38; Gupta also cites him in this regard), are seen as "incarcerated, or confined, in those places," adapted to them both ecologically and in their ways of thinking. Appadurai suggests thinking of (Western) anthropologists voluntarily displacing themselves to study the natives, the involuntarily localized "others" (1988a:16). But the Japanese and Punjabis displaced themselves; they came to and settled in California, despite American popular notions that stereotyped them as "other" and despite immigration and citizenship laws that viewed them as natives of other places. The law was used to confine them to "their" place, a place of powerlessness and of cultural "otherness."

Not only did the Japanese and Punjabis come to California, but some also saw themselves as warlords and landowners in their new home. Their evocations of familiar landscapes, of similarities and resemblances to their old homes, helped create collective identities in California, identities demonstrably different from and larger than those left behind but not exactly the externally imposed identities that stressed their subordination. Strikingly, representatives of the dominant culture played no role in these articulated visions. Were Asian farmers somehow denying the fact of their migration, of the new context overseas in which they found themselves? Both groups had chosen to migrate, to settle, and to fight for political rights in the United States, therefore it seems more likely that by thinking of themselves as rulers on the land, they were subverting the imposition of the racial and ethnic stereotypes that portrayed them as powerless laborers in California agriculture. Just as race, ethnicity, and gender all helped shape the political economy in rural California, so did they help shape the identities worked out by Asian immigrants. Some things were gained, some new formulations and alliances made, in rural California. Those other actors, members of the dominant culture, were even more strongly present in the immigrants' accounts just because of their absence. The "precarious discourse" of the immigrants may omit explicit references to the dominant culture, but that serves only to emphasize the implicit power relations, the "politics of location" of the time (Keith and Pile 1993). There is still much to learn about the changing historical configurations of "we" and "other" as the Japanese and Punjabi immigrants shaped and reshaped their senses of place and community, but certainly they made this land their own.

NOTES

This piece benefited from comments made by my colleagues Liisa Malkki (an early reading) and Jim Ferguson (a final reading) and by the anonymous readers for the Press as well.

1 See Gary Okihiro et al. 1988:214–37 for Sucheng Chan's annotated bibliography. The *Amerasia Journal,* published from the University of California, Los Angeles, also puts out annual bibliographies.

2 I would like to thank Dr. Sucheng Chan, director of Asian American Studies at the University of California, Santa Barbara, for telling me about this book and giving me a copy of the English typescript.

3 *El Centro Progress,* 5 December 1919, 122.

4 For their educational level and the fact that more Japanese spoke English in 1910 than did any other immigrants save the Scandinavians and Germans, see Iwata 1962:25–37.

5 The story is on page 18 in the 21 October 1988 edition of *India-West,* a South Asian weekly newspaper published in Fremont, California.

6 See Jordan 1982, a pioneering study of Mexican, German, and southern American graveyards in Texas.

7 *El Centro Progress,* 13 August 1918. I would like to thank Joseph Anderholt, Holtville, California, for this and other clippings.

8 Werner Menski, Department of Law, School of Oriental and African Studies, London, in a personal conversation with the author, South Asian Diaspora Conference, Toronto, Canada, 10 December 1989. The early Punjabis in California found it difficult and expensive to ship ashes home, and many of them had also let ties with relatives there lapse.

9 This information derives from personal observation of the Hindu plots in El Centro and Sacramento.

10 Again, see Chan's bibliography in Okihiro et al. 1988, particularly 223–26 and 234–36; and Ichioka 1988.

11 California's antimiscegenation laws were dropped in 1948 but stayed on the books until 1951.

12 These statements come from interviews by the author with Mola Singh and Susanna Mesa Rodriguez Singh (Selma, Calif., 1983), Norma Saikhon (Brawley, Calif., 1981), Rose Canaris (Calexico, Calif., 1986), Elizabeth Din Hernan-

dez (Burbank, Calif., 1981), and Fernando Sanga (Brawley, Calif., 1981), and from recollections of Sunder Amer Dhutt Singh by his daughter Vicenta (Kulkarni 1984).

13 Outstanding work by Harjot S. Oberoi (1988 and 1994) and Peter van der Veer (1994) shows the formation of increasingly differentiated and internally uniform Hindu, Muslim, and Sikh religious communities in nineteenth- and early-twentieth-century India.

14 The men also talked about things that were different—social practices no longer appropriate. Most mentioned behaviors conditioned by caste and religion back in India, but they behaved differently in California. The dominant Jat Sikhs could point out Untouchables in their midst, but those men socialized with the others daily. The men remarked on prohibited Sikh-Muslim-Hindu interactions in India, but members of all three religions generally worked, ate, and socialized together in California. Social practices from the Punjab were consciously discarded; children remarked on their father's refusal to teach them about the Punjab, refusals justified by the uselessness of such knowledge and by a need to become American. (Some fathers resurrected the ghosts of caste, sect, and region from their pasts as their children began to date and marry, but since the wives and children had not learned about these distinctions, the fathers' concerns came too late.) Author's interviews with Mary Garewal Gill (El Centro, Calif., 1981), Kishen (Domingo) Singh Deol (Corona, Calif., 1981), Bob Mohamed (Yuba City, Calif., 1983), Ray Sidhu and Isabel Sidhu Villasenor (Yuba City, Calif., 1982), and Janie Diwan Poonian (Yuba City, Calif., 1982).

15 See Leonard 1992 and La Brack 1988 for discussions of the immigrants who have come from India since the 1965 changes in U.S. immigration law.

16 Mary Garewal Gill, interview by author, El Centro, Calif., 1981.

17 There may be some basis in reality for the statements about size, because many of the pioneers had served in the British military and police services, services that had physical requirements for enlistment. These statements derive from interviews by the author with Verdie Abdullia Montgomery and Emma Smiley (Sacramento, Calif., 1982), Olga Dad Khan (Sacramento, Calif., 1982), Isabel Singh Garcia (Yuba City, Calif., 1983), and Nellie Shine and Caroline Shine Sunghera Resendez (Huntington Beach, Calif., 1982).

JAMES FERGUSON

Anthropological thinking about the rural and the urban has long taken place within a familiar story line of "urbanization," with the urban conventionally understood as the site of modernization and change, and the rural, as the locus of tradition and continuity with the past. Especially in Africa, urbanization has tended to be merged with industrialization, Westernization, and the penetration of capitalism into a single figure, both in the conceptions of scholars and often in those of the "ordinary people" whose experiences anthropologists have tried to describe and explain.

Nowhere is this more true than in Zambia, where the contrast between the rural and the urban has long been taken as a commonsensical spatialization of such dichotomies as primitive/civilized, tribal/Western, traditional/modern, or precapitalist/capitalist. In such a dualistic conception of a country suspended "between two worlds" (Burdette 1988), the process of urbanization takes on a special salience, as a literal journey from one "world" to the other. For this reason, urbanization in Zambia has long signified something much more than a merely demographic process. On the Copperbelt, as in countless other settings around the globe, the shift from rural to urban life has been understood, by scholars and others, not just as manifestation of but also as metonyn for the whole package of modernization, industrialization, and capitalist development. (The literature on urbanization on the Copperbelt is reviewed and critiqued in Ferguson 1990; compare also Ferguson forthcoming).

Wherever the urban has been experienced and understood in this metonymic fashion, conceptions of rurality or "the country" have been ready symbolic materials for the construction of local critiques of urban, capitalist, industrial encroachments. In a variety of settings familiar to anthropologists, notions of "the country" as natural, pure, authentic, or whole have provided powerful alternative moral images to be contrasted against urban realities conceived as artificial, immoral, corrupt, and anomic. Thus Raymond Williams, (1973) has explored the ways in which concepts of the country and the city in England over the centuries have provided central tropes for conceptualizing the social and economic changes associated with capitalist industrialization. In the same spirit, John Comaroff and Jean Comaroff (1987) have shown in their work on the Tshidi of South Africa how, where historical consciousness is not formulated according to the conventions of "narrative realism," dualistic contrasts involving notions of inside versus outside, work versus labor, and rural versus urban have provided an implicit critical commentary on the exploitative system of migrant wage labor. As I will show in the first part of this essay, constructions of "the country" in Zambia during the 1950s, 1960s, and early 1970s were contrasted with urban ills in similar ways, both by localist workers with strong links to rural areas and by some cosmopolitan urbanites.

The recent economic history of the Copperbelt, however, has undermined the established meanings of country and city on which such critiques of contrast have rested. In the last twenty years, Zambia has suffered catastrophic economic decline, reducing it from one of the wealthiest countries in Africa to one of the poorer ones (Jamal and Weeks 1993; Clark and Allison 1989). The mining industry on which the urban centers of the Copperbelt depend has been especially hard hit. Employment has declined, standards of living have plummeted, and real wages have shrunk, all while prices of essential goods have skyrocketed (Jamal and Weeks 1993). Once the industrial heartland of an urbanizing, industrializing, "emerging" Zambia, the cities of the Copperbelt today see their industrial base in rapid decline and their populations actually shrinking in relation to the national population (Potts 1995:254).

Within this changed context, country and city have taken on different meanings, as urban workers' life trajectories have increasingly been brought into conflict with places long imagined and idealized at a certain distance. In the second and third sections, I argue that this fact may help to explain why contemporary Copperbelt mine workers have turned away from a familiar critique of contrast that opposed indigenous rural virtue to imported urban vice, and toward a more inwardly directed critique that locates the blame for urban ills in the supposed "selfishness" of Zambians.

The Country and the City

People have often said "the city" when they meant capitalism or bureaucracy or centralised power, while "the country," as we have seen, has at times meant every- thing from independence to deprivation, and from the powers of an active imagina- tion to a form of release from consciousness. At every point we need to put these ideas to the historical realities: at times to be confirmed, at times denied. But also, as we see the whole process, we need to put the historical realities to the ideas, for at times these express, not only in disguise and displacement but in effective mediation or in offered and sometimes effective transcendence, human interests and purposes for which there is no other immediately available vocabulary. It is not only an absence or distance of more specific terms and concepts; it is that in country and city, physically present and substantial, the experience finds material which gives body to the thoughts.

—Raymond Williams, *The Country and the City*

A reading of ethnographies and other material on the Zambian Cop- perbelt from the 1950s and 1960s suggests that much popular com- mentary on the urban industrial order there was organized by meta- phors of rural/urban contrast. Specific images of "the country" and "the village" seem to have been used to comment on urban life in at least two different ways, corresponding to two different modes of rela- tionship to rural areas.

From the 1920s onward, workers settled in the towns of the Copper- belt, often on a semipermanent basis—dwelling in town with their immediate families, while maintaining links with rural "home" areas to which they might (or might not) return upon retirement. The connection an urban worker might have with such a rural "home" ranged along a continuum, from one extreme (which I call "localist") in which a rural home village was conceived as a primary home, to which the worker might return at intervals, to the other (which I call "cosmopolitan") in which the (often better-off) worker regarded the "home" region as a faraway place, rarely if ever actually seen or visited, to which one was connected more by nostalgia and sentimental attachment than by social and economic ties or life trajectory (compare Ferguson 1990, forthcoming).

The more localist urban workers — those with a strong investment in the "home" village or region — seem to have used a dualist scheme to critique the urban order implicitly by contrast with the rural, much as Comaroff and Comaroff have reported for the Tshidi. Ethnographies from the 1950s provide many examples of moralistic thinking that opposed moral "village women" to immoral "town women"; rural generosity to urban selfishness; rural cooperation and social ties to urban competition and monetary ties; and, most generally, rural morality to urban immorality. A. L. Epstein (1981), for example, describes a number of instances in which an idealized rural tradition provided a point of contrast for Copperbelt workers to the perceived immorality and disorder of urban life during the 1950s (see, for instance, 1981:351, 85, 65). Often this contrast was drawn most sharply in images of women, as in the following popular song of the period (Epstein 1981:351):

> The girls of the railway line
> Are destroying the country
> They abandon the customs of home
> And simply follow their own.
>
> Painting one's lips
> Does not become a Black.
> Look in the mirror,
> You are an entirely different creature.
>
> Tattoo marks on the temples,
> A *lupande* shell about the neck,
> And a string of beads around the waist:
> These are the customs of home.

Women loomed large not only in workers' conceptions of urban vice but in their ideas of rural virtue as well. "Home" was, after all, the place to which one was connected by the bonds of kinship — bonds reckoned, for the matrilineal majority of workers, through the mother. Indeed, Bemba-speaking workers even today give one definition of "home" as the place where one's umbilical cord is buried, the implication being that one's home is properly among those with whom one has a uterine connection, those to whom one is thus tied (compare Epstein 1981:136). If the town could be represented as a corrupt, money-hungry, immoral young woman who had forgotten who she was, the village could always be represented as a loving mother to whom one would always be connected.

A similar moral contrast between rural authenticity, virtue, and connectedness, and urban moral decay was sometimes drawn in the legal sphere, as by one "Traditional Elder," who claimed a superior moral authority to the Urban Courts on these grounds:

Nowadays the people on the mine just live like animals in the bush. They have no big leaders [*ntungulushi bakalamba*]. If a man and his wife are having a tiff in the house, all they can do is go to the Compound Office, and there they are given a letter to take to the Boma. There they have to leave much money, for at the Boma [i.e., the Urban Court], there is no charity, *uluse*. The Court Members just work on a ticket basis, not like ourselves who work for *ubuteko*, for the sake of governing just as we do in the villages, without receiving any pay. . . . We follow the law as it is in the village, but there at the Court they work for the salary they get every month. They do not follow the law of government as we know it at home. (Epstein 1958:59)

The moral contrast between an immoral, urban world of money and an authentic, morally pure rural community of people was colored, too, by the judgment that the urban world was foreign, a creation of the Europeans, themselves often viewed as immoral (Powdermaker 1962:168, 267).

More generally, J. C. Mitchell notes that all over southern and central Africa during this period, "morally and aesthetically evaluative images of town life were common" (1987:101), observing that Africans often shared the dominant European judgment of African town life as disorganized and even morally degraded. Similar themes of town as locus of immorality have, of course, been reported for localists in other urban sites in Africa, for example, by David Parkin for Nairobi (1978) and Kampala (1969) and by Philip Mayer (1971:72–75) for East London. T. Dunbar Moodie (1994) has recently given an especially vivid account of the moral geography that sustained migrant workers in South African gold mines during the same period.

Many images of town were, to be sure, positive, and these were perhaps the dominant ones, especially among women, for whom town life was often seen as a "modern" liberation from the drudgery and social constraints of village life (Hansen 1984; Parpart 1986). But such evaluations usually existed in a complex mix, as J. C. Mitchell (1987) has emphasized: "Derogatory images of town life and towns-folk are usually balanced by contrary images in which cities are perceived as the centres of development and change. In terms of this image the countryman is the ignorant and backward yokel as against the urbane and progressive townsman. The countryman is thus morally upright but unprogressive, the townsman is degenerate but an agent of change and development" (102). The same ambivalence is seen in tales from primary school readers from the 1960s, in which assertions of rural virtue and moral superiority are balanced by such stories as "Town Mouse Goes to the Bush" and "Bush Mouse Goes to Town," which emphasize the contrasting virtues and faults of progressive but morally degraded urbanites and morally pure but backward villagers (Higgs 1979:332). But however ambivalent the final judgment, the moral contrast was always available as a resource for social critique.

The growing and cosmopolitan urban middle class, meanwhile, was using an imagined, idealized rural "tradition" in a different way: to attack colonial domination and to open up some space between their own urban modernity and the specifically Western modernity of the white settlers. In political terms, African nationalists in this period glorified rural folkways and explicitly sought to construct an authentic "Zambian-ness" out of ruralist themes as an alternative to Westernism. Kenneth Kaunda was only an articulate spokesperson for a tendency that was shared by many cosmopolitans during this period when he declared (1966:32):

I am a firm believer in a co-operative way of life as it was practiced in simple village-life fashion. Here family life was intact. The general rule was everyone helping their relatives and friends. The infirm were the responsibility of the entire village unit. The aged found hope and joy in their grand-children. The spiritual and moral side of life was the responsibility of grannies, uncles and aunts, mothers and fathers alike.

I refuse to agree with those who say this was all very well for a unit as small as a village, before the advent of the powerful forces that exist in the Western type of colony. Surely it is not beyond the capacity of man to devise ways and means— especially in a place like Northern Rhodesia, where we have a big country with a comparatively small population—that would make it possible for us to accommodate the powerful forces in the Western type of economy, as well as preserve the man that is found in the small village unit who is not de-humanized, heart, soul, mind and body.

I would like to be bold here and declare that to me independence would be meaningless if Northern Rhodesia is going to continue, just like any other country, a floating unit of human beings, travelling toward human destruction.[1]

Notions of an idealized village life as a moral anchor for a new socialist society were in this way deployed by the most urbanized and cosmopolitan of Zambians in nationalist political discourse. A similar set of themes may be seen in the morality plays that are prominent in the fiction of the period, in which rural folk are almost inevitably cast both as backward in some ways and as the bearers of wisdom and morality, which the typically young, urban, male protagonist ignores only until he sees the error of his ways and integrates their wisdom and virtue into his modernity (Reed 1984).

Similar themes were to be seen in the political struggles surrounding the workers' movements of the period. In the mining industry, in the strikes of 1935 and 1940, workers had already challenged colonial attempts to channel workers' activism into such neotraditional and ethnically local organizational structures as the "Tribal Representatives." The prolonged struggle in the 1950s between the emerging trade unions and the old Tribal Representatives revealed the split between, on the one hand, conservative and rurally oriented workers who saw rural community as the counterweight to urban exploitation and, on the other, progressive workers who demanded urban, working-class structures as the only way to address urban inequalities (Epstein 1958; compare Moodie 1994). But after Independence in 1964, the new Zambian government consistently countered the wage demands of these organized urban workers with a moral geography that opposed their urban "greed" to supposedly more authentic national interests located in the countryside. The idealized images of rural cooperation and generosity that had informed the nationalist movement were in this way opportunistically yoked to a managerial ideology of worker motivation and wage restraint, all in the name of rural interests for which the state claimed to act as guardian (Bates 1971; Burawoy 1972; Ault 1981). As the minister of labour declared in 1967: "If we are to give way any further to demands for increases we would very likely place in jeopardy the programme of development on which we place our main hope for a better future for the mass of the nation, most of whom at present live in rural areas at far lower standards of life than the urban average earner" (cited in Bates 1971:38). In the event of strikes, the president asked in 1965, "Who is going to gain? Who suffers? . . . Your Mother, Father, Brother and the like at home will never forgive you for having failed to get a local clinic, school, roads, etc." (cited in Bates 1971:36). What was needed, Kaunda added in 1968, was for workers to be less selfish and to work harder for the nation, whose real roots were in the rural areas: "If, countrymen, I can not move you on principles, I do not move you ideologically, morally, to hard work, then at least I can ask you if you do not want to work hard . . . [to] remember where we come from. The village. Your own mother is there. My own mother is there. . . . They are all there in the village. . . . If morally, ideologically, philosophically, I cannot move you to hard work, at least I can remind you now your own mother, your own aunt, your own uncle, your own father is there in the village, suffering. . . . What is your contribution? . . . What is your contribution? This is my question" (cited in Bates 1971:33).

Here we find the identification, already noted above, of the rural areas with the kin group, and especially with the mother, and an appeal to mutuality and cooperation over selfish material gain. But the implications of these uses of ruralist themes was rather different than the localists' condemnation of immoral urbanism. For the point was not to reject modern urban life in its totality but to make use of ruralist themes, first to reform or replace the colonial system and then to legitimate the postcolonial order as a genuine African urban alternative. The critique was not of "urban civilization" but of the specifically white, colonial cast it had taken on; "the village" was invoked not as an alternative to the city but as a moral image that should inspire or discipline urban behavior. For cosmopolitan African urbanites whose life trajectories were at this point quite removed from actual villages, the idea of an authentic, rural, African village life was a resource to be used in the projects of constructing an alternative urban modernity and of legitimating postcolonial rule.

Localist criticism, then, cast a moral indictment on the entire urban order via its comparison with an idealized rural one, and comprised an implicit and sometimes explicit critique of modernity. Cosmopolitan criticism, on the other hand, sought to undermine Western domination of the urban order (and later to undermine the claims of urban workers) by invoking a cooperative Zambian tradition conceived as having its most authentic locus in the country. The critique of Westernism was here linked to the promotion of an alternative African modernity. In both strains of criticism, however, "the country" served as symbolic anchor for a critique of urban ills as external to and imposed on the *real* country and its people.

The "Selfish Zambian"

Who must we blame for all these wild changes?
Obviously it is the black man himself.

—Joseph Bantu, *A Straw in the Eye*

In recent years, the ruralist themes in social criticism described above seem to have fallen into relative disuse, even in the face of the collapse of the urban economy (associated with a decline in copper prices and a severe debt crisis) and the consequent decline in the quality of urban life (Clark and Allison 1989; Jamal and Weeks 1993; Ferguson forthcoming). In fieldwork with mine workers in the Copperbelt town of Kitwe in 1985–86 and 1989, I did find some social critiques still anchored in an idealized ruralism, and urban social and economic ills were sometimes attributed to such external or "foreign" origins as — in descending order of plausibility — the International Monetary Fund (IMF), the South Africans, or Indian merchants. But the more prevalent theme by far was a striking, inwardly directed moral critique.[2]

Why are things falling apart? Again and again I was told, in a variety of contexts, that it is because Zambians are "selfish." On the job, Zambian supervisors are "only looking out for themselves." Unlike the white colonial supervisors, many informants insisted, the black Zambians are corrupt and selfish and have no regard for their workers. What is more, there was wide agreement that these same moral flaws could be located in the workers, who, I was told (by workers themselves), are "lazy," "thieving," and "selfish." The government, of course, received its share of the blame: informants considered civil servants corrupt and "out for themselves." But such moral blame was by no means restricted to government and industry. Indeed, what was most striking was the way that the cardinal fault of "selfishness" was applied most vigorously to the "self." The most sweeping moral judgments often began with the word "we." Why has the country fallen on such hard times? As one informant put it, "We, the citizens, are to blame. Today, the collectivity is dead. There is nothing but selfishness. All we think about is ourselves."[3]

This view was often applied to personal life as well as to public affairs. Spouses were inevitably faulted for not trusting each other, and wives specifically (by male informants), for being interested only in money and selfish pleasures.[4] A pronounced misogyny on the part of men, along with mistrust and suspicion of the motives of wives and lovers, long noted by ethnographers of Zambian gender relations (for example, Schuster 1979:126–39; Powdermaker 1962:151–69; Epstein 1981), appears to have intensified in recent years. Rural kin too were regularly denounced for their avaricious greed and selfishness. "My mother is coming [from the village] to visit," an official of the mine workers' union declared to me in conversation one day. "Oh, wonderful," I replied. "No!" he retorted with a bitter laugh. "Terrible! She has only come to try to take more of my money!" Such attributions of selfish motives not only to spouses but even to such formerly idealized categories as mothers and rural kin may have profound consequences, as I will argue shortly.

Coupled with these harsh denunciations of Zambian selfishness was often a conception of a future in which progress could come only through outside agency. These conceptions often found expression in embarrassingly regressive political fantasies. How might things get better? "If the Europeans would come back . . . ," "If the IMF can help . . . ," "If they can bring in some people from outside, from Ghana, from Europe, whatever. . . ." There was the powerful sense here that a progressive moral trajectory could come only from outside. Indeed, it proved extremely difficult to elicit from most informants any morally positive images at all of a Zambian-made future. It is in this sense, I think, that we might understand the response of one mine worker who, when asked what the future might hold for Zambia, replied sadly: "We black people are unable to speak of the future. We can only talk about the past." Without a credible moral trajectory, how indeed is one to talk about the future?

Strikingly similar themes are to be found in recent Zambian fiction. It is easy to find continuity with older themes of rural purity and of lessons to be learned by arrogant young urbanites. But there is also and unmistakably a new ambivalence and pessimism about self and society—a sense of a selfish and morally corrupt world no longer redeemed through rural authenticity.

For instance, *Matteo Sakala,* a play created through improvisation by a group of University of Zambia students in 1977 (Kerr and Shoniwa 1978), replays the familiar theme of the arrogant young man who rejects the counsel of his rural elders, learning only through his urban misadventures that he doesn't really know it all. In a climactic scene, the protagonist, Matteo, opts for a criminal career (1978:52–53):

MATTEO: I had a good job you know. And I wanted to improve. It's a long story. Anyway, things didn't work out. You know, when you're up there, it's like being in a little boat on the sea. There's poor bastards swimming, and drowning and splashing and trying to crawl into the boat where it's comfortable.

STEADY: But the sonofabitches inside push'em out.

MATTEO: Sure. That was me.

STEADY: Kick'em in the teeth.

MATTEO: Right. But even in the boat it's not really so comfortable. Because you just make one careless slip, and they'll push you out as well.

STEADY: That's what happened?

MATTEO: Exactly.

STEADY: Friends dumped you?

MATTEO: Right.

STEADY: Tough!

MATTEO: Bastards! (PAUSE.)

STEADY: Anyway, brother, you don't have to drown.

MATTEO: Hell no, I'll crawl back into that boat.

STEADY: Even here in the water, *mwana* you do fine fine. You just become like a mother-rapin' shark. Like me. No problem.

MATTEO: (THOUGHTFUL): You mean . . . (MATTEO STANDS AND ADVANCES TOWARDS THE AUDIENCE WHILE HE CONTEMPLATES THE LIFE OF A THIEF.)

STEADY: Join our goondy. (PAUSE) Me and my buddies . . . We need someone with brains.

MATTEO: Why not? (PAUSE) It's better than drowning.

STEADY: That's right brother.

By the play's end, Matteo has returned ignominiously to the village, but—in striking contrast to the fiction of an earlier period—the village provides no salvation. Not only is the chief himself a thief, but Matteo finds no real community and feels instead like a social outcast.

He concludes the final scene by reflecting on the boat image quoted above, observing that although he has now had "to swim to land," "I don't really fit here either. Maybe I just belong in the water like a big snake" (1978:85). The play's pathetic end thus involves a failure of social and moral connectedness, leaving the hero suspended in the water, belonging neither in the boat nor on the land. The old gendered symbolism of maternal connection to the rural "home," meanwhile, is inverted: instead of being socially and morally tied to the land by the umbilical cord, there is the image of floating free in the water "like a big snake"; instead of an ethic of caring for one's rural community as if for one's own mother, the hero chooses to be "a mother-rapin' shark."

Killian Mulaisho's more recent play *Tragedy of Pride* (1988) offers an even more bleak resolution of the same general plot line. Again the story revolves around a young man, Milimo, who has rejected rural ways and the wisdom of his elders, this time by spurning an arranged marriage with a village girl, Juliana. Milimo comes to town, where he lives a fast life and becomes known by the name "Poggy Wizard." Eventually the fast living runs out, and Milimo loses everything. He sees his foolishness and plans his return to the village, where "all is at peace." "Surely," he reflects, "my salvation lies in the village and in Juliana, the village girl whom they hoped I would marry!" (24). But again, there is a twist in the so-far conventional story line. For instead of learning his lesson and being reintegrated into society, Milimo finds that Juliana has married another man and that the village has no place for him. When he complains that he is "no longer a man of the city," his own father tells him, "Yet you neither belong here my son." The play concludes with Milimo reflecting on his despair, observing: "And the village — so cold and indifferent, sleeps soundly when I, its child, is having a sleepless night. I had come to make amends, to lead a new life. But this (points to various places on the ground), this, this is all I get . . . 'You neither belong here' my father has said" (24). The play ends here, with the following stage directions: "Milimo lies prostrate on the floor and uncontrollable wailing is heard in the background for half a minute. Lights go off again and play ends. N.B. No mourners to come on stage."

These themes of selfishness and moral disintegration are captured even more sharply in Joseph Bantu's complex novel *A Straw in the Eye* (1989). In this book, the town is again a place of moral decay, where "man has lost his self-conscience and he does not know who he is or where he is going," a place where Zambians have forgotten their own old cultures and blindly imitate an imported and inauthentic Western way of life (116–17). But it is striking that "the country" is *not* presented as a moral contrast but only as another arena for corruption and immorality. The village is a place where witchcraft is rampant, where relatives are continually trying to kill one another out of jealousy and malice. Such practices are seen as widespread — "Nobody who has lived in Zambia can doubt that [witchcraft] throws its shadow over every activity of the country's subjects" (90) — and increasing: "Just as the white man is advancing in technology, the black man is advancing in witchcraft. It has grown tremendously" (91). As the story unwinds, "the village" is gradually revealed to be not a cooperative, moral community but a cruel and fearsome setting crisscrossed by corruption, treachery, and murder. In the course of his adventures, the young, male narrator is abused and mistreated by a range of unsavory rural characters, including corrupt and selfish schoolmasters, bullying students, and a cruel and immoral uncle, who is himself eventually murdered in cold blood by his neighbors and enemies (88–92, 129, 133, 138, 144, 147, 170–71). Even more striking, the narrator himself is implicated in the same immoral order of things, both categorically ("The European is going, but our own people are just as bad" [156]) and individually, as in the following startling passage:

Nobody by now, can deny the fact that most men lead two lives — a normal life and a secret life. Society is, of course, only able to judge a man's character by his own normal life. If he makes a mistake, however, and his secret life becomes public, then he is judged by his own secret standards and is, more often than not ostracized as punishment. In spite of this, he is still the same man who, a moment before received the praises of society. At least he is the same man with one important difference: he has been found out.

By now, because of my complete frankness, you may have come to the conclusion that I am exceedingly unpleasant. You may even have decided that I'm unethical, dishonest, vain and worthless. These conclusions are not due to your own insight and perception. They are due to my own frankness. (159)

Recent Zambian works of fiction thus reproduce many of the same themes of "selfishness" and inner corruption that I discovered in the interviews with mine workers. They also hint at a connection between the moral standing of "the country" and the moral standing of the self, which I wish to explore in the final section.

The Country and the Self

For the wars that are raging again
Is African goodness good enough?

— Taban Lo Liyong, *Ballads of Underdevelopment* [5]

The question I want to pose is this: Why did the social critiques of the 1950s and 1960s — critiques that attributed urban social evils to an origin *outside* and external to an African society conceived as authentic, morally pure, and essentially *rural* — give way to such a destructive and self-denigrating contemporary critique locating these evils in an internal and essential Zambian selfishness? What happened to the authentic, pure, morally centered "country" that served so long as a basis for critique? To explain this, I suggest that it is necessary, among other things, to examine the changing relationship between urban workers and their rural dependents.

Very schematically, the workers I have described as "localists" have strong ties to a rural nexus of dependents and kin in a "home" village or region, and they invest heavily in maintaining their social position there. They may visit often or contribute clothing and money to their rural kin, and they expect to return "home" upon retirement at age fifty-five or earlier. The workers at the other extreme, the ones I have called "cosmopolitan," have more or less severed their social links with a rural "home" and have made their life choices on the assumption that they will not have to retire to a rural area but will manage to live out their lives in town. Today, with the urban economy in collapse, many of these "cosmopolitans," even at rather high socioeconomic levels, are finding it impossible to remain in town after leaving employment and are facing the possibility (which they never expected or prepared to face) of being forced to return to the rural kin they have ignored and snubbed for so long (see Ferguson 1990, forthcoming).

What does this mean for the ruralist critique of urban industrialism? Given this set of relations between urban workers and rural dependents, as the urban economy continues its downward spiral, two things happen at once. First, of course, the need for a critique grows. The collapse of living standards and the rise in social evils such as crime, hunger, and destitution must be in some way explained and blame attributed. But, second, the antagonism between urban workers and rural dependents intensifies. The economic decline means not only that dependents have greater needs but also that they have greater power, for workers must now count on returning "home" and are therefore under greater pressure to make their peace with their rural kin. This new power in the hands of the rural dependents finds expression in new demands made on workers' earning power, even as workers' shrinking real income means that they are less and less able to satisfy even the old demands. Under the changed circumstances, even the most loyal urban localists feel besieged with unfair and impossible demands. For male workers, of course, such demands by rural, often female, relations only exacerbate the misogyny and the suspicion of women that already characterize their relations with their wives and lovers in town.

Meanwhile, cosmopolitans (who have largely cut their links with rural dependents) now must face a return to rural life for which they are wholly unprepared. Indeed, having defied rural opinion and denied rural claims for so long (in the mistaken belief that a return "home" would never be necessary), "the village" is for many of these squeezed cosmopolitans a potentially hostile and frightening environment. For increasing numbers, "the country" now no longer appears as a nostalgic fantasy but as a terrifyingly real destination. The village, far from being the locus of an authentic morality, appears rather as an object of intense fear, often articulated as fear of witchcraft. Here, too, a political economy of misogyny is at work, because women (especially older women) are often imagined as the perpetrators of witchcraft.

As the economic collapse worsens, then, "the country" comes more and more to appear as (in the first instance) the locus of selfish, greedy, parasitic demands on strapped localist workers and (in the second) a fearsome and threatening site of potentially violent and vindictive acts against noncompliant cosmopolitans. The rural kin once invoked as the very paradigm of a morally centered world of love and reciprocity — "your own mother, your own aunt, your own uncle, your own father" (Kaunda, cited in Bates 1971:33) — are increasingly likely to be perceived as potential antagonists, or even enemies.

This creates a double bind at the conceptual level, for the powerful forces demanding a critique of urban life are at the same time generating changed circumstances that undermine the suitability of "the country" to serve as the internal base for such a critique. As the economic crisis deepens, "the village," long conceived as somehow constituting the moral heart of society, the "*real* Zambia" — must come to seem more and more of a selfish and even sinister place. Such a turnabout in the moral standing of what had been understood as the true social locus of authenticity, purity, and wholeness necessarily undermines the effectiveness of the old critique that contrasted the artificial, urban, industrial immoralities of imposed capitalism with the authentic, morally centered social core located in rural life. With the urban image of "the country" increasingly dominated by themes of selfishness and treachery, it becomes more comprehensible that social critique should have nowhere to turn but inward and that the failings of the urban economy should come to appear as attributable not to any external force but to the internal moral faults of the Zambian character. Given the gendered nature of both the symbolism and the social relations linking male workers with "the country," it is perhaps not surprising if it involves an intensification of men's hostility and suspicion toward women as well.

In the classical European pattern of urbanization, as Raymond Williams (1973) showed, urban images of rurality have sometimes been remarkably free-floating, related strongly to the conceptual needs and political fantasies of urban society and only weakly to actual rural conditions. Where country and city are socially and experientially segregated, it is perhaps easy for conceptions of "the country" to become largely and sometimes almost completely deterritorialized, insofar as "the country" figures in the lived world of such permanently urbanized populations principally as a metaphorical "other" to urban life and only occasionally or secondarily as a lived social context in its own right. In Zambia, however, as in much of the rest of the world, "the country" as ideal and "the country" as locale are less easy to separate, and the deterritorialization of rural images may be in some measure checked or complicated by the intrusion of rural lived experience. It is in this way, I have argued, that in Zambia, "the country" as imagined locus of moral purity and wholeness is today increasingly in tension with "the country" as the seat of actual and antagonistic social relations.

I suggest, too, that wherever "the country" is in this way partly, but not wholly, deterritorialized or free-floating, such tensions are always potentially present. Among migrant and semimigrant urban communities, the way in which rurality is imagined (and thus the way it can figure in a critical apprehension of the urban) is necessarily conditioned both by the politico-symbolic demands of the urban present and by the political and economic character of the gendered social relations linking the country and the city. To say this is not to suggest that imaginations of place are crudely or mechanically determined by political economy but only to insist that people acquire their conceptions of places in the context of social lives and biographical trajectories that are, as so many Zambians have been so cruelly reminded of late, often at the mercy of structural processes over which they have no control.[6]

At a time when anthropologists are becoming more concerned with such things as displacement, migration, and exile, it is perhaps useful to remind ourselves that such conditions are rarely experienced as absolute, unambivalent, or final. There is a temptation to see displacement as a specific social condition, a form of life that follows from some definitive break with a social life rooted in ancestral places.[7] Yet dislocation is more often a partial and conditional state of affairs, an uncertain predicament that entails neither a clear sense of membership in one's community of origin nor an uncomplicated conviction of having left it behind. For the experience of displacement is full of ambiguity and indeterminacy; one may not know oneself whether one is a "temporary migrant" or a "permanent immigrant," an "exile" or a "visitor," an "urbanite" or a "villager," for such fixed statuses may hinge on the unknowable dice toss of the future. In such circumstances, the nature and significance of continuing connections with places left behind may be extremely variable and may, as in the case discussed here, shift in unexpected ways over time. The empirical exploration of how such shifting connections may frame experiences of place, community, and society among the partially and provisionally dislocated offers rich ground for future anthropological research.

NOTES

This paper is based in part on one year of anthropological fieldwork conducted in Kitwe, Zambia, from October 1985 to September 1986 and in June–August 1989. The research was made possible by grants from the Africa Program of the Social Science Research Council and the American Council of Learned Societies. The research was done in affiliation with the Institute for African Studies of the University of Zambia and with the cooperation of the Zambia Consolidated Copper Mines. All conclusions, opinions, and other statements in this publication are those of the author and not necessarily those of the above organizations.

1   See also Kaunda 1966:14–15, 138, 232. Similar themes were, of course, developed by other African nationalists of the period, most notably Julius Nyerere, whose ideology of African socialism centered on an idealized picture of African village life governed by the familial, communal spirit of "*ujamaa.*" For a comparison of the governing rhetoric of this period with the technocratic rhetoric of contemporary "structural adjustment," see Ferguson 1995.

2   For a discussion of the relation between the technocratic development discourse associated with "structural adjustment" programs in Africa and regional traditions of moralizing critique, see Ferguson 1995.

3   Interviews and conversations with mine workers were conducted by the author in 1985–86, via tape recordings in Kitwe, Zambia. Informants were promised that they would not be quoted by name.

4   My fieldwork was principally with mine workers, who were nearly all men. I am naturally much more confident in characterizing their views than those of Copperbelt women. But although I have less information than I would like about how women felt about their husbands, I did see (like other Copperbelt fieldworkers before me) ample evidence of distrust, suspicion, and antagonism.

5   Taban's poems refer more to the Kenyan context than the Zambian but evoke powerfully the sense of self-doubt and unworthiness that seems to grip Africans all over the continent nowadays.

6   An articulate statement of an approach to place that preserves such a recognition of political-economic determination while striving to grasp the culturally and locally specific forms of lived experience may be found in Pred and Watts 1992.

7   Compare Liisa Malkki's critique (1995b) of studies of displacement that take for granted "emplacement" as an unproblematic or natural state of affairs.

Rethinking Modernity: Space and Factory Discipline in China

LISA ROFEL

The search for the modern is the zeitgeist, if there is one, of China's recent period of economic reform (1978–89).[1] This is but an intensification of a process that has marked at least the entire twentieth century in China. One of the most telling ways to examine this process is through changing representations of urban space. Spatial relations, as cultural, political and economic practices, have featured prominently in discussions of modernity (Harvey 1989; Davis 1990; Foucault 1979; Holston 1989; Rabinow 1989). Urban design is, arguably, the epitome of modernity (Rabinow 1988:361). How can we evaluate this project in China? There are two aspects of this question I wish to address. The first is the matter of globalization. As the Chinese party-state rather self-consciously claims to be borrowing at least selected Western practices, can we therefore conclude that modernity there is similar to that described for "the West"? Most important, does post-Mao modernity in China present a confirmation of or a challenge to more recent discussions in the United States and Europe that have involved rethinking this category? In what follows, I argue that hegemonic transnational flows of commodities and values create a powerful discourse on modernity spreading out of the West, but we must nonetheless remain wary of creating unified readings out of local Euro-American practices and allowing those to overpower interpretations elsewhere.[2]

The second, related matter is the question of resistance within modernity. The argument has already been eloquently put forth that resistance never exists outside fields of power — that it does not simply

oppose power but occupies a strategic field coterminous with networks of power (Lila Abu-Lughod 1990; Butler and Scott 1992; Timothy Mitchell 1990). With these poststructuralist revisions in mind,
many scholars find it important nonetheless to mark the limits of
domination in deeply coercive social contexts. How can we theorize
modernity as a technology of power/knowledge that reconfigures
what will count as resistance? Rather than approach the situation in
China as one in which the state provides a set of external constraints
which coerce citizens' behavior or which subaltern subjects manage to
evade, I argue that, in this case, workers' negotiations of the spatial
disciplining they experience occur within spatial technologies that
transform their conceptions of themselves and their very embodiment
of identity as subaltern subjects. Their implicit and explicit challenges
are produced in the interstices provided by the collisions and paradoxes in the palimpsest of architectural histories that reside in factory
space.

OF PANOPTICONS AND POLYSEMY

The idea that spatial relations have the power to shape subjectivities
has recently led Western intellectual practitioners on a journey in
search of cross-cultural panopticons.[3] The panopticon, that visionary
architectural plan of Benthamite utilitarianism, was transformed by
Foucault into a metonym of the modern disciplinary gaze (compare
Foucault 1979). Intended as a design for prisons, the panopticon is a
circular building with a guard tower in the center. The peripheral
building contains individual cells structured such that the inmates are
visible at all times, but they can see neither their fellow inmates nor the
person in the guard tower. According to Foucault, the panopticon is
the perfected apparatus of discipline by means of a hierarchized, continuous, and functional surveillance independent of any person who
might exercise it — a gaze that never stops gazing. It produces subjects
who assume responsibility for self-discipline, because the power of the
gaze is visible to them but unverifiable. The power created through
this architectural structure is thus pervasive, anonymous, and productive, rather than repressive. It fosters a regulated and productive population. Foucault argued that this "disciplinary regime" marked a turn
in European history beginning in the eighteenth century. Since that
time, individuals have increasingly become subjects and objects of
surveillance and knowledge by various institutions (for example, pris-

ons, medical clinics, schools) as well as by the disciplines of the human social sciences (compare Dreyfus and Rabinow 1982; Foucault 1973, 1975, 1978).

Although Foucault addressed himself specifically to the cultural history of Europe, lately his work has been read as a more general statement about the rise of an episteme called "modernity."[4] What is now meant by this term? The explosion of recent writings on "modernity" (compare Berman 1988; Escobar 1988; Habermas 1987; Harvey 1989; Horn 1988; Latour 1993; Rabinow 1989; Urla 1988; Yang 1988) has presented us with sophisticated analyses about the links among epistemology, power, and subjectivity.[5] These descriptions of modernity's effects contain an urgent sense that we reexamine some of the most cherished Western ideals of liberty and progress. They also convey an implicit assumption that modernity constitutes a unified set of practices, in part because it takes place amidst an implosively interconnected "global ecumene" (Hannerz 1989). That is, transnational interconnections make modernity appear to be a whole new way of experiencing the world. Thus, for example, Marshall Berman claims that "there is a mode of vital experience — experience of space and time, of the self and others, of life's possibilities and perils — that is shared by men and women all over the world today. I will call this body of experience 'modernity' " (1988:15). The term "modernity," as recently employed, encompasses the belief in the triumvirate of Reason, Progress, Truth; the rational planning of ideal social orders; and the standardization of knowledge and production that takes Man as the norm for understanding — in short, the European Enlightenment project (compare Harvey 1989). This further includes the belief in an objective science, a universal morality and law, and autonomous art. Modernity manifests itself in metanarratives (for example, Marxism, liberalism, and so forth) whose teleological tales grope for idealistic utopias. It is a positivistic, technocentric, and rationalistic stance toward the world that espouses an active break with what it constructs as the irrationalities of religion and superstition found in "tradition" — its dependent and relational "other." Following Foucault, modernity has been taken to mean a particular focus of power on the welfare of the population, on regulating its physical and spiritual health, life, and growth (Yang 1988). Finally, as Berman has argued, modernity is the experience of life as radically contradictory, ceaselessly revolutionizing itself while searching for the ultimate stability, a world in which "all that is solid melts into air" (1988).[6]

Nowadays, one seems to come on this project of modernity virtually everywhere. Contemporary nation-states adopt visions and methods for creating "efficient," "productive," and "functional" social orders from the crisscrossed terrain of transnational flows. Architectural plans for a "rational" urban life; assembly-line techniques for producing mass-consumption goods, often for export; increasing surveillance of bodies through new reproductive technologies; sophisticated military methods of torture; satellite communications technology; literary narratives and popular culture forms; plastic surgery to make Asian women look Western — these form the transnational cornucopia from which "citizens of the world" (to paraphrase Kant) are seemingly created.[7] Whether one envisions these global connections as center-periphery relations (Hannerz 1989; Wallerstein 1974) or as multiple "scapes" of overlapping disjunctures (Appadurai 1990), it is clear that this search for modernity occurs in an unequally balanced world, where the position of the United States as a model to be emulated remains hegemonic.

How do the revolutionary transformations of the past decade in China speak to these issues of modernity? State discourse in China on the Four Modernizations (industry, agriculture, military, and science and technology) has inscribed its version of the universal efficacy of science, progress, and rationality. There was a rigorous attempt to create an empiricist separation of economics from politics, as the state urged the populace to leave off with ideology and "seek truth from facts."[8]

As elsewhere, structural designs that induce effects of power in China are most obviously sought in the industrial discipline of urban factory work. The factory is the icon par excellence of modernity. In this respect, China is no different from Lowell, Lancashire, or Juárez. Factory managers, urged on by the party-state, have adopted "capitalist" techniques of scientific management in the intensive pursuit of that quixotic thing called "profit."[9] And factory cadres have begun to redesign factory architecture in the name of efficiency. In the silk industry, the focus of my research, the emphasis on exports has led to intimate interweavings into the global political economy. All these transformations have wrought their disciplinary effects on the subjectivities of workers.

Yet even the panoptic gaze of industrial discipline needs to be captured in its historical and cultural specificities. Even in a space as seemingly global as an urban factory geared toward export, spatial productions of modern subjectivities collide with polysemous histories of past spatial relations. For space — and the authority to construe it — is a contested domain of relations of production because of its recognized connections to power. These polysemous histories are located in several sites: in the specific interpretations of scientific management by local factory managers; in architectural histories rooted in the early years after liberation (1949), as well as in the prerevolutionary era; and finally, in workers' memories of past spatial relations, memories that have taken on the hue of subversion in the context of economic reform. As a result, modernity in China does not neatly replicate the hypothetical transnational — that is, European — model.[10]

In the midst of my several years of fieldwork in China (1984–86), I joined the work force of a silk-weaving factory in Hangzhou, a moderately sized eastern coastal city that serves as a center of light industry. Managers assumed I would join in a supportive dialogue with them about the best ways to interpret and implement scientific management successfully. Their approach led me to realize that workers' interpretations of management's interpretations of "discipline" constituted one site where local histories were being expressed. Throughout the factory, I found prep workers sitting off the shop floor chatting, young men leaving their looms to have long, leisurely cigarette breaks, and inspection workers who would sit outside during their shift and relax in the sun. Western tourists who visit similar factories often comment on the lack of "industriousness" of Chinese workers. There is not a little irony in this characterization, given the orientalist notion of Asians as hardworking. And the obvious essentialism of this observation makes it easy to dismiss. Yet, one is still left with a puzzle: the spatial logic of the factory can be read as conducive to certain disciplinary effects; the current self-conscious efforts of the state even more so. Why, then, are they only partially effective?

In addressing this question, I eschew an approach that would assume a sovereign autonomy of consciousness on the part of the subaltern that generates the source of agency internally. Those engaged with subaltern studies have provided a rich debate on subaltern subjectivity. They have maintained a productive tension between subalternity as discursive effect and the subaltern as social agent (Chakrabarty 1989; Guha and Spivak 1988; O'Hanlon 1988; O'Hanlon and Washbrook 1992; Prakash 1992, 1994). Subalternity, as Gyan Prakash has argued, "by definition, signifie[s] the impossibility of autonomy" (1994:1480). It is constituted not in spite of but by dominant discourses. Yet, in the very manner in which they are constituted, sub-alterns represent a radical difference for dominant forms of power. This makes it all the more critical to analyze the ways subalterns sub-vert, recast, dislocate, or exert a limit on power, even as power never ceases to operate.

In what follows, I hope to suggest an approach to spatial disciplining of workers — and thus to the issue of modernity — that takes account of the way history comes into play with epistemic structures. That which has been taken as homogeneous and called "modernity," I argue, obscures a range of diverse practices, for memories are not erased by the introduction of newer epistemes. Memories are a prominent site in which the specificities of workers' subject formation in post-Mao China are located. These memories are not foundational; they do not carry forward an unmediated sense of the past. Rather, as Lisa Yone-yama (1994) has so eloquently argued, attention to memory high-lights contestatory processes of historical representation.

At the very least, then, we might want to begin speaking of "alterna-tive modernities." This essay can be read as a cautionary tale, urging us to be wary of creating a new master text of modernity from Foucault. After all, we have already been through modernization and depen-dency theories. We need to retain the sense of modernity as an ideo-logical trope — both in Europe and elsewhere. As such, it generates meaningful struggles because people have a commitment to the term. More than a specific set of practices, modernity is a story that people tell themselves about themselves in relation to "others." It is a power-ful story because nation-states organize the body politic around it (Dirks 1990). As a story, it can illuminate matters, and it can affect people's consciousness. But it can also fool and mislead us. Even in those moments when, for example, the party-state in China declares itself to be faithful to the Western version of modernity, specific histo-ries that reside in various people's memories turn it into another form. For like all tales, its meanings acquire different valences with its vari-ous narrations.

SPATIAL DISCIPLINING

China's party-state imagines new levels of wealth and power it might attain in global networks of culture and capital. To that end, factory cadres have adopted Western "capitalist" techniques to induce dra-matically higher levels of "efficiency" and "productivity" in urban factories.[11] They have embraced "scientific management," that quintessential biopowerful technique for producing disciplined workers. In the silk-weaving factories of Hangzhou, state bureaucrats and factory managers yearn for a perfectly ordered, spatially disciplined, and therefore productive work force. Their visions have been created in opposition to the spatial modes of authority prevalent in the Cultural Revolution (1966–76).

The Cultural Revolution, currently portrayed as a maelstrom of meaningless violence, in fact raised several deep-seated issues: the relationship between economic development and hierarchical work structures, especially social divisions of labor; the place of intellectuals, long part of China's ruling class; the production of social inequalities within a socialist society; and China's relationship to the capitalist world system (Dirlik and Meisner 1989). In the seemingly distant past of that Maoist era, workers, through various political campaigns, were periodically encouraged to leave their work positions to focus on other concerns, namely, their political consciousness. In the initial years, virtually all workers left their work posts to reinvigorate that consciousness through factory-wide meetings in which they forced managers to confess crimes of following the capitalist road. The more radical workers, mainly from the younger generation, left the shop floor in pursuit of political rights; they challenged managerial authority by dragging managers out of their offices and forcing them to do manual labor on the shop floor. Workers continuously moved on and off the shop floor, one moment weaving some cloth or spinning thread, the next moment participating in a political meeting. When not engaged in political struggle, workers' work regime still involved political discussion meetings with other workers.

High political consciousness often became equated with refusal to participate in production.[12] The sign of a politically "red" worker was her or his zeal in political struggles rather than in production of commodities. Leaving the shop floor was thus a peripatetic statement of political rights to challenge managerial authority. The combination of struggle sessions against managers with "bourgeois" ways, factional fighting among workers, and disruptions in regional supply networks meant that workers took a measure of control over organizing their own daily movements, mixing the space of the factory with domestic space by doing their laundry, shopping, and washing bicycles at the factory or during work hours. Workers during the Cultural Revolution thus challenged the meaning of their place, both physically and in terms of social divisions of authority and power. Walking away from one's work position to engage in politics put one at the forefront of the radical faction.[13] Even after 1973, when managers returned to their place in the offices, they did not punish or pressure workers to produce more silk goods. For then, too, the most important product to come off the shop floor was supposed to be political consciousness.[14]

Just as significant, the labor process during the Cultural Revolution era was structured such that it did not matter at which position any particular worker prepared thread or wove cloth, for workers were conceived of as laboring in collective groups. Collectivity was the hallmark of Maoist production processes. Even when bonuses were restored after the Cultural Revolution, they were initially allocated to groups of workers. Amounts produced were measured but were not tied either to individuals or to particular workstations.

That system has been rigorously criticized as one of the many inefficiencies of the Cultural Revolution. With economic reform, the intensification of production placed a new measure of importance on the individuation of workers. The abandonment of the collectivism production of the Cultural Revolution and the objectification of the individual worker through spatial arrangements, measurement, and quantification are part of the same political project. The creation of the individual subject — minus the exhortations toward bourgeois freedom of expression — has been very much a project of the state.[15]

Silk factory managers sought to root each worker spatially in one work space through an appropriately named position-wage system (*gangwei gongzi zhi*), instituted in 1985. Each worker receives wages based on the position on the shop floor that she or he occupies; bonuses are calculated by piece rate, again tying individuals to work positions. In the prep shop, each worker's number of filled spindles is recorded by the shift leader at the end of the day. In the weaving shop, each worker's name is sewn into the side of the cloth produced. Alienated labor it might be; still, the identification of individual, product, and position is total. Even when one worker substitutes for another, the spatial ordering of individuals is such that the cloth or thread from that workstation is recorded under the original worker's name. Workers are thus spatially ranked and specified so that anomalies in the working body can theoretically be more readily discerned.

That ranking is magnificently displayed on a gigantic production board hung on a shop floor wall where Mao's larger-than-life picture once stood. Mao had exhorted workers to discipline their political consciousness. Now, the production board exhibits the monthly amounts that each worker has produced. Yet this is not only a spatial disciplining of bodies but a spatial disciplining of consciousness as well. Each worker is to identify with a particular workplace and with the thread or cloth produced there.

In the imagined plans of Party cadres and factory managers, each worker remains fixed to his or her designated spot on the shop floor, leaving it only for meal breaks and at the end of the shift.[16] As part of this spatial disciplining, each worker is to stand at a set interval from the next worker, the distance prescribed by the number of spindles or looms at the workstation. The machines are evenly spaced so that the shift leader, shop supervisor, or master teacher can readily discern production problems when she or he walks up and down the central aisle of the shop floor. To ensure that workers do not leave their positions, management has instituted a number of disciplinary rules, discipline having been lost, they said, during the Cultural Revolution. Workers are not allowed to chat with one another during their work shift. Because of the pounding, deafening noise of the looms and spinning machines, chatting would require leaving one's work space. Nor are workers allowed to leave the shop floor to accommodate the kinds of "personal" labor chores they had incorporated into their work during the Cultural Revolution. Neither, however, can workers remain unduly attached to any workstation. A worker must accept a change in assignment — for example, from twisting the silk threads to sweeping the floor — without protest. Individuation also means interchangeability of the parts.

In rearranging spatial modes of authority in the factory, state cadres have imagined a space of national wealth and modern nationhood (Anderson 1983) — a reformed nation-state. The paradox, however, is that these silk factory spaces have been constructed as sites of global interconnections. Factory managers proudly told me of their efforts to mimic faithfully Western techniques for disciplining workers. During my sojourn in Hangzhou's silk factories, a German manager came to lecture; factory engineers and cadres went to Como, Italy, to study dyeing techniques; and the American best-selling manual of business success, Thomas Peters's *In Search of Excellence* (1982), was popular.

The silk itself, as both a commodity and a cultural artifact, signifies the transnational nature of the factories. Once worn only by the Imperium, silk has become one important sign of China's place in a global cultural and political economy.[17] Over 40 percent of Hangzhou's silk production is for export. But China does not export its own patterns and uses of the silk, which are mainly elaborate symbolic designs for wedding quilt covers. Instead, they "blank out" their notions of beauty and utility by producing plain white silk for Western designers. Or they weave Western desires and tastes into the cloth.[18] In this case, then, one cannot simply conclude that transnational flows consist of an Asian appetite for Western culture, for here, things "Chinese" are increasingly difficult to distinguish from things "Western." These silk factories, though recognizably in China, in effect are no longer solely of China. These sites have been reterritorialized. The place of the factory is shifting underneath workers' feet, even as they remain in "place." In this sense, workers in China, too, can be thought of as transnational.

These intimate microconnections of power that link artifacts to bodies should not obscure the specificities of China's search for the modern. The introduction of Western techniques does not erase history, much as this might be factory managers' intent. For their visions of scientific management embody a particular history. In pamphlets written in 1979 and 1980, silk corporation cadres broke down and subdivided the body's movements in space to have a better handle on them. Their inspiration, they told me, came from American Taylorism.[19] A section of one pamphlet on prep work reads:

For the task of rewinding pure silk thread that has not been twisted:
1. Relieving the previous shift:
   Accomplish the one link, three checks, one do well.
   "One link": Enter the production position fifteen minutes early, link with the previous shift over the production situation (including the raw material, the batch number, etc.); check the machinery's condition.
   "Three checks": Check the last shift's markings for mistakes; check the ring frames for roundness; check the patterns of the thread spinning on the spools for regularity.
   "One do well": Do well the markings for dividing the shift.
2. Making the rounds:
   The path for making the rounds must be rational (heli). When inspecting for quality, use hands, eyes and ears together. Differentiate the weight and tension of the thread. Do the easy first and then the difficult. Stop the spools or the ring frames to fix problems.
   The path for making the rounds should follow the shape of the character for

"bow," starting from the head of the first line of spindles to the end of the second line. The second round should still begin from the head of the first line, in proper order, and not return along the path.

Both eyes should look to the left and right at the ring frames and spindles and not stare idly. Concentrate without rushing.

Both hands should be industrious. Accurately lift the thread, accurately correct the tension.

When checking the quality of the filled spools, do not entangle the ends, get grease or sludge on the thread, or other defects. If it does not meet quality standards, do not go on to the next production process.

Should the ear hear a strange sound in the machine's operation, immediately take care of it. (Hangzhou Silk Institute 1984)

Microtechniques of the body these may be, yet they have their specificities in the way that consciousness and literacy come into play. Taylorism in the West treated the body as if it were a machine, so that movement would become rapid and automatic without involving any thought. In contrast, here one finds an emphasis on the need for workers' participatory consciousness in their actions rather than on a mere physical reenactment of motions in space. The pamphlet recalls recent Maoist history that took consciousness as the site of political possibilities and political threats. Cultural Revolution sessions consisted of yelling and beating people into a conscious realization of their class-errant ways. But consciousness in this case is not the repository of a unified subject's inner truth. It is rather a permeable site that is reflected through outward actions.[20] With economic reform, Maoist consciousness-raising has continued in the form of "thought work" (*sixiang gongzuo*). Party cadres in the factory now do thought work to bring workers' thoughts to bear on production. There is no work without thought. The opposite also holds true.[21]

Perhaps most striking in the pamphlet is the importance of tracing characters as a form of discipline. The characters themselves are significant. Writing, in this instance, is not simply the transparent medium of Western communication, in which signs represent or mirror reality. Rather, signs are an outline of the body's actions, a display of action that both imitates and constitutes the form of its signified.[22]

Body manuals have a rich history in China. This handbook is reminiscent of earlier choreographies, especially prerevolutionary ritual manuals, in which writing was viewed as an enactment of the world

(Zito 1989). As Angela Zito has argued, writing was treated as a way to discern the pattern of interpenetration between natural and social worlds and as a way to keep reproducing that pattern. Together with painting, ritual, and architecture, it was viewed as one of the significant forms that shaped consciousness and human agency. The writing was crucial to a good ritual performance, because it was in itself a performative enactment of the world.

It is in this sense that following the correct characters with one's body is so essential to good production. Characters can be known only from the consciousness and perception of the person performing the action. There is no "rational" reason to require literacy of workers. Yet workers must skill their bodies up rather than down, for they need to train their bodies to move in strict accordance with the strokes for "bow."

This form of rationality in production does not replicate Western notions of deskilling (Harry Braverman 1974). Rationality is often invoked as a key sign of the modernist project (Harvey 1989). In our post-Foucauldian haste to chart modernity, it might be useful, then, to remind ourselves, as Max Weber (1991) argued, that rationality has no a priori content and makes sense only in a given cultural context. Scientific management does not, as they say, lend itself to the free play of signification. In specific material worlds, people invest categories with meaning based on imaginations that are shaped by historical developments.[23]

SPATIAL SUBVERSIONS

These, then, are the spatial disciplinary efforts that Party cadres and factory managers put into practice and imagined would come to fruition. They have partially succeeded. Yet these same factory spaces and the bodies and consciousnesses that are objects of control contained memories of past spatial arrangements that held a different semiotics of production. Managers were not rearranging blank spaces. The history of earlier eras — the 1950s and the recent Cultural Revolution — still resided in them. Certain workers questioned and contested the new authority of efficiency with memories of previous spatial relations through which they still moved about on the shop floor. Through these memories, they created spaces of subversion, both subtle and direct.

During the time I spent at Zhenfu Silk Weaving Factory, I was struck by three particular spatial sites in which distinct cohorts of workers marked out their identity. The most dramatic, it appeared to me, was the one entailing the reappropriation of public space. In the context of economic reform, resting rather than working formed part of a political assertion about the identity of a good worker. A group of six or seven women on the A shift of Zhenfu's Number Two Prep Shop had claimed a comfortable and visible place to take breaks, where it would be clear to all that they were not at their work positions: a small table just off the shop floor, in full view of the shift leader's desk and the front entrance to the shop. It was the only place to sit down.

This was no simple matter of taking long breaks. These women flaunted their presence by sitting and loudly complaining about the new production pressures. Occasionally Xiao Ma, the shift leader, yelled at them to return to work, but they simply responded in kind. Once, angry about having been penalized for spinning the wrong box of silk yarn, one of the women joked to the others about needing to get back to the old method of hanging signs on people, like in the Cultural Revolution, and calling them "capitalist roaders." Theirs was an overt and brazen challenge to the reform attempts to re-form them into new kinds of subjects. They postured against the authority of efficiency. This was the generation who had come of age in the Cultural Revolution.

Most of this generation no longer held onto the specific politics of the Cultural Revolution. They too had become disillusioned with its excesses and the sense, as one person put it, that "we had a carrot sitting on our heads and didn't know it."[24] Yet, they went to great lengths to retain their political rights to challenge managerial authority or, perhaps more accurate, their political rights not to have managers challenge them. They remained conscious that work experiences in the factory were political—as against efforts by the state to separate the "economics" of the factory from the "politics" of the state. Once I asked Xiao Bao, a thirty-one-year-old member of this cohort, the delicate question of whether she planned to become a Party member. Xiao Bao responded that she had no interest in joining the Party, because it was simply a method to mold her into a model worker, which in turn only meant pressuring other workers to produce more.

In newspaper articles and cartoons, in statements by factory cadres and by intellectuals, workers had become naturalized into people who tended toward laziness and who understood only the power of material incentives. They were a problem to be solved. But the Cultural Revolution generation contested this sign of laziness with which the state has tried to refigure their bodies by retaining the memory of what it had previously meant to be a good worker: to maintain a consciousness of class and therefore of the ability to move on and off the shop floor without managerial authority to position them.

Adding to their refusal of spatial disciplining was the sense among several of these women that they might have attained the status of intellectual had it not been for the Cultural Revolution's shutting down of all schools. Their insistence that they were not really workers but just stuck in the factory by the ill will of history reflected a dominant discourse fostered by the economic reform state that replaced workers with intellectuals as the heroes of China's future.[25] Through their retrospective claim to the possibility, now lost, of an intellectual identity, these women refused the spatial authority of reform that placed them in the category of mere worker by forcing them to remain on the shop floor. This Cultural Revolution cohort were thus a recalcitrant presence formed through discourses on class categories and on the absolute distinction between intellectuals and workers. They shared in the abjection of the subject position of worker, but it was precisely their desire not to be made abject that led them to recall the historical meaning of their place in the factory.

A second site in which an older generation marked out their identity appeared to me more marginal than the table, yet just as crucial. This was the dense and massive space of the spinning, twisting, and combining machines. For memories also resided in these machines and their alignment, memories that, in Raymond Williams's terms, were now residual in their counterhegemonic form (1977). These machines loomed a head taller than workers, so that prep workers disappeared among the rows of spindles. No central vantage point — no panopticon — existed from which to gaze on them. To see what they were up to, management had to walk up and down each and every row, a disciplined disciplining in which they rarely engaged. Older groups of workers, women who had begun working in the silk factories in the 1950s, gathered periodically amid the thick forest of machinery to rest and chat with one another. Their activities recalled previous practices: these older workers, as part of the so-called conservative faction of the Cultural Revolution, had taken refuge from and refused to participate in the ever more chaotic and vindictive political winds of revolution. Their identity was tied to the memory of work just after liberation, when silk work was a skill displayed with pride, a skill that women worked hard to attain. These women countered efforts to turn their bodies into ever more efficient producers by insisting on recognition for the hard work they already performed. Yu Shifu, a woman in her late forties who had entered the silk factories at the age of thirteen, once remarked that the women of her mother's generation were in much better health than the women of her own. This was despite the fact that, as she implied, her mother's generation was often portrayed as more physically constrained by feudal gender ideology (iconized through foot-binding). This oldest cohort accepted the socialist state's discourse that labor is the essence of meaningful identity. In crafting their identity through that discourse, they marked the limit of post-Mao visions of modern order through an embodied memory of previous arrangements of space.

The final site of spatial subversions resided in the very sinews of the bodies of the youngest generation, in their gestures and movements around the shop floor. These women, in their late teens and early twenties, were newly arrived from the countryside and had just begun to enter the factories in the previous year. Subject(ed) bodies, they nonetheless refused to remain spatially rooted in one place or move in the prescribed circuits. There was a steady stream of visiting one another back and forth. Their bodily movements did not mimic new standards of rationality. They did not work quickly enough. They made mistakes in the tension of the thread. They did not look carefully to the left or to the right; they did not check, link, or make clear markings. They did not use their hands, eyes, and ears to inspect for quality. For this group, quality was well below the standards of the other shifts in the prep shop. Their consciousness did not participate in production problems. They rarely concentrated. Few made a "rational" inspection of their spindles, and none followed the character for bow. After all, as management complained to me, these peasant women could barely read.

Shop managers characterized these women from the countryside as being slow and dull witted. Their comments were an ironic twist on the "nimble fingers, patience" litany that has shaped Asian women in the context of transnational industries' relocation to Asia (compare Ong 1987). That gendered technique of biopower was also employed by managers about women workers in China as part of a reform discourse essentializing women's capabilities. But these "dull-witted and clumsy" peasant women displaced the gendered disciplinary regime of space by acknowledging their differences from city women, while continuing to move freely about the shop floor.

These various cohorts' elusions of and momentary confrontations with post-Mao spatial discipline appear to resonate with Michel de Certeau's discussion of poaching on the power of social space (1984). De Certeau suggests that urban citizens poach on urban design by walking through cities in a manner not originally laid out in the architectural design. The problem with his analytical schema, however, is that de Certeau assumes a fully autonomous consciousness that stands apart from the exercise of spatial power. In contrast, these women workers are, in the moment of displacement, linked with power in the formation of their subjectivities.

ARCHITECTURAL HISTORY

Workers' abilities to challenge the reform disciplinary regime were fostered by a seeming paradox in the factory architecture. Factory spatial relations are not just the setting for disciplinary actions but are themselves part of the same mode of power and authority. Factories are sensuous embodiments of productive power (producing both goods and subject positions).

The architectural paradox begins with the relationship between the offices and the shop floor. Each workshop — prep, weaving, and inspection — is housed in a separate building, each with its own shop office. But the workshop offices are virtually hidden from the shop floor. At Zhenfu, the office is set off to the side in the prep shop, a few floors above the shop floor in the weaving shop, and in a separate building in the case of the inspection shop. The main offices of the party secretary and factory director are in homologous fashion, set in a separate building well apart from the workshops. The offices are completely walled off from the shop floor. Separation is effected through thick concrete walls. Office windows look out toward the other buildings, but no windows exist to look out into the shop. These offices were spaces in which managers separated and distanced themselves from the shop floor. The office, then, did not serve as a site from which anything even approaching a panoptic gaze could emanate. Equally significant, workers could not observe managers in their exercise of power but could only imagine their activities. In fact, it appears that this spatial relation was not so much for managers to look out at workers but to keep workers from looking in at the managers.

This structure has its roots, I believe, in two cultural schemes, one having to do with a prerevolution "metaphysics of display" and the other having to do with recent revolutionary history. When these factories were built in the early 1950s, their architectural design stood as a display of hierarchy. They still bear a striking resemblance to prerevolutionary design, specifically, to the imperial palace in Beijing, known as the Forbidden City. The Forbidden City's architectural logic was in turn echoed in the homes of the previous gentry elite, in the dynastic tombs, and in the numerous local official residences known as *yamen*.[26] In nearly identical fashion, contemporary factories, the Forbidden City (now a museum), and old gentry homes are walled off from the rest of the city, though set within its midst, by thick brick walls more than high enough to discourage any outsider's gaze.[27] Each is a mimesis of an entire universe unto itself.[28] The main factory office building, known as the *changbu*, houses the highest-level management. It sits, like the Emperor's Inner Court, in the center of the factory grounds well apart from the shop buildings where manual labor occurs. Within this two-story main office, Party cadres sit on the floor above technical managers. As a group, they sit apart from the shop supervisors and, of course, from workers. The shop buildings radiate outward from the changbu in linear fashion to the front, to the back, and to either side. Again, this layout mimics the Outer Audience halls of the Forbidden City and the successive courtyards of wealthier urban homes (Pruitt 1979).

The features of the imperial palace embodied the king's power to center the universe. The symbolism of the center was constructed as the nexus of inner/outer and upper/lower (Zito 1989). That which was most inner (*nei*) equaled that which was most upper (*shang*). The architectural design symbolically displayed and reinforced imperial power. The display of hierarchy by itself sufficed as a stratagem of power. It was meant to be enough to rein in the populace. This is the cultural schema I found still embodied in Hangzhou's silk factories. Managers, it appeared to me, still relied on a metaphysics of display through which to discipline workers. Newspaper articles urging factories on to ever more efficient production tellingly focused on the "problem" of factory mangers who always sat in their offices and never walked onto the shop floor (for example, *Baokan Wenzhai*, 19 November 1985). This, I would argue, was not simply a matter of bureaucratic bumbling and laziness, as the media would have it. It was equally a matter of changing cultural logics of power — moving from a hierarchy of display into a disciplinary regime.

The second cultural schema informing factory architecture over-determined the first. This schema lies in the more recent history of the 1949 revolution in China. This was, after all, a revolution in the name of workers and peasants. The party-state therefore set about inscribing in space their mythologizing gestures toward the proletariat. Conse-quently, factory construction of the 1950s was, in part, high socialist realism. Inspired by the Soviet example (and by Soviet aid), the state built workshops of massive concrete, with straight lines and a solid utilitarian look. They were a paean to proletarian lives.

Yet these factory spaces embodied a contradiction, for the workers did not run them. In the Maoist era (1949–76), at least, a certain discomfort existed in any brazen display of power over workers. The office–shop floor arrangement enabled managers to avoid the dis-comforting gaze of workers. Equally important, knowledge in the form of state directives, Party documents, and personal dossiers (all tellingly referred to as "inside section," or *neibu*) resides in the offices. Those who have access to the knowledge contained in these documents have power because they can interpret the state's will to control popula-tions. Managers therefore keep workers out of the offices and away from such knowledge.

It is striking, then, that during the Cultural Revolution, workers challenged hierarchical class relations by storming the offices and, besides pulling managers out of them, reading and burning their per-sonal dossiers. The old hierarchy was toppled, if only for a brief mo-ment. Yet that moment still lives on in the memories of workers who have resumed their place on the shop floor. Their daily resistances indicates that the hierarchy of display, overdetermined by socialist realism, is no longer sufficient in itself to discipline. These earlier cultural logics have not been erased but rather incorporated into the search for modernity. At Zhenfu, a new six-story weaving shop was built at the start of 1985. It was a monument to the reform calls for higher productivity. The shop towered over the *changbu*, the main office building, which stood directly opposite. But Zhenfu's party sec-retary let me know that they planned to erect a new *changbu* that would equal the height of the weaving shop. The logic of display is alive and well in China's search for the modern.

RETHINKING MODERNITY

I have argued that changing spatial relations exemplify projects of modernity. These changes are perhaps most vividly displayed in urban factories, architectural paeans of modernist aspirations. In China's silk factories, global exchanges fostered by the party-state's economic reform have sutured China into a world political economy. The silk factory site, though shaped by nationalist aspirations, is no longer bounded by them. It has become reterritorialized into a veritable transnational landscape, where Western and Chinese commodities and desires have literally become interwoven.

Yet, this spatial reordering is no simple matter of a unitary set of practices called "modernity" being reworked on a local basis. The cultural and historical specificities of spatial relations in Chinese factories manifest themselves along several dimensions. Scientific management in China does not mean turning bodies into machines but rather implies a level of self-consciousness and an approach to literacy and writing that echoes both more recent Maoist notions of consciousness and earlier ideas of writing as performance. Architectural reform means that a disciplinary regime is overlapping and incorporating a hierarchy of display. The relationship between disciplinary gazes and microtechniques of power is not one of the panopticon. History has not been erased by the search for the modern. Indeed, as Nicholas Dirks (1990) so cogently reminds us, History is one of the most important signs of the modern.[29] Whatever counts as the modern episteme — should we even want to employ such a singular term — derives from the ways in which China and other "local" places interpret modernity. There is no singular transnational standard, with its local digestions.

The Chinese state aspires and claims to enact a faithful reproduction of Western modernity — a claim echoed (until the Tiananmen Square demonstrations) in the Western press. Yet the state carries out its program in sites and through bodies that hold memories of past spatial relations. It is in the disjuncture between these specificities and transglobal borrowings that managers' interpretations and workers' subversions have their effect.[30] Thus, the connection between space, memory, and resistance must be brought to the fore in any analysis of spatial disciplining.

To maintain that the order of power in China does not exactly replicate our own is not to exoticize it. Nor is it to place China in a world of essentialized Oriental difference. To the contrary, by arguing for the specificities of Chinese workers' experiences, I hope to further the critique of the universalizing tendencies of Euro-American social theory.

How, then, does my argument about China's search for the modern require us to refine Foucault's and others' notions about space and discipline? It is not my intention here to engage in a textual exegesis of Foucault. For we need not be "text-positivist" (Rosaldo 1989a) in our approach to poststructuralist theories. I want to encourage us rather to engage in a "faithful blasphemy," to paraphrase Donna Haraway (1985), of the "Master." A serious commitment to end metanarratives requires more than its mere assertion.[31] Suffice it, then, to raise two points in brief. First, we should be cautious about assuming a bourgeois subject, with its attendant consciousness, as the site of all disciplinary regimes. Whether one argues that Foucault disregarded his own positionality in theorizing subjectivity and therefore reinscribed the West as subject, we might usefully heed Gayatri Chakravorty Spivak's reminder that contemporary relations of power, including the role of Western intellectuals within them, rest on the intersection of representations, colonialism, and the political economy of global capitalism (Spivak 1988a). The subject positions available to Chinese cadres and workers have been forged through neocolonial hegemonies as well as by a Chinese Marxist state. As such, they display historical configurations that fracture consciousness along specific fault lines.

Second, the project of Foucault, as I read him, is to excavate — and then hold in tension — the discursive productions of subjectivities and equally the ways that ordinary people embrace, appropriate, and sometimes transform these as they recast their embodiment of past practices. Indeed, this dual analytic focus is one of the challenges now facing anthropology. We need to attend to the power of dominant cultural narratives, while paying close attention to the resistances as well as reaffirmations by subjects positioned in particular relations of inequality. For us to resist a textualist reading of modernity that inadvertently privileges Western voices requires tracing how subjects absorb representations and what they do with them.[32] Or, in de Certeau's terms (1984), we must pay attention not just to the production of discourses but to their consumption as well — and to how consumption unexpectedly and in small ways subverts the dominant order. For the consumption of discourses is ultimately part of their production.

Modernity, then, is an empty set category, a site of continuous hegemonic power plays and thus shifting meanings. And the relationship between history and modernity is contested terrain. The state in China has created one version of a story about modernity as a force that will overcome China's "feudal" past — a past extended to include the Maoist era. The power of that narrative was made vivid for me when I returned to China in 1991 and discussed with friends my analysis of the relationship between space, history, and the search for the modern. Feeling sure of the need to emphasize specificity, I was reminded of the power of representations and my own positionality when they sympathetically cautioned that an argument in favor of historicity was fraught with political implications that China was still mired in feudalism. Yet, as Spivak has argued, such periodization of modes of production is itself part of the history of imperialism (1988a). On the other side of the political spectrum, my argument equally transgresses that of young Chinese radicals who condemn the entire history of "Chinese culture" as signifying "weakness" and who consequently call for an embrace of "modernity," though not on the state's terms. (The controversial serial *River Elegy* exemplifies this theme. Compare Wakeman 1989.) My claim, in my engagement with these voices, is for the need to recognize the vital role that China has always played in the creation of contemporary meanings about parity and inequality among nation-states.

NOTES

Twenty months of field research in China (1984–86) were supported by a grant from the Committee on Scholarly Communication with the People's Republic of China. The writing was supported by a University of California, Berkeley, Center for Chinese Studies Postdoctoral Fellowship. Special thanks to Anna Tsing for taking the time to think through these issues with me. I also thank Christine Gilmartin, Akhil Gupta, Gail Hershatter, Carma Hinton, Emily Honig, Jean Jackson, David Keightley, Renato Rosaldo, Orin Starn, Sylvia Yanagisako, Marilyn Young, and Angela Zito.

1   China's party-state claims that economic reform is still on, but they essentially signaled its death in their terrible parody of its effects in the June massacres of 1989. Of course, it was just these sorts of destructive effects that Nietzsche and others, including Horkheimer and Adorno, saw as part of, not counter to, the project of modernity. For an especially lucid summary, see Harvey 1989.

2   Partha Chatterjee (1990) has made a compelling argument in this vein about the universalizing tendencies in Western philosophical discussions of the concept of "civil society."

3   As will become evident below, I mean "panopticon" metaphorically. Those who have contributed to the reassertion of a spatial perspective in contemporary social theory include Pierre Bourdieu (1977); Michel de Certeau (1984); Anthony Giddens (1984); David Harvey (1989); Fredric Jameson (1984); Henrietta Moore (1986); and Edward Soja (1989).

4   I suspect that scholars are interested in this category in part because, following Foucault, it seems to bring together the specificities of our academic practices with political and artistic ones.

5   Explorations of postmodern themes implicitly and sometimes explicitly address themselves to the issue of what constitutes "modernity." See, for example, Foster 1983; Haraway 1985; Huyssens 1984; Jameson 1984; Kaplan 1988; Kroker and Cook 1986; and Nicholson 1990.

6   Those who are exploring this topic do not by any means agree on the stance one should adopt toward this project of modernity. Jürgen Habermas (1987) and Berman (1988), for example, argue that modernity still has liberating potential and that we should continue it. Michel Foucault (1979), Jean-François Lyotard (1984), and many who support a postmodern stance criticize modernity for being a project of domination through its claims to absolute truth and universal answers. Although their positions are thus radically opposed, I would argue that their differences are of degree rather than kind.

7   The paraphrase of Kant is found in Foucault 1961:27 as cited in Rabinow 1988:355.

8   Of course, China's search for the modern is not new. Some would date this process back to the sixteenth-century Ming dynasty to emphasize the importance of China's internal history (Spence 1990); others would begin in the nineteenth century, with China's response to the territorial onslaught of Western imperialism (Hsu 1990); still others emphasize the early-twentieth-century efforts at state-building (Duara 1988); and, finally, some would insist on the Revolution of 1949 as the key turning point of the state's full penetration into the government of everyday life (Yang 1988). Each of these periodizations is defensible, for, to get ahead of myself, the meaning of modernity is ideologically variable. But, with economic reform, the search for modernity acquired a new intensity in China, in large part because of the party-state's virtual abandonment of Marxist-Maoist theory and its enthusiastic embrace of things Western.

9   I do not mean to say that China is becoming a capitalist country. "Capitalism" and "socialism" are tropes of very contested meanings in contemporary China.

10 The history of "modernity" as a contested political category in Europe, especially in the context of colonialism, needs excavation. Such a history would illuminate and deconstruct the center-periphery nature of the trope. For an excellent, more recent example, see Comaroff and Comaroff 1993 on colonialism and modernity in southern Africa.

11 For a discussion of the cultural construction of productivity, see Rofel 1989.

12 Worker creativity was also stressed at different moments during the Cultural Revolution.

13 After the initial battles, many workers would come to work and then leave because lack of supplies left them with virtually nothing to do. These actions have also been reinterpreted as signifying laziness.

14 For analyses that address the issues of ideology and consciousness in Mao's writings, see Schram 1969 and Wakeman 1973.

15 Ann Anagnost (1989) has written of the homologous program to individuate peasant households in China's rural areas.

16 Here I follow Ann Anagnost's (1997) notion of the "imagined state" to emphasize the symbolically constructed character of the party-state.

17 Export of silk from China began at the turn of the century and has continued, with only a brief interruption in the two years after the Communist Revolution of 1949. Rofel 1989.

18 In his otherwise excellent discussion of bourgeois distinctions in taste, Pierre Bourdieu (1984) pays little attention to the decisive role of neocolonial hegemonies in the construction of European tastes.

19 Taylorism, derived from F. W. Taylor's *Principles of Scientific Management* (1911), attempts to increase labor productivity by breaking down each labor process into component motions and organizing fragmented work tasks according to rigorous standards of time and motion study (compare Noble 1977).

20 See Cheng 1986 and Hu 1944 for a similar sense of the concept of "face" in China.

21 Yet I would maintain that this form of disciplining is distinct from other forms found in the Maoist era (1949–76). To lump them together as China's singular project of modernity would, I think, miss the specificities of history. With the economic reform regime, for example, Party cadres have turned to "psychology" as a repository of truths to be mined for thought reform.

22 A simultaneous Western intellectual tradition of questioning the transparency of signs begins with Saussure 1986 and continues through Derrida 1974. But their point is to question the correspondence between signifier and signified. They do not theorize about how writing might bring the world into existence. Kristeva (1980) and Lacan (1985) raise this point with respect to the Symbolic but do not discuss it as performance. Compare Zito 1989 for an excellent discussion of these issues.

23 This point is cogently argued in a different vein by Kathleen Weston (1993) in her critique of performance theories of gender.

24 This quip refers to inner-Party struggles at the highest levels that increasingly became common knowledge near the end of the Cultural Revolution and led many people to feel manipulated by the very leaders, especially Mao Zedong, that they had followed.

25 See Barlow 1991 for a discussion of the place of intellectuals in the period of economic reform in China. For a history of intellectuals in the early twentieth century, see Grieder 1981.

26 Thanks to David Keightley for pointing this out to me. See Chang 1977 and Pruitt 1979.

27 Ida Pruitt writes of a Beijing gentry home: "There was, I knew, endless variety

within the pattern in those compounds guarded by the great gates and by the spirit screens inside the gates and shielding them. Credited with keeping ghosts and demons from entering the compounds and wandering through the courtyards and house, the spirit screens effectively kept out the peering eyes of those who passed on the streets" (1979:10).

28 For state-run factories, this often means a literal attempt to build a self-contained social world by including a dining hall, nursery, beauty salon, showers, and a small shop that sells sundry goods. Workers receive everything from food rations to permission to marry from their work units. See Walder 1986.

29 Dirks's argument (1990) that history has been colonized even as it has produced the nation-state is suggestive of my point about modernity.

30 Emily Honig's study of women workers in 1930s Shanghai textile mills (1986) makes a similar point about the complexity of these women's lives, situated in the intersections between foreign-influenced work structures and their own practices of, for example, Buddhist-type sisterhoods.

31 Dipesh Chakrabarty (1989) has recently engaged in just such a critical reading of Marx and the problem of applying Marxist theory to Indian working-class history.

32 One might address this critique to postmodern readings of space. Fredric Jameson's compelling description of the Bonaventura Hotel (1984), for example, lacks any positioned gaze. Yet Jameson presents his reading as the universal meaning of that architectural design.

The Song of the Nonaligned World: Transnational Identities and the Reinscription of Space in Late Capitalism

AKHIL GUPTA

The nation is so deeply implicated in the texture of everyday life and so thoroughly presupposed in academic discourses on "culture" and "society" that it becomes difficult to remember that it is only one, relatively recent, historically contingent form of organizing space in the world. National identity appears to be firmly spatialized and seemingly immutable, becoming almost a "natural" marker of cultural and social difference. In this paper I problematize nationalism by juxtaposing it with other forms of spatial commitment and identity, particularly transnational ones. In so doing, I seek to illuminate the specificity of nationalism in the postcolonial world. Beginning with the premise that the structures of feeling (Raymond Williams 1961:48–71) that produce a location called "the nation" are not identical in differently situated places, I wish to conceptualize the vastly dissimilar structural positions occupied by First and Third World nationalisms by locating them with respect to late capitalism and to the postcolonial world order.[1] Connecting such global phenomena with questions of place and identity is consonant with recent moves in anthropological theory that urge us to go beyond "the field" to see how transnationalism refracts and shapes "the local."[2]

The changing global configuration of postcoloniality and late capitalism have resulted in the repartitioning and reinscription of space. These developments have had profound implications for the imagining of national homelands and for the discursive construction of nationalism. To grasp the nature of these changes, we need to be bifocal in our analytic vision. On the one side, we need to investigate processes of place making, of how feelings of belonging to an imagined community bind identity to spatial location such that differences between communities and places are created. At the same time, we also need to situate these processes within systemic developments that reinscribe and reterritorialize space in the global political economy.

To spell out the argument, I make extensive use of two examples of nonnational collectivities: the Nonaligned Movement (NAM) and the European Union (EU) or European Community (EC). The examination of imagined communities that transgress the spatial order of nation-states offers some important insights into nationalism. In the section that follows, I offer a historical narrative of the Nonaligned Movement, after which I look at the differences between the Nonaligned Movement, the European Union, and nationalism; consider nationalism in greater depth; and draw out some of the theoretical connections between space, place, identity, and the problematic of nationalism.

"SONG OF THE NON-ALIGNED WORLD"

In 1987, a little-noticed, long-playing album was released in Belgrade. The cover has a photograph of the leaders of twenty-five nations in full national regalia at the first Nonaligned Summit held in Belgrade in 1961. Above and below the borders of the photograph is the album's title, "Song of the Non-Aligned World," repeated in Serbo-Croatian, Hindi, Arabic, Spanish, and French. The back sleeve has a more recent color photograph of smiling children from what appears to be a veritable United Nations. Inside are photographs of the meeting sites of various Nonaligned Conferences and the words of the (only) song in the album, repeated in all the languages mentioned above, whose lyrics follow:

From Brioni[3] hope has come to mankind
Hope and justice for all men as one kind
Tito, Nehru, Nasser gave us peace of mind
When they built the movement of the Non-Aligned

In making us believe in the right things
They gave us a song which the world sings
Wisdom listens, violence is blind
The only promise is that of the Non-Aligned

The creators of the Non-Aligned world
Will be hailed forever by the whole world
In the world of justice all men will be free
Everyone will live in peace and harmony.

In its form, this song resembles those other songs that we call national anthems. Yet the type of community that is being invoked here is clearly not a national one. In this essay I propose that it is only by examining such nonnational spatial configurations that the "naturalness" of the nation can be radically called into question. Therefore, the study of nationalism must necessarily refer to phenomena that transgress "the national order of things."[4] In other words, we need to pay attention to the structures of feeling that bind people to geographical units larger or smaller than nations or that crosscut national boundaries.

The Nonaligned Movement serves as a good example of such a transnational imagined community. Although an analysis that centers on late capitalism alone fails to explain the *political* impetus for a transnational organization of third world nations,[5] an analysis that centers exclusively on the political changes resulting from decolonization cannot explain why the Nonaligned Movement has been less successful than expected in forging third world unity and why the European Union, despite some dramatic drawbacks, has made impressive moves in that direction.[6] The powerful structural forces acting differently in these two cases can be grasped only by paying attention to their differential locations within a postcolonial world and to the reinscription of space in late capitalism (Jameson 1991; Harvey 1989). Spatial identities have been powerfully shaped by the accompanying processes of deterritorialization and displacement (Kaplan 1987; Martin and Mohanty 1986). Yet, as the Nonaligned Movement demonstrates, in parallel to this are equally important, although less noted, processes that are involved in the repartitioning and *re*territorialization of space. It is in this changing relationship of space and identity that the problematic of nationalism needs to be situated.

The genesis of the Nonaligned Movement is usually traced to a meeting of twenty-nine countries in the Indonesian resort city of Bandung in 1955. The conference was the first, groping expression of the idea of Afro-Asian unity, bringing together the leaders of independent states in the two continents. Many who were to become the most important government leaders on the world stage attended this meeting, including Nehru, Chou En-Lai, Nasser, and Sukarno. Although the meeting resulted in no concrete institutional changes, the presence of almost half the member states of the United Nations laid the framework for third world unity in the interstate system. The "spirit of Bandung" was to be evoked in all subsequent efforts to create a new "third bloc" in the postcolonial world.[7]

The pace of efforts to forge unity among third world countries accelerated after Bandung, particularly following a meeting between Nehru, Tito, and Nasser in Brioni, Yugoslavia, in 1956, culminating in the summit that formally launched the Nonaligned Movement in September 1961 in Belgrade. To understand the particular conjuncture that led the twenty-five participant states and the three "observers" to come together, one has to look at those eventful six years that separate Bandung from Belgrade. This period witnessed the Suez Canal crisis and the Soviet invasion of Hungary in 1956, the admission of sixteen newly independent African countries to the United Nations in 1960, the escalation of cold war tensions following the downing of an American U2 spy plane over Soviet air space in 1959, and growing U.S. military involvement in places as diverse as Cuba, Vietnam, the Congo, and Laos. For third world nation-states, especially newly independent ones, these actions only highlighted the fragility of their sovereignty. Superpower conflict and direct military intervention were grave external threats to the nationalistic goal of preserving and consolidating their independence.

The principles of nonalignment enunciated at the Belgrade summit emphasized a commitment to nuclear disarmament, a reduction of Great Power tensions, and noninvolvement in the cold war. Nonalignment was differentiated from "neutrality," which implies a passive, isolationist policy of noninvolvement in all conflicts. Indeed, it was an assertion of *agency* on the part of third world nation-states that defined what it meant to be "sovereign" and "independent." For this reason, nations whose sovereignty was sullied by their participation in multilateral or bilateral military agreements with the superpowers were barred from membership. Hence, it would be a mistake to see the Nonaligned Movement entirely in the context of political conflicts among the superpowers. From the beginning, some of its most important themes have been the opposition to colonialism, neocolonialism, imperialism, and racism.[8] Nonalignment was thus predicated on nationalism at the same time as it helped consolidate it.

A particularly controversial position maintained by the nonaligned states has been their consistent criticism of the "cultural imperialism" of the West.[9] Here U.S. control of communication systems, news and information services, and mass media–based cultural production has received particular condemnation. In calling for a New World Information and Communications Order, the nonaligned world has earned the undying hostility of the corporations that control these services in the West. Dissatisfaction with the present information order led to the innovation of a Nonaligned News Agency Pool that takes reports from various third world countries and distributes them horizontally instead of going through wire services controlled by the West (D. R. Mankekar 1978a, 1978b, 1978c, 1981). Asserting the power to control the distribution of news flows and cultural products in this way, the Nonaligned Movement is attempting to "bind" space in a new manner.

The News Agency Pool is one of a small body of formal institutions run by the Nonaligned Movement. Other organizations include a permanent executive committee that plans the summits held every three years; a United Nations caucus group; and a series of economic working groups, such as the International Centre for Public Enterprises, in Yugoslavia, the Centre for Science and Technology, in Peru, and the International Centre on Transnational Corporations, in Cuba. Nevertheless, the Nonaligned Movement, true to its self-designated status as a movement, has maintained a diffuse and decentered profile. Its strength lies as much in its *interstitial* location between the superpowers as in its ability to resist the metanarratives that they attempt to impose on it. This proves annoying even to sympathetic first world scholars: "The itinerant nature of the intra-Third World diplomatic process has been an *obstacle* to a well-informed understanding of the role of the developing countries in international politics. *The process appears to lack continuity in the absence of a central vantage point from which to view it*" (Mortimer 1984:4; emphasis added).

Conventional explanations of the formation of the Nonaligned Movement emphasize the pressure of contingent events in world politics. Although such events were undoubtedly important, they have to be contextualized with respect to the structural shifts accompanying decolonization. Among the most important of such shifts was that which occurred with the end of direct rule: the new global political economy moved to exploitation through division of labor and unequal exchange. This significantly altered the spatial and political contours of resistance by colonized groups. The postcolonial context of sovereign, independent nation-states created a space for lateral political connections between formerly colonized nations, where previously such relations had been mediated by the colonial powers. In the Non-aligned Movement, we therefore have a recognition of the political significance of the formation of independent nations in the third world and at the same time an acknowledgment of the heavily over-determined and tenuous nature of that independence. In the next section I explore this contradictory position by comparing the Non-aligned Movement both with nationalism and with the European Community.[10]

NONALIGNMENT, THE EUROPEAN UNION, AND TRANSNATIONALISM

As a form of imagined community, the Nonaligned Movement shares a great deal with nationalism. Nonetheless, it is instructive to examine the ways in which it is different. Much of the impetus for the move-ment came from the *nationalist* desire on the part of weak third world nation-states to preserve some measure of independence for them-selves. There is something paradoxical about the fact that nationalism should need *trans*nationalism to protect itself. This paradox cannot be explored by staying within the problematic of nationalism — the ideo-logical claims it makes both about historic possibilities and the practi-cal forms in which they can be realized (Chatterjee 1986:36–53). Why nations come to be such potent forms of imagining community can be understood only by contrasting them with other forms of imagined community, both supranational and subnational. Although one can debate the efficacy of the Nonaligned Movement in creating a su-pranational imagined community, far more important for the pur-poses of my argument are the challenges that such an organization poses for the analysis of nationalism. How does the Nonaligned Move-ment (as an organization that includes most nations of the world) contrast with such other forms of imagined community as nations or ethnic groups? How are these differences to be characterized? What is it that distinguishes and privileges nations as a form of imagined com-munity and that makes them so compelling to the hearts and minds of their citizens?

Like nationalism with respect to regionalism or ethnic movements, nonalignment is itself a metanarrative that incorporates the particular struggles of its member states within the "general" struggle of the third world. The "Song of the Non-Aligned World" is a variant of the national anthem, one that seeks (quite literally) to create a poetics of a new kind of transnational, third world identity. The effort to create a nonaligned identity and to give the notion of "third world" a positive valence can be interpreted, analogously to nationalism, as a move to create new, homogenizing narratives of resistance to domination by nation-states that constitute the capitalist core. But the Nonaligned Movement too has to be located within yet another overarching narrative of world community — that provided by the United Nations. The self-understanding of themselves as a "third bloc" constitutes an important unifying strategy for these nations and enables a degree of resistance to the UN's master narrative of the world as a body of equal but different nation-states. In this context, nonalignment plays a role analogous to that played by the subnational vis-à-vis nationalism. In seeking an alternative identity, it rejects as fact the homogenizing premises of the United Nations — separate but equal. At the same time, it uses those premises as an ideal to assert another kind of identity, pointing to the discrepancy between the formal recognition of equality and actual practice. We can think of the Nonaligned Movement as representing a "rainbow coalition" of dispossessed nations: united by their common exploitation by the superpowers and demanding their constitutional rights as citizens of the world of nation-states. The Nonaligned Movement's efforts at imagining collectivity are thus caught between multiple levels of spatial commitment and organization.

It is for this reason quite revealing to compare attempts at building such transnational imagined communities as the Nonaligned Movement and the European Union with the system of practices that constitute nationalism. In addition to practices oriented externally — that is, toward other states — some of the most important features that enable the nation to be realized are flags, anthems, constitutions and courts, a system of political representation, a state bureaucracy, schools, public works, a military and police force, newspapers, and television and other mass media. The Nonaligned Movement possesses some of these features, such as an anthem, a founding charter, a bureaucracy, a spokesperson who represents the movement to the "world" media, and so forth. Similarly, if one considers Europe after Maastricht, the line between a "national" and some kind of larger unit becomes even more fuzzy (Allan Williams 1994). Internal travel without visas; a European parliament; a European bureaucracy; the relaxation of trade barriers, tariffs, and taxation; the free movement of labor (Teague

1993); perhaps a common currency (Kondonassis and Malliaris 1994; Molle 1994) — these features resemble the practices of nation-states so much that it could be argued that what is being proposed is the dissolution of old national boundaries and the creation of a new, united nation of Europe (Milward et al. 1993). Yet it is unlikely that the nations that constitute Europe today will just disappear (Stone 1993). What may be happening is the creation of a hybrid form that lies somewhere between federal nation-states like India and the United States, and a singular European state-nation. This tension between a federation and a confederation, between *integration* and *interdependence*, has been implicit in the notion of "Europe" since the beginning.[11] The European Union has resulted not just in the redivision and repartitioning of space but in its reinscription — something new that shares many, but not all, the practices that constitute a nation-state (Everling 1992; Koopmans 1992).[12]

Some of the problems arising in the integration of Europe bear a striking resemblance to dilemmas of nation-building that continue to be experienced in a multiethnic, multilingual, religiously pluralistic, administratively divided federal political system such as India's. (Let me immediately add that I do not want to equate the integration of Europe with nation-building but merely to point to their similarities.) Take, for example, the schools that have been set up for the fifteen thousand children of the employees of the European Community to "create a whole new layer of identity in these kids" (Mapes 1990:A1). "Graduates emerge [from these schools] superbly educated, usually trilingual, with their *nationalism muted — and very, very European*" (A1; emphasis added). The schools strive to educate students "not as products of a motherland or fatherland but as Europeans" (A1); but administrators find that the education ministries of the twelve EU countries are not "fighting for the European view in education . . . maybe they *think European* in the finance and trade ministries, but not in education. It will be the last thing to be harmonized" (A16). History textbooks, usually published for students in one nation, pose further problems. "They tend to be blinkered histories of the great powers" (A16). Schools are one of the crucial sites where the nation comes to be imagined in the minds of generations of future citizens. It is for this reason that so much attention is given to the curricula in newly independent nation-states, especially the constructed "national" traditions embodied in history texts.

The European Community schools are creating new sets of relationships between peoples and spaces, forging a different type of identity in their students. The relationship they find between space, time, and historical memory in existing textbooks may be "blinkered," but what will be the blinkers on the new sense of community produced? Will this alternative production of Europe as "home" be one that, while not national, is still built on violence and the exclusion of others (Closa 1992; Martin and Mohanty 1986; Miles and Thränhardt 1995)? For who will now be classified as the "other" of a "European"? Will Europe become a "fortress" to be defended against immigrants?[13] What the schools are attempting to do is to redescribe cultural differences, embedded so naturally in national traditions, so that the new kinds of cultural differences they produce no longer coincide with old boundaries. The European Community schools are thus actively involved in producing the reterritorialization of space.

According to Benedict Anderson (1983:16), one of the most important mechanisms for imagining the "deep horizontal comradeship" that a citizen feels for a fellow national is the mass media. In his view, the ability to imagine the nation is closely tied to print capitalism. Newspapers enable the nation to be represented by the juxtaposition of stories from different "parts" to be assimilated under one date; similarly, the nation is differentiated from others by the presentation of "international" and "foreign" news. In this regard, transnational organizations like the Nonaligned Movement and the European Union contrast with nation-states in that they have no widely circulating newspapers or widely watched televisual programs that enable them to be represented to "their" citizens.[14] It is the failure to construct a "European audiovisual space" that leads David Morley and Kevin Robins to argue that "the European Community has so far failed to develop an adequate political culture or a basis for European citizenship. Questions of identity and citizenship have become disassociated" (1995:19). This is perhaps one of the reasons why such transnational communities have been less successfully imagined than have nations.

Although less successful overall, clear differences nevertheless exist in the degree to which distinct nonnational communities have been realized. The Nonaligned Movement and the European Community are so different as federations because of their respective locations in the postcolonial world system of late capitalism. Despite its longer history as a formal organization, the Nonaligned Movement has not managed to create the same bonds of solidarity linking peoples, locations, and spaces that the European Union has managed to do in a relatively short time span. This is in part because of the long historical project in which many European nations were, if not united, at least in cohort: colonialism. Margaret Thatcher invoked this "common experience" of European colonialism in a speech in 1989 in which she declared that "the story of how Europeans explored and colonised and — yes, without apology — civilized much of the world [is] an extraordinary tale of talent, skill and courage" (quoted in Morley and Robins 1995:50). European unity in the postcolonial world is therefore predicated on a structural position entirely different from unity among nonaligned nations.[15]

A convincing argument could also be made linking the reinscription of space in Europe and the third world with the nature of late capitalism (Mandel 1975; Harvey 1989). Perhaps the most important reason for the relative success of the European Union is that integration has been driven largely by the need to make European capital competitive on the global market. Starting with the European Coal and Steel Community, industrial and financial considerations have loomed large in the direction and pace taken by the European Union. In fact, it could be argued that the coordination of social policies and political institutions has been largely a response to the needs of a unified market rather than an independent goal in the construction of European identity (Allan Williams 1994:150–214). Ernest Mandel predicted almost twenty years ago that the growing centralization and concentration of capital was likely to lead to the reterritorialization of space as ever larger capitalist conglomerates ran up against the limits of specially protected but spatially segmented national markets (see also Harvey 1985a). He visualized several scenarios, the most likely of which foresaw the creation of three regionally based capitals, one centered in Japan, the second in the United States, and the third in a united Europe. This is not to argue that the move toward a united Europe follows in some direct fashion from the changing "requirements" of late capitalism or even that it depends on it "in the last instance" but to emphasize that transformations in the global political economy are a central component in any explanation of the reterritorialization of space.

In contrast to the European Union, the Nonaligned Movement has had a much more difficult time in forging a common identity for its member nations because building unity from the fragmenting experience of subjugation and displacement under colonialism is a difficult task in the best of circumstances. It is also because the rapid geographical expansion of the largest capitalist combines of the world system have put third world countries, which are producers of raw material and sellers of inexpensive labor power, under greater and greater competitive pressure vis-à-vis one another. Where third world countries have attempted to band together and promote regional economic cooperation to preserve their sovereignty, multilateral "development" aid has seduced them into a pattern of debt and dependence that has pried open their economies to multinational capital (see Ferguson 1990). The debt crisis that currently afflicts most of the developing world, leaving it completely vulnerable to control by the most powerful capitalist nation-states (and their proxies, the International Monetary Fund and the World Bank), reinforces the vertical links characteristic of colonialism rather than horizontal cooperation and unity in the third world. Powerful structural forces such as these work against intra–third world unity: hence, building an identity based on nonalignment is more challenging than building one based on European-ness. The contrast between the Nonaligned Movement and the European Union illustrates the different ways in which postcoloniality articulates with late capitalism in the production of transnational imagined communities.

NATIONALISM IN A TRANSNATIONAL WORLD

If we examine the nature of the "independence" won by formerly colonized peoples and places (in most cases, it would be anachronistic to call them nations), three features stand out: the modernist form taken by the nation, the formal equality enjoyed by newly independent countries in a postcolonial global discourse about the "family of nations," and the ambiguity of sovereignty in an unequal world.

What emerged from decolonization was a distinctively modernist institutional and ideological formation: the nation-state. One of the first things that new nation-states do is to write the history of the "nation" (itself an entity consolidated during or after colonial rule) stretching into the distant past (Dirks 1990). Such modernist practices have led two of the most influential theorists of nationalism, Partha Chatterjee (1986) and Benedict Anderson (1983), to emphasize the "secondary" character of twentieth-century nationalist discourse. Whereas Chatterjee sees third world nationalism as a derivative discourse that inevitably, perhaps reluctantly, participates in the "thematic" of the Enlightenment, Anderson sees it as a modular form that draws on "more than a century and a half of human experience and three earlier models of nationalism" (1983:123). It is possible to attain a somewhat different understanding of anticolonial national struggles by placing them within a more macro perspective. One could fight the colonial power to "liberate" the nation only because the nation was already recognized as something that was waiting to be born. In other words, the discursive availability of the imagined geography of the nation allowed it to exist as a potential entity and made it a form of organizing space that had political legitimacy. The significance of this fact can be judged by comparing the relative success of nationalist movements with the relative failure of international working-class movements: as generations of marxists after Marx found out, it is one thing to liberate a nation, quite another to liberate the workers of the world.

Second, just as the formal equality of citizens in the nation-state is often constitutionally enshrined (Anderson's "deep horizontal comradeship" [1983:16]), so the equality of nation-states in the world system is given concrete expression in the charter and functioning of international organizations such as the United Nations. The independence of third world countries, dependent as it is on the international order of the United Nations, thus redirects spatial identity from the nation at the same time that it produces it.

Finally, independence from colonial rule made it imperative for postcolonial third world nation-states to examine the nature and meaning of sovereignty (Onuf 1991; Shapiro 1991). They soon realized that the independence they had fought so hard to obtain could not be sustained under the pressure exerted by the superpowers to incorporate them into clientistic relationships. The only way to resist this pressure was to band together and form a common front and to use this union strategically to prevent absorption into either bloc. Sovereignty does not only depend on the protection of spatial borders: it is above all the ability of state elites to regulate flow across those borders of such items as commodities and surpluses; the passage of people in the form of labor, tourists, and so forth; and the movement of cultural products and ideas. It is significant that the agenda of successive meetings of nonaligned nations moved from an initial emphasis on the cold war and colonialism to questions of imperialism, unequal trading relationships, and the new information order. It was realized that economic dependence, indebtedness, and cultural imperialism were as great, if not greater, dangers to sovereignty as was military invasion. The Nonaligned Movement thus represented an effort on the part of economically and militarily weaker nations to use the interstate system to consolidate the nation-state.

The other way in which newly independent states attempted to protect their fragile sovereignty was by aggressively employing nationalist discourses and practices *within* the country.[16] Nationalism as a distinctively modern cultural form attempts to create a new kind of spatial and mythopoetic metanarrative, one that simultaneously homogenizes the varying narratives of community while, paradoxically, accentuating their difference (Brackette Williams 1990). Taking an implicitly omniscient perspective, "a national narrative seeks to define the nation, to construct its (typically continuous and uninterrupted) narrative past in an assertion of legitimacy and precedent for the practices of the narrative present—its own relation of the national 'story' most especially" (Layoun 1990:7). The national narrative incorporates the local as one element in the "larger" spatial and temporal story of nationalism. In the Indian case, for example, rulers of small kingdoms who fought the British to preserve their own power are now considered nationalist heroes whose efforts contributed to the demise of colonialism. It is in this way that local struggles waged for local reasons are "written into" the nationalist narrative, either as a geographically limited instance of the whole or as a moment (perhaps an originary moment) in the gradual unfolding of the master narrative. Nationalism therefore gathers into its fold the dispersed historical narratives of diverse and often unrelated communities.

On the other hand, nationalist narratives also acknowledge and sometimes celebrate difference. It needs to be emphasized that shaping union through difference is also a mode of creating subject positions for subordinated narratives. As a reinscription of narratives of community, nationalism does not so much erase existing narratives as *recast* their difference. The recognition that different ethnic groups, different locales, and different communities and religions have each their own role to play in the national project underlines their difference at the same time that it homogenizes and incorporates them. The Indian national anthem, for example, sequentially names the different regions (hence languages, cultures, religions, histories) that are all distinctive parts of the united Indian nation. Such an incorporation of difference hierarchically organizes subject positions for diverse groups of citizens. Mary Louise Pratt (1990:6) notes the fundamentally androcentric bias of nationalist longings: "Women inhabitants of nations were neither imagined as, or invited to imagine themselves as part of the horizontal brotherhood." Women are generally recognized only in their role as the producer of citizens and are thus precariously positioned as subjects of the nation.

To the extent that nationalism attempts to rewrite already existing narratives of community (mistakenly analyzed as "primordial"), resistance to it takes the form of a renewed emphasis on oppositional ethnic, subnational, or religious identities. Any emancipatory movement that tries to fashion a new, coherent identity (as nationalism attempts to do) carries with it its own repressive agenda (Radhakrishnan 1987:208). The containment that nationalist narratives seek to impose on their constituent elements — actors, actions, histories, and, most pertinent to this paper, spaces — are predictably, but with varying degrees of success, resisted by those so confined. But to the extent that it is successful in incorporating the recognition of difference, nationalism serves to negate in advance — to anticipate and thereby to diffuse, reshape, and contain — particular forms of resistance.

Whether a hegemonic master narrative of the nation succeeds in establishing itself depends a great deal on the *practices* of the state. The nation is continually represented in such state institutions as courts, schools, bureaucracies, and museums that employ the icons and symbols of the nation — flags, currency, seals, and so forth.[17] But, very important, the nation is also constituted by a state's external dealings with other states, which recognize these practices as belonging to an entity of the same kind as themselves, thereby validating the ideology of nationalism. Such "externally oriented" practices, which constitute what it is to be a nation, include things as marking borders (by erecting fences, maintaining troops to guard it, checking and stamping passports, issuing visas, levying duties, and so on [Timothy Mitchell 1989]); maintaining embassies in one another's countries; keeping or breaking off diplomatic relations; signing treaties; declaring war; recognizing regimes; gaining admission to the United Nations, participating in the Olympics, the World Cup and other international sports events, and the like. These are some of the practices through which the "nation" is represented to *other* nation-states.

A consideration of these practices makes it clear that the potential forms that states can take in the modern world are severely circumscribed. It is for this reason that movements *against* the nation-state themselves aspire to the status of autonomous nationhood. The pervasiveness of nationalism as a system of practices and as a form of

ideology cannot therefore be adequately explained simply by referring to the appeal that it has for those nationalist elites who clearly
stand to gain the most from it. Instead, to understand why the nation
comes to be such a privileged form of statehood, we need to locate the
question of nationalism *centrally* within the context of the postcolonial
interstate system. It is difficult to imagine what a state that is not a
nation would look like and how it would operate in the contemporary
world. By reflecting on the larger historical context, we can mark the
circumstances that have led to the emergence of the nation-state as a
dominant organizational form (Ruggie 1993), which also enables us
to speculate about the conditions that may lead to its demise and the
eventual development of an alternative hegemonic spatial formation.
The reinscription of space in the context of late capitalism, by de-
stabilizing the complacent equilibrium of the contemporary world
system of nation-states, may very well be tending in that direction.

One conclusion that follows directly from this is that the processes
that position people as citizens of nations *and* as members of larger,
smaller, or dispersed units of agglomeration need to be conceptualized together. Morley and Robins argue along similar lines in thinking
about identities in the European Union: "To be European now is to be
implicated in all three — continental, national, and regional — and . . .
[is] about managing some amalgam of these different scales of identity" (1995:20). Citizenship ought to be theorized as one of the multiple subject positions occupied by people as members of diversely spatialized, partially overlapping, or nonoverlapping collectivities. The
structures of feeling that constitute nationalism need to be set in
the context of other forms of imagining community, other means of
endowing significance to space in the production of location and
"home."

A powerful mechanism for imagining the national community in
most nations has traditionally been the mass media. Efforts to employ
the mass media to that end, however, are persistently undercut by the
transnational character of those media. In fact, representing the nation in an age when the public sphere is thoroughly transnational is a
major challenge facing state elites. The control exerted by multinational corporations in particular sets severe limits on both the extent
and form of nationalism practiced in different parts of the world today. The dominant social blocs of third world nations find that the
power of nationalism as a unifying metanarrative is thus inherently
compromised. In the transnational public sphere, peoples' identities

as citizens of a nation are multiply refracted by their inventive appropriation of goods, images, and ideas distributed by multinational corporations.[18] There are thus processes at work that bind space and construct communities of people in a manner that dilutes the power of the nationalist project.

Such a challenge is not only being raised by transnational cultural and commodity flows but also arises when loyalty to oppositional identities, especially subnational ones, dominates feelings of nationalism. Three kinds of examples could be given here: subnationalism, identities that crosscut the boundaries of contiguous nations, and transnationalism. Considering subnationalism first, in South Asia alone, one could point to the examples of Bengalis in the former East Pakistan (Bangladesh), Sikhs in India, and Tamils in Sri Lanka. Then there are ethnic loyalties that cut across national boundaries without, however, being transnational in the same sense as the Nonaligned Movement. Here, one could point to Kashmiris in India and Pakistan; Tamils in India and Sri Lanka; and Kurds in Turkey, Iran, Iraq, and the former Soviet Union. Finally, one could point to a few genuinely transnational identities like that forged on the lines of Islamic community. Hence any effort to understand how identity and location become tied through nationalism must examine those situations where the imagined community does *not* map out a national terrain. The displacement of identity and culture from "the nation" forces us not only to reevaluate our ideas about culture and identity but also enables us to denaturalize the nation as the hegemonic form of organizing space. To place nationalism within a transnational context therefore allows one to pose new questions about spatial identities and commitments.

STRUCTURES OF FEELING AND THE REINSCRIPTION OF SPACE

Efforts to create identities based on transnational imagined communities, epitomized by the Nonaligned Movement and the European Union, throw into sharp relief the structures of feeling that go under the name of nationalism. It becomes clear that any attempt to understand nationalism must set it in the context of other forms of imagining community, other mechanisms for positioning subjects, other bases of identity. Some of these loyalties refer to units of space larger than the nation, some smaller, and yet others to spaces that intersect nations or are dispersed. The analytic challenge is to explain why certain forms of organizing space — specific boundaries, particular places — attain the singular importance that they do in a given historical context. Why the hegemonic representation of spatial identity in the world has become that of the naturalized borders of nation-states cannot be understood by just studying the processes within a nation that enable it to be imagined. One of the ways of stepping "outside" the nation (and the problematic of nationalism) is to see how nations are created and reproduced as a consequence of the global interstate system. By doing this, we can fathom what effects specific patterns of the reinscription of space in the postcolonial, late-capitalist world have on the nation-state. Will nations as we know them today continue to be the hegemonic form of spatial organization in an increasingly postmodern world? And, if not, in what ways will the structures of feeling that characterize nationalism be transformed? It seems to me that any answer to these questions of identity, location, and nationalism must begin with the redefinition of space in the context of postcoloniality and late capitalism.

In addition to the theoretical limitations of studies that ignore these transnational factors, the burgeoning scholarship on the "national" question in recent years runs into a problem similar to that faced by those attempting to understand the state. Just as analyzing "the state" may involve the scholar in an unwitting collusion with state elites in their efforts to represent a naturalized, unified entity called "the state," so may the studies of nationalism unknowingly contribute to its privileging as *the* most important form of imagining community and shaping identity (Duara 1995).

Another direction from which the discourse of nationalism receives unexpected, if dubious, support is what may be termed "third worldism." Fredric Jameson (1986:69), for example, argues that all third world texts are necessarily *national* allegories. His reasoning is that what is particular to literary production in the third world is that it is always shaped by the experience of colonialism and imperialism. The binary opposition between a first and a third world embedded in the Three Worlds Theory leads to the overvalorization of nationalist ideology; indeed, since the third world is constituted through the singular experience of colonialism and imperialism, there is nothing else to narrate but the "national" experience (Ahmad 1987:5–8). The problem with employing a monologic ideology such as "third worldism" is that it encapsulates all narratives of identity within the master narratives of imperialism and nationalism. It thus serves to foreclose a richer understanding of location and identity that would account for the relationships of subjects to multiple collectivities.

In this essay I have argued that nationalism, as a model of imagining community, articulates with, rewrites, and often displaces other narratives of community. The production of a location called "nation" thus involves the creation of a new order of difference, a new alignment of "self" in relation to "other." Yet the positioning of subjects as citizens of nation-states is multiply refracted by their identities as members of other collectivities. It then becomes pertinent to inquire why the hegemonic representation of spatial identity in the world continues to be that of the naturalized border of nation-states. For to call the nation a hegemonic spatial form is to foreground the fact that the identity it gathers in and encloses is often contested and unstable (Hall 1986).

The unstable character of national identity becomes especially evident when one examines the makeup of contemporary third world nationalism. The unitary nature of analyses and critiques of nationalism makes it impossible for one to appreciate the depth of the differences in the construction of the nation between, say, Canada and Sri Lanka (both countries with "ethnic" minority problems). A more contextualized understanding of third world nationalism would begin by accounting for its specific location within two macrologies. On the one hand, it has to be located within the postcolonial world order, because everything from territorial boundaries to administrative and judicial systems and international alliances is tied to the political changes surrounding decolonization. On the other hand, it cannot be understood without paying attention to the global system of production and distribution within late capitalism.

But what is the relationship between these two contexts? The central objective of this essay has been to discuss attempts to forge such transnational forms of community as the Nonaligned Movement and the European Union with the aim of demonstrating the manner in which late capitalism and postcoloniality converge to produce and simultaneously to problematize the nation. Hence, I argue that the multiple spatial grids through which identity is mapped need to be conceptualized in such a way as to de-essentialize and denaturalize nationalist discourses of authenticity. Processes of migration, displacement, and deterritorialization are increasingly sundering the fixed association between identity, culture, and place. In this context, nationalist narratives are being brought under increasing critical scrutiny by those marginalized or excluded from them. It is perhaps not surprising, therefore, that there is a renewed scholarly interest in nationalism.

To understand these phenomena, we need to pay bifocalized attention to two processes. On the one hand, we need to study structures of feeling that bind space, time, and memory in the production of location. By this I mean processes by which certain spaces become enshrined as "homelands," through which ideas of "us" and "them" come to be deeply felt and mapped onto places such as nations. On the other hand, we need to pay attention to those processes that redivide, reterritorialize, and reinscribe space in the global political economy. Only then can we understand why the naturalized divisions and spaces that we have always taken for granted become problematic in certain circumstances, and only then can the "problem" of nationalism be posed adequately.

NOTES

This paper is dedicated to the memory of D. R. Mankekar. I thank Purnima Mankekar, Lisa Rofel, Roger Rouse, and C. Rajamohan for their critical comments; Arun Kumar for bringing some important material to my attention; and Yoo-Jean Chi for research assistance. Earlier versions were presented at the Faculty Seminar on Cultural Nationalism at Stanford University on 2 May 1990 and at the 113th Annual Spring Meeting of the American Ethnological Society, Charleston, South Carolina, March 1991.

1   Although I am aware that the notion "Third World" is often employed in "the West" to homogenize what are in fact quite distinctive histories and places (to construct in effect a space of "otherness") (Mohanty 1988), it has become a positive tool of solidarity in the postcolonial world system. Self-identification as Third World has served a central constructive purpose in movements such as the Nonaligned Movement. For this reason, I have chosen not to put Third World in capital letters, quotes, or italics in the rest of this essay.

2   I have been especially influenced by the work of Arjun Appadurai in this regard. See Appadurai 1986; Appadurai and Breckenridge 1988b and the journal *Public Culture*, Hannerz 1987; George Marcus 1986; and Morley and Robins 1995.

3   Brioni, Yugoslavia, was the site for the first tripartite summit between Nehru, Tito, and Nasser, which first led to speculation in the world press that a new third world bloc was in the process of formation.

4   The phrase is Liisa Malkki's (see the essay in this volume).

5   It also fails to appreciate the genuinely *popular* aspects of an admittedly largely elite-based postcolonial nationalism.

6   I want to emphasize that I see the European Union as a contested, conflictual entity in the process of formation. Roger Rouse (private communication) has suggested that a distinction be made between "transnational," "international," and "supranational" such that "transnational" refer to phenomena that crosscut or intersect national boundaries, "international" be used to denote that which occurs between and among nations, and "supranational" denote spatial configurations that stand above and incorporate nations. The Nonaligned Movement displays all three features.

7   Not all scholars of the Nonaligned Movement accept that Bandung marked the beginning. For example, Peter Willetts (1978:3) says, "In the states that attended, in the tone of the debates and in the resulting decisions, Bandung was not a forerunner of the Non-Aligned conferences."

8   The last theme was particularly prominent in the third summit at Lusaka, Zambia, in 1970, where the issue of continuing first world support of South Africa occupied center stage. The increasing importance of concerns dealing with problems of economic development and structural dependence on the superpowers is reflected in the call for a New International Economic Order (NIEO) at the fourth summit in Algiers in 1973.

9   Despite ritual invocations acknowledging the power of the ethnographer, the full implications of this fact for anthropological theory have not been realized (for an exception, see Talal Asad's essay [1986] on the inequality of languages).

10 My discussion of the Nonaligned Movement does not focus on its institutional structures and everyday operations because, for the purposes of this essay, I am less interested in how, or whether, the Nonaligned Movement "worked" than in what it symbolized and aspired to achieve. I would agree with most critics that the Nonaligned Movement was a historical "failure" in its inability to construct alternative futures for third world nations and their inhabitants.

11 Alan Milward et al. argue that the European Union is integrationist only in the plan for monetary union; on topics such as immigration, defense, and foreign policy, the goal of coordinated policies is an attempt at interdependence (1993:20–30). Another way of stating this proposition has been put forth by Etienne Balibar: "The state today in Europe is *neither national nor supranational,* and this ambiguity does not slacken but only grows deeper over time" (1991a:16).

12 It should be clear that I am not implying that Europe after Maastricht is a forerunner to developments in the rest of the world.

13 The evidence indicates that a coordination of immigration policies is leading exactly to "Fortress Europe." An excellent treatment of the relation between migration and European integration is to be found in Miles and Thränhardt 1995.

14 It must be noted, however, that one of the more successful programs of the Nonaligned Movement has been its wire service, which feeds stories horizon-

tally to other nonaligned nations. This has the advantage of creating stronger links within the third world, but it does not necessarily create a new form of identity analogous to national identity.

15   For basic overviews of the history of European integration in the postwar world, see Milward et al. 1993; Urwin 1991; Weigall and Stirk 1992; and Allan Williams 1994.

16   See, for example, Sudipta Kaviraj's (1992) important argument that nationalist leaders in India failed to propagate the idea of the nation after independence because they considered it as something already achieved rather than an object yet to be created.

17   In some cases, institutions like Britain's National Theatre serve as a medium of national representation (Kruger 1987).

18   See Appadurai 1990 for an effort to map these different transnational flows theoretically.

PART TWO

CULTURE, POWER, RESISTANCE

Exile to Compatriot: Transformations in the Social Identity of Palestinian Refugees in the West Bank

GEORGE E. BISHARAT

Studies of the mass movement of peoples, whether through labor migration or through displacements caused by war, natural disasters, or development projects, have achieved what would seem to be an unprecedented centrality in current social scientific concern.[1] On the one hand, this merely reflects in the academy the global reality of the postmodern world, in which the presumptions (never other than mythological) of the ethnic purity of nations and of the "natural" relationships between territories and culturally unitary groups seem increasingly ludicrous and insupportable (compare David Scott 1992). On the other hand, this flurry of academic interest belies the profound sense in which this postmodern global reality has challenged fundamental social scientific paradigms, particularly in the field of anthropology. What can it mean to study the "other" — the stock in trade of traditional anthropology — in such a thoroughly intermixed social world, one in which "familiar lines between 'here' and 'there', center and periphery, colony and metropole, become blurred" (Gupta and Ferguson 1992:10), often beyond recognition?

Ironically, perhaps, if this is the era of the greatest mobility of peoples and permeability of national boundaries, it is also the era of the resurgence — sometimes savage, as in the conflict in the former Yugoslavia — of ethnic nationalism. Clearly, these are not unrelated phenomena, at least in some contexts — for example, in the xenophobic riots in contemporary Germany, where socially disenfranchised ethnic "Germans" vent their frustrations against newer "non-German" or "immigrant" communities. Indeed, as David Harley (1993:12) suggests, "Place is becoming more important to the degree that the authenticity of dwelling is being undermined by political-economic processes of spatial transformation and place construction." In other words, it is precisely under conditions of challenge and threat to connections between peoples and places that identities are most vehemently, even lethally, spatialized. But if the relationship between the postwar movements of peoples and the resurgence of ethnic nationalism is patent in some cases, it may not be in others. Nor may the relationship always be identical in different places or historical moments.

In this essay I explore the relationship between displacement of a group of people—those Arab residents of Palestine who left their homes in large numbers in 1948, in the months surrounding the establishment of the State of Israel, and sought refuge in what became known as the "West Bank"—and transformations in their social identity. I will argue that the fundamental transformation undergone by West Bank refugees has been from a community defined by the lived historical experience of flight, and united in the purpose of a physical return to a Palestine geographically and tangibly conceived, to one bound by the specific experience of life in exile and committed to a "return" to a Palestine conceived abstractly—that is, as a purportedly natural society free of Israeli occupation. This transformation in social identity is manifested in, among other ways, the leadership roles that a number of West Bank refugees assumed during crucial periods of the Intifada, or "Uprising," which convulsed the Israeli-occupied territories through the late eighties and early nineties—roles that, though diminished, have not been entirely relinquished in the period following the signing of the Oslo accords by Israel and the Palestine Liberation Organization (PLO) in 1993 (Brynen 1995).

The perspective taken here is that Palestinian refugee identity, as other social identities, is a continuing "production" (Hall 1994), based on sets of oppositions between the self and an other—or, more accurate, multiple others. As a general proposition, then, social identity is the unstable, contingent reflection of a dialogic process in which a number—and at times a cacophony—of voices are raised. The information exchanged in this dialogue is constituted in, on the one hand, positive assertions of individual or group self-identity and, on the other hand, statements about or labels affixed to the identities of others. Some of the voices in the dialogue may be more compelling than others, speaking to deeper aspects of consciousness, and conjuring up more stirring symbols of inclusion and exclusion. Some may be, moreover, more authoritative than others, possessing the capacity to enforce their interpretation of identities through the attachment of either benefits or liabilities to them, thereby creating distinct experiences for groups and deepening what may have originated as inconsequential cleavages. Yet the dialogue is ongoing, and while all voices contribute and condition, not one is finally determinant; none really has the last word. The most meaningful interlocutors in the negotiation of West Bank Palestinian refugee identity, apart from the refugees themselves, have been the nonrefugee communities of that region, the international community in the particular embodiment of the United Nations Relief and Works Agency (UNRWA), and, later, both the Israeli occupation administration and the PLO.

There is a second sense in which social identity is shifting and provisional, apart from its being a production of an ongoing, incomplete dialogue and therefore variable over time. I would venture to say that statements about identity are virtually never idly made but are typically coded with implications for future action and sometimes with claims, being fielded with reference to some, not necessarily conscious, purpose. The negotiation of an identity is thus a step toward an end, not an end in itself; identity is always "identity for" something. It follows that the social identity of an individual or group "for" one thing may shift and be transformed as it is constituted "for" something else. Identity is thus contextually variable as well. Partly for this reason, Palestinian refugee identity has had profoundly ironic meanings: on the one hand, as a signifier of statelessness, the ultimate negation of nationality; and on the other hand, as the embodiment of exile, that most defining, constitutive experience of "Palestinian-ness" and the very means by which Palestinian nationalism became distinctive.

If, as I have said, identities are elaborated only in confrontations with some categorical other(s) and are simultaneously freighted with implications and claims, it is but one step further to recognize that at least one context in which identities are spatialized is on contests between groups for the control of space. The negotiation of identity is part of a more general narrative transforming blind, featureless "space" to knowable, familiar, intimate "place" (Tuan 1977, 1980), naturalizing the links between a people and their "homeland"—the possessory aspect, above all else, implying the power and right to exclude others. This is quintessentially so of Palestinian national identity, which developed in the crucible of violent contestation between Arab residents of Palestine and the Zionist movement for control of that land.

Some 360,000 to 380,000 Palestinian refugees presently live in the West Bank, nearly 100,000 in the twenty refugee camps scattered throughout the region (Jabr 1989; McDowall 1989). The camps range in size from 646 (Ein es-Sultan, near Jericho) to over 12,060 (Balata Camp, adjacent to the city of Nablus) (Jabr 1989). Together, the refugee communities constitute approximately 42 percent of the total population of the West Bank (excluding the 130,000 residents of East Jerusalem). A survey of the events leading to the establishment of the West Bank refugee communities is essential to understanding the transformations in social identity and political role mentioned above.

THE PALESTINIAN EXODUS OF 1948

As many as 770,000 Palestinians left the areas of former Palestine either allocated to Israel in the UN partition plan of 29 November 1947 or actually conquered by Israel in the ensuing fighting (most of which occurred in 1948). The areas slated in the same plan to become the Palestinian state were seized either by Jewish military forces moving from the coastal regions eastward or by Jordanian forces moving across the Jordan River to the west. The latter portions were shortly thereafter annexed by Jordan, acquiring the name "West Bank" in distinction from the "East Bank" or portions of Jordan lying to the east of the Jordan River (Hurewitz 1968). West Bank residents, including the refugees, were granted Jordanian citizenship (Mishal 1978; Amnon Cohen 1982).

The causes and circumstances of the Palestinian exodus in 1948 constitute one of the great controversies in a region that abounds in them. The official Israeli line on the matter for many years has been that Palestinians were induced to leave their homes by radio broadcasts emanating from the surrounding Arab countries, the better to facilitate Arab military operations against the nascent Jewish state. Such claims have recently been questioned by "revisionist" Israeli historians, whose perusal of newly revealed archival materials suggests instead that, although the flight of the Palestinians during the months surrounding the establishment of Israel cannot be reduced to a single cause, a large percentage of Palestinian refugees were more or less deliberately expelled by Jewish military forces, with the tacit if not explicit approval of political leaders of the Zionist movement (Benny Morris 1988, 1990; Flapan 1987; Segev 1986).[2] Be that as it may, it is clear that this cataclysmic period, referred to by Palestinians simply as

an-Nakba, or "the Catastrophe," has passed into their national historical consciousness as one of unexpected, unnatural, and forced exile.

It should be noted that the *gradual* displacement of the Palestinian
peasantry from the land and accompanying rural to urban migration
was a phenomenon that well predated the 1948 Catastrophe. The
complex socioeconomic and political causes of this phenomenon are
beyond the scope of this essay. Suffice it to say here that although some
of these causes were linked with the integration of Palestine into the
capitalist world system and thus were typical of transformations occurring in many similarly situated societies of the Third World, others
were somewhat more specific to Palestine. Of the latter, for example,
was the program of Zionist colonization of Palestine, which, by 1948,
had resulted in the purchase by Jewish individuals or agencies of between 1.7 and 2 million dunums of land (a *dunum* is equivalent to one-
quarter acre). This amounted to a relatively scant 7 percent of the total
land area of Palestine, but it may have constituted more than a quarter
of the total *cultivable* land at the time. Thus, from one angle, the
massive displacement of Palestinians in 1948 was simply the rapid
acceleration and effectuation by new means (military force as opposed
to economic pressures) of an ongoing *process* of displacement. Of
course, the pre-1948 stages of the process did not result in the physical
ejection of the peasantry from Palestine but rather their relocation
within it, mainly to urban areas — doubtless one of the reasons (but
only one) that the Nakba is seen by Palestinians as something sui
generis and not as a part of a continuous process.[3]

It has been argued that one of the key vulnerabilities of Palestinian
society leading to its fragmentation and dispersal in 1948 was the
fact that its ostensible leadership, drawn from the middle and upper
classes, had already abandoned Palestine in the months before the
announcement of the partition plan in late 1947 and the formal outbreak of war between the newly formed Israel and the Arab states in
May 1948. As Benny Morris (1991) posits the claim: "Did this flight of
the privileged weaken Palestinian society economically, politically, and
militarily? Did it undermine the staying power and self-confidence of
those left behind, especially the increasingly unemployed masses in
the towns and cities? Did it provide a model of escape for those who
were to take to their heels in April–June [of 1948]? The evidence all
points to the affirmative, and not too much imagination is required to
understand the dynamics of the situation" (100).

Indeed, there seems little doubt that up to seventy-five thousand

Palestinians of middle- and upper-class town origins had begun a relatively deliberate and orderly withdrawal (expectedly temporary, much
as had been the case when the same groups left Palestine during the
1936–39 Arab revolt) from the areas falling within the planned Jewish
state and by the time of the 1948 war, had already ensconced themselves, with their movable assets, in the towns of the West Bank and
other areas safely within Arab control (Benny Morris 1988; Tamari
1994). And that the evacuation of the middle and upper classes served
as an example for and hastened the flight of others seems convincing,
at least, in relation to the Palestinian urban poor — the majority of
whom, as we have noted, were relatively recent "economic refugees"
from rural areas.

There are reasons for caution, however, in accepting the claim of
Morris and others with respect to the Palestinian peasantry still resident in the villages. In the first place, the claim bears disquieting
similarities to conventional interpretations of the 1936–39 Arab revolt, the demise of which has been seen as the product of the peasantry's accession to leadership in the vacuum left by the departed
urban elites. This view of the revolt has been convincingly critiqued by
Ted Swedenburg, who marshals evidence of considerable resourcefulness and ingenuity on the part of the peasant rebels, arguing that their
defeat was ultimately due to the formidable military strength brought
to bear against them by the British. In fact, although the revolt gave
the Zionist movement an opportunity to build its military capabilities
(Atran 1989:736), by the end of the revolt the Arab community was
substantially disarmed. This military imbalance, accentuated during
World War II, was a critical factor leading to the disaster of 1948
(Swedenburg 1988:197).

It is not self-evident that, at least at the village level, the Palestinian
peasantry was in fact "leaderless," and such fragmentary evidence as
we have hints of much the same resourcefulness and ingenuity as was
demonstrated in the previous decade during the revolt. For example,
Elias Shoufani's description of the wartime activities in his native village, Mi'ilya, in the Galilee, chronicles the mounting of elaborately
planned and coordinated expeditions behind Israeli military lines in
search of food (Shoufani 1972). There are suggestions that the neighborhood committees that became such an effective part of the sustained uprising in the Occupied Territories that began in late 1987
may have had precedents in the period of the 1948 war (Giacaman
1989). Neither is it entirely clear that the outcome of the conflict in

1948 would have been greatly different had the middle and upper classes remained in Palestine, given the limited efficacy of the regional and national leadership they provided, the relative weakness of Palestinian national consciousness in the villages, and the aforementioned military imbalance between the Jewish and Arab communities.[4]

Virtually none of those who left their homes and land during the Nakba expected to be gone more than a few days or at most several weeks. The majority carried with them only their valuables and provisions for a few days. Needless to say, not all Palestinians fled their homes in 1948, nor did all flee to the West Bank. Those who did flee generally sought safety in the nearest territory held by Arab armies. For residents of the northern Galilee and coastal areas, this tended to mean Lebanon and Syria, whereas for those of the southern coast, it meant the Gaza Strip, which fell under Egyptian military control. Large refugee camps sprung up in each of these locales (Janet Abu-Lughod 1971). Families with kin outside Palestine often relocated in the towns and villages of their relatives, if not immediately, then in the process of regrouping that continued for months, if not years, following their initial exodus.

Most of the refugees who ended up in the West Bank — perhaps 350,000 of the total of 450,000 Palestinians who entered Jordan in the months surrounding the 1948 war (Jabr 1989; Plascov 1981) — came from the villages and towns in the central coastal plain, such as Lydda, Ramla, and Yaffa, having fled directly eastward and upward into the highlands. Families and often entire villages fled together, reassembling in part spontaneously and in part at the bidding of Jordanian troops in the West Bank, adjacent to routes of transportation and to towns, where services and markets were available. In 1950 a number of these encampments were subsequently moved by Jordan to a position at least twenty kilometers from the western borders, to prevent infiltrations into Israel and thus to avoid resultant friction between the Jordanian and Israeli governments (Plascov 1981).

UNRWA AND THE INSTITUTIONALIZATION OF REFUGEE STATUS

Emergency relief services were initially offered to the Palestinian refugees by local town councils, the International Committee of the Red Cross, and such charitable agencies as the American Friends Service Committee and UNICEF, which first reached the field with tents and other provisions and supplies in 1948–49 (Jabr 1989). By November

1948, the United Nations General Assembly created a special fund, the United Nations Relief for Palestinian Refugees (UNRPR), to be disbursed by a director, who was also charged with coordinating the relief efforts of local governments and international and voluntary agencies (Buehrig 1971). After more than a year and with the likelihood of a quick return of the refugees to their homes fading, the United Nations General Assembly further acted by granting a three-year mandate to a special agency to provide for refugee needs (Adam Roberts 1989). The mission of the United Nations Relief and Works Agency was to conduct, in coordination with local governments, "direct relief and works programmes" among the Palestinian refugees and to "prevent conditions of starvation and distress and to further conditions of peace and stability" (Angela Williams 1989:156).[5]

UNRWA began work in May 1950, distributing more tents, emergency medical supplies, and minimum food rations to the refugees. To properly apportion these benefits it registered the refugees, issuing them identity cards, for the first time creating a formal institutional category of that group. UNRWA's definition of a refugee entitled to registration was one "whose normal residence was Palestine for a minimum period of two years immediately preceding the outbreak of the conflict in 1948 and who, as a result of this conflict, has lost both his home and means of livelihood" (Buehrig 1971:39).

Just what kind of proof UNRWA required, or could have required, to establish eligibility for registration as a refugee is not evident, given the chaos surrounding the Palestinian exodus. No doubt many Palestinians left their former homes with sufficient documentation to establish residency in Palestine for the requisite two-year period; equally clearly, many others did not. It appears that, in some cases, West Bank town councils "certified" individuals as refugees by sending letters to UNRWA officials (Plascov 1981).

Nevertheless, in the first years of Palestinian exile, there was considerable contention not only as to the application of the definition to specific individuals and groups but also as to the definition itself. For example, many residents of villages bordering Israeli-held territory, though never having left their homes, were nonetheless separated from their lands by the armistice lines and thus lost their livelihoods. Twenty-five thousand such persons were eventually registered as "refugees" by UNRWA and were granted half rations (Buehrig 1971), presumably as they met only half the formal definition. A number of destitute West Bankers sought refugee status and the meager benefits attaching thereto, claiming to have come from Gaza.[6] Efforts by UNRWA to conduct a census of the refugees—seen as a prelude to the curtailment of relief aid—met with fierce opposition in the form of numerous and strident demonstrations in the camps. Some wealthier refugees demanded identity cards from UNRWA, arguing that they "should be issued to all refugees regardless of their need for relief, for they were a symbol of separatism" (Plascov 1981:49). These "better off" refugees sought an identity card not as proof of entitlement to relief benefits but as a signifier of a temporary, unique status and a tangible representation of UN commitment to effect their return to Palestine. On the other hand, it is clear that a number of middle-class Palestinians refused registration and the dole offered by UNRWA as a fundamental humiliation (see "Refugee Interviews" 1988).

Importantly, UNRWA also helped to establish refugee camps on government lands or on lands leased by host governments. Although many refugees never took up residence in the camps, many others did, which gave the refugee population at least a partial spatial segregation from the nonrefugee population of the West Bank and simultaneously gave rise to a division *between* refugee communities (namely, *camp* communities) and those settled within towns and villages—a division to which we will return below (compare Malkki 1990, 1995a). Later UNRWA built rudimentary open-air sewage systems in the camps and provided materials for the construction of semipermanent huts (UNRWA 1987).

UNRWA came to be viewed by Palestinians with a combination of appreciation and resentment. On one hand, it evolved gradually into an important provider of health, welfare, and educational services, the latter especially highly prized among Palestinian refugees (Badran 1980; Cossali and Robinson 1986). In 1989, in the West Bank alone, UNRWA was running ninety-eight primary and preparatory schools serving some forty thousand students (Arafat 1989; Schmida 1983). In the Occupied Territories, UNRWA was for many years the sole legal administrative agency existing in the camps (whereas in Lebanon, for example, the PLO assumed many administrative and social welfare functions).[7] Many of its lower- and middle-level staff eventually were Palestinians, mostly from the camps themselves, who brought a kind of missionary zeal to their work. Thus, until the establishment of the Palestinian Authority in parts of the West Bank and Gaza Strip pursuant to the 1993 Oslo accords, UNRWA was the closest thing to legitimate self-government the camps were permitted by Israeli authorities.

Suspicion among Palestinian refugees concerning UNRWA stemmed from the sense that it was the instrument through which the international community sought to depoliticize their plight and lull them into a dependent, "refugee consciousness."[8] In the words of one Palestinian, Hamdi, interviewed by Paul Cossali and Clive Robinson (1986:12): "Everyone was always waiting for things, handouts, forms, cast-off clothes, applications, and so on. The whole sense of rootlessness created a sort of paralysis. The world saw our cause as a refugee one instead of a political one."

Hostility toward UNRWA intensified whenever the agency appeared to take steps that would either encourage or accede to the permanence of Palestinian exile.[9] For example, the movement to replace tents in the camps with cinder block or asbestos huts, begun in the early fifties, was completed in all of the camps administered by UNRWA in the region only in 1959, largely because of resistance by the camp residents. Even these ostensibly permanent structures were referred to by the refugees as "shelter" (malja'), rather than "home" (bayt). Likewise, refugees flatly refused to participate in several large-scale irrigation projects designed in the fifties by UNRWA for Jordan and the Sinai Peninsula to facilitate refugee settlement and employment. In the mid-1950s, refugees in the Dayr Ammar camp destroyed a nursery established by UNRWA — symbolically resisting the implantation of "roots" in their community of exile.[10]

Interestingly, UNRWA's later eventual focus on education was apparently impelled by the demands of the refugees themselves, who craved individual advancement and distrusted only UNRWA projects aimed at the collective body of refugees as such (Ernst 1989; Schiff 1989). A more recent and equally intriguing example of the Palestinians' ability to transform UNRWA's mission occurred during the Intifada, when the agency's tasks were enlarged to encompass "general assistance" protection of refugees, not merely humanitarian aid. So, for example, newly appointed "refugee affairs officers" were deployed in the Occupied Territories to monitor demonstrations, and reduce violent encounters with Israeli troops by establishing a visible UN presence. "Legal affairs officers" were sent to observe military court trials of Palestinians and to provide legal advice to UNRWA field directors. UNRWA also began for the first time to distribute aid without regard to refugee status, primarily out of recognition that other Palestinians were, in the circumstances of the Intifada, equally in need of relief (Schiff 1989).

In general, then, the refugees have been anything but passive in dealing with UNRWA, instead vigorously articulating their concerns and pressing their demands, often with success. And as we have seen, ultimately they negotiated an effacement of the administrative distinction between themselves and the surrounding nonrefugee population.

LOCALISM AND INCORPORATION INTO WEST BANK SOCIETY

Despite the lengthening of the period of exile and all the accumulating signs of its permanence, refugees for a number of years after 1948 continued to conceptualize their status as temporary and to hope for a return to their homes and villages. If the futility of such hope is apparent in retrospect, it is important to remember that sporadic but never-ceasing diplomatic efforts for repatriation and for a general resolution of the Arab-Israeli dispute always admitted some feeble ray of optimism.

It is fair to say that in the initial years of exodus the predominant idiom for articulating this urge to return was the sentiment of "localism," a powerful undercurrent of which continues to run through Palestinian society. Palestinians voice very strong attachments to the villages and towns of their origins. Residents of particular villages and towns are often identifiable by distinct speech patterns and intonation, women by the patterns of embroidery on their dresses. In the past, people of the various towns and villages were renowned for their occupational specialties (Parmenter 1994:22). There is much lore about the purportedly "typical" characteristics of people from certain towns or villages (Khalilis, or people from Hebron, are widely believed to be somewhat brutish — stupid and gullible, but physically powerful; Nabulsis, from Nablus, are seen as clever, but ruthless in business). The oldest Arab organization in the United States — and one of the liveliest — is the Ramallah Federation, linking immigrants and their offspring from the West Bank town of that name.

These local attachments were both perpetuated and transformed in the diaspora in a number of ways. First, residents of many villages who fled simultaneously in 1948 settled in the same quarters of refugee camps, thus preserving a degree of spatial and social cohesion.[11] In the months following the war, refugees organized committees composed of former notables and *makhateer* (petty village officials; the singular is *mukhtar*) to ensure appropriate shares for their former villages in the distribution of relief, in some instances attempting to revive prewar local organizations in exile (such as the Haifa Cultural Association in Nablus and the Jaffa-Muslim Sport Club in Ramallah) (Plascov 1981). Streets, alleys, shops, and markets that sprouted in the camps were named for the villages and towns from which the residents or proprietors hailed (Said 1986; Sayigh 1979).

Refugees continued to refer to themselves as "coming from" their original home villages. This practice was accepted and somewhat formalized in the society at large. Even today, for example, nearly fifty years after the Nakba, a refugee in a West Bank court (where witnesses are required to state their names and hometowns prior to testifying) will identify himself as *fulaan ibn fulaan, Ramla, iskaan ad-Dheisheh*, "so-and-so, son of so-and-so, from Ramla [his town of origin] — *residence Dheisheh* [a refugee camp just south of Bethlehem]," and this is duly recorded by the court scribe. Many families retained the keys to their homes, prominently displaying them in their camp shelters as symbols of their determination to return.

The strong localism among Palestinian refugees was equally characteristic of the West Bank society into which they were cast. Although they shared language, religion or sect, and general culture with West Bank Palestinians,[12] the refugees for the most part were outsiders to the kin and other networks which constituted the functioning units of social and political life there and which provided the "security of an individual and his social standing" (Shoufani 1972:115). One might say they had no more place in the West Bank *socially* than they did spatially or geographically (Lutfiyya 1969).

In fact, it appears that the refugees were viewed by West Bankers with a mixture of pity and contempt — pity, of course, because the refugees were the most obvious victims in what came to be seen as the great national catastrophe. The contempt perhaps stemmed from more complex sources — the sense that the refugees were "defeated," "losers," perhaps even somehow responsible for their state of destitution, complicit in their degradation.[13] The refugees, of course, were landless in a society in which there was a close nexus between land ownership, wealth, social status, and political influence, exemplified in the folk proverb "*ardi 'irdi*" (my land is my honor). Though anomalies with respect to West Bank social structure, the category or class with which the refugees were most closely analogous was the landless peasantry, which endured the lowest status in the social hierarchy. Or, perhaps still worse, as Rosemary Sayigh suggests, the refugee was like a gypsy or bastard, or "a person of no known social origin, and therefore of no respect, the lowest level of human being" (1979:126).

Liisa Malkki has proposed that refugees are a "categorical anomaly" in the order of nations and as such represent a political and symbolic threat to that order (1990:33). This may also be true of refugees vis-à-vis the social order of the host communities in which they take refuge. Liminal social beings—those who do not fit easily into conventional social categories—especially tend to threaten social order in societies in which social norms are enforced in the first instance through mutual exchange and reciprocity between known social groups, such as West Bank Palestinian society. Liminality in such circumstances implies a lesser susceptibility to social control. Thus, as Shimon Shamir reports, camp-based refugees complained that nonrefugee Palestinians considered them "outside any binding code of traditions and customs," refused to give them loans, and were reluctant to sanction intermarriages with their children (1980:150).

There is little question, furthermore, that the massive influx of the refugee population into the West Bank was profoundly disruptive to local society in a variety of ways. Town councils, after an initial period of cooperation in relief efforts, chafed at the problems of sewerage, flooding, hygiene, water, inadequate space for burials, and the like created by the refugee presence. Many refugees squatted on the private property of local landowners. Economic friction emerged as shops opened in the camps, offering cheaper goods than did merchants in the towns and attracting even town-based patrons, and as refugees competed with poor nonrefugees for jobs (Plascov 1981).

If the refugees were resented and looked down on by the local population, it is also plainly evident that the refugees judged themselves by the same standards and criteria that the surrounding West Bank society did, suffering deep senses of shock, shame, and humiliation at their condition. The camps, in a sense, became nearly as much refuges from the surrounding society, full of reminders of the refugees' degraded status, as from the conditions of war that first gave them birth (Shamir 1980).

There was considerably less resistance to the assimilation of the middle- and upper-class Palestinians who had migrated from towns in the coastal plain to towns in the West Bank, probably because the elites enjoyed greater supralocal ties, a function of their historically greater mobility, which eased their entry into West Bank society.[14] Moreover, in their more orderly withdrawal (more akin to a "transplantation" than an "uprooting"; Malkki 1992), the well-to-do had managed to preserve more of their material assets and with them a greater quantum of their previous social status. Thus the spatial division between camp and noncamp refugee communities reiterated and perpetuated preexisting sectoral (rural-urban) and class differences in Palestinian society.

It is also apparent that sect played a role in the differential acceptance of refugees into West Bank town society. Virtually all Christian refugees in the West Bank settled in towns and villages. In some locales, such as Ramallah, coreligionists welcomed the Christian refugees and relied on their votes in municipal elections to retain control over town councils. Again, in Ramallah, it was to Christian refugees that local land was first sold and with whom the first intermarriages with the nonrefugee population occurred (Plascov 1981).

Those who fled to the towns are now seldom referred to colloquially as "refugees" (*laji' iin*), although they still might identify themselves as such, for effect in speaking to a foreigner, for example. The term *laji'*, singular for "refugee," has come to connote a social and demographic category, along with *qarawi* (villager) or *fellah* (peasant) and *hadari* or *midini* (town dweller). It means primarily a "resident of a refugee camp." It thus subsumes some who never actually experienced flight — namely, the children of the original refugees from 1948 who have remained in the camps — and excludes others — those who settled in the towns — who are true refugees in the respect that they actually participated in the exodus.

Traces of discrimination even against the town-based migrants are still evident, however. In my research on the West Bank legal profession, for example, I found that people are generally reluctant to entrust sensitive financial matters — especially those involving land — to lawyers who are not members of the putative founding clans of their villages or towns (Bisharat 1989). And while individuals of nonlocal origins have become increasingly active in elections for municipal councils and local Chambers of Commerce in the West Bank, those with "original" linkages to the community still enjoy a decided political advantage.

Camp dwellers began to find work as agricultural laborers and as both skilled and unskilled workers in the West Bank. Some were able to parlay their educations into petty bureaucratic positions or to enter the free professions, such as law and medicine (Bisharat 1989). A large number of others — typically young men — found employment further afield, in Jordan, Saudi Arabia, and the Gulf States. Their remittances were essential to the survival of their families in the camps (see Graham-Brown 1983; Benvenisti 1984; Janet Abu-Lughod 1983; and Saleh 1990). Interestingly, these families moved out of the camps at a rate considerably slower than mere economic barriers dictated. There is no doubt that for many the refusal to leave the camps was a deliberate, conscious statement of the determination not to be assimilated but to return to their ancestral villages,[15] and their UNRWA identity cards were like the "promissory note" on their right to return to their lands (Shamir 1980:152).

At the political level, West Bank Palestinian refugees in the 1950s and 1960s, like Palestinians in Lebanon, Syria, and elsewhere, pinned their hopes for salvation to the nationalist Arab governments. This was the era, it should be recalled, of the greatest effervescence of Arab nationalism, under the leadership of Nasser in Egypt and the Ba'th Party in Syria and Iraq. Palestinians largely shared in the vision of the creation of a great Arab Nation of which they would be simply one constituent element (see Mishal 1978; Amnon Cohen 1982; and Sahliyeh 1988, 1992). This did not diminish their longing for return, but again, this was articulated predominantly (not exclusively) as the longing of individuals to return to homes and less so as the longing of a people or collectivity to return to a *homeland*. Thus the lyrics of the famous song sung by the Lebanese artist Fairuz were "*khuthuni ila Beisan,*" or "take me to Beisan," a village in Palestine lost in 1948, rather than "*khuthuni ila Filasteen,*" or "take me to Palestine." Still, as Barbara McKean Parmenter convincingly argues (1994:70–77), the intense focus of diaspora Palestinians on the intimate, sensual details of their remembered landscapes reflected in their literature and elsewhere was not the same as the unstudied, spontaneous attachment to home that preceded exile. Rather it represented an early step in the construction of a more self-conscious relationship to place and an attempt to reconcretize a connection to the land that had been violently sundered. To use Yi-Fu Tuan's terms (1980), "rootedness" was giving way to a "sense of place."

THE IMPACT OF ISRAELI OCCUPATION AND THE RISE OF THE PLO

A number of developments were set into motion by Israel's resounding defeat of the Arab states in the war of 1967, which radically disrupted the pattern thus far described. Not all these developments unfolded at the same rate; some were more gradual than others, their effects becoming apparent only in the last few years. One of the relatively immediate ones was the profound discrediting of the Arab nationalist governments, which, for all their bluster, were no more successful on the battlefield than the corrupt regimes from whom they had seized power. A specifically Palestinian national movement, incarnated in the various organizations that together formed the Palestine Liberation Organization, arose out of the ashes of the June war.[16] Palestinian national consciousness crystallized around and was greatly strengthened by the emergence of the PLO. Young Palestinians in the diaspora flocked to the resistance organizations (Cobban 1984; Taraki 1990).

The PLO was based primarily in the Palestinian community in exile — first in Jordan, until King Hussein's ejection of the movement in "Black September" of 1970 — and later in Lebanon. The principal goal of the movement was defined as the liberation of Palestine and the creation there of a "democratic secular state." The very word "return," in Arabic, *'awdeh,* acquired special meaning in the parlance of the national movement. Thus journals entitled *al-'awdeh* (*The Return*) cropped up, as did poems, calligraphy, and other artwork, all playing either on the word itself or on the concept of return. So the emblem of the Popular Front for the Liberation of Palestine, one of the resistance organizations encompassed in the PLO, cleverly superimposed the first letter of the organization's name, a "*jiim*" or "j," over a map of Palestine, with the initial arc of the letter representing the unwilled ejection of the Palestinians, while the finishing stroke, a direct line with an arrow pointing back to Palestine, their purposeful, though still-to-be-realized, return. Palestine itself was intensely romanticized — and I mean this quite literally. A recurrent theme in Palestinian poetry of the diaspora, for example, was the likening of the homeland to a lost lover (Aruri and Ghareeb 1970; Elmessiri 1982; Parmenter 1994).[17]

The West Bank (along with the Sinai Peninsula, Gaza Strip, and Golan Heights), of course, fell under Israeli occupation. The 1967 war witnessed a second mass exodus of Palestinians, primarily from the West Bank to the East Bank; some 175,000 were second-time refugees, previously registered with UNRWA, whereas another 250,000 were fleeing Israeli jurisdiction for the first time (Buehrig 1971; Barakat and Dodd 1969).

One effect of Israeli occupation for the refugees who remained in the West Bank (and, in fact, for Palestinians living outside the region and bearing non-Arab passports) was renewed access to the towns and villages of their origins. Shortly after the war, Israel virtually eliminated the borders between itself and the Occupied Territories.[18] Although West Bank Palestinians were not permitted to stay in Israel overnight (let alone resettle), many refugees living in camps and further abroad were able to visit their homes and villages for the first time in nineteen years and to introduce their children born in exile to these nearly fabled locales. There is scarcely a refugee child who has not made this pilgrimage with his or her family at one point or another since the occupation (compare Kapferer 1988). Unquestionably, it is a profound experience, fraught with meaning for seemingly all who undergo it.[19]

It would seem a logical assumption that this renewed access would strengthen the refugees' will to return by breathing new life into aging memories for some and providing tangible visions in the place of previously only imagined ones for others. Ironically, the opposite may have occurred.

It is crucial to recall here the demographic profile of the West Bank. In 1987, 46 percent of the population of the region was under the age of fourteen, which reflects the Palestinians' very high birth rate (Benvenisti 1987). Considering that the occupation is now approaching its thirtieth year and notwithstanding recent and anticipated extensions of the powers of the Palestinian Authority, it is clear that a considerable majority of the Palestinian population of the West Bank and Gaza Strip now has no direct or personal memory of anything *but* occupation. It should be equally evident that the number of people who actually suffered the exodus is diminishing and that the living link they constitute to the experienced past is weakening.

The "Palestine" to which children of the refugees were introduced after 1967 was vastly different from the one which their parents had fled in 1948 and which had remained frozen in the memories of the older generation (Swedenburg 1991).[20] For one, Israel, as conscious as the Palestinians of the legitimizing effects of familiar places (Swedenburg 1991), had taken considerable pains to efface the signs of a Palestinian presence, razing approximately 385 of the 475 Palestinian villages that fell within its borders in 1948 and reforesting around many of them (Janet Abu-Lughod 1971; Benny Morris 1988). All that remained of many villages was the odd foundation stone or the telltale cactuses that ringed most Palestinian settlements to discourage human and animal intruders.[21] Whereas the parent who left in 1948 had vivid images of homes or of the well or threshing floor of their village, there was little more than trees and empty land for their children to see. Attachments formed on the latter limited exposure simply could not match the intensity of those held by the original exiles and were inescapably different and more abstract (Parmenter 1994).

I suspect, moreover, that the renewed accessibility of Palestine robbed it of a good deal of its mystique. The "land of Palestine" and the dream of a geographical, bodily return were compelling metaphors for an end to the Palestinians' woes as long as they were not juxtaposed to an unconforming experiential reality. And that reality could not sustain the weight of all the hopes and longings of the refugees for a better life. Thus, although the intense romanticization of Palestine that I mentioned typified the discourse of the Palestinians outside the Occupied Territories,[22] the same was not true within the Territories. There, understandably, the poetry, art, and political discussion increasingly focused on the travails of life under occupation (Taraki 1990).

Israeli occupation also contributed to the broadening of opportunities for wage labor for residents of the Occupied Territories. Israel experienced an economic boom from 1968 to 1973, during which up to 140,000 Palestinian workers from the Occupied Territories migrated daily to work in Israeli agriculture and industry (Graham-Brown 1983). The numbers have varied in the years since, but the trend has generally held up; in the mid-1980s, daily migrants to Israel numbered some 115,000, swelling to as many as 250,000 during harvest time (Shelley 1989; Saleh 1990). During the Intifada, however, large numbers of Palestinians who worked in Israel engaged in prolonged strikes, at least some of whom have been permanently replaced by hirings of new Jewish immigrants to Israel from the former Soviet Union. Moreover, following the Gulf War, when many Palestinians exhibited open support for Iraq, large numbers of Palestinian workers were fired from their jobs in Israel. Still more have lost employment in the period following the Oslo accords, as a consequence both of popular Israeli reactions against Palestinian bombing attacks on Israeli civilians and of official government policies aimed at weaning Israel of dependence on Palestinian labor.

Contemporary developments notwithstanding, the cumulative effect of almost three decades of access to jobs in Israel, along with the labor migration to the Gulf and elsewhere during the Jordanian period (which only continued, even increased, during the period of Israeli occupation), has been the relative economic emancipation of the landless peasantry and the refugees from dependence on the landed class in the West Bank. The result was a decline in the latter group's political influence in the region. This process was already apparent in 1976, when PLO-affiliated nationalist leaders swept to victory in municipal elections, defeating the old-guard, landowning notables linked with Jordan (Ma'oz 1984; Sahliyeh 1988). Needless to say, a relentless program of Israeli land acquisition in the West Bank further undermined the material basis of the notables' social and political power (Bisharat 1994).

Another dimension of the growth of the nationalist movement was the emergence of an alternative scale of values and status that emphasized service to national political goals. By no means insensitive to wealth, religiosity, and such traditional elements of social status, the new scale accordingly opened the door to alternative social and political leaders who possessed few of those advantages (Brynen 1995; Stein 1991).[23]

NATIONALIST CONSCIOUSNESS AND THE UPRISING

The Intifada initiated in December 1987 in the Occupied Territories represented the further fruition of these processes. One of the remarkable features of the Uprising was that its leadership was decidedly younger than any of the previous nationalist figures — and that a sizable contingent of it apparently came from the refugee camps (Peretz 1990; Rashid Khalidi 1988).[24] It is important not to exaggerate this point, however; by no means have the new members of the leadership of the Uprising totally supplanted previous social and political elites. Although the Uprising actually began in Jabalia refugee camp in Gaza, quickly spreading to other camps there and in the West Bank, after six or so weeks other segments of the population, including urban merchants and village youths, joined in and assumed equally active roles.

Eventually, the Unified National Leadership of the Uprising (UNLU) emerged and began to issue directives to the population concerning activities of resistance (strikes, demonstrations, boycotts of Israeli goods and services, and so on). Membership in this group was secret, and little was known about its composition beyond the fact that each of the four principal secular nationalist groups in the Occupied Territories — Fatah, the Palestine Communist Party (rechristened in 1991 as the Palestine People's Party; Tamari 1992:17), the Popular Front for the Liberation of Palestine, and the Democratic Front for the Liberation of Palestine — were equally represented. It is apparent, however, that as the Intifada lengthened and became more routinized, the notables and prominent nationalist personalities who traditionally dominated local politics regained some of the momentum they had lost in earlier stages of the Uprising (see Tamari 1990b; Jarbawi 1990; Sahliyeh 1988; and Yahya 1990). For example, the leaders of the Palestinian delegation to the peace talks that commenced in October 1991 were solid representatives of the pre-Intifada nationalist leadership, as are many of the appointees of the current Palestinian Authority (Brynen 1995; Amy Docker Marcus 1995).

Matters might not have progressed to this point if the prior leadership either within or outside the Occupied Territories had been more successful in realizing community goals — ultimately, bringing an end to Israeli occupation and, at least more modest, defending the land from expropriations and defending the people against the relentless pressures toward permanent emigration. In 1982 the nationalist municipal leaders had been expelled from office for refusing to cooperate with changes in the Israeli military administration, never subsequently regaining political efficacy (Ma'oz 1984). In the same year the PLO was forced out of Lebanon, then embarked in a period of infighting that extended to the followers of its factions in the Occupied Territories, with ruinous effects on the general community's morale. The stagnancy and inefficiency of the movement created a vacuum into which the new leadership of the Uprising stepped virtually without competition.

What were the factors that allowed for the participation of the formerly powerless refugees in the leadership at crucial stages of the national movement in the West Bank? I have already referred to the increase in wage labor and the resulting decline of traditional landowning political elites, as well as the emergence of a new scale of nationalist values. By this new scale, the camp residents shined, over the years offering up more to imprisonment, injury, and death in demonstrations and generally suffering consistently more severe repression by the Israeli military government than any other demographic sector in the society (a pattern that was largely continued during the Intifada; Zureik, Graff, and Ohan 1990–91). Imprisonment and torture by Israeli military personnel became the contemporary "rites of passage" for young Palestinian males (Peteet 1992; on Israeli practices of torture, see Human Rights Watch 1994). There is a palpable esprit de corps in the camps built on this reputation of sacrifice toward the national cause (Yahya 1990; see also Baumann 1988).

Most important, the sharing of the camp youth in the Intifada leadership also reflected the gradual weakening of the current of localism that ran so strongly in the generation of their parents and the strengthening instead of a transcending national Palestinian identity.[25] The emergence of the PLO was certainly a major factor in this, giving the national movement organizational expression and international recognition. So too was the intermingling of Palestinians from different backgrounds in universities, workplaces, and other institutions where they met abroad, through which the commonalities of their respective experiences were revealed (Rashid Khalidi 1987).

In the West Bank, refugees mixed with town and village residents in high schools and in the fifteen or so institutions of higher learning that were founded in the West Bank since 1967, through their jobs, and — very significant — through membership in political organizations. It is difficult to exaggerate the importance of the political groups in the lives of many West Bank youths. They eat, sleep, and breathe politics, spending most of their waking hours with political compatriots. It is these groups, which crosscut local and demographic sectoral ties, that now appear to fulfill the primary social needs for a sense of solidarity and purpose in young Palestinians' lives.[26] Political activity led to imprisonment for thousands of West Bank youths, whose membership in Palestinian organizations afforded protection, education, emotional sustenance, and a variety of other benefits.[27]

By now, of course, members of the upcoming generation of Palestinian refugee youth share a more compelling and immediate experience — that of Israeli occupation — with their contemporaries from the towns and villages than they share with the generation of their parents, who endured the Great Catastrophe. It is a minor but nonetheless telling fact that by the late 1980s, those street names in the camps, drawn from the ancestral villages, were beginning to be renamed after individuals who were killed (*istashhad,* or "martyred," in Palestinian terms) in the then current Uprising (Stork 1988). And, finally, the aforementioned Israeli expropriations of Palestinian lands in the West Bank — conservatively estimated by some to have reached 34 percent of the total land area of the region (McDowall 1989:20) — have steadily eroded the most meaningful distinction between refugees and the nonrefugee population, namely, landlessness versus ownership of land.

FROM PALESTINE AS GEOGRAPHY TO PALESTINE AS NATION

I suggested at the beginning of this essay that the transformation in the political role of the West Bank refugees manifests a transformation in their social identity, from one defined by the experience of flight and exile and united in the purpose of a physical return to Palestine, to one bound by the experience of occupation and committed to a return to "Palestine" conceived abstractly. Let me turn to the specific issue of the relationship between this identity and the ideal of "Palestine." One of the most obvious clues that the relationship has undergone change was that the avowed political goal of the secular mainstream during the Uprising was an end to Israeli occupation and the creation of a Palestinian state in the West Bank and Gaza — *not* a geographical return to all of Palestine, as the first generation of refugees had fantasized. This, of course, was in accord with the political program of the PLO, which since 1974 had increasingly explicitly expressed its acceptance of a "two-state solution" to the Israeli-Palestinian dispute (Jarbawi 1990; Rashid Khalidi 1988; Stork 1988; Sahliyeh 1988).

This does not mean that the concept of a return no longer has currency or that images of the past no longer hold any sway. The *imagined* past is still a powerful motivating image (compare Anderson 1983); historical narratives of a people's past are retrospective only in form but are future-directed in all their meaningful implications. With the passage of time, Palestinians generated a semiofficial national historiography that foregrounded an idealized rural life and venerated the Palestinian peasantry (Swedenburg 1991, 1990; Parmenter 1994). As Swedenburg (1990) points out, the Palestinian peasant was uniquely fitted as a signifier of the national movement, symbolically reestablishing and naturalizing the challenged relationship of the Palestinian people to the land of Palestine, while also eliding the differences between the largely middle-class leadership of the PLO and its following of more diverse social background.

For example, during my period of field research in the Occupied Territories (1984–85), I attended a popular play entitled "*Wadi al-*

Ward," or "Valley of the Rose," which presented a schematic history of the Palestinian experience, beginning with the precolonial period. As the title of the play hints, this period was depicted as something akin to an original state of nature, with happy peasants singing and dancing together—with never a hint of material hardship, class conflict, or Ottoman Turkish domination—which is brought to an abrupt and brutal close only by the intervention of the unnatural forces of first British and then Israeli colonialism.

Lisa Taraki (1990) refers to the "museumization" of Palestinian culture, which reached its zenith in the full-scale styrofoam re-creation of a Palestinian village on the campus of a West Bank university during its annual "Palestine Week"—this at a time when nearly 70 percent of the population continues to live in villages nearly identical to the model! Again, this hyperemphasis of the pastoral connections of Palestinians to the land is reflective not of genuine rootedness but of an intellectualized, stylized assertion of place under conditions of rupture and threat. As Tuan (1977:198) observed, "A truly rooted community may have shrines and monuments, but it is unlikely to have museums and societies for the preservation of the past."[28]

Imagery that contrasts the purportedly natural serenity of indigenous Palestinian life, allying it with the earth and elements, against the unnatural, artificial Israeli intrusion is a common theme in Palestinian cultural expression (Parmenter 1994). One famous poem addresses the Israelis as "Enemy of the Sun" (Aruri and Ghareeb 1970), while another incants:

> From you the sword—from us the blood
> from you the steel and fire—from us our flesh
> from you yet another tank—from us stones
> from you tear gas—from us rain.[29]

Poetry of the Intifada recurrently employed the image of the stones thrown at Israeli soldiers by Palestinian youths as pieces of the dismembered homeland (Atran 1990:492)—as if the very earth itself were rebelling against the Israeli presence.

Thus the colonial episode seems to be conceptualized as a kind of perversion of nature and a deviation from history. The return that is now sought is a return to history and to that imagined, purportedly natural Palestinian society free of Israeli occupation.

ISLAMISM AND THE POST-OSLO ERA

A casual observer of events in the Middle East can hardly have failed to be aware that there is a current within the West Bank and Gaza Strip that offers a different, partially competing vision for the future of Palestine linked with a similarly different conception of social identity from that described thus far. The current is embodied in the various Islamicist movements and organizations that have gained considerable strength in the Occupied Territories (particularly in the Gaza Strip) since the late seventies. Initially tolerated, even encouraged by the occupation authorities as rivals to the nationalist organizations (Rashad 1993), some of the groups achieved an uneasy but nonetheless working alliance with the nationalist forces during the Uprising (Tamari 1990a; Legrain 1990). They have since surged to the forefront of active opposition to the Oslo accords, at times resorting to highly publicized, violent attacks on both Israeli soldiers and civilians and proclaiming their goal as the complete liberation of Palestine and reestablishment there of Islamic rule. Since the waning of the Intifada in the beginning of the nineties, the political fortunes of the Muslim organizations have ebbed and flowed in approximate inverse relation to the achievements and failings of the secular national movement, now incarnated in the Palestinian Authority and commanded by Fatah and Yasser Arafat (Hajjar 1993; Tamari 1992).

Although, as the Muslim organizations themselves often point out, Islam has composed an element of Palestinian identity since the early days of the national movement,[30] it is only in recent years that it has been propounded as the primary basis of that identity — that is, as one that would supersede the previously dominant vision rooted in conventional notions of national community.[31] Indeed, it is possible that the shift in emphasis to an at least partly nonspatialized, transnational basis of unity represents a fundamental recasting of Palestinian identity. Such is certainly hinted in the words of Hamas ideologist Mahmud Zahhar (Hijazi 1995:84): "A pebble tossed in a pool leaves a series of concentric circles. I live in the Rimal Quarter. This quarter is in Gaza. Gaza is in Palestine. Palestine is in the Arab world. The Arab world is in the Islamic world. The error arises when you try to substitute a little circle for a bigger one, for instance, making the small circle of narrow nationalism a substitute for the large circle of the great community of believers." But there are reasons to be cautious of how far this transformation has yet gone. First, evidence exists to show that the preeminent ideology of the young Palestinians is still secular and nationalist and that apparent support for Muslim organizations primarily manifests discontent with concessions to Israel made by the PLO leadership in earlier peace talks (Hajjar 1993) and now in mapping out the powers of the Palestinian Authority.[32] Moreover, as Musa Budeiri (1995) maintains:

It is clear that Hamas [the Islamic Resistance Movement] has a nationalist rather than an Islamic agenda: it is virtually impossible to come to grips with a substantive Islamic program Hamas is trying to implement. Hamas was able to gain recognition as a legitimate Palestinian faction through its involvement in the Intifada. . . . It must be stressed, however, that the legitimacy the Islamists now enjoy is the result of nationalist activity, and not of a greater receptiveness among a more militant and desperate Palestinian generation to their religious message. (1)

Equally clearly, of course, and to reiterate a point made at the outset of this essay, Palestinian national identity is fluid, not static, and subject to ongoing negotiation. Indeed, Salim Tamari (1995) chronicles the bewilderingly rapid changes in the articulations and uses of such formerly fixed symbols as the Palestinian national flag and national anthem — three versions of which were employed in the first year after the signing of the Oslo accords — and sees in this a veritable "crisis of Palestinian national identity" (1995:10). There is little question that the new conjuncture of political circumstances prevailing in the region since the Oslo peace accords and the establishment of the Palestinian Authority establish new challenges, present new sets of oppositions (for example, between long-time residents of the West Bank, "insiders," and Palestinians returning to serve in the new administration, "outsiders," and between nonrefugee residents of the West Bank and Gaza, for whom Israeli withdrawal is a relatively complete remedy, and camp residents, for whom it is not), and create opportunities for new claims, on which identities may be further elaborated.[33]

Refugee status for those who fled parts of Palestine falling under Israeli control in 1948 to the West Bank and for their offspring has been, alternately, a brand of disrepute, a strategy for survival, a badge of entitlement, and a moral claim. In the first years following the Great Catastrophe, this status was legally concretized by UNRWA through its issuance of identity cards and was spatially represented through the establishment of refugee camps. Ultimately, the distinction between the refugee and nonrefugee communities in the region, which was not otherwise supported by any significant differences in ethnicity, language, religion, or culture, has been eroded by socioeconomic forces and political developments — principally, the diminishing significance of land ownership and the rise of both daily and long-distance labor migration, on the one hand, and the development of a transcendent Palestinian national identity, embodied by the PLO, on the other. The once unifying experience of collective flight from Palestine faded and was superseded by the gripping drama of life under and opposition to Israeli occupation.

Even in the post-Oslo period, refugee status has not been completely occluded as an element of social identity. When a Middle East peace treaty was only imminent in the early 1990s, raising the possibility of compensation for lost properties, some Palestinians once registered with UNRWA but who, over the years, allowed their refugee status to lapse, began to seek to regain their UNRWA identity cards (Seteney Shami, letter to the author, October 1992). It remains to be seen whether future socioeconomic and political developments, including the unfolding of further forms of Palestinian self-rule in the Occupied Territories, again recall refugee status to salience.

NOTES

I thank Jim Ferguson, Seteney Shami, Liisa Malkki, and the two anonymous reviewers for Duke University Press for their comments on various drafts of the essay.

This essay is based largely on my experiences during numerous trips to the Occupied Territories, Lebanon, and Jordan and on several extended stays in the region, including one of fourteen months in 1984–85 (during which field research was conducted on the Palestinian legal profession in the West Bank). An earlier version of the essay was printed in Seteney Shami, ed., *Population Displacement and Resettlement: Development and Conflict in the Middle East* (New York: Center for Migration Studies, 1994); I thank the publisher for permission to publish this revised version.

In a region as intensively studied as the Occupied Territories, it is remarkable how little sociological or anthropological attention has been paid to the West Bank refugees. There are, of course, exceptions, most notably Plascov 1981; Ben Porath and Marx 1971; Cheal 1988; Shamir 1980; Roy 1989; and the various articles in the *Journal of Refugee Studies* 2, no. 1 (1989) devoted to the Palestinian refugees in the Occupied Territories. The Palestinian refugees in Lebanon have been more frequently studied; see especially Sayigh 1979, 1977a, and 1977b; also Brynen 1990 and Peteet 1987. Halim Barakat and Peter Dodd (1969) have studied the exodus of Palestinians from the areas occupied by Israel in the 1967 Arab-Israeli War.

1   Witness for example, the appearance of the three English-language journals in more recent years substantially devoted to studies of population movements or transnational studies: the *Journal of Refugee Studies, Diaspora,* and *Public Culture.* Numerous journal articles, monographs, collections, and conferences have treated these same themes.

2   Not surprisingly, the controversy has not ended with the revelations of the "revisionist" school. Benny Morris, the most prominent of the new Israeli historians, has firmly rejected claims that there was a preexisting Zionist plan to depopulate Palestine of its Arab residents, holding out for a "multicausal, multistage" explanation of the exodus. For a review of his and some of his critics' arguments, see the exchanges between Norman Finkelstein (1991), Nur Masalha (1991), and Morris (1991) in the *Journal of Palestine Studies* 21, no. 1. For a more conventional Israeli critique of Morris, see Teveth 1990. Morris (1995) has gone on to show that Zionist leaders willfully altered historical records in such a manner as to conceal their hand in effecting the Palestinian exodus.

3   Readers interested in these broader issues might consult Atran 1990b; Stein 1984; Miller 1985; Ruedy 1971; and Taqqu 1980. It must be further noted not only that the 1948 war immediately created nearly thirty thousand *internal* Palestinian refugees in Israel but also that the more gradual process of the transfer of Arab land to Jewish ownership or control did not halt with the war. The medium, however, was not land purchases, as it had been before the war, or massive evictions, as had been effected during the war, but a variety of legal mechanisms amounting essentially to expropriation. See Lustick 1980; Jiryis 1973; and Bisharat 1994.

4   So resourcefulness and ingenuity at the village level were no substitute for effective regional and national leadership. Of the level of nationalist consciousness among his fellow villagers, Shoufani noted: "The *Mi'ilyan*'s world was his village — the land and the people. Matters of national, or even regional, politics were the concern of one or two people in the village. The farmers were totally indifferent to developments elsewhere, even in the Galilee itself. They did not, for instance, view an attack on Yanuh a few miles to the south as something they should worry about" (Shoufani 1972:120). Also, the deprivation of its most educated and articulate segments doubtless contributed to the observed fragmentation, demoralization, and the absence of corporate solidarity or identity among the Palestinian community that remained in what became Israel (Nakhleh 1975).

5   As UNRWA is unique as an international relief organization created specifically to address the needs of one refugee population, so are the Palestinians unique as the single group in effect excluded by the Statute of the Office of the United Nations High Commissioner for Refugees (UNHCR) and by the 1951 Convention Relating to the Status of Refugees, which together establish the funda-

mental international legal regime pertaining to refugees. Paragraph 7(c) of the statute and Article 1D of the convention, respectively, exclude persons receiving aid through some other organ of the United Nations. This exclusion reflected the judgment that the "competence of the High Commissioner in the political issues surrounding the Palestinian cause was once thought incompatible with the proclaimed non-political character of the UNHCR's work." Still, in principle, if either UNRWA assistance is terminated before resolution of the situation of those it serves or particular individuals leave the sphere of UNRWA's operations, Palestinians may then qualify for refugee status under the 1951 UN convention (Goodwin-Gill 1983:56–57). Palestinian refugees in the West Bank, however, still might not qualify by virtue of their Jordanian citizenship: Article 1E of the convention excludes a person granted by the country in which the person resides the rights and obligations attached to possession of the nationality of that country. It is not clear whether this problem is cured by Jordan's formal legal and administrative disengagement from the West Bank in 1988 and its claim to consider residents of the West Bank from that point Palestinian citizens, not Jordanians.

6   This occurred in late 1950, when there were large-scale movements of persons from Gaza across Israeli-held territories to the Hebron area (Plascov 1981).

7   The popular committees that assumed many administrative functions in and outside the camps during the Intifada were banned by Israeli authorities, as had earlier youth and student organizations affiliated with factions of the PLO and which, before the Intifada, regularly engaged in small-scale public work efforts in the camps.

8   On the creation of the category "refugee" as a systematized, "routine" technique for dealing with and containing the growing number of refugees in the postwar period, see Malkki 1995a, 1990.

9   In fact, the UN has never granted UNRWA more than a three-year mandate, instead renewing it repeatedly—primarily to avoid apparent acceptance of the permanent or even long-term nature of the Palestinian diaspora.

10   On the ubiquity of trees as analogies for the rootedness of nations in particular territories, see Malkki 1992.

11   The degree to which this cohesion was maintained varied considerably from camp to camp. Some camps, for example, concentrated residents of as many as eighty different villages (such as one adjacent to Tulkarm), whereas others were built practically for a group of previously linked villages or even for extended families (such as Azzah Camp, named for that family) (Plascov 1981:16). Barbara McKean Parmenter (1994) points out that Palestinians' self-conscious narrative of connection to the land of Palestine, or "sense of place," was partially expressed through literary evocations of the antipodes of place, particularly the deserts, cities, and refugee camps of exile. Although the deserts and cities were depicted as formless and alienating, the camps were intermediary between "place" and "antiplace," as "re-creating certain aspects of home imbues the camp with form and meaning otherwise absent in exile" (1994:67).

12   This distinguishes them from Palestinian refugees in some other Arab countries. In Lebanon and Syria, the peasants were predominantly Shiite Muslim, Druze, and Christian, and the Sunni Muslim majorities were primarily urban. Palestinian refugees who settled there, overwhelmingly Sunni peasants, faced either class or sectarian differences in the host societies — differences from fellow Sunnis in being peasants, and differences from fellow peasants in being Sunni (Sayigh 1977a).

13   The causes of the Palestinian exodus may not have been well understood in the surrounding Arab societies; many apparently believed that the refugees had sold their land, or fled out of cowardice (Sayigh 1979:108). This may, however, have been more true of some Arab countries (Lebanon) than of others (Jordan).

14   It also seems plausible to assume that villagers who fled the shortest distances in 1948 — from areas close to the armistice lines to villages just within the West Bank — would have had kinship ties and other functioning networks that would have facilitated their acceptance into the communities of refuge as "known" social beings, thus partially sparing them the debilities suffered by other refugees. Furthermore, some of those who fled in 1948 were relatively recent migrants from areas in the West Bank and elsewhere and doubtless had a considerably easier time returning to their towns and villages than did others who were total strangers. This was true, for example, of a number of refugees from Haifa, who had moved there during the Mandate years from Nablus and its environs (Plascov 1981).

15   Precisely that sentiment has been repeated by many Palestinian refugees in conversations I have had in Lebanon, Jordan, and the Occupied Territories. Nonetheless, it is important to note that by 1987, only one in five Palestinians globally resided in a refugee camp (Rashid Khalidi 1987).

16   The PLO itself was formed by the League of Arab States in 1964, but its leadership was appropriated by independently formed Palestinian guerrilla organizations in 1965. It rose to prominence as the voice of Palestinian nationalism in the post-1967 period. See Cobban 1984.

17   This kind of imagery emanated not solely from the Palestinian community in exile. For example, in 1980, Taghreed al-Butmeh, a university student from the West Bank village of Batir, was killed by an apparently deranged Israeli soldier while waiting for a bus. Her family modeled her burial procession after a traditional wedding ceremony, proclaiming her a "bride of Palestine."

18   Of course, Israel has at times restricted and even barred access for Palestinians from the Occupied Territories into Israel, imposing prolonged closures of those areas on security grounds. The lengthiest such closures occurred during the Intifada and in the post–Oslo accords period.

19   For example, see two written accounts of these visits by Noman Kanafani (1995) and Muhammad Khalidi (1995). Both writers happen to be Palestinians living in Western countries.

20   As to this "freezing" of memory, Fawaz Turki, a Palestinian author raised in a refugee camp in Lebanon, comments: "To my parents' generation the present

was insanity. Not a natural continuum of what was. The only way they could relate to it was to transform it into an arrested past, governed by Palestinian images, rites, rituals, and dreams. . . . They looked at themselves in the mirror of their past, for had they looked at the present the mirror would have cracked. . . . A whole mosaic of folklore began to emerge that captured, and froze in the mind, the portrait of Palestine as our parents' generation had left it" (1988:33).

21 As Ted Swedenburg (1990:20) points out, young Palestinians are trained to recognize the cactus as a sign of their former presence in the land of Palestine. The extent of Israel's success in obliterating traces of former Palestinian existence is manifested in the disorientation and disempowerment experienced by Palestinian visitors to their ancestral homes. Says Kanafani (1995:41): "Soon I realized that one can get lonely and lost in 'his' city. One may have to ask others how to find his house. At first I thought I would find it myself if only I passed near it. I know its architecture, the color and shape of its stones. . . . Once I admitted defeat, I declared myself the lost son of the city to the first passerby." And Muhammad Khalidi states (1995:74): "It is not so much that the Israeli presence is alien, but that it makes you feel so exposed, vulnerable, and suspect, as if you were an undercover operative in a political thriller." There are, nonetheless, triumphal tones sounded in such writings as the familiar eventually takes form through the shadows of occlusion.

22 Consider the response of the Palestinian woman in a refugee camp in Jordan questioned as to the meaning of "Palestine" in May 1994 (cited in Abdallah 1995:65): "I don't know. . . . I know it through my parents' stories, their memories. And then there is television, photographs, the news. I imagine a place where the weather is pleasant, where water to cultivate the earth is plentiful. I think that everything you need, everything you want, you can find it there."

23 This process, as Julie Peteet (1987) points out, was also observable in Palestinian communities in Lebanon.

24 One of the interesting indexes of the ascendancy of the camp youths to social and political leadership, described in Peteet 1992, is the community's resort to them to mediate disputes — the role of mediator being a venerated one in Arab society.

25 This phenomenon is paralleled among the young militant Palestinians in Lebanon, who, as Rosemary Sayigh (1979:11) documented, criticized the localism of their elders: "All their talk is about their own particular case, their land, their trees, their home, their position."

26 Membership in "hostile organizations" — any group affiliated with the PLO — is a violation of military security regulations punishable by imprisonment (see Shehadeh 1988). As a consequence, it is impossible to gauge accurately how many young Palestinian men and women actually belong to political groups. My comments about the importance of membership in the lives of the younger generation in the West Bank are accordingly impressionistic.

27 According to Israeli military sources, 83,321 Palestinians were tried in military

     courts in the five-year period 1988–93 alone (Human Rights Watch 1994); the conviction rate in these courts was approximated at 95 percent (Hicks 1992:12).

28 Such societies also flourished in the Occupied Territories. As Swedenburg (1991:168) notes: "Nationalists tend to regard tradition as something to be preserved in its pristine form rather than opened up for revolutionary uses. In such an atmosphere, it is to be expected that local institutions concentrate on salvaging the past rather than elaborating historical narratives. The feeling that Palestinian history is threatened with extinction encourages preservationist work."

29 Mahmoud Darwish, "Those Who Pass between Fleeting Words," *Jerusalem Post,* 2 April 1988; translation from the Arabic by the *Jerusalem Post.*

30 The name of the Izzedin Qassam Brigades — armed wing of the organization *Hamas* (an Arabic acronym for *harakat al-muqawima al-islamiya,* or the Islamic Resistance Movement, and also meaning "zeal") — for example, is derived from that of the famous Syrian Muslim sheikh who was killed while leading armed resistance to the British in the Arab Revolt of 1936–39 (Rashad 1993:16; Swedenburg 1991:152).

31 While many Palestinian secular nationalists have tended to view Islam itself as a significant part of the Palestinian national culture, much in the way that Arab nationalists such as Michel Aflaq and Abd al-Rahman al-Bazzaz viewed Islam as the "national religion of the Arabs" (Aflaq 1968; al-Bazzaz 1962), their perspective on an *organized* Islam in and outside the Occupied Territories has been jaundiced by the suspected alliance between Muslim organizations and political competitors of the national movement, particularly the Hashemite throne.

32 For further discussion of these issues, see Bowman 1990; Hammami 1990; Tamari 1988; Bishop 1988; and Taraki 1990. It appears that Israeli closures of the Occupied Territories, employed with rising frequency during the post-Oslo period in response to attacks in Israel mounted by the Islamicists, may actually have contributed to the Islamicists' popularity. One of the ways the Muslim organizations entrenched themselves in the Occupied Territories was through the provision of social services such as medical treatment, support to businesses, educational scholarships, and the like. These services become all the more vital when Palestinian workers are barred access to employment in Israel (Hajjar 1993:12).

33 Not surprisingly, the Oslo accords provoke similar uncertainties for the identities of Palestinian communities outside the Occupied Territories, as Laurie Brand (1995) demonstrates in the case of Jordan.

Third-Worlding at Home

KRISTIN KOPTIUCH

As a student of the history of social formations located in what has come to be known as the "third world," I was intrigued by a more recent report recounting the experiences of a score of American Christian pilgrims who only five years earlier had established home and mission deep in the jungle. According to the report, these new missionaries had reasoned that, if their efforts were to have "authenticity," they would have to share the daily hardships, gloom, and fear that permeate a blighted and primitive environment. They knew it would not be easy to gain the trust of the local inhabitants. Indeed, many of the natives suspected that the pilgrims constituted the vanguard of a new wave of colonization. Only recently, similar colonizers had occupied a nearby community from the same language group, obliging the locals to flee deeper into the shadows of a jungle increasingly encroached upon by the implacable, moving frontier of civilization. But the pilgrims felt prepared for their task. One had been raised in Indonesia and thus was already acquainted with the "peace and joy" that comes from "living on little," whereas others had spent several months getting ready in Latin America, which often exhibited less extreme manifestations of "third world" life than they later encountered in the mission territory. Interestingly, the report tells us little about the natives themselves, and the only positive reference comes in a pilgrim's exuberant reaction to a local wedding ceremony. They "really know how to celebrate life," he declares. "They know how to celebrate a moment." The collective "they"; ritual otherness; present tense.

Where can we find this imperial frontier? A French traveler described it as "the only remaining primitive society" (Baudrillard 1988a:7). It is located in the world's fifth largest Spanish-speaking nation; but it is also an important African country, and its Asian and Caribbean diasporas are increasingly significant as well. As you undoubtedly have guessed, it is here in the United States. The particular frontier described in the report is a dilapidated, drug-infested, trash-strewn, graffiti-riddled, Puerto Rican barrio in the *urban* jungle of North Philadelphia. And the determined missionaries are nondenominational, charismatic Christian yuppies: young, white, highly educated professionals, among them lawyers, physicians, an occupational therapist, a nurse, and a theology student (Carvajal 1989). Most work in lucrative occupations outside the barrio where they purchased or rent homes — but of course *they* are not the dreaded white colonials, even though the fifteen-minute "commute between class and culture" led one Center City Philadelphia lawyer to imagine himself "hurtling through the skies on a plane to Managua!" The pilgrims try to ward off suspicions that they represent the Anglo vanguard of gentrification by not renovating the facades of their common row houses with "historically correct colors," brass lamps, or other emblems of affluence. And they ward off their own fears of the urban jungle's perils with alarm systems and by avoiding solitary nighttime strolls.

Oxymoronically then, Philadelphia, the nation's oldest colonial city, city of the Liberty Bell and the signing of the U.S. Constitution, has become the site of a largely uncolonized imperial frontier situated at a transnational intersection of language, labor, and everyday life. But it is by no means unique. Instead, it simply manifests a process of "third-worlding" that, in the last fifteen to twenty years, has become apparent throughout the United States. In this essay, I shall begin an exploration of the paradoxical cultural politics entailed in this process by focusing on the Philadelphia case. My tone is deliberately polemical, the better to jar many conventional anthropological apperceptions that, unless reframed in today's transnational scene, risk complicity with the ethnologics of a revamped imperialism.

The colonial project of the nineteenth century implemented what Gayatrii Chakravorty Spivak has described as the " 'worlding' of what is now called the 'Third World' " (1985b:243), producing at once the contours of the modern world economic order and its epistemological ethic, a systematic construction of otherness that Edward Said, in reference to one region of the globe, has called orientalism (1978). But since the early 1970s, the modern imperial field has been fractured and deterritorialized by the upheavals of a new transnationalized division of labor and global restructuring of regimes of capital accumulation. Among the effects of these shifts has been a spatial and symbolic reterritorialization resulting in the "third-worlding" of the West.[1] I have purposely chosen "third world" as concept-metaphor to gloss this new practice of othering here in the United States not to collapse what are distinctly different historical formations but as a reminder that "third world" is a *name*, a representation, not a place (compare Spivak 1985a:149). It specifically names the effects of a process of exploitative incorporation and hegemonic domination — and its fierce contestation by subjugated peoples — that used to take place at a safe, reassuring distance. But the third world can no longer be geographically mapped off as a space separate from a seignorial first world. Across the latter we can trace the path of a postmodern imperial frontier marked by inscriptions of a virtually unreconstructed colonial discourse etched with a repetition of the nineteenth-century colonial episteme.

This process is marked by numerous material signs that make it difficult to distinguish the third world from the first. The unfathomable U.S. federal indebtedness of $4.9 trillion in 1995 (the first trillion was reached only in 1981), the unfavorable balance of trade, substantial investment and ownership of business and real estate by foreigners, a declining middle class, and increased economic and social exploitation all conspire to make the nation look increasingly comparable with third world countries that receive its foreign "assistance." This "development of underdevelopment" most visibly afflicts the nation's major urban centers. One begins to wonder whether the only recourse for Philadelphia, the only U.S. city in 1991 with a junk bond rating on Wall Street and teetering on the brink of bankruptcy, is to bite the bullet, acknowledge itself to be a third world city, and apply for foreign aid from the federal government.

The shift toward desperation is also apparent in the growing disparities between the dominant white population and the "minority" populations of the inner cities, and in the growing similarities between the latter and people in countries conventionally associated with the "third world." As of 1990, trends in health and education make this readily apparent. The United States ranks a low twenty-second among industrial countries in terms of infant mortality rates, and statistics show a widening gap between whites (8.6 deaths per 1000 live births)

and blacks (17.9), the latter approaching third world levels. In Philadelphia, whose minority population includes about half its citizenry
(some 40 percent black, 10 percent Latino), the overall rate is 16.9.
The general mortality rate in Harlem, where 96 percent of the population is black and 41 percent is poor, is more than double the rate for
white Americans, and as a study by doctors at Harlem Hospital revealed, the chances of living to age sixty-five are markedly worse for
African American men in the area than they are for men living in
Bangladesh (40 percent versus 55 percent, compared with 70 percent
for white Americans) (Maykuth 1990). In education, the failure rate
on final exams of students in New York City high schools with pre-
dominately African American enrollment is comparable to that of
black high school seniors in South Africa (Sam Roberts 1990).

Yet such statistical measures are not the only indications of a growing process of third-worlding at home. Forms of power/knowledge
generally associated with the colonial and postcolonial exploitation of
a distant third world are also becoming increasingly apparent in the
treatment of U.S. minorities. Alongside the influx of pilgrims and
missionaries already described, these include the use of disciplinary
techniques that meet violent forms of challenge with a combination of
direct state repression and spatial transformation, the mass marketing
of goods (including those no longer considered safe for elite use),
forms of representation that constitute people as proper objects of
control, and well-meaning but myopic forms of scholarship whose
users are ultimately complicit in the onerous processes they seek to
render more humane. I shall illustrate each of these procedures in
turn as played out in the more recent history of Philadelphia, beginning with the interplay of repression and spatial reconfiguration.

In 1964 a violent struggle wracked a North Philly African American
community reeling from the first flush of deindustrialization and the
initial throes of what has by now become a wholesale extinction of
labor-market options for young blacks (compare Mike Davis 1988):
the Philadelphia riot on "Jump Street," the once-lively business district along Columbia Avenue. The area has yet to recover from the
devastation that seemed like a cancer to engulf, ghettoize, and significantly depopulate it, but this lack of improvement has not been the
result of self-inflicted wounds. Instead, it owes much to bankers' red-
lining, realty disinvestment, middle-class black exodus, and federal
cutbacks that Republican administrations have used since 1980 to
starve the cities and thus undermine the traditional power base of the

Democrats. Interestingly, a *Philadelphia Inquirer* article commemorating the silver anniversary of the riots noted with approval that the stores that had once flourished along the nine blocks of "Jump Street" were nearly equal in number to the shops located in the more recently new Gallery Mall (Ferrick and Carvajal 1989). This mall was built to complement the 1980s' corporate renaissance of Center City Philadelphia. Safely enclosed within glass-encased, postmodern ramparts, the mall ironically simulates — by a double displacement via the suburbs — exactly the sort of commercial urban space that in the ghetto had been redlined into oblivion.

The era succeeding the 1964 riots witnessed both an emergent national movement for the extension of civil rights and, in Philadelphia's urban jungle, an intensification of repression under the direction of police chief/mayor/party turncoat (turned Republican) Frank Rizzo. In the late 1970s and early 1980s, the gentrification of Center City Philadelphia required a strenuous struggle for political stability. The struggle was continually fraught with racist politics intensified by the local repercussions of global Fordism, which displaced across a global field the city's industrial employment base or compressed labor requirements under the weight of new technologies (as happened, for example, to the dockworkers). Urban experience in the space of the city itself has been recomposed in accordance with shifts in the transnational economy and culture (Harvey 1989), and contours of the post-Fordist regime of accumulation (Lipietz 1987) have been monumentalized by phallic corporate images etched into a newly emergent skyline of glamorous, glassy skyscrapers, whose postmodern pinnacles mimic those of high-modernist architecture or pastiche pastoral rural dwellings (a barn, a "village"). These buildings now dwarf the early-modern architecture representing monopoly capital's stately mastery through its earlier mimicry of the Parisian Champs Elysées (City Hall, the Free Library, Ben Franklin Parkway) and classicist Athenian glory of the Philadelphia Museum of Art. Meanwhile, a de-skilled, insecure urban labor force awash in a low-wage service economy struggles in the shadows of the corporate skyline and its accompanying moat of corporate parks nestled in the affluent suburbs that surround the city. The homeless are left to navigate the interstices of this new social spacialization, nagging reminders of the displacements it entails.

In 1985, another explosive event marked the end of this period, bringing notoriety to the erstwhile City of Brotherly Love and incendiary destruction to an entire neighborhood in West Philadelphia. A fiercely resistant community of black radical utopians was besieged in its fortified row house by counterinsurgency Special Weapons and Tactics (SWAT) teams and literally bombed by helicopter into a firestorm of oblivion. This was, of course, the infamous MOVE "incident," which killed eleven MOVE members, five of them children (Margot Harry 1987). No Star Wars umbrella of protection could have preempted *this* attack on U.S. territory. Little matter that the orders for the well-planned operation were given by a post-Rizzo city administration led by an African American mayor, W. Wilson Goode, who has since been regarded by many as a turncoat of another color. At the time, a special commission absolved police and city officials of any wrongdoing. It produced no criminal indictments, nor did a local federal grand jury investigation in 1988. Before the five-year statute of limitations ran out in May 1990, a last, unsuccessful attempt was made to reopen social wounds and investigate the case as a violation of civil rights of MOVE members, who reportedly turned back to perish in the flaming house rather than risk the bullets that SWAT teams are alleged to have showered on them to block their escape. The officialized narrative both assuages the shock of America dropping a bomb on itself and serves as a warning to those who would challenge its postmodern civilizing mission that the state's repressive apparatuses are ready and waiting in the wings.[2]

Subtler protocols thereby receive credibility. In 1987, Columbia Avenue, site of the 1964 riots, was rechristened after Cecil B. Moore, then leader of the National Association for the Advancement of Colored People. But while the political nuance of the new appellation symbolically invests with African American ethnicity the planned urban renewal of the North Philadelphia ghetto, the riot's scars indelibly mark the deep fissures rent in the social and architectural body of the neighborhood, as if in cumulative, collective refusal to forget an important moment of popular struggle. The scars resist recoding or erasure, even as the entrepreneurial acumen of new-immigrant Asians attempt to reinscribe them with the luckier characters of a libidinal, underground economy now flourishing in the interstices of the crisis-ridden economy of late capitalist America. But the new minimum-wage sweatshops valorize female, new-immigrant labor, and in the proliferating service economy, African American and Latino males also lose out to more "docile" immigrants, legal and undocumented, and to that newly created caste of poverty-level wageworkers — women. Mike Davis, writing about Los Angeles, points out that it was precisely these transformations that "incubated the counter-economy of youth crime and drug dealing" (1988:49). The prejudicial repercussions of this new urban plague on black youth registers strongly in the name of the rap group Public Enemy (1988). They are, indeed, "Too Black. Too Strong."

This violent tale of state repression and popular resistance, a tale familiar to other major U.S. cities, increasingly evokes apt comparisons with America's imperial outposts: Vietnam, Lebanon, South Africa, Central America. But this mixture of violence and spatial reconfiguration is not the only form of discipline associated with capitalist involvement in the third world. Mass marketing is also exercising an increasingly powerful influence. On Philadelphia's new imperial frontier, billboards boldly cajole viewers to consume brand-name alcohol and nicotine via sexually suggestive ads that target the ghetto's and barrio's "minority" population. The ads deploy fantasies of sexual power and self-possession to construct as consumers those most locked out not only as consumers but as producers as well. Just as the illegal status of the bulk of Philadelphia's thousands of billboards (Ferrick 1989) is belied by their commercial slickness, so the drugs they deal are sanctified by their circulation as value within federally approved commodity circuits, a legitimation unavailable (formally, at least) to the corner dealers of crack cocaine.

This process attracted unusual attention in 1990 when R. J. Reynolds announced its plan to produce a new menthol cigarette called "Uptown," clearly aimed at poor blacks, and to test-market the product in Philadelphia's African American neighborhoods. The military metaphors used to describe the ad "campaign," with its "deployment" of race as a "strategic" marketing "attack" on black lungs, are as apt as the ghetto's spatial geographics and idealized social inversion that are mapped into the brand name: North Philadelphia is as "uptown" as Harlem, and its inhabitants, just as downtrodden. The campaign also doubles at home another imperial trope familiar to third world nations abroad—that of transnational corporate "dumping" of those drugs, chemicals, technology, and waste eschewed by the West and, in this case, the whites.

Faced with heated opposition from a local coalition of community, clergy, and public health groups and an outraged African American secretary of health, R. J. Reynolds attempted to appeal to the broader public by engaging the debate on a slippery semiotic field, conjoining in a sliding chain the celebrated signifiers of free speech, civil rights, and protection of its cigarette sales pitch to American blacks, who after all, the corporate parent argued, needed no paternalistic protection from public-interest groups. This argument may have been too transparently self-serving, and for once, the company backed down. But the process as a whole continues. Previously excluded from dominant consumer commodity circuits, the black or Latino subaltern body is increasingly recast as a culturally relativized Other targeted for colonization by new transnational commercial empires.

As if in response, graffiti answers back with its ephemeral but insistent repetition of the signature tags of those most cut off from consumption. Efforts to defuse and transfigure what many perceive as graffiti's desecration and violence have proved far from effective. In Philadelphia as elsewhere, it quickly became fashionable to venerate graffiti as gallery art or even as a city-sponsored antigraffiti that attempts to discipline its youthful perpetrators for their improperly placed critique of urban desolation. But employing young graffiti writers to depict reassuring faux cityscapes or trompe l'oeil images that epitomize civic taste cannot recuperate graffiti's definitive rage and implicit threat to the bourgeois value systems that undergird each of these reformist efforts: the uniqueness of the artistic artifact, the privilege of propertied, privatized consumption (compare Susan Stewart 1987). More accurate, I think, Jean Franco reads New York City graffiti as cultural inscriptions of resistance etched in the "war zone" along a new frontier where ghetto meets gentrification (1985).

Linked to strategies of marketing, spatial and labor reconfiguration, and periodic violence are other more hegemonic practices of representation. The newspaper report with which we started serves as apt example. Clearly inscribed in a colonial discourse now rehabbed for home use, its narrative bears the markings of the early-nineteenth-century travelers' accounts of colonial Africa analyzed by Mary Louise Pratt: depopulation of the landscape, homogenized collective "they," timeless present tense, effacement of the speaking self of the reporter. Just as such early explorer-writers as John Barrow produced "Africa" for the European imagination (Mary Louise Pratt 1985) or, later, just as Fredrick Jackson Turner's westward "moving frontier" thesis secured the imagined origins of the American nation about to be deluged by turn-of-the-century immigrants (1962), today's explorer-reporters mediate for us an increasingly vivid image of a little-explored interior frontier demarcating the borders of a new third world here at home.[3]

Through accretion, this image becomes more descriptively concrete with each daily paper or TV news report, for media representations engage in the sort of indigenous self-documentation (and documentary othering) that confounds traditional notions of ethnographics (compare Dorst 1989). The image, too, becomes more allegorically forceful with each new film that narrativizes imperialist nostalgia (such as Sydney Pollack's *Out of Africa* of 1985)[4] or indulges in Asian-bashing (for example, *Best of the Best* [Bob Radler, 1989], *Black Rain* — Ridley Scott's 1989 version, not Shohei Imamura's, also 1989), each new education proclamation (William Bennett's "intellectual heritage" plan), each new immigration regulation, each new "official language" debate, each ready acceptance of those simulated racial assaults purportedly carried out by blacks (for instance, Charles Stuart's murder of his pregnant wife in Boston, which he blamed on a fictitious black assailant, and Camden's law-and-order prosecutor Sam Asbell's faked chase and shoot-out with black would-be assassins), each ready denial of those actual racial assaults perpetrated by whites (consider Bensonhurst, Howard Beach), and each new rescission of laws that once secured labor and civil rights (for example, legalization of home work, restrictions on affirmative action and abortion).

Registered in the discourses of hegemonic purveyors of culture, politics, and policy is a palpable anxiety about the micrological effects of shifts in the international scene as the third world is structurally reconstituted within the first. The cover story of a 1990 *Time* magazine ambiguously announced "America's Changing Colors" and asked, "What will the US be like when whites are no longer the majority?" (9 April). The title cut of Public Enemy's 1990 album names the anxiety more bluntly: *Fear of a Black Planet*. Similarly, inside the reporter's *de*scription of the North Philly barrio with its "graffiti freshly painted across porch steps, the jarring noise of powerful stereo boosters blasting through the street, smashed car windows, trash and syringes scattered in the park and street corner sales pitches for drugs" (Carvajal 1989), we can read the *in*scription of panic provoked by the defamiliarizing effects of what seems to many to be an increasingly alien nation. This well-known litany makes up in popular imagery what Ruth Glass, in reference to the similarly repetitive, alarmist idioms used by international planning prophets, labels "clichés of urban doom" (1989). These are the current icons of urban illness, part of a widely replicated system of representations, images, and concept-metaphors that *precede* the empirical data world they purport to describe. Articles in Philadelphia's newspapers abound with such affirmations of these stereotypes, offered as explanation, when it is precisely these representations that must be explained and analyzed. And even the richest current urban ethnography is held back by anthropology's own litany of concept-metaphors, such as the lingering concept of the culture of poverty, now reincarnated as the "urban underclass" (Di Leonardo 1990).

With such vivid images readily at hand, the iconography of ghetto or barrio (a modified iconography applies to Asia-towns) recodes as primitive cultural difference what might be read from another perspective as an antagonistic disarray and destruction that flagrantly taunts a slipping but still prevalent middle-class value system, giving the lie to an ideology of equal opportunity that covers over widening disparities along class, race, and gender lines.[5] Even as a persistent humanist ethic ensures that these culturally different Others will be subject to the laws of a restructured imperialism, the iconography of otherness is evidence of subtly revised normalizing strategies that mobilize social and cultural difference the better to constitute new identities and subjectivities proper to this neoterritory. Thus in complex and contradictory fashion, perhaps what is most proper (from the point of view of power) about these subaltern subjectivities is their impropriety: naming as Other makes *figurable* otherwise unavailable resistant energies that henceforth become potentially liable to domestication, displacement, reeducation, incarceration. Clearly, for those of us committed to a counterhegemonic cultural politics, caution is warranted here against contributing to the consolidation of such structured otherness, a contradictory pitfall into which even well-intentioned studies of cultural resistance might tumble.

In characteristic colonial fashion, then, the North Philly missionaries followed on the heels of urban militias, merchants of the economic underground, and explorer-reporters in a new internal imperializing effort to regain control of a territory previously consigned to wildness. As in the early modern moment, anthropologists and folklorists are right behind them. Only now we need no longer voyage to distant, exotic field sites, because "the field" has come to us. In the case of Philadelphia, two projects evince this process in a particularly interesting way.

Staffed by anthropologists from Temple University, which is itself located in the heart of the ghetto's war zone, a Ford Foundation project has been set up in North Philly to research the "changing relations" between "newcomer" immigrants and more established U.S.

residents. From the few materials publicly available earlier on, the project's sanguine cultural relativism seemed an anachronistic anthropology in the postmodern era, safely encoded in the well-tempered anthro-speak of adaptiveness and social interactionism, valiantly confronting conundrums such as whether the " 'real' problems are differences in language or culture" (Schneider and Goode 1989; *Temple Times* 1988).[6]

The project's focus on schools and businesses is instructive. For hegemonic authority, these institutions constitute two important sites for the recomposition of power relations and changes in the form of crisis management within the state, as well as new sites of resistance to social reproduction, with wholesale abandonment of schooling by early dropouts and flight into an underground economy in the absence of secure employment (compare Katz 1990). Situated at these sites, new deployments of class, race, and gender as strategies of subject formation *and* subaltern struggle supplement, on the one hand, the less subtle and more conventional repressive state apparatuses and, on the other, the more easily controllable organizations of labor and party politics. Despite unprecedentedly large numbers of inmates overcrowding the U.S. prison system (more than doubling in the 1980s) and as of 1989 the incarceration (either jailed or paroled) of an astounding 25 percent of young black men and despite enormous investment in police forces, these repressive apparatuses are no longer sufficient to discipline the deteriorating urban immune system — the metaphor now appropriately shifts to AIDS rather than cancer, conforming well with the current proliferation of self-disciplinary measures into the body (politic).

The Philadelphia Folklore Project, equally well endowed with funds, also has adopted an approach to culture based more on the model of "ways of life" than on "ways of struggle" (compare Hall 1981), thus replicating folklore's nineteenth-century function of allegorizing national unity. The project highlights the distinctive contribution of different folk cultures that are "still" vital to the integrated fabric of city life, fetishizing "authentic" folk cultural practices of Philly's old and new ethnic communities, even as the folklorists act as their advocates, and shying away from the folk's often conflictual relations with the dominant society. To my mind, this is a failed opportunity to consider whether the figure of "ethnicity" is being deployed now to reinterpellate postmodern subjects as subaltern within a transnational frame, to enable communities to enact their own distinctive resistance to mass-mediated cultural assimilation in the United States, or to encourage new immigrants in this post-VCR world to sustain up-to-the-minute transnational links with the cultural struggles under way *in their homelands,* where "tradition" may be inflected with a very different political force (I am thinking of Korean Americans here, who can rent last week's news broadcasts by Korean networks in many Korean-run corner stores).[7]

I hasten to add that the overall thrust of these two projects reaches beyond the best intentions of the individual researchers involved (as several who have resigned from the projects discovered). I also recognize that even critical cultural studies often seems to evaporate beneath the spectral light of what Susan Stewart aptly describes as the capacity of the postmodern commodity system for the "re-inscription of negation as novelty" (1987:161). But this constitutive disciplinary discrepancy between intention and the handmaiden effect that historically aligned anthropology with the hegemonic side of the imperial divide also seems compulsively to repeat the earlier colonial episteme. In this case, the deepest damage caused by pluralist, relativist liberalism lies in its covering over of historical *discontinuity* by arguing that we've *always* been a society of immigrants; there have *always* been sweatshops, racism, homelessness, battered women, intrafamily abuse, gang warfare, youth suicide, and so on. It may well be that many of these social practices never disappeared altogether; but the point is, their significance has been refunctioned in concordance with the changing globe. Supplying a national, linear, and continuous history pseudo-archaizes the irreducibly *new* relationship that such cultural and economic practices now hold to the structures and discourses of domination and exploitation. The "truth" of these practices no longer coincides with the space of the nation within which they occur (if, indeed, this was ever the case). Anthropologists who do not take into account the transnational reinscription of these discursive and neo-imperial "fields" may find themselves unwitting parties to a postcolonial discourse whose effect is to validate with social-scientistic authority an imaginary historical authenticity that makes invisible the ruptures that produced contemporary conditions of postmodernity.

In sum, the third-worlding of America proceeds apace under crisis conditions of late capitalism, disgorging racial, ethnic, and new-immigrant enclaves as the contradictory legacy of empire strikes back (compare Center for Contemporary Cultural Studies 1982). A little-explored interior frontier has been constituted right at the West's core, abutting the diasporas of these exotic others-come-home and the internal communities constructed as Other (by class, race, or gender), whose constituents have long struggled for inclusive parity in the hallowed pronominal phrase "*we* the people." As if straight out of some sci-fi plot, the distant wild frontiers dramatized in early travel accounts have, to our unprepared astonishment, imploded right back in our midst! The globally expanding universe of modernity seems finally to have exceeded its outer limits and begun to burst inward, its internal fissures readied as formerly unimagined battlefields of colonization and resistance.

The vast novelty of these imploding "fields" lies not in their (re)appearance. Indeed, their economic configuration does not look novel at all but seems only to simulate the most primitive forms of capital accumulation that earlier had been banished from the modern industrial landscape of advanced capitalist nations by hard-won, protective labor legislation. The new industrial sweatshops, the putting-out system, and child labor practices of the not-always-so-underground economy stage one *local* form of the *global* reterritorialization of the relations between labor and capital. And cultural forms along the interior frontier often evoke what seems an almost stereotypically familiar sort of distanced primitivism, whose savage panic is heightened by its incorporation of post-VCR accoutrements. Yet we cannot justifiably invest these cultural and economic forms and practices with nostalgia — unless that be the postmodern equivalent of an origin myth for a copy without an original (the simulacrum).[8] For their history is incontrovertibly discontinuous, displaced from modernist narratives, determined Other-wise. The agency of those Others makes indeterminate the outcome of America's third-worlding.

My project here has been to begin to narrate some of these events occurring along the new interior frontiers of Philadelphia's third world at home. I've borrowed from critical inquiries into an old genre (travel literature) to crash through new imperial idioms readily accessible in popular and public culture, idioms that would seem to defy or eclipse any representation of radical difference. But on many fronts, oppositional cultural practices have already ruptured the modern imaginary by infusing it with what Cornel West vividly calls "the ragged edges of the real": "of not being able to eat, not to have shelter, not to have health care" (1989:93). Then, too, there remains the utopian but distinct possibility that the aftereffects of the third-worlding of the West may ultimately prove constructive for the emergence of a truly multicultural, equitable, noninterventionist (trans)nation. Much remains to be done to examine and cultivate those diverse resistant strategies that might transform the panic simulation of primitivism and subvert the dominant efforts to reinterpellate national subjects in a transnational frame via new deployments of gender, race, and ethnicity.[9]

It is especially important to intervene with a critical anthropological voice in this present context. At risk is the appropriation of anthropology's earlier, unfortunate contributions to a colonial discourse, an appropriation that insidiously brings home those orientalist logics to fuel the recomposition of technologies of power and domination. Our intervention must include delegitimating those earlier models and representations and challenging the culture area concept-metaphors they depend on so as to forge more effectively a link with the subaltern voices that have initiated the current debates on gender, race, and politics.

NOTES

Versions of this essay were presented in 1989 at both the American Anthropological Association Annual Meetings, Washington, D.C., and the Marxism Now Conference, Amherst, Mass. For their helpful comments on an earlier draft, I thank Julie Graham, Cindi Katz, Smadar Lavie, Fred Pfeil, Roger Rouse, Eric Santner, Ted Swedenburg, and Kara Tableman. Thanks also to my students at Temple University, who indulged my formulating in classes many of these ideas about third-worlding and who wrote insightful papers based on their own fieldwork in the "third world at home." Frances Negron and I produced an audio accompaniment to this discussion of Philadelphia's third-worlding (Koptiuch and Negron 1991).

1   In this analysis I have adapted the notions of deterritorialization and reterritorialization devised by Gilles Deleuze and Felix Guattari in their "schizoanalysis" of both libidinal and political economies (1983). The same basic notions are theorized differently as global Fordism by the French regulationists (Lipietz 1987) or more optimistically as flexible specialization (Piore and Sabel 1984). But see the lucid and cautionary critique of these formulations by Julie Graham (1991).

2   In rougher cities, like Los Angeles, where the third-worlding process is even more accelerated, the police qua occupying army have exercised far less restraint. See Mike Davis 1988.

3   Although it's tempting to do so, in my opinion conceptualizing this frontier in terms of the Wild West metaphor remains enclosed within the ideology of the nation-state and uses as analytic category precisely the figure that covers over the nation's rupture by irrepressible global transformations come home to roost. Compare Neil Smith's (1992) otherwise wonderfully insightful piece on

struggles over gentrification in New York City, in which he reads the Lower East Side as Wild West.

4   Compare Renato Rosaldo (1989b) on "imperialist nostalgia."

5   Mike Davis (1989) explicitly places in polarized counterpoint the middle-class, mostly white, homeowner-based "slow growth" associations in and around Los Angeles and the urban street gangs of black "homeboys," each epitomizing equally dystopian responses to the international corporate restructuring of the *Blade Runner* city's spatial economy. See also Kate Braverman's essay "Nostalgia for the Empire" (1989), in which she narrates the urban heart of darkness in postapocalyptic Los Angeles as experienced by the story's main character. The protagonist's figuration as a low-income, white female single parent is prototype for yet another third-worlded group in the United States.

6   The results of the Ford Foundation research project are available in Goode and Schneider 1994.

7   Thanks to Hong-Joon Kim for pointing this out from his research on the Korean American community in Philadelphia.

8   Compare Jean Baudrillard 1983b. In a different vein, Kathleen Stewart (1988) shows how even nostalgia can be inflected by counterhegemonic resistance in her discussion of Appalachians, whose recuperative memory-narratives mark a refusal to forget—even while parodying their own discourse—the familiar world that had deserted them.

9   For example, Ted Swedenburg (1989) shows how rap music's selling of social insubordination engages precisely this terrain of struggle.

The Demonic Place of the "Not There":

Trademark Rumors in the Postindustrial Imaginary

ROSEMARY J. COOMBE

In the habitus of death and the daemonic, reverberates a form of memory that survives the sign. . . . And then suddenly from the space of the not-there, *emerges the re-membered historical agency "manifestly directed towards the memory of truth which lies in the order of symbols" . . . the temporality of repetition that constitutes those signs by which marginalized or insurgent subjects create a collective agency.*

—Homi Bhabha, *The Location of Culture*

From Upton Sinclair's grisly description in The Jungle *of how workers who fell in vats of fat emerged as Durham's Pure Leaf Lard to the recent belief that McDonald's uses worms in its burgers, one of the most prevalent folk ideas in 20th-century American life is suspicion of big business.*

—Gary Alan Fine, "The Goliath Effect"

Although Philip Morris manufactures more than 160 other cigarette brands in some 170 countries, Marlboros have been the key to its global success. A succession of marketing entrepreneurs steered the company's phenomenal expansion. But the most valuable figure in the company by far is the mythic billboard idol, the Marlboro Man. Forbes *magazine once estimated that the Marlboro Man by himself had a "goodwill" value of $10 billion.*

—Richard Barnet and John Cavanagh, *Global Dreams*

These undecipherable markings on the captive body render a kind of hieroglyphics of the flesh whose severe disjunctures come to be hidden to the cultural seeing by skin color. We might well ask if this phenomenon of marking and branding actually "transfers" from one generation to another, finding various symbolic substitutions in an efficacy of meanings that repeat the initiating moments.

—Hortense Spillers, "Mama's Baby, Papa's Maybe"

The bizarre rumors that consumers spread about the origins and meanings of corporate trademarks are phenomena of consumer culture that indirectly articulate social anxieties about the intersections of culture, power, and place in the condition of postmodernity.[1] Demonic rumors, I will suggest, provide a means by which people culturally express commercial power's lack of place—the simultaneously pervasive but incorporeal presence of corporate power. Moreover, such rumors serve to remark upon the consumer's own place—making audible her lack of voice—and her sense of powerlessness in the ubiquitous but evanescent world of commercial media culture. Rumors give presence to the consumer's cultural absence; they assume power and momentum as they insinuate themselves into the "mediascape" (Appadurai 1990). Traveling anonymously, without clear meaning, authority, or direction, rumors colonize the media in much the same way that commercial trademarks do—subversively undermining the benign invisibility of the trademark's corporate sponsor while maintaining the consumer's own lack of authorial voice.

To make sense of such practices it is necessary to summarize some of the socioeconomic conditions from which they spring. The corporate trademark is a signifier that proliferates in the mass media communications technologies of postmodernism. As production moves elsewhere and the industrial landscape fades from public view (emerging, of course, in export processing zones, women's kitchens, and immigrant's garages), the power of the corporation in the "imaginary space of postmodernity" (Kester 1993; Lazarus 1991) is most evident in the exchange value of the brand name, the corporate logo, and the advertising lingo—the "distinction" these signifiers assume in the market. Rumors, suggests Homi K. Bhabha, "weave their stories around the disjunctive 'present' or the 'not-there' of discourse" (1994:200), and in the "not-there" of production, I propose, we may find new meanings in the devil rumors that circulate in conditions of postmodernity.

The proliferation of signification is often understood to be a peculiar characteristic of postmodernity and its hyperreality of self-referential signs (Harvey 1989; Jameson 1991; Baudrillard 1981, 1983a, 1983b, 1988a, 1988b, 1988c; Kellner 1989; McRobbie 1994; Poster 1988). In a series of works, Jean Baudrillard theorized the postmodern by examining the extension of the commodity form to textual phenomena—in contemporary capitalism, he suggested, the pervasive penetration of mass media enabled the hegemony of a "signifying culture," in which the social world became saturated with shifting cultural signs. The Western world, he posited, has reached the end of an era dominated by industry and now constitutes itself "postindustrially" through the circulation of image and text.[2] In *Simulations* (1983b), the "code" of marketing signs comes to subsume the distinction between objects and their representations: "Instead of a 'real' world of commodities that is somehow bypassed by an 'unreal' myriad of advertising images, Baudrillard discerned only a hyperreality, a world of self-referential signs" (Poster 1988:1).

As I have elaborated elsewhere (Coombe 1991a, 1991b, 1993, 1997) the corporate trademark is one of the most significant cultural goods in conditions of postmodernity—the quintessential self-referential sign—as indicated by the slogans with which they are lobbied into the public sphere: "What's good for General Motors is good for America," General Electric "brings good things to life," and Coca-Cola is "*the* real thing." These signifiers serve as a locus for cultural investments and social inscriptions by those who manufacture mass-market goods. In postmodernity, the focus of commodity fetishism shifts from the product to the sign values invested in products. The "value" of a product, in other words, lies in the exchange value of its brand name, advertising image, or status connotations—the "distinction" it has in the market. Monopoly of the trademark or "commodity/sign" is crucial to corporate capital and an important site for capital growth and investment (Coombe 1997). In many companies, the value of such intangible textual properties as trademarks equals or surpasses the value of tangible assets, and in some corporations a single distinctive symbol may be one of the most valuable assets the company "owns" (Drescher 1992).

Corporate trademarks are key symbols in postmodernity. Corporations invest huge amounts monitoring their use in the public sphere. When a corporation has proprietary rights in a sign, it may also attempt to maintain control over its connotations and to police critical commentary. The more famous the mark, the greater the legal protection that is accorded to it. In practice, this means that the more successfully the corporation dominates the market, the more successfully it can immunize itself against oppositional cultural strategies. But attempts to restrain the tactical appropriations of those signifiers which embody corporate presence in postmodern culture are not always successful.

This is especially evident in the case of rumor. Rumor is elusive and transitive, anonymous, and without origin. It belongs to no one and is possessed by everyone. Endlessly in circulation, it has no identifiable source. This illegitimacy makes it accessible to insurgency, while its transitivity makes it a powerful tactic, one that Gayatri Chakravorty Spivak calls a truly subaltern means of communication (1988b:23). According to Bhabha, it represents the emergence of a peculiar form of social temporality that is both iterative and indeterminate: "Its intersubjective, communal adhesiveness lies in its enunciative aspect. Its performative power of circulation results in the contagious spreading, . . . the iterative action of rumour, its *circulation* and *contagion,* links it with panic — as one of the *affects* of insurgency" (1994:200). Rumors, he suggests, remark "an infectious ambivalence" of "too much meaning and a certain meaningless . . . panic is generated when an old and familiar symbol develops an unfamiliar social significance as sign through a transformation of the temporality of its representation" (202). In rumors, everyday and commonplace forms are transformed into forms that are archaic, awesome, and terrifying; the circulation of cultural codes is disturbed by new and awful valences.

The ubiquity and the anonymity of trademarks in consumer societies seem to invite such appropriations. When the reconfiguration of corporate symbols is articulated in the form of rumor, it may be impossible for a manufacturer to stop aliens from speaking its language with their own voices or colonizing its systems of exchange value with their own experiences or lifeworlds. Procter & Gamble, a company that bombards North America with cleaning products, discovered this phenomenon at quite some cost. First, a word about the sponsor. Procter & Gamble is the largest American corporation producing cleaning and food products (Fine 1990:137) and, until quite recently, the single largest American advertiser.[3] Its daytime radio and television commercials engendered the term "soap opera" and the marketing of its brands (Tide, Crest, Ivory Snow, Pampers) has been the paradigm case in business school textbooks for years. Yet despite all this public cultural activity, the company itself keeps a remarkably low corporate profile (*Globe and Mail* 1982; *Montreal Gazette* 1985). Like any good corporate citizen, it lets its trademarks do the talking.

Corporate capital, however, cannot always control the conversations in which its trademarks become engaged. From about 1978 until the late 1980s a rumor campaign linked the company to Satanism. A survey by *Advertising Age* during this period indicated that 79 percent of the public could not name *any* specific product made by Procter & Gamble (Fine 1985:72), one of North America's oldest soap companies and owner of some of the oldest and most venerable brand names in American mass markets (Crisco, Folgers, Duncan Hines). Despite the ubiquity of its products, the multiplicity of its brands, and the mass dissemination of its trademarks, few people actually understood the company to be the maker of these goods.

Anonymous social groups ascribed occult significance to the man-in-the-moon logo it used on most if not all its products.[4] This corporate insignia (originating in 1851) was seen to be the mark of the devil. One woman, for example, claimed that when you turned the logo up to a mirror, the curlicues in the man's beard became 666 — the sign of the Antichrist: "I just don't understand the coincidence" (*New York Times* 1982:D10). An anonymous leaflet asserted that a company official appeared on national television and "gave all the credit for the success of the company to SATAN. . . . They have placed their satanist symbol on all their products so that they can get SATAN into every home in America" (D10). Others reported hearing that Procter's "owner" appeared on a talk show where he admitted selling his soul to the devil for the company's success.

Procter & Gamble hired private investigators and established a toll-free hotline to deal with twelve to fifteen thousand monthly phone calls from concerned consumers. As their public relations office put it, "Procter is going after the rumor with all the diligence that it devotes to a new product" (D10). The anti-rumor campaign cost millions.[5] Yet, in 1985, when the hydra-headed rumor surfaced again, the company acknowledged a form of defeat. It removed the 134-year-old trademark from its products, a decision described by marketing experts as "a rare case of a giant company succumbing to a bizarre and untraceable rumor" (*Globe and Mail* 1985:B6).

Incredibly, in a decade when the Federal Centers for Disease Control linked the company's tampon with fatal toxic shock syndrome, feminists protested the use of sex in Procter & Gamble's advertisements, fundamentalists boycotted the company for sponsoring violent television shows, and unions urged boycotts to back their struggles for recognition, it was the battle over the meaning of a tiny moon-and-stars symbol that brought the diffident corporation most prominently to public attention. In other words, the biggest threat to the company's benign, if somewhat empty, public image came not from organized groups with expressed political agendas but from the anonymous appropriations of mysterious agents whose interests and motivations remain inscrutable.[6]

Scholarly work on urban and "mercantile legends" (for example, Brunvand 1984, 1986), although replete with references to well-known trademarks, fails to see such signifiers as anything but equivalent to the corporations which control them or the products for which they serve as marketing devices. Folklorist Gary Alan Fine, for example, sees trademark rumors as reflecting an American ambivalence toward bigness, manifested in the pervasive portrayal of well-known corporations as distinctly malevolent: "The popularity of mercantile legends suggests that the public is sensitive to the nuances of corporate capitalism. The legends reveal attitudes within modern capitalism that cannot be easily and directly expressed. . . . Most of these narratives are identical thematically: there is danger from corporations and danger in mass-produced and mass-distributed products. In some legends the corporation itself is guilty for producing a shoddy product; in others an employee is to blame. . . . In few stories can the corporate entity be considered heroic . . . and even here the stories revolve around the enormous size, power, control, and wealth of the corporation. In American mercantile legends there is a strong undercurrent of fear and suspicion of size and power" (1985:79). The mistrust of corporations is most fully expressed, he suggests, in mercantile legends that name the firm or product with the largest market share in that product area (or at least market share *as it is perceived* by the public). Fine makes no distinctions between legends dealing with prominent corporations (either in terms of market share, advertising saturation, or size of operations), those that make reference to products by brand name, those that identify products by brand name, or those in which the corporation, the product, and the brand name are linked in public perception. Indeed, he does not address the trademark at all, except to acknowledge that brand names figure as signifiers in the mercantile legends he recounts (often as a means of effacing their corporate authors).[7] Fine makes a more promising suggestion, however, when he remarks:

The social-psychological rationale of these attitudes seems based on the separation of the public from the means of production and distribution. Corporations are perceived as caring primarily about profits and only secondarily about the needs of consumers. . . . Marx was correct in claiming that separating people from the means of production under capitalism will result in alienation; this alienation provides a psychological climate in which bogey legends can flourish . . . one must accept that the "folk" (in this case the postindustrial public) are capable of conceiving folkloric content in economic terms that reflect the structure of mass capitalist society, feeling constrained, at least subconsciously, by their own lack of control. The resultant sense of constraint and frustration explain this pattern of mercantile legends that is so prevalent under American capitalism. (80)

In later work (1990) Fine suggests that the companies at the center of such rumors are well known (or at least their trademarks are) and deal almost exclusively in consumer products and services. The management and production operations of such corporations are far more anonymous: "These rumors symbolically mirror the ambivalence between knowledge of the product and ignorance of the individuals who direct the creation and marketing of these products" (144).

Despite references to the "postindustrial state" and the "postindustrial public," Fine does not ask why people in a so-called postindustrial society would be any more suspicious of corporate power than those of a more obviously industrial age. The content of the rumor drawn from Upton Sinclair's novel — that workers were being cannibalized in the mass production process — is, however, suggestive. Here, it is the monstrous nature of mass production itself that figures an unnatural form of human consumption for the sake of maintaining a consumer society. The human fodder consumed by the mechanics of mass production is then literally consumed by those loyal to the brand name.

Let us return to the mark of the devil — the Satanic figuring of the corporation in consumer rumors. In *The Devil and Commodity Fetishism*, Michael Taussig (1980) explored the significance of devil symbolism to the emergent proletariat in Bolivia and Colombia. He persuasively showed that proletarianizing peasants used the devil, a fetish of the spirit of evil, as a powerful image with which to express culturally an ethical condemnation of the capitalist mode of production, their hostility to wage labor, and the unnatural subjection of humans to the commodity form. The maintenance and increase in production under capitalism was understood to result from secret pacts made with the devil.

I shall speculate here on the role of the devil in the current stage of capitalism and its feverish proliferation of media signifiers in the service of maintaining and increasing consumption (appropriating and detourning Taussig's terms to make them speak to a postmodern context). The devil contract may be operating in postmodernity as an image with which to indict a system in which consumption is the aim of economic activity, signs circulate without meanings, symbols are divorced from social contexts, the images that convey commodities are abstracted from the sources of their production, and trademarks are held to be their own sources of value. It may be against this obfuscation of power that satanic rumors are directed — the fetishization of evil, in the image of the devil, directed at the fetishism of the commodity/sign. The meaning of late capitalism may be emerging in the fantastic fabulations through which trademarks are given evil reenchantments.

The devil in North America may adopt a variety of forms. Demonic others figure in many consumer rumors, but the devil will assume the image of evil most compelling in the subaltern spheres in which it circulates. This is clearly evident in the perpetuation of Ku Klux Klan rumors that circulate among African Americans in a black counterpublic that flourishes in postindustrial America.[8] Two centuries of American support for the sale of black bodies; the branding, marking, and wounding of African Americans; official tolerance of white on black violence; and an insidious fascination with and fixation on controlling black male sexuality have inevitably left legacies of hostility, anger, and distrust. These legacies are registered in rumors — which increasingly target corporate powers. Drawing on the comprehensive accounts furnished by folklorist Patricia Turner (1993), I will elaborate upon the particular prevalence of trademarks in the subaltern consumer counterculture she describes.

Turner links contemporary rumors or legends in African American communities to a provocative corpus of related oral and written lore concerning race relations and the imperiled black body that can be traced back to the early-sixteenth-century encounters between white European explorers and sub-Saharan Africans. Similar, if not identical, rumors have circulated back and forth between black and white communities in mimetic circuits of exchange ever since this mythic moment of "first contact."[9] As Walter Benjamin might appreciate, mechanical (and electronic) modes of reproduction have increased the speed and velocity of these rumors, as corporate control of imagery has mystified the sources of control over the black body. Turner (1993) traces the continuing operations of the mimetic faculty in the multiple modernities that African Americans have experienced and the demonic others who populate their appropriations: "Concerns about conspiracy, contamination, cannibalism, and castration . . . run through nearly four hundred years of black contemporary legend material and prove remarkably tenacious" (xv).

As both whites and blacks attempted to fit the other into their own worldview, they both adopted the figure of the cannibal, with flesh eating representing the epitome of barbaric and uncivilized behavior for both groups during that period (Turner 1993:9). In the era of slave trading, rumors about the other circulated and were mimicked by their alters, as evidenced in the continued currency of the trope of man-eating: "New World cannibalism rumors continued well into the nineteenth century, as the mutiny on the Spanish slave ship *Amistad* revealed; although the African men had been subject to all the horrors of experience as cargo in the Middle Passage, they did not attempt to take over the ship until they were told by the cook that the white men intended to eat them" (14). The term "man-eater" had a literal meaning for both the slave traders and the slaves, the majority of whom were men, and rumors that black men are the particular targets of white animosity and most at bodily risk have persisted over the generations. For blacks, Turner suggests, "such as those in West Africa where economies of commodified labor were unknown, the rumor satisfied basic explanatory needs; slave traders kept coming back for live bodies to satisfy their hunger for human flesh" (30).

The commodification and the vilification of black bodies in the United States — their simultaneous status as objects of property and subjects of physical danger and sexual potency, branded as chattel and targeted with violence — have a long and sordid history that lives on in the embodied memories of African Americans. Apologists for slavery in the eighteenth and nineteenth centuries claimed that Africans had been visited with an ancient, if not biblical, "curse" that "marked" them for slavery: "God has placed a mark on the Negro as distinctive as that on Cain" (Harriet Schoolcraft 1860, cited in Diane Roberts 1994:58). Such marks served to deem those who bore them (blacks, women, natives) subservient to their unmarked (white, male) masters. The witnessing of abuse visited on black bodies lingers in collective memory and continues to inscribe the bodies of African Americans to the present day. Elizabeth Alexander movingly evokes these corporeally inscribed memories, repetitively provoked by white on black violence, as consolidating "group affiliation by making blackness an unavoidable, irreducible sign which, despite its abjection, leaves creative

space for group self-definition and self-knowledge" (1994:78). Ku
Klux Klan rumors are one example of this memory and creative self-
recognition.

After the civil rights struggles, rumors linked reprehensible violence against blacks to the KKK—tying the Ku Klux Klan to consumer goods conspiratorially designed to prohibit black reproduction. "To many African-Americans, the Klan exists as the agency on
which whites depend to mitigate or eliminate black access to those
rights and privileges that white adults take for granted" (Turner
1993:58). The Klan's verifiable abuses of black bodies—lynching, castration, burning, and mutilation are sufficiently well documented;
"Reconstruction-era Klansmen devised many cruel fates for blacks,
which contributed to their emerging reputation as demonically inspired monsters determined to sexually humiliate those who threatened white supremacy. Sexual metaphors abound in stories of KKK
violence" (64). In the Reconstruction era, for example, Klan members padded and enlarged their own crotches when pursuing their
presumably overendowed victims—a mimicry of the alterity they so
fantastically constructed. In many accounts, the desire to destroy the
victim's sexuality is literally realized, as when black genitalia served as
the trophies of a successful hunt.

Black engagement in the defense of international democracy during World War I did not bring them democratic rights and privileges
when they returned home. Wearing uniforms and carrying weapons
were privileges that white American men saw as properly their own
preserve—black male adoption of these insignia provoked an anxious
backlash of white supremacy. Associations between male sexual prow-
ess and military acumen were registered in the lynching, mutilation,
and dismemberment of black men in uniform (71). Later, post–World
War II Klan attacks on male genitalia and the bombings and burnings
of institutions central to the reproduction of black community life
made rumors linking the KKK to the insidious sterilization of black
men particularly compelling.

The KKK has figured prominently in at least four contemporary legend cycles in
which modern corporations are the mechanism by which late-twentieth-century
white supremacists pursue the bodies of blacks. The KKK, in other words, has
traded its white sheets of yesteryear for the white shirts of corporate America. In
one rumor, the KKK, who [sic] allegedly owns Church's Fried Chicken, has tainted

the chicken recipe so that black male eaters are sterilized after consuming it. In a second, young African American male consumers are unwittingly supporting the KKK by purchasing overpriced athletic wear manufactured by the "Klan-owned" Troop clothing company. Third, many believe that the KKK owns Marlboro cigarettes, a brand popular among black smokers, and is not only accruing financial benefits from but also deliberately causing cancer in African American consumers. Finally, the Brooklyn Bottling Company, maker and distributor of a soft drink called Tropical Fantasy, which is said to contain a mysterious ingredient capable of sterilizing black men, is similarly alleged to be a front for the KKK. (82–83)

In these rumors of KKK manipulation of mass production, the agendas of the suspect corporations mimic those traditionally pursued by the KKK—conspiratorial attempts to limit and destroy the reproduction of the black population. Church's Fried Chicken was targeted, Turner suggests, because its persona in the market—its public signature, trademark, and trade name—reminded blacks of houses of worship: "Churches played a pivotal role in the civil rights movement. In many communities houses of worship were the only public spaces in which African-Americans could meet. Moreover, many of the best-known leaders in the civil rights movement emerged from the ranks of the clergy. In its attempts to prevent civil rights advances, the Klan was proven to be responsible for the bombing and burning of numerous black churches throughout the South. This flagrant disregard for the sanctity of churches no doubt left a lasting impression on the African-American mind. The notion that 'Church's' [a company with ownership based in the South] could be responsible for such destructive behavior as the sterilizing scheme thus gained a perverse, ironic appeal" (85).

Moreover, Church's "product" involved the preparation of foods typically associated with the soul food of the folk. Such foods were sold exclusively in inner-city black areas—Church's was one of the last fast-food franchises to move into suburban locations (86). Its retail operations were highly visible in black communities but largely unknown in white areas, whereas its advertising budget was (contrary to Fine's expectations) the *lowest* in the industry. With few other connotations to attach to the company's mysterious "presencings," only its disembodied trademark remained for inner-city consumers to invest with meaning. The very anonymity of the company might have invited rumor, suggests Turner—although the franchises provided some employment in heating and serving precooked food, these were jobs that reinforced servile and emasculating images. Like Kentucky Fried Chicken, Popeye's, and other southern food franchises, moreover, Church's figured in rumors that its fried chicken recipes were stolen from black maids. In such rumors, even the history of exploitation is further expropriated for white profit when an "imitation of life" is sold back to blacks under the signatures of Southern white men — descendants of slaveholders — who claim food for the soul as trade secrets and circulate it by means of trademarks — taking possession of the literal sustenance of black bodily well-being.

In 1985 another company introduced a line of sportswear under the name "Troop," capitalizing on an incipient military aesthetic in the male urban underclass. It marketed these intimidating combat-style goods almost exclusively to black and Latino youths in inner cities where the clothing became incredibly popular. Soon it was reported on community radio stations that the Troop trademark was owned by a company controlled by the Ku Klux Klan — the trademark, in other words, was employed to create the perception of a threatening, oppositional "army" that would legitimate *and fund* the Klan's own paramilitary operations.[10]

In fact, Troop Sport was a New York firm owned by Korean and American entrepreneurs with production operations based in Korea. It had no Klan affiliations that could be established. But rumor is never error but basically errant (Spivak 1988b:23), and this one, capturing the public imagination, swept the nation. As the *San Francisco Chronicle* reported: "A Chicago variation of the rumor has rap singer L. L. Cool J. ripping off a Troop jacket on the Oprah show and accusing the firm of hating blacks. The singer has never appeared on the talk show. . . . In Memphis, the rumor was that the letters in Troop stood for: To Rule Over our Oppressed People. And in Atlanta some believed that the words 'Thank you nigger for making us rich' were emblazoned inside the tread of Troop's tennis shoes. . . . Troop's [black] marketing director . . . [claims] that he has gone to great lengths to disprove the alleged Klan connection. 'I went to Montgomery, Alabama to a store and cut open five pairs [of shoes] to prove it wasn't like that' " (1989).

In contrast to Procter & Gamble's defensive countertactics, Troop Sport responded overtly. It decided to "do the right thing" and affirm its allegiance to civil rights. A two-hundred-thousand-dollar public relations campaign enlisted the aid of Operation Push, the NAACP, and black musicians and athletes. Church rallies were held, black students were publicly awarded scholarships, and anti-Klan posters were distributed. According to Turner, Troop officials in Chicago also engaged the executive secretary of the African American Alpha Phi Alpha fraternity to request that they use their chapter network to dispel the rumors. Despite these efforts, the company fell into dire straits, closed its stores, and filed for bankruptcy in the summer of 1989. Its downfall may have been due to changing fashion trends, but it is difficult to deny the injuries that the rumors visited on the company's reputation.

The objective falsity of this rumor makes it difficult to understand at first why people find it persuasive. Although Ku Klux Klan rumors may be empirically false, they articulate compelling truths about the history of black social experience in North America. In marketing goods to the black population, these companies were not unusual. But elements specific to these endeavors make them unique. For example, instead of addressing blacks as part of a market in which everyone could now be seen to consume the same goods — an inclusionary gesture — the Troop marketing strategy was designed to *mark* a *difference*. The pseudomilitary character of the product itself physically interpellated young black men as identifiable targets and marked them (while inviting them to brand or tattoo themselves) as recruitable subordinates. If this seems far-fetched, this excerpt from the *Metro Word* ("Toronto's Black Culture Magazine") indicates that such possibilities are never far from consciousness in black urban communities: "On a warm autumn day, Rick is easy to spot wearing his Black leather jacket imprinted with an X along with his Malcolm X cap. . . . As Rick turns to catch the bus, the large white X smack dab in the middle of his back takes on an ominous meaning. The X appears almost like a target and Rick appears to have become human prey. From Public Enemy's Rebel Base One in New York, [Harry] Allen says, 'This is why Public Enemy has taken the image of a Black man with his arms crossed defiantly and his head held upward in a rifle sight as their logo. Most Black people see themselves in the same situation — in the sights' " (Beaumont 1992:7).[11]

The Troop marketing strategy seems to have evoked disturbing associations in black cultural memory and the social unconscious. The disproportionate numbers of young black men recruited to serve as subordinate "grunts" in Vietnam was a powerful memory. The experience of serving as capital's reserve army of labor, increasingly mobilized according to the demands of the military industrial complex, was potentially evoked, along with memories of the rewards expected and postponed after serving in two world wars. Indeed, race rumors during the two world wars demonstrate profound racial distrust. According to Turner: "The antiblack rumors that circulated during wartime reflect the ambivalence, insecurity, and uneasiness felt during a time of crisis. The dominant culture did not embrace the idea of training black men to shoot, but the idea that they share the risk of being shot at was perfectly acceptable. Blacks were empowered, in short, by America's need for them. A nation that had always tried to limit black access to weapons suddenly needed to train black soldiers. Few roles reinforce masculinity more than that of soldier. Whites knew, moreover, that they could not easily ask blacks to be soldiers while denying them the full rights of citizenship and increased access to the American dream" (1993:45). Black rumors focused on the second-class treatment of black soldiers and on the individual bodies of black soldiers serving as fodder for American troops: "Yet from the Revolutionary War through World War II, the weapons, pay scale, food, and training provided to black soldiers were nothing like those afforded to whites. . . . Given the disregard with which blacks were treated before World War II, the possibility that the military establishment wanted to place them between Axis bullets and white Allied bodies undoubtedly rang quite true" (45). Later, race riots also provoked (and were provoked by) rumors about the relative treatment of black and white bodies by members of the other race.

Michelle Wallace adds further dimensions to this emphasis on the black body:

Afro-Americans, as ex-slaves, are not only permanently exiled from their "homeland" (which now exists most meaningfully only in their imaginations), but also from their bodies. Their labor and their reproduction can be considered to be in a state of postcoloniality—no longer colonized but not yet free. In a manner that may be characteristic of "internal colonization," Afro-American culture has traditionally seemed fully aware of its own marginality to the white American mainstream. Accordingly, it combined (and often cleverly disguised) its political objections to Afro-American "invisibility" with a progressive integration and reinterpretation of those qualities and features that first marked the "racism" of white images of blacks. In other words, black culture continually reincorporates the "negative" or "racist" imagery of the dominant culture. (1990:2)

As Manthia Diawara phrases a similar insight, "Blacks often derive the good life from repressive institutions by systematically reversing the significations of those institutions" (1994:42). With these insights, we might see black male adoption of army surplus camouflage gear and military insignia in the service of a "BAD " aesthetic as ironically inverting this symbolism to create and affirm black solidarity. The gesture is one that Henry Louis Gates Jr. (1988) might see as a form of "Signifyin(g)" — the employment of figurative rhetorical strategies that repeat and imitate elements of dominant culture while critically marking a difference — that enables blacks to respond indirectly to an exclusionary white culture. Gates discusses literature and the oral tradition, but Wallace (1990) argues that Signifyin(g) tactics are even more characteristic of African American popular culture and its mass culture derivatives (2). As Grant Farred remarks: "Subjugation in contemporary America is an insidious process because it silences constituencies even as it gives voice and face to their culture and histories. It adopts black dress and posture, it facilitates black interpellation without enfranchisement, it addresses blacks without providing channels and forums for response and critical engagement; it takes on repertoires of black representation without respect for the conditions under which the history of that community is made" (1995:26).

The conversion of the signs of physical conscription and betrayal into a subcultural aesthetic of resistance might be Signifyin(g), but it was as signification that they were rerouted by Troop Sport to serve the endless needs of commerce for new sources of distinction. The appropriation and projection back on blacks of their own Signifyin(g) by anonymous forces of capital — an inversion of their inversion — inevitably sparked racial anxiety about white enmity. This enmity was most aptly represented by the Ku Klux Klan. Black response to the Troop marketing strategy (the Ku Klux Klan rumor), however "false," served to connote historical "truths" about black male subordination. The Troop marketing strategy stirred something in the political unconscious of black Americans that surfaced in the form of a fantastic recognition of black social identity; the rumor might be understood as a return of the repressed in the black social imaginary.

British Knights and Reebok, both manufacturers of athletic shoes, have also been visited with accusations of Klan affiliation, although in the Reebok case, the funneling of funds to South Africa to maintain apartheid was a more pervasive theme. As Patricia Turner notes, the

Knights trademark was easily associated with the knights of the Ku Klux Klan, but the Reebok rumor was more mysterious. The rage for athletic footwear did cause concern within black communities, and the Reebok rumors circulated just as celebrity condemnations of South African apartheid became dominant in American media (1993:127–28). Perplexed by these allegations, Reebok marketing personnel chose to interrogate the trademark with which the company purveyed its goods so as to determine if it held any clues to the origins of the rumor. Implicitly they recognized that the authorial mark under which the goods were marketed and with which black consumers marked their bodies might contain clues to the nature of African American distrust: "The company's founders, Joe and Bill Foster, turned to the dictionary for a name for the bootmaking company in the late 1950s; they 'picked the name Reebok . . . a light, nimble gazelle.' . . . Coincidentally that species is found almost exclusively in South Africa. [Vice-president for corporate communications] Lightcap, in speculating on the source of the rumor, mentioned . . . the similarity between the words *reebok* and *springbok*— an annual South African rugby match — and the fact that the corporate symbol for the Reebok brand is the British flag" (129).

Turner claims to have found few informants for the rumor who knew anything about the gazelle or the South African rugby team (although informants with a British Caribbean heritage did associate the British flag used in Knights shoe advertising with a history of racist colonial oppression) (129). "To the company, its status as the first major U.S. shoe company to withdraw its products from the South African market makes the allegations even more disturbing. Proud of its record on human rights and its support of the African-American community, Reebok has gone to great lengths to dispel the rumor. . . . Lightcap spends a great deal of time on the road, pleading Reebok's case to African-American college groups as well as community and political groups. Signs disavowing the South African connection are very much in evidence at Reebok outlets. A handsome flyer entitled 'Reebok: On Human Rights' contains disclaimers from both African-American athletes and well-known anti-apartheid groups" (130). The flyer also contained a letter to Reebok employees that reiterated the company's determination to reproach other American corporations doing business in South Africa and its commitment to "a responsible corporate America" (131). Although it is the largest athletic footwear manufacturer in the world, Reebok's vision of corporate responsibility does not include the provision of any manufacturing jobs for the African Americans who constitute so great a share of its market. Like other corporations, it has adopted strategies of flexible capital accumulation, shifting the places of its production operations to take advantage of low-wage labor and legislative regimes that impose the least onerous regulatory constraints on its operations.

The effects of global capitalist restructuring have been particularly grave for African Americans: "The shift to a system of flexible accumulation which led to smaller workplaces, more homogeneous work forces and the weakening of labor unions, meant that the moderate-waged bases of the Black working and middle classes were eviscerated. Moreover, under the new regimes Blacks were more likely to suffer from racial discrimination in the labor market. Further, the spatial aspects of this transformation left inner-cities economically devastated as their economic base was removed, and large sectors of urban minority residents lived in increasingly impoverished neighbourhoods" (Dawson 1994:209). Like Troop and other athletic-wear companies, Reebok's manufacturing operations are now located in China and Southeast Asia, a typical corporate strategy that has moved manufacturing jobs out of the country and, more significant, out of the areas in which most African Americans live. Providing only low-wage, low-skill service jobs without benefits or security to those black youth able to commute to distant retail outlets, Reebok is typical of a larger pattern of disinvestment in black communities that has prevailed since the 1980s. The shoes sold to young black men retail for prices that often exceed fifty dollars — sometimes three times that — but are physically produced (largely by women) in minimal-wage, sweatshop conditions or subcontracting arrangements to inflate profit margins. These factors are still largely unknown to many consumers. The invisibility of these conditions of production or indeed of any places of manufacture for those consumer goods with which African Americans mark status distinctions makes such rumors more compelling than they might be if African Americans had any role in the goods' manufacture.

Athletic wear has special significance for African American male youth — celebrity sportsmen are role models for many who see their greatest chance for legitimate financial success to lie in professional athletics (Turner 1993:173). Black leaders have accused athletic-wear companies of stoking violence by inspiring lust for expensive goods. In

1990, for example, the Reverend Jesse Jackson urged black consumers to boycott products manufactured by Nike because the company had shown so little corporate responsibility in the black community.[12]

Cigarette companies are also linked in black popular imagination to the KKK. During the 1960s, rumors circulated among African Americans about Kool, a menthol cigarette that was a top brand among black smokers. "By misspelling a word prominent in the folk speech of African-Americans to arrive at the product's name," Turner suggests, the manufacturer set itself up for speculation (1993:98). Today, rumors alleging Klan affiliations are targeted at Marlboro, the phenomenally successful brand controlled by the Philip Morris Corporation. Many blacks claimed that the letters KKK could be found in the logo on the cigarette package (Turner 1993:100). One of Turner's informants recalled a caution received when lighting up a Marlboro:

The logo design incorporated 3 representations of the letter K. . . . So far is plausible, the final "proof" was that if you tore the bottom of the packet open [in a particular way] . . . there would be revealed the head of a hooded klansman, the two spots, in black and gold, standing for eyeholes. To this was added the "fact" that Philip Morris, in person, was a noted Klan member and financier. . . . Although I personally never heard or saw the story carried in printed sources or on T.V. . . . Marlboro nevertheless stopped using the two spots on their boxes. . . . With the withdrawal of the two spots, this story seems to have died a death, but even so, every now and then somebody will say to Marlboro smokers (there are a lot of us unfortunately), "you shouldn't smoke Marlboro, you know." (Cited in 1993:100)

The three *K*s on the package that supposedly indicate the Ku Klux Klan "signature" and the work in which black consumers engaged to "discover" the Klan's presence in the manufacture of the cigarettes display in particularly graphic fashion the dance of mimicry and alterity at play in the market. Out of the trademarks and logos the corporation disseminated, black consumers constructed the signature of the demonic other—they manufactured marks of alterity in the countertrademarks they created with those offered to them. They detected other authorities behind products that harmed them and did so by evoking the figures that most thoroughly represented their bodily vulnerability in white society.

Philip Morris is not a singular owner of a manufacturing concern but the original English tobacco merchant who achieved success in the mid–nineteenth century (and was a rather minor player in the global tobacco market until the birth of the Marlboro Man in the 1950s). The American company is now publicly owned by thousands of shareholders. This differentiation of corporate ownership is rarely represented in the commercial marketplace per se, and trade names that incorporate the names of individuals are far more common on packages and in the advertising of goods that consumers encounter. Ownership is much more easily conceptualized in individual terms, and the prevalence of white patriarchs in consumer culture (Colonel Saunders, Orville Redenbacher, Dave Thomas, "Mr. Christie," Frank Purdue) legitimates a misrecognition of personal control over the manufacture and distribution of goods.

The toxicity of tobacco and the dangers of its consumption require little comment; a product with detrimental effects for black bodies might well attract attention. More salient perhaps are historical memories of tobacco harvesting and black exploitation in conditions of forced labor. After emancipation, intimacy with southern tobacco fields continued: "A fancy coffee table book, published in 1979, on the Philip Morris company's commitment to the art world . . . contains several artistically rendered black-and-white photos of African-Americans working in tobacco fields" (Turner 1993:102). Today, black and Hispanic communities are particular targets of tobacco company advertising; as wealthier and more educated Americans stop smoking, cigarette companies aim more and more of their marketing at the poor:

Much of Harlem looks like a war zone, but the ubiquitous billboards featuring scantily-clad women advertising Kools, Camels, and Virginia Slims and the fully clothed cowboys welcoming all to Marlboro country are bright and shiny. In early 1990, the *New England Journal of Medicine* published the shocking findings that black men in Harlem were less likely to reach the age of 40 than men in Bangladesh. Six of the top seven killers in Harlem are, according to the great weight of medical opinion, tobacco-related or alcohol-related. According to the Centers for Disease Control, cigarettes and alcohol are the two most heavily advertised products in African-American and Latino communities. Indeed, about 90 percent of all cigarette and alcohol billboard advertising in the country is located in these communities. (Barnet and Cavanagh 1994:196–97)

These rumors focus on the racial body and its vulnerability and surveillance in the United States. They remark a suppressed subaltern truth when they stress the vulnerability of those bodies that American industry has controlled, contained, and ultimately abandoned in conditions of postmodernity. Both Fine and Turner view the rumor as a form of resistance—one of the few weapons of the weak in a society where culture is commodified and controlled from indeterminate places. The "folk idioms of late-twentieth-century life" are potent resources with which black consumers contest "ubiquitous billboards, glossy advertisements, coupons, and television commercials" (Turner 1993:178). Significantly, the modes of discourse with which consumers spread rumors mimic the tactics through which the trademark itself makes its way into daily life, provoking alternative forms of authorship and new sources of authority.

This is particularly evident in the Brooklyn Bottling Company's battle with Klan rumors, which began in 1990. Tropical Fantasy was resisted in communities heavily populated by Caribbean-born blacks and Hispanics (Turner 1993:142). In 1991 young blacks were handing out photocopied flyers reproducing the allegation and authorizing it with "evidence"—an exposé that had supposedly appeared on the television show *20/20*. Graffiti artists further perpetuated the rumor: "The *Wall Street Journal* describes this scene: 'A burned-out building covered with graffiti includes the slogan: "Oppressors are not our protectors." Just under the spray-painted warning a chalk-scrawled postscript adds: Tropical Fantasy'" (169).

These anonymous others mimic the mass circulation of the commodity text with whatever means of reproduction are available, authoring alternative versions to the commodified narratives that mass marketing provides, and claim the authority of the mass media to validate their own authorship. Many rumors contain accounts of their own verification—pointing to the media as authenticating the account. The mediums that interpellate us as mass subjects (Warner 1993) operate for America's others as authorities that legitimate their own knowledge of their perceived bodily excess and real corporeal vulnerability. Nationally syndicated news and entertainment shows appear to be the vehicles of choice. As one of Patricia Turner's African American students put it: "Oh well, I guess that's like what they say about eating at Church's Chicken—you know the Klan owns it and they do something to the chicken so that when black men eat there they become sterile. Except that I guess it isn't really like the one about the Kentucky Fried Rat because it is true about Church's. I know because a friend of mine saw the story on '60 Minutes'" (1993:84). In

response to the Tropical Fantasy rumor, corporate authorities sanctioned alternative forms of authority — black authorities — to validate
their own benign intentions; they sought black authorship, provided
black employment, and publicly recognized the specificities of their
consumer base:

> While the most potent folklore genres of the postindustrial age — rumor, graffiti,
> Xeroxlore — were being put to work to spread the notion that Tropical Fantasy was
> a KKK-inspired aphrodisiac, the company fought back with all the standard damage-
> control tools. They had their products tested by the FDA and made the results
> public; they hired a truck to drive around black neighborhoods with a billboard
> denying the KKK allegation; they hired a black public relations team to propose
> strategies by which they could reclaim their customer base. Individuals respected in
> the black community were enlisted for the campaign. The mayor of New York,
> African-American David Dinkins, guzzled the soda on television; community cler-
> gymen denounced the rumor. (169–70)

Like the Procter & Gamble rumor, these anonymous appropriations
had the effect of pulling invisible companies into the public limelight.
Rumors may provoke corporations to renounce their lack of public
presence and make political commitments. Procter & Gamble, whose
implicit motto is that cleanliness is next to Godliness (its products are
marketed with biblical referents), may have been compelled only to
reaffirm its advertising commitments to purity, cleanliness, and light
against the forces of evil, filth, and darkness. Troop Sport, Reebok,
and the Brooklyn Bottling Company, however, were pushed into overt
political engagement, solidarity, and connection with African American communities and concerns.[13]

Like Fine, Turner does not explore the pervasive significance of
trademarks, brands, or trade names in rumors concerning corporate-
controlled, antiblack conspiracies that threaten black bodies and the
fate of the black race. Although she recognizes them as features of
"modern motifs" or indicia of "contemporary legends" (1993:5), we
are not told what is peculiarly modern about them. I would suggest
instead that they are postmodern phenomena, peculiar to late capitalist, post-Fordist, or "postindustrial" conditions.[14] Trademarks promise
a unique source of origin for mass-produced goods of identical appearance, but this site can be traced in postindustrial societies only
with great difficulty. The brand name or trademark floats mysteri-

ously—a corporate signature endlessly reproduced by mechanical means, it marks an invisible and imaginary moment of manufacture—conjuring a source of origin while it magically garners goodwill for its invisible author.

Rumor campaigns such as those directed at Procter & Gamble, Church's, Reebok, Philip Morris, and Troop Sport must be understood in the context of a consumption society in which corporate power maintains silence and invisibility behind a play of media signifiers without referents, a circulation of signs without meanings. In a world in which the presence of power lies increasingly in the realm of the imaginary, such rumors may be understood as cultural guerrilla tactics—"political" in their significance, if not in their self-consciousness. As Bhabha phrases it, "What articulates these sites of cultural difference and social antagonism, in the absence of the validity of interpretation, is a discourse of panic that suggests that psychic affect and social fantasy are potent forms of political identity and agency for guerilla warfare" (1994:203).

The nature of signifying power influences the form of the appropriations it engenders. Arguably, such rumors constitute a "counterterrorism" of sorts to the "terror" of postmodern hyperreality. If the "terror" of hyperreality[15] lies in its anonymity, its fleetingness, its dearth of meaning and excess of fascination, then it is not surprising that it provokes "counterterrorist" tactics that have the same characteristics. It constitutes an "alter" in its own seductive image.[16] As social psychologist Frederick Koenig puts it, "Next to an act of terrorism, what corporations fear most is that they may be targeted with an outlandish tall tale" (cited in Turner 1993:166). The rumor campaign seems to have the same superficial senselessness and indeterminacy as the media that it combats, into which it simultaneously insinuates itself.

These rumors concomitantly challenge visions of the masses as silent majorities capable only of passive yes/no signals in response to power, while they add more subtlety and dimension to claims that people are capable only of making arbitrary and ineffective connections among floating signifiers. Faced with only the signifier, people construct a signified; in a world of empty signification, people may invest their own meanings. The connections people make may well be arbitrary, they may even be absurd, but the massive investments that manufacturers make to counter their influence suggest that they are hardly ineffective.

Finally, these rumors indicate popular refusal of a dominant cultural logic that replaces exchange value with sign value to the extent that even the memory of use value is lost. To put this more succinctly, as manufacturers erase and obscure all traces of production through their investments in decontextualized media signifiers, they encounter consumers determined to reembed these signifiers in myths of origin or narratives of production. These narratives bespeak an anxiety about the abstraction of symbols from lifeworlds and the invisibility of production relations in Western societies, giving voice to a profound suspicion of corporate power and its contemporary lack of place.

NOTES

I thank Kathleen Pirrie Adams, Gail Faurschou, and Mick Taussig for early insights and support. Don Moore also played a key role in providing inspiration for this project. Roger Rouse made helpful comments on an early draft in 1989. An abbreviated version of the argument was contained within "Tactics of Appropriation and the Politics of Recognition in Late Modern Democracies," *Political Theory* 21:411–33. I am grateful to the editors for allowing me to expand and elaborate the argument here.

1   I should make it clear at the outset that I don't believe it is possible to adopt the position of a detached observer who studies practices of rumor. In a mass-mediated society and culture, the practices involved in spreading a rumor, reporting it, commenting on it, and analyzing it necessarily collapse into one another, as they do here.

2   The term "postindustrial" must be approached with great caution — the idea that we occupy a "postindustrial" culture is part of an ideological structure that denies the industrial work being done "out of sight." Good criticisms of some usages of the term are provided in Kester 1993 and Lazarus 1991. I employ it here to refer to a felt sense of industrial production's disappearance and its cultural manifestations.

3   Barnet and Cavanagh 1994:197, 221. Since 1991 its advertising expenditures have been exceeded by Philip Morris, the tobacco giant of Marlboro Man fame, who acquired General Foods and Kraft and with them a roster of famous trademarks — Jell-O, Kool-Aid, SOS, Maxwell House, Cheez Whiz, and Miracle Whip — and is now the single largest advertiser in the world. By acquiring General Foods and Kraft, Philip Morris now controls about 10 percent of all food products in U.S. supermarkets. With relationships with 165 banks, over $19 billion was available overnight to accomplish the hostile takeover of Kraft. Philip Morris accountant Storr refers to himself as a shaman: "At a meeting in Nigeria for senior managers, he put on an African mask and waved a wooden snake to make a point. He knows that when he telephones for money, he is

certain to get it because his request is backed by the full faith and credit of the Marlboro Man" (Barnet and Cavanagh 1994:229).

4   Fine suggests that even though the trademarks belonging to Procter & Gamble were unknown, rumors suggesting that the company was controlled by Satanists, a witches' coven, or the Unification Church were believed because "the psychological dominance of the corporation as a whole made such beliefs credible. . . . Such rumors need not be grounded in knowledge, but only in general emotions about the corporation" (1985:72). This begs the question of how a company becomes "psychologically dominant" and ignores the very signifier around which the rumor circulated—the medieval stylization and religious resonance of the logo of the moon and stars, which no doubt suggested an association with the devil, witches, and "Moonies" in a fashion that a more streamlined or modern logo would not.

5   The company hired detectives from Pinkerton and Wackenhut to track down rumormongers, instituted lawsuits against rival Amway distributors who were alleged to be spreading the story, and in Canada enlisted provincial police in its efforts to track down producers of flyers disseminating the story.

6   Threats to a company's public image are necessarily based on perceptions of perceptions and therefore cannot be measured in quantitative terms. Press surveys for the 1980s, however, indicate that the rumor campaign received more press coverage than did Procter & Gamble's other difficulties and suggest that its public relations department devoted more energy and resources to deflecting the rumor publicly than to meeting other challenges simultaneously faced by the company.

7   According to Fine: "Some companies so dominate their product areas that their names are almost generic. We refer to Xerox machines rather than copiers, Jell-O rather than flavored gelatin, Kleenex rather than facial tissues, or Oreos rather than sugar cream sandwiched between two chocolate wafers. People use these names even when they refer to other brands because these corporate names symbolize the products. In legends and rumors dealing with these products ('Xerox machines cause cancer') we use the corporate name without necessarily claiming that the corporation named is the only corporation involved. When informants talk about 'Jell-O' hardening into rubber and being indigestible, the target of the story may not be General Foods. However, the mention of such corporate names reflects psychological dominance. If asked directly which corporation was involved, informants typically confirmed that it was the corporate leader even though the source for the account might have used the product reference generically" (1985:71).

Fine does not explore the possibility that there may be social significance to and distinctions made between the name of the corporation, a legally protected trade name (which may also be the name of the corporation), a brand name legally protected as a trademark, and the product itself, conflating all these when he decides "for ease of reference" to "use 'corporation' to refer to corporations and products" (71). Thus it becomes impossible to determine whether specific rumors manifest distrust of known corporations, surround trademarks of especial renown in their own right (through advertising, for example), attach to brand names known to have particular corporate owners, or are associated with especially popular products that are most easily referred to by a mark that is becoming generic (for a discussion of the fear of "genericide" and its cultural consequence, see Coombe 1997). It is difficult for Fine to explain why in the anxiety surrounding certain technological innovations (e.g., microwave ovens) rumors do not attach to a certain manufacturer or any particular brand name but to the product itself, whereas with others (e.g., soft bubble gum), a brand name (Bubble Yum) figures prominently (except to suggest that perhaps in the microwave field no one brand is publicly perceived as dominant, whereas in the bubble gum field, the new brand became the bestseller — but we have no way of knowing if members of the rumormongering public were aware of this). Only by examining the particular products, their consumers, and the corporate marketing strategies that accompanied their introduction into the market would any rationale emerge. To the extent that children form the penny candy market and are perhaps the most mystified segment of the consuming population — when it comes to recognizing and distinguishing corporate ownership, production processes, marketing strategies, trademarks, and the products to which they refer — their rumors are likely to name products exclusively by trademark (Pop Rocks and Bubble Yum are examples Fine cites).

8 The ideal of a singular public sphere for civil society has come under much critical scrutiny. In the context of a discussion of the possibility of a black public sphere, Steven Gregory (1994) evokes Nancy Fraser: "Fraser notes that members of subordinated groups, such as women, people of color, lesbians and gays have found it politically important to constitute alternative, or 'subaltern counterpublics'; that is, parallel discursive arenas where those excluded from dominant discourses, invent and circulate counterdiscourses, so as to formulate oppositional interpretations of their identities, interests, and needs. The proliferation of such counterpublics allows issues that were previously shielded from contestation to be publicly argued. . . . The presence of a counterpublic can direct attention to the public arenas where micro-level discursive interactions are shaped by wider institutional power arrangements and discourses" (153).

   Although Gregory clearly has a more articulate and rational discussion in mind, a counterdiscourse is no more likely to adopt a rationalist tone than the discourses it counters. Hence, in the case of the subaltern practices I discuss, the rumor adopts a mode of address and circulation that simultaneously mimics and disrupts the mass-market media significations to which it indirectly responds.

9 My use of mimesis and alterity as related to moments of alleged "first contact" and what might be deemed the phenomenology of primitivism draws extensively from Taussig 1993. For a longer discussion of Taussig's theory of mimesis and alterity and its relevance for considering the cultural power of trademarks, see Coombe 1996.

10 I am grateful to Kathleen Pirrie Adams for her insights into this issue and for helping to give linguistic shape to my inchoate sense of rage on learning of the Klan's purported involvement in the marketing of these goods.

11 Margaret Russell (1992) describes how California police use certain brand-name clothing to target minority youth. They are seen as de facto indicators of gang status in "gang profiles" that are used to justify the harassment, inter-rogation, and detainment of minority youth and as grounds for denying La-tinos and Afro-Americans entry into public amusement parks or ejecting them if they are inadvertently admitted.

12 According to Patricia Turner: "Although African-American consumers pur-chase 30 percent of all Nike shoes, blacks had no Nike executive positions, no subcontracting arrangements, and no seats on the company's board of direc-tors; moreover, the footwear giant did not advertise with black-owned media outlets. With the possible exception of such celebrity spokesmen as film direc-tor Spike Lee and basketball superstar Michael Jordan, both of whom received large sums in exchange for product endorsements, Nike simply was not shar-ing its profits with blacks" (1993:20).

13 However cynically one might view the support that tobacco companies give to African American causes, there is little doubt that such corporate donations to community public interest groups are much needed and appreciated.

14 For further discussion of the role of the trademark in the configuration of African and African American identities and the politics of the black public sphere in globalizing conditions, see Coombe and Stoller 1995.

15 The concept of hyperreality as developed by Jean Baudrillard and Umberto Eco is ably summarized in Woolley 1992:190–210.

16 The concept of the seduction used here is drawn from Baudrillard 1988b:149.

Bombs, Bikinis, and the Popes of Rock 'n' Roll: Reflections on
Resistance, the Play of Subordinations, and Liberalism in
Andalusia and Academia, 1983–1995

RICHARD MADDOX

RESISTANCE IN ACADEMIA AND ANDALUSIA

In 1986 and 1987, there was much concern with the topic of resistance within a segment of the anthropological community. In the
Department of Anthropology at Stanford University, for example, it
seemed that whenever graduate students and junior faculty members
met, they talked about struggle and domination and the tactics of
resistance that people employ in the affairs of daily life. That this was
not merely or primarily a local concern was brought home to me when
a group of visiting anthropologists, some of whom were seeking jobs,
gave a series of guest lectures that either referred to or directly focused
on how people in subordinate positions managed to oppose and evade
the predations of higher powers.[1] At the time, I too was much engaged
by the topic of resistance. I was completing an ethnohistorical disserta-
tion on tradition and hegemonic processes in Aracena, a hill town of
sixty-five hundred people in southwestern Spain, and was confronted
with the problem of how to describe the ways in which townspeople
had responded to the political, economic, and cultural liberalizations
that had occurred in the late 1970s and early 1980s, during the transition from the Franco dictatorship to parliamentary democracy. Resistance, I hoped, would be one of the keys to organizing my account
of what had been occurring in Aracena.

Unfortunately, though, the talks by visiting anthropologists were
more perplexing than helpful. Although, in my view, they demonstrated a laudable zeal to uncover seeds of hope and traces of freedom
in the mundane business of daily life, they often seemed to join to-

gether under the notion of "resistance" a disparate array of discourses and dispositions that ranged from expressions of alienated resentment to rueful complicity. Probably because I had recently been dealing with the overt revolutionary forms of resistance involved in violent anticlericalism during the Spanish Civil War, I was disturbed by their tendency to "see resistance everywhere." This tendency not only appeared to underestimate the forces operating to contain and incorporate counterhegemonic practices but also seemed to obviate the need for direct political action in some subtle way that I found difficult to accept. Even though I could often perceive the oppositional character rather than simply the alternative character of what was being described by the speakers, I was reluctant to agree with their general notions of resistance. Yet my own tendency to toe a sort of party line that devalued forms of opposition that seemed disconnected from "politics" in the common sense of the term was not particularly comforting.

In these circumstances, I decided to reexamine three different incidents that occurred in Aracena in the summer of 1983. The incidents seemed to be of the same general type in which the visiting speakers had discovered evidence of resistance, for each of them involved a perception that social boundaries were being transgressed, each provoked a response that entailed a reassertion of local values in opposition to the values of the larger society, and each reanimated traditional "sociocentric" themes that many ethnographers of Spain, beginning with Julian Pitt-Rivers (1969), have long regarded as central to understanding the character of radical social movements in Andalusia. What follows here is a summary of the incidents and my estimations of their significance or lack of it as instances of resistance. The insights gained from this discussion will provide a point of departure for an attempt to account for the prevalence of talk of resistance among anthropologists in the 1980s and to explore the prospects for critical anthropology and comparative studies of resistance in the 1990s.

CULTURAL LIBERALISM AND THE PLAY OF SUBORDINATIONS IN ARACENA, 1983

One summer morning in 1983, a garbageman in Aracena happened across a peculiar-looking box that had been deposited in the trash bin in front of the branch office of a national bank. The day before, a terrorist bomb had devastated another office of this bank in the Basque country, and the incident had been extensively reported on the television news. The trashman poked the box anxiously a few times and decided to call for the municipal police to investigate. As he waited, a group of about twenty people gathered and began to tease the increasingly embarrassed garbageman. Most of the jokes were about the unlikelihood of Aracena as a terrorist target. One man, for example, ventured the opinion that the ETA (Euskadi Ta Askatasuna) revolutionaries had finally discovered the secret submarine base of the Guardia Civil hidden under the nearby ruins of a castle. A friend of mine pointed an accusatory finger at me and loudly asked what business I had in the town—a reference to the rumor that I was a spy for the Central Intelligence Agency, a rumor that had circulated during the first weeks of my fieldwork. But despite the joking, when a police officer arrived on the scene, the crowd spontaneously backed up twenty feet or so, a distance that would have done little to protect them from the effects of an explosion but one that apparently seemed to embody a sense of caution appropriate to the occasion. Then just as the officer approached the trash bin, a young boy popped an inflated plastic bag, and the startled onlookers began to scatter in all directions. Everyone except the police officer was much amused by this. And particularly amused was the trashman, who turned the tables on the onlookers and began to taunt them for reacting so strongly to what he called "a little noise."

A week or so after the incident of the bomb (which, to be more accurate, could be called the affair of the discarded adding machine), I was involved in another matter in which a certain ambivalence prevailed about the insulation or lack of it that local people felt in relation to broader social forces. This time, the incident involved a dispute about reputation, customary propriety, and the integrity of the domestic domain. One Saturday afternoon, my wife and I accompanied Miguel, the son of a prosperous merchant and clothing distributor, to the house of his much poorer fiancée in a nearby hamlet. Our intention was to collect Miguel's fiancée, her younger brothers and sister, and her mother and drive to a nearby reservoir for an afternoon of swimming and picnicking. When we reached the hamlet, however, we encountered some reluctance on the part of the mother to carry out our plan. The mother, whom everyone called La Madrecita both because of her diminutive stature and because of her aura of childlike innocence, was sixty years old and had been widowed ten months earlier. Despite the fact that she and her husband had been estranged for several years, she had been strict about observing the long period of mourning and confinement that local custom required. Recently, she had even refused to indulge in her great passion for bullfights, choosing not to attend the *corrida* celebrated in association with Aracena's annual fair. Yet in partial surrender to the enchantment of the arena, she had persuaded her future son-in-law (Miguel) to make a home movie of the event, which she had watched in the privacy of her house; and in return for this favor, she had promised him that she would bring her period of seclusion to an end.

When the moment of truth arrived, however, La Madrecita, dressed from head to toe in traditional black as she had been for months, declared that she was not going anywhere, because, as she said, people would certainly talk. This stance infuriated her daughter, who pointed out that her mother no longer felt really saddened by the loss of her husband, that she had promised Miguel that she would resume normal life, and that it was hypocritical to maintain the appearance of mourning while she enjoyed herself in private. Her daughter's charge put La Madrecita on the defensive, but she still refused to budge. Miguel, however, unbeknownst to anyone else, had anticipated La Madrecita's stubbornness and intervened in the argument by declaring that he had a marvelous solution to the problem that would surely silence wagging tongues and still permit La Madrecita to enjoy the afternoon with her children. With this statement, he reached into a bag that he had been carrying, pulled out a bikini bathing suit, and began waving it in the air. As he repeatedly and solemnly stressed, the bikini was black and therefore was totally appropriate for the occasion. Even La Madrecita smiled at this mock concession to tradition, and amid peals of laughter from her children, she was more or less carted off to the beach. Nevertheless, once there, she kept on her mourning garb and also remained firmly tucked inside the car, saying that she preferred to stay there in her *casa,* or "house."

A certain stubbornness also characterizes the final incident I want to describe. During the town fair, a nationally famous rock band gave a concert in Aracena. Most (though not all) young people enthusiastically welcomed the concert, and the performance was a glitter rock spectacular with images from 1950s horror films and commedia dell'arte mixed in. For weeks afterward, it seemed that every bar with a youthful clientele was constantly blaring the band's songs into the streets — much to the annoyance of many of the town's older inhabitants, who were almost equally vocal in expressing their disapproval of the whole affair. Antonio Vargas, a man whose opinions on the matter were especially vehement but otherwise consistent with those of his neighbors, was particularly offended by the crowds of youths from nearby towns who had camped in the streets and plazas after the concert ended at four in the morning, and as a Communist sympathizer, he was also enraged that the Socialist town council had officially sanctioned the concert. Again and again, he denounced the whole business to anyone who would listen. One his more colorful speeches went like this:

Why did the town council bring them here? They have no public here. Those *sin vergüenzas* [shameless ones] sleeping in the streets are not from Aracena. That rock group is Basque, and they sing about drugs. . . . *Qué barbaridad!* [How barbarous!] They are nothing but an instrument of propaganda promoting drugs because they want to appear to have a special truth. They are as bad as the priests, who never stop whispering of the mysteries of the faith and obedience to the Pope. No, they are worse. They are the true anarchists *sin formalidad* [without formality, manners, and a sense of correct action or virtuous behavior], and the authorities brought them here. This is what happens in this so-called democracy. It is an abuse, and the fault is with the parents, the teachers, and the sons of whores on the town council. . . . But let me tell you, better the Pope than these degenerates with respect for nothing.

How are we to understand this diatribe and the other incidents described above? First, each of the incidents involved a sort of transgression of boundaries of the body, the home, or the community by a dominant power. In the case of the imaginary bomb, it was not Basque terrorists but televised images of carnage and destruction that penetrated the community. These images, though fleeting and commonplace, were sufficiently strong to induce a state of nervousness that led to the anxious and startled reactions to the threat of the bomb, despite almost everyone's conscious estimation that a terrorist act in Aracena was extremely unlikely. In the case of the black bikini, the home movie of the bullfight undermined the distinction between domestic and public domains, and the reference to it, as well as the sudden materialization of the black bikini itself, subverted the significance and coherence of traditional mourning customs. Finally, the local appearance of the popes of rock 'n' roll transformed a conventional folk fiesta into a performance of modernity and in so doing introduced a cleavage both within the community and within the ordinarily largely undifferentiated category of "popular culture." Thus, the "free" (or at least fluid) flow of information, commodities, and performers — a phenomenon that townspeople closely associate with the global processes of liberalization that intensified during the post-Franco period — was experienced by many townspeople as a violation of the social body.

Second, we can note a range of responses to these experiences of penetration, transgression, and violation. In the bomb incident, the response took the form of a rather weak reassertion of distance and insulation and a less than completely confident reaffirmation of reason as a tool for mocking the unlettered and anticipating the sort of events likely to occur in a town like Aracena. In the matter of the black bikini, the response of La Madrecita was somewhat stronger and more defiant because she was able to recover some of the ground she had lost by transforming her future son-in-law's car into a home away from home. In the third instance, the man who railed against the rock concert made a still stronger response. By associating the rock band with the Pope and by associating drugs with the mysteries of the faith, Antonio Vargas conveyed the message that one form of cultural hegemony that reinforced authority and discipline (the Catholic Church) was rapidly being supplanted by another form that was centered on consumption and diversion; and in so doing, he challenged conventional notions of cultural, socioeconomic, and political progress and reaction.

Third, in each of the three instances, we can recognize signs of a culture of opposition that depends, above all, on the sense of difference between the community and the larger society. Despite the manifest impact of processes of suburbanization on local life, the residual force of what Pitt-Rivers (1969:13) long ago called the principle of the "moral unity of the *pueblo*" continues to offer townspeople a way of defining their identity that is at odds with dominant contemporary modes of representation. Thus, the people who gathered during the bomb incident were convinced that it "can't happen here" because of the conditions of local life and the moral character of the townspeople; La Madrecita acted in accordance with her profound respect for her neighbors' notions of proper behavior; and Antonio Vargas continued to insist that members of the rock band were outsiders with no "public" in Aracena, ample indications to the contrary notwithstanding. From this perspective, each incident might be construed as "resistance" because it reaffirmed local values in a way that opposed them to dominant tendencies in the larger society.

But despite the common roots of these various expressions of op-

positional sociocentrism (Caro Baroja 1957) in traditional Andalusian culture, it seems to me that only Vargas's jeremiad should be
considered an instance of full-blown resistance. In their response to
the bomb threat, members of the crowd recognized cultural differences between their town and others; but along with this, their response embodied a tacit acceptance of isolation, marginality, and a
lack of autonomy and in this sense was merely reactive. La Madrecita's
defiance of her family's wishes was more active, but it was still predominantly defensive in spirit; and by reaffirming the legitimacy of the
mourning customs, she thereby committed herself to continuing her
seclusion in a way that not only reproduced oppressive notions of
women's duties but also flew in the face of her barely contained desire
to get on with her life. Thus, the first two incidents involved an accommodation to prevailing rural and national conditions, an accommodation that was facilitated rather than impeded by the cultural capacity
to oppose the local and traditional to the urbane and modern.

In contrast, Vargas's diatribe attempted to alter his listeners' sense
of the possibilities present in both tradition and modernity and to
redraw the lines of local community in terms of a strongly etched
political and cultural position. On the one hand, his invocation of the
frustrated will of the people of the community recalled and reanimated the old anarchist ideals of local autonomy that had shaped local
politics during the civil war period. On the other hand, his speech was
designed to criticize and undermine the emergent Socialist hegemony
of the town, region, and nation by directing attention to the complicity and involvement of the local Socialists with contemporary forms of
domination closely linked to the dissemination of the commodity culture of international capitalism. As a result, his speech had a defiant,
"offensive" edge to it that was more than implicit. To all who heard
it — including townspeople and not just the ethnographer — it was recognized as a challenge which was bound to antagonize sectors of the
community and which entailed some risk to Vargas's own reputation.

For these reasons, Vargas's speech can be construed as a far clearer
example of resistance than were the two other incidents described.
But the broader point is that the analysis of resistance requires the
ethnographer to consider matters from at least two points of view.
Consideration certainly must be given to the motivations and modes of
interpretation of the people immediately involved in and engaged by a
particular statement or act. But it is also necessary to make some
critical, distancing, and objectifying judgments concerning the extent

to which that act or statement represents a way in which "difference" is incorporated within hegemonic regimes, which always allow some more or less limited forms of opposition and diversity and, indeed, may well encourage and be reinforced by them.

RESISTANCE, PROFESSIONALISM, AND MULTICULTURAL LIBERALISM IN ACADEMIA, 1986–1987

With this point in mind, I will turn now to a brief consideration of why talk of resistance gained such prominence in anthropology in the mid-1980s, what the significance of the tendency of some anthropologists to "see resistance everywhere" might be, and to what extent the academic talk about resistance itself constituted a form of resistance. In exploring these questions, I will begin by considering the complex structure of feeling (Raymond Williams 1977) that appeared to exist among visiting anthropologists, graduate students, and some faculty members at Stanford at the time.

Despite the seemingly less-than-risky circumstances that prevailed within the department and university, the talks and occasional comments of this group of anthropologists seemed in many instances to be more direct and forceful expressions of resistance than were some of the actions of other people that they described in these terms. The pointedness of many of the remarks by the anthropologists and the tone in which they were delivered bespoke a commitment to the struggles of women, African Americans, Chicanos, and oppressed groups of migrants and workers within California and the United States and in more remote regions, and they also expressed open hostility and barely contained outrage toward everything "Reaganism" meant in the mid-1980s. As a result, what was said seemed at least to evoke or simulate resistance and perhaps even to enact it. From this perspective, talk of resistance could be seen as a particular way of striving to reanimate the long and worthy anthropological tradition of using the tools of research and reason to defend and support those exposed to the most oppressive aspects of the power of capital and the state. In addition, talk of resistance represented a way to express solidarity with increasing efforts within the academy to broaden the curriculum in order to overcome "Eurocentric" bias and give greater attention to non-Western and minority cultures and to use affirmative action to open up admissions and hiring procedures.

But more was involved than proclaiming allegiances to and engagement with these kinds of struggles. Talk of resistance also clearly had a specific intradisciplinary resonance and force. For many, focusing on resistance represented one of the key ways to define themselves in opposition to the supposed ills and fallacies of "value-neutral," "objectivist," and "scientistic" tendencies within anthropology. Centering ethnographic attention on resistance held forth the promise of synthesizing approaches to the study of social discourses and practices that derived both from "symbolic" or interpretive anthropology and from Marxism and political economy (see Ortner 1984). It also seemed consistent with the "postmodern" project of developing new forms of ethnographic writing that would let the voices of others be heard in ways that would constitute a powerful critique not only of conventional social science but also of dominant sociopolitical ideologies (see Marcus and Fischer 1986).

Indeed, in the anthropology department at Stanford at the time, these intellectual commitments were of more than usual academic interest because of simmering conflicts about new faculty appointments and a brewing debate about the future direction of the anthropology program as a whole. The central issue was whether new appointments should be made primarily to strengthen the department's predominantly sociocultural orientation or to lay the groundwork for developing a program in human biocultural evolution that would attract outside funding. Although a departmental schism was ultimately avoided, rhetoric and emotions ran high during this period, and the intensity of the disputes gave notions of resistance an immediate piquancy, especially for those inclined to associate an interest in human evolution with relatively "conservative" intellectual and political orientations.

It is small wonder, then, that talk of resistance was overdetermined, for it represented one of the key ways in which to forge and proclaim a complex political and intellectual identity and to condense and unify a number of somewhat disparate themes and interests. On the one hand, concern for resistance permitted anthropologists to build bridges to broader struggles both within and outside academia, and on the other hand, it offered a rallying point for what many were inclined to think of as a newly emergent critical community within the discipline of anthropology. As a result, talk of resistance not only represented a crucial point of integration for anthropological theory and practice but also had an offensive edge to it that challenged certain key aspects of dominant cultural and political arrangements.

Yet it seems to me that consideration of these positive articulations of resistance is not completely sufficient to understand either the peculiar structure of feeling involved in concerns about resistance or the tendency to "hyperpoliticize" other people's often highly ambiguous and ambivalent actions. To gain a broader sense of what was at stake in talk of resistance, it is helpful to give heed to Michel Foucault's observation (1978:27) that "silence itself — the things one declines to say, or is forbidden to name, the discretion that is required between different speakers — is less the absolute limit of discourse, the other side from which it is separated by a strict boundary, than an element that functions alongside the things said, with them and in relation to them."

From this perspective, what was left unspoken in the discourse of resistance was any critical consideration of the changing role of the university and the class position of anthropologists as professionals within academic institutions. Despite an acute awareness of the ways in which gender, race, and ethnicity have affected university life in general and individual careers in particular, those who were most interested in analyzing other people's modes of resistance nonetheless failed to reflect much on the broader ways in which many anthropologists as anthropologists are involved in academic institutions that today tend to function as virtual multinational corporations of higher learning that are crucially involved in the production and reproduction of relations of cultural and class inequality in advanced liberal societies.[2]

For one thing, there was virtual silence concerning the increasingly intense pressures of professional socialization that seem to be forcing or inducing many junior anthropologists to act as academic entrepreneurs and maximize their marketability by pursuing aggressive career strategies for building cultural capital. Such strategies are sometimes hard to distinguish from the gritty competitive individualism and smooth corporate conformism that pervade the dominant sectors of American society. For another, there was no sustained critical reflection on how anthropologists ought to understand and engage the contemporary politics of cultural diversity in the academy. Rather, there seemed to be unquestioning support for the emergent redefinition of universities as "multicultural, diverse communities" dedicated to the values of "interactive pluralism."[3] Although there were and are good reasons for endorsing many aspects of this new wave of academic liberalism, the enthusiasm with which this redefinition of the university community as a set of distinct cultural groups was being promoted in certain quarters of academic administration ought to have raised some serious questions for anthropologists. At the very least, close scrutiny ought to have been given to the apparent contradictions between the emergent definition of the academy as a multicultural community and the dominant institutional constitution of universities as highly bureaucratized and rationalized corporate structures designed to produce qualified elites. How, for example, should we regard the tendency of university officials to represent themselves as both the upholders of traditional standards of academic excellence and the benign regulators and mediators of cultural differences? And how and to what extent should anthropologists act as professional experts, consultants, or brokers for these officials? Should we envisage the postmodern university as a cosmopolitan and diverse but otherwise blind and absolute meritocracy?

The absence of much critical reflection on these matters is difficult to understand, especially in light of the fact that the great majority of those most interested in resistance were people in subaltern and insecure positions—graduate students, job seekers, and untenured faculty—whose interests in the present and future state of the profession were intensely personal, urgent, and uncertain. Yet if we follow Foucault, then this silence itself opens a new horizon for interpreting talk of resistance. From this point of view, the defiant edginess and assertiveness with which people expressed their solidarity with the struggles of subordinate groups and indicated their allegiance to a critical community of ethnographic theory and practice can in part be understood as an indirect effort to come to terms with the hegemonic pressures and constraints of professional academic life. But at least with respect to anthropology as a profession and the institutional structure of the academy, the talk of resistance probably ought to be regarded more as a means of achieving an uneasy accommodation to difficult circumstances than as a manifestation of resistance, because it failed to bring to critical consciousness its own social conditions of production. Rather, the talk of resistance attributed a will to political engagement to the incidental and often highly ambiguous actions of distant others, and in doing this it tended to locate the truly critical sites of struggle elsewhere. As a result, the discussions of resistance were not recognized by other members of the academy as a serious challenge to their own professional policies and practices. Moreover, the displacement of the will to resist onto others tended to disenable the people most directly concerned with political engagement from giving voice to specific aspects of their own situation of subordination. From this perspective, the talk of resistance was less a sign of a willingness to take up arms than a symptom of an alienating and repressive sublimation.

But in stating this rather extreme and negative view of the significance of what Lila Abu-Lughod (1990) has called the "romance of resistance" that existed in the mid-1980s in American anthropology, my intention is not to disparage the importance of commitments to continuing struggles within the academy. Rather, it is to stress that there are few (if any) "pure" acts of resistance and that because of the multidimensionality of relations of power, the heteroglossia of ordinary speech, and, perhaps most crucial, those things that are left unsaid and undone, it is necessary to consider how opposition to one form of domination may involve complicity with or greater vulnerability to others. To bring out the complexity of this play of subordinations and resistance, it is essential to consider the silences and the unacknowledged and unintended consequences that accompany even the most explicit, challenging, and dramatic political acts.

RESISTANCE IN ANDALUSIA AND AMERICAN ACADEMIA IN THE 1980S AND PROSPECTS FOR CRITICAL ANTHROPOLOGY IN THE 1990S

Points similar to those outlined above have been persuasively made by Sherry Ortner in the review article "Resistance and the Problem of Ethnographic Refusal" (1995). In this essay, Ortner criticizes investigations in anthropology and cultural studies for their failure to provide adequate contextualization of forms of resistance. According to Ortner, the lack of ethnographic "density" and the neglect of holistic perspectives have led to discussions that are politically "sanitized" and "culturally thin." To counter these liabilities, Ortner calls for work which better distinguishes "creative" and "transformative" resistance from other forms of cultural and sociopolitical opposition and which also reveals "the ambivalences and ambiguities of resistance itself" (190–91).

Yet as valuable as Ortner's suggestions are, it is doubtful that good ethnographic intentions and conscientiousness alone will be sufficient to meet the challenge that studying contemporary forms of resistance poses. As my juxtaposition of events in Andalusia and events in American anthropology during the 1980s is intended to illustrate and reflect, not only is understanding the nature of resistance in any particular place a complex matter, but multifaceted and shifting circuits of relations also condition and interlink how ethnographers represent to themselves and others what is going on both "out there" in "the field" and "back home" in the academy. Thus, to construct more compelling accounts of resistance would seem to require more than just a commitment to doing better ethnography "out there," because ambiguity and ambivalence also often characterize the anthropologists' situation at home in ways that are likely to influence and at times seem to condition rather strongly what is being understood as resistance. For this reason, we also need to cultivate an ability to participate in anthropology and the life of the academy and simultaneously to observe it with the same sorts of holistic concerns and systematic rigor that we strive to bring to our investigations of the relations between cultural discourses and sociopolitical practices in the field.

In other words, as we go about our work, we should also continually consider how it is being affected by our identities as subjects and agents of various sorts of cultural and sociopolitical authority in academic and other contexts. To cultivate such a critical stance is, of course, no easy matter and may lead to a kind of self-absorbed introspection that runs the risk of being as frustrating as it is ultimately unproductive. Probably the best way to avoid this, however, is to develop broad synthetic and comparative perspectives that will enable us to understand better the nature of the connections and divergences between our own varying political and cultural situations as anthropologists and those of others elsewhere.

One such comparative perspective that is implied, though not developed, in the discussions above would involve analyzing the manifestations of resistance in Aracena, American anthropology, and elsewhere in the 1980s as episodes in the global history of political, economic, and cultural liberalism. From this perspective, much of the explanation for the divergent expressions and characteristic strengths and weaknesses of resistance in Andalusia and American academia would lie in the differing ways in which the two places were integrated into particular liberal regimes. Thus, it was perhaps primarily because Aracena was a marginal, relatively isolated, and homogeneous town in one of the poorest regions of western Europe that asserting a highly localized form of tradition-based cultural autonomy seemed for many townspeople to be a viable and desirable possibility in the early 1980s. But the town's very insulation probably also contributed to the greatest weakness in its prevailing styles of resistance: the lack of any practical ideas about how to restructure a politicoeconomic order in which liberal ideals of freedom of choice, freedom of expression, and so forth were increasingly being invoked in ways that expanded the capacity of corporate and state technobureaucratic elites to regulate social life. In contrast, in American academia, it was largely because universities were already relatively diverse, liberal institutions that expressions of solidarity with broader struggles, coupled with specific demands for the inclusion of underrepresented groups and perspectives, held forth such promise for change both within the university and within the larger society. Yet while the movements within American academia suffered from no shortage of concrete proposals for broadening participation in campus life and reworking the curriculum, they demonstrated a perhaps excessive (and characteristically liberal) faith in the strategy of "winning concessions" from other more or less enlightened and progressive professionals in positions of power, and they did not involve much effort to increase faculty or institutional autonomy in ways that would reduce the vulnerability of reform movements to external pressures and constraints.

Such an approach to the comparative analysis of resistance appears promising for a number of reasons. For one thing, it would enable us to understand better why it appears so often to be the case that the strengths of one form of opposition and resistance are the weaknesses of another, and it would thereby help us to guard against whatever inclinations we may have either to inflate the importance of or to underestimate the force of particular forms of resistance. It would also help us to avoid lapsing into extreme forms of ethnographic particularism that revel only in "difference." Most important, developing such comparative modes of analysis might well lead us to explore new ways of thinking about the relationship of ourselves and others to contemporary processes of globalization and redifferentiation that are affecting the dynamics of domination and resistance virtually everywhere these days.

For critical anthropologists to reach these goals, however, steps have to be taken to correct what remains the discipline's most glaring weakness: the refusal to "study up." There have been many calls for this (for example, Marcus and Fischer 1986:137–38) and some important work in the anthropology of science, medicine, law, development, and other fields; but ethnographic and comparative literature on traditional dominant groups and classes, particularly Western ones or ones influenced by the West, does not fill many library shelves, and culturally complex and sociologically focused accounts of the "new classes" of officials, experts, scientists, bureaucrats, policymakers, planners, and executives are even rarer. The huge present imbalance in the discipline in favor of studies of resistance and the broader politics of identity among subaltern groups inevitably skews our understanding of the contemporary world because it makes it difficult, if not impossible, to trace and analyze the linkages between what is going on in places near the top and centers of the global pecking order and what is happening in sites near the bottom and on the margins. Thus, much more investigation is needed on topics such as how new elites, who are increasingly cosmopolitan and global in their perspectives, are being recruited, trained, and disciplined; how the technobureaucracies of states, transnational corporations, and the auxiliary organizations that support them operate from day to day; how various groupings of experts and specialists communicate with one another across cultural and occupational boundaries; and how objectified forms of knowledge and instrumental rationalities are employed to generate strategies, policies, technologies, and products that affect the lives of millions.

In the absence of more detailed ethnographic knowledge of such matters, the already pronounced tendency in studies of domination and resistance to rely too heavily on abstractions about late capitalism, Eurocentrism, technoscapes and mediascapes, power/knowledge relations, and similar concepts when discussing the broader contexts that condition local events will be likely to continue. Yet to understand better both the pressures and the constraints shaping the development of anthropology as a discipline and also to be better able to trace the ambiguities, limits, and potentialities of contemporary forms of resistance and opposition, nothing can really substitute for ethnographic, comparative, and synthetic work that directly addresses all the complexities and contradictions of what there is to resist in the "New World Order." If critical anthropologists neglect this crucial task, then instead of being able to take a message to the streets with Antonio Vargas, we will continually find ourselves in one or the other of three situations: rummaging through the odds and ends of daily life looking for bombs where none in fact exist; locked in the car with La Madrecita in order to defend our own virtue; or enthralled by the latest popes of rock 'n' roll and jumping to someone else's postmodern beat.

NOTES

For comments on earlier versions of this paper, I am grateful to Akhil Gupta, Mark Handler, James Ferguson, Peter Kivisto, Andrea Klimt, Claudio Lomnitz, Tom Lutz, Sharon Keller Maddox, Michael Taussig, and anonymous reviewers and am especially grateful to Roger Rouse. Research in Spain from 1980 through 1995 has been supported by grants from the Commission for Educational Exchange between the United States of America and Spain, the Social Science Research Council and the American Council of Learned Societies, the National Science Foundation (grant number BNS 8107146), the Program for Cooperation between Spain's Ministry of Culture and United States' Universities, and the Wenner-Gren Foundation for Anthropological Research. Any opinions, findings, and conclusions or recommendations expressed in this publication are those of the author and do not necessarily reflect the views of the people or agencies acknowledged above.

1   The published literature on resistance is large and growing in anthropology and other disciplines. But rather than focusing on published works, in this essay I focus on the oral culture of anthropology. I have avoided citing the particulars of who said what and when in informal talks and exchanges, because it would be counterproductive and pointless to hold individuals responsible for works in progress. To gain some sense of the range of the work that was being done on resistance in the mid-1980s, readers may wish to consult de Certeau 1984; Limón 1989; Martin 1987; and James Scott 1985. In their fine critical essays on resistance, Lila Abu-Lughod (1990) and Sherry Ortner (1995) cite a broader sample of the literature on the subject.

2   For extended and highly illuminating discussions about the university as an institution of social and cultural production and reproduction in France, see Bourdieu 1984 and 1988.

3   The phrases "multicultural, diverse communities" and "interactive pluralism" were the primary ones being used to describe the project of academic redefinition at Stanford University in the 1980s. A glance at almost any edition of the *Chronicle of Higher Education* from this period reveals that identical or virtually equivalent terminology was being used by many universities and colleges in the United States.

The Remaking of an Andalusian Pilgrimage Tradition: Debates Regarding Visual (Re)presentation and the Meanings of "Locality" in a Global Era

MARY M. CRAIN

Recent scholarship has focused on the mastery of the visual, and vision has often been deemed the privileged sense in both modern and postmodern culture (Clifford 1986a; Hal Foster 1988; Fabian 1983; Pollock 1988). According to Luce Irigaray (cited in Owens 1983:70): "More than the other senses, the eye objectifies and masters. It sets at a distance." Irigaray has argued that in Western culture, "the predominance of the look over smell, taste, touch, hearing, has brought about an impoverishment of bodily relations." She notes that "the moment that the look dominates, the body loses its materiality."[1]

Dick Hebdige (1994), Fredric Jameson (1984), and Hal Foster (1985) have drawn attention to the recent shift under conditions of late capitalism in the West from societies based on "production" to those increasingly oriented toward "consumption." With the onset of the era of consumption, the cultural sphere is no longer granted a relative autonomy. Instead, the cultural realm undergoes further expansion and is commodified, as economic privilege is replaced by a semiotic privilege in which we consume the coded differences of commodity signs (Foster 1985:171–73). In his analysis of this new cultural moment of postmodernism accompanying late capitalism, Jameson (1983:125) also foregrounds the field of vision, arguing for the emergence of a social order marked by "the transformation of reality into images" and by a "surface culture of appearances."[2] Similarly, Jean Baudrillard (1988c) has commented on the regulating power of "the image" and "media codes" in formulating what passes for "the real" in contemporary consumer societies. Domination proceeds through the appropriation of significations of other groups as elites strive to control signification through the monopoly of the code. Subaltern groups resist domination and the systematizing logic of the code through a bricolage that makes a parody of the privileged signs of class, race, gender, and nation. Such critical activity calls attention to the arbitrary and artificial character of the code and may reveal a symbolic disaffection with it (Foster 1985:170).

What does it mean to be a member of a "local community" in such a world of simulations and commodified differences? If, as many have argued, even the most peripheral and "out of the way" places (Tsing 1993) are increasingly caught up in a transnational, mass-mediated social reality (Appadurai 1992), how does this change the way in which such things as locality and community themselves are lived and understood? Objects of urban nostalgia, putative sites of a disappearing "real," rural communities frequently find their sign value becoming their chief economic asset, their very "localness" a packageable good to be served up to the touristic gaze (Urry 1990) that, in a hypercommodified "society of the spectacle" (Debord 1983), remains ever hungry for novelty, difference, and authenticity. But local actors are never simply the passive victims of such processes of commoditization and specularization. For when locality and community themselves begin to appear as simulations, the stage is set for a complex and elaborate symbolic politics, a politics in which, as I hope to show, resistance can take diverse forms and varied tactical paths.

I will illustrate the links between visual representation, mass media, and the constitution of locality by examining the case of the Andalusian pilgrimage tradition of El Rocío that is celebrated in rural Spain. During the past three decades the mass media and the tourist industry, as well as new social groups, have become increasingly implicated in this event, initiating its transformation from a local *romería* (religious pilgrimage) to a festival with regional, national and secular dimensions. The rite falls within the purview of "public culture" as formulated by Arjun Appadurai and Carol Breckenridge (1988b:5–9) and draws attention to "global cultural flows" and the increasingly interpenetrating spheres of modern cultural life. Similar to William Kelly's (1990:65) analysis of Noh festivity in Japan, El Rocío registers "the cross talk" of permeable spheres in which "the national culture of the state, a mass culture of the media, subordinate regional culture," and, in this case, also village all claim this tradition as their own (compare Appadurai and Breckenridge 1988b).

As part of "the worlding" of this pilgrimage, a ritual that formerly confirmed community and subregional identities, images typically associated with the event are now teletransported by the culture industries across a much vaster spatial terrain. Separated from their historical and social context and reformulated in new settings, such refashioned images often conflict with local imaginings of community as it is presently defined. While internally differentiated along class, gender, and generational lines, village culture in the area of Andalusia considered here is characterized by a staunch localism and a sense of singularity in which villagers imagine themselves residing at "the moral center of the universe" (Caro Baroja in J. C. Mitchell 1987:3; compare Driessen 1989). A traditional distrust of both neighboring villages and broader entities, such as the nation-state, informs this orientation of village autonomy (compare Pitt-Rivers 1974).

I begin by focusing on the ways in which the media and tourist industries have represented the rite as a site of consumption and in doing so have often privileged the field of vision. I outline the ways in which particular visual regimes insinuate themselves as new forms of domination within the context of the ritual. This is followed by a consideration of the transformational processes reshaping the pilgrimage itself as the rite has evolved from being an event primarily for pilgrims to a mass event with a more heterogeneous audience, largely concentrated at the shrine. The number of people who participate in only one portion of the pilgrimage, that of the shrine, has grown enormously. That has created an incipient contrast between a large audience of tourist-spectators who arrive at the shrine primarily to view the ritual and "the *rocieros,*" those individuals who undertake a rigorous pilgrimage to the shrine. The analysis that follows illustrates how the romería presently serves as an arena in which competing sacred and secular discourses intersect, as the rite holds divergent meanings for distinct audiences. Finally, I examine the manner in which pilgrims from the Andalusian community of Marisol (pseudonym) respond to this transformation by negotiating the dominant meanings assigned to the event. With regard to the field of vision, I demonstrate that in certain instances the pilgrims divest the new visual modes of domination of their primacy in order to emphasize dialogue and touch. In other instances, the local sense of visuality is grounded in bodily forms that resist appropriation. What is at stake in these struggles, I will show, is not only how one ritual is to be experienced and interpreted but also how the meaning of membership in a local community may itself be transformed and reconfigured through the encounter with the specularizing tourist gaze (Urry 1990).

ETHNOGRAPHIC CONTEXT: THE PILGRIMAGE OF EL ROCÍO

The pilgrimage to the shrine of El Rocío, located in the Spanish region of Andalusia some sixty-five kilometers south of Seville, consists of a cult to the Virgin Mary, who is referred to in this context as the Virgin of El Rocío. One authoritative account holds that, during the thirteenth century, Alfonso X, king of Castile, ordered that a primitive sanctuary be constructed at the site and that a sculpted icon of the Virgin be placed inside (Archives of the Hermandad Matríz). Popular accounts dating from the fifteenth century, however, claim that the Virgin of El Rocío appeared before either a lowly shepherd or a hunter, who found her hidden in a wild olive tree in a dense thicket of the *marismas* (the area of marshlands created by the Guadalquivir River). According to the latter accounts, a brotherhood devoted to the Virgin was founded in the nearby town of Almonte, and a chapel was built at the site where the miraculous icon first appeared. In the late seventeenth century, filial brotherhoods representing distinct communities from Lower Andalusia, each subordinate to the founding brotherhood of Almonte, were formed. Every spring, during the holy day of the Pentecost, the brotherhoods make a pilgrimage to the shrine, each following its own itinerary. Referred to as *el camino*, this journey is a strenuous undertaking of seven to eight days, with three days lapsing between departure from the home community and arrival at the shrine, followed by two days spent at the shrine and then three days to travel home. Each community carries along its own banner bearing an emblem of the Virgin, traveling on foot, horseback, and in jeeps and covered wagons. In May 1989, the first year that I accompanied some forty families from Marisol to the shrine, there were a total of seventy-eight brotherhoods.[3]

During the celebration at the shrine there are endless processions of brotherhoods filing according to seniority, before both the icon of the Virgin and the members of the Almonte religious hierarchy. Individual pilgrims attend mass and leave candles for the Virgin. Amid the aroma of home-cooked foods, people mill around, eat with friends, and renew acquaintanceships. This is followed by drinking and dancing and perhaps four hours of sleep, and then, in a dizzying flurry, the whole process begins anew.

The climax of the celebration occurs between Sunday night and the Pentecost, which falls on Monday. Sunday night is the vigil during which no one sleeps, as the entire crowd waits for hours until the Virgin is brought out of the chapel. The Virgin's entrance into public space carries potentially dangerous implications, as church official-dom has less control over the icon and she is embraced as "the peo-ple's Virgin." Arms and bodies struggle to touch her and many gasp for breath in this harrowing process. The pilgrims begin their dia-logue with her fetishized figure shouting Andalusian *piropos* (compli-ments) such as, "Viva la Virgen de las Marismas!" (Long live the Virgin of the Marshlands!). As soon as the icon exits the church, it is swept through the streets by young Almonteño men. Numbering over one million in 1989, the expectant, heterogenous crowd included the cus-tomary group of pilgrims devoted to the Virgin but also a much larger group of tourist-spectators as well as film crews.

READING REPRESENTATIONS OF EL ROCÍO:
EXOTIC SPAIN OR BARBAROUS CULT?

Contemporary mass media representations of the celebration of El Rocío — and, by extension, of the surrounding region of Andalusia — construct two quite different images of the region and the rite itself. The first image is that of an exotic and frontier Spain with which elites and certain sectors of the growing middle class seek to identify. Thus, the traditions of flamenco dancing, sevillanas-style dress, and *peñas rocieras* (bars typical of El Rocío) have become coveted by the rest of Spain (*International Herald Tribune* 1989:11). The surge in popularity of "things Andalusian" has been further abetted by the fact that the head of Spain's Socialist government as well as many of his cabinet members are Andalusians. Thus markers of Andalusian identity have been appropriated by trendsetters in non-Andalusian settings and have been converted into signifiers of distinction. Such signifiers have also entered into a transnational circuit of prestige forms, evinced in the current French, Swiss, and British fascination with Andalusian music and fashion. Foreign interest was further encouraged by the government's decision to locate the 1992 World's Fair in Seville, the capital of the region.[4]

In the rhetoric of the national press, the celebration of El Rocío itself is glamorously depicted as a place to be seen, where one can rub shoulders with members of the royal family, bankers, politicians, bull-

fighters, and celebrities, such as Julio Iglesias (García 1988:23).[5] At
the same time, travel posters from state tourism offices underscore the
"return to tradition" that the festival is said to epitomize. The images
presented in these posters are often nostalgic ones providing visions of
a slower way of life, rooted in the rural village, where oxcarts still
appear as a mode of transport. Scenes of nature that depict the Virgin
encircled in a grove of pine trees are also frequently portrayed. These
visual representations offer a seductive contrast to the saturated ar-
teries of Spain's major cities, which are often choked with cars. Such
images work ideologically as an "other" and appeal to an emergent
middle-class ideology in Spain. El Rocío is offered as an escape fantasy,
a place to go to get away from it all (Romero 1989:27–30).[6]

In recent Spanish history, abandonment of rural areas, rapid social
change, the growing urbanization of the nation's population, as well as
the contamination of the environment have created a nostalgia for
rural roots and traditions, especially among upwardly mobile groups.
The increased presence of such urbanites during the past decade at El
Rocío is partially the result of the "economic boom" sweeping Spain
that has fueled a rise in domestic tourism. The traditions of the rural
village and its reputed integrative mechanism remain a source of longing for at least some urban dwellers, as the experience of face-to-face
relations in the village still forms part of their personal memories.

However, the growing popularity of El Rocío is not only the result of
the arrival of urbanites from all over Spain. It must also be explained
in the light of the cultural politics of "the New Spain," of the period of
the democratic transition (1975–present). This period has been characterized by movements of regional autonomy in which regional elites
and the middle and working classes have fashioned a self-conscious
politics of identity vis-à-vis the central state. Aiming to "decenter" the
hegemony of diffusive national culture, these groups underscore internal differences and the plurinational composition of contemporary
Spain (compare Comelles 1991; Moreno 1985). They have promoted
the revival of many regional traditions that Franco's iron-handed policies often erased. Thus there has been a ubiquitous call in contemporary Spain for the recuperation of "authentic" festive traditions, distinct from those exalted under Castilian hegemony, a process that
to some degree implies the reinvention of these regional traditions
(compare Crain in press and Hobsbawm and Ranger 1983). Thus
Andalusians of various persuasions are increasingly drawn to El Rocío,

for this rite has become a secular emblem, an important marker of Andalusian regional identity and cultural pride.

The second image of Andalusia and the pilgrimage carries more negative connotations and portrays both the region and the rite as signifiers of lack. Rather than being used to represent all Spain, this image is often concealed from the outside gaze. In this narrative mode, contemporary Andalusia is the economically backward south where gypsies and bandits are known to roam. Instead of emphasizing the region's proximity to Europe, this representation stresses its position as the gateway to the Third World, to the Arab nations, to black Africa, and to Latin America. This alternative Andalusia plays an important structural role in the discourse on Spain and provides an image against which other regions of Spain may define themselves in favorable terms. As Spain charges forward to enter the European Economic Community, Andalusia is characterized by officials in both Madrid and Andalusia as the primary sight/site of "economic and cultural lag," as that region which is not quite "up to European standards" (Dale 1988:1, 17). In keeping with these dominant representations, the pilgrimage of El Rocío itself often evokes an image of a collective "blowout," of an extravaganza in "the south" in which the work ethic is undermined by excessive merrymaking on the part of festive devotees. Similarly, the rite is referred to as the scene of "collective madness," as a barbarous and passionate cult characterized by irrational extremes and latent violence (García 1988:23). What is implied is that the event is a national embarrassment, a *mancha*, or "stain," best kept a deep, dark secret (compare Dubisch 1988; Herzfeld 1986).

A WORLD TRANSFORMED: ON VIEWING VIRGINS AND THE RECONSTRUCTION OF HERITAGE

Some thirty-five years ago, the site of El Rocío was a sleepy hamlet where stood the sanctuary that housed the Virgin. Surrounded by the marismas, few people lived near the shrine on a permanent basis. During the late 1950s, however, a public road traversing this area was finally completed. By the 1960s the shrine had been declared an official tourist site, which thereby allowed the Spanish nation to reaffirm its association with one of the country's most widely visited shrines. Linking regional and microlevel heritages with "the national," such a policy enabled the state to lay claim to the lengthy history of this tradition, thereby underscoring both "the eternal" and the quasi-sacred character of the Spanish nation (compare Hobsbawm and Ranger 1983). Furthermore, by rooting national culture in "the popular," in the festive traditions of El Rocío as celebrated in numerous Andalusian villages, the reigning Franquist government sought an identification of such municipalities with the projects of the state (compare Crain 1990).

Although pilgrims have traveled to this site since at least the fifteenth century, the majority of people attending the romería today are not pilgrims but spectators of primarily domestic but also foreign extraction. Partially to accommodate this tourist boom, the old sanctuary was demolished in 1963 and replaced in 1969 by a more spacious chapel. During the past fifteen years, tourist shops have been built near the shrine, restaurants now proliferate, and luxury condominiums are being completed (compare *El País* 1990). Some seventeen kilometers to the south, an international beach resort was opened during the 1970s. Such profound transformations in local spatial relations have been effected largely by the intervention of three secular agencies: the municipal council of Almonte, the tourism office of Almonte, and the Junta de Andalusia (a regional governing body). Plan Romero represents the coordinated activities of these three agencies, activities that complement those of the founding brotherhood of Almonte in the realization of this rite. In line with the guidelines of Plan Romero, the area near the shrine was reorganized in 1979 with "zones for new housing opened, a town hall constructed and electrical services, telephones and sanitary facilities installed for the first time" (Comelles 1991:23). Such improvements promoted the growth of the romería as a mass event for tourists.

Beginning with the assertion that "our culture needs constructs of difference to signify itself at all," Judith Williamson (1986:101) has underscored the relentless search of the contemporary culture industries for new areas to colonize, zones that will enable them to capture "difference" and recode it for mass cultural consumption. Enticed by media depictions of El Rocío which identify it with difference and which redefine the rite both as a site of historical tourism and as an encounter with the natural wilderness surrounding the shrine, cosmopolitan urbanites of both Andalusian and non-Andalusian extraction who are attracted to the transformed space of the contemporary Rocío seek to construct more satisfying images of themselves. As trendsetters, they are concerned with the presentation of self, embodied in "the look," and they establish novel patterns of consumption that distinguish them from others at the sanctuary. At present they keep the fashion industry busy delivering the latest in sevillaña-style clothing, which can be displayed at the annual event. These urbanites rent the newly constructed houses, whereas those who built the houses sleep in the alleyways and augment their income by renting their homes (Comelles 1984). Although the majority of pilgrims sleep on the ground or in buildings owned by the brotherhoods and have never paid for a place to sleep, the new housing may rent for as much as one thousand U.S. dollars for the celebration.

In 1989 when I accompanied the Marisoleños on their pilgrimage, I found that when we arrived at the shrine, 226 representatives of the media, from such diverse corners of the world as Spain, Japan, Germany, France, Brazil, and the United States, were already on hand and ready to broadcast this event worldwide. On asking an Almonteño for official information regarding this year's celebration, I was escorted to the press office, which had been set up in the chapel, adjacent to the altar housing the Virgin. There I was issued a press packet containing a map, a program of scheduled events, and a glossy commercial brochure advertising an upcoming pilgrimage to Rome. I was told to come back the next day for an appointment. I began to feel as though my entire experience was being mediated by the communications industry and was painfully reminded of Jean Baudrillard's (1988c:167) argument that we are suffering from "a gradual loss of the real."

These sentiments were confirmed when I stopped at a tourist shop near the church. The young couple who owned the store, which had been in operation for less than one year, were ensconced in the back room of their shop. Wandering back there to see what was going on, I found the couple glued to the television set watching "live coverage" of the pilgrimage. They were more fascinated with watching how they were being represented visually than they were in stepping outside their door where the pilgrimage was unfolding all around them. Thus, the Pentecostal pilgrimage at El Rocío, which Marisoleños spend all year preparing for and which they regard to be their ritual home, has been partially turned into a media spectacle.

The spectacle, as analyzed by Guy Debord (1983:24), "is the existing order's uninterrupted discourse about itself." In his analysis he places power at the root of the spectacle, arguing that both human relations as well as the administration of society are increasingly mediated by a communications industry that is "unilateral." In such a context, which presupposes the existence of the modern state, dialogue is interrupted and "capital is accumulated to such a degree that it becomes an image" (Debord 1983:10). Similarly Hal Foster (1985:80) argues that "the spectacle works as a simulated reality, ... [and as] ... a set of effects that replaces the primary event." In this new visual regime the active agency of participants is replaced by the passive consumption of images by spectators.

The extent of this shift toward "the spectacular" and the conflict it provoked among the pilgrims were illustrated with particular force on Monday morning at 2:00 A.M. when the Virgin was taken out of the church by the young Almonteño men. In a manner different from what I had experienced during the previous year, this climactic moment was interrupted by an army of TV camera operators, who positioned themselves between the Virgin and the crowd, thereby cutting off the public's access to the sacred. Many became furious as it was disclosed that the church hierarchy of Almonte had allocated the media a first shot at filming the Virgin before she was passed on later to an impatient crowd. Two people panned a camera shot across the crowd, toward several women of Marisol who stood beside me. One of the women raised her hand in front of her face, attempting to deter the operator's gaze and shouting in disgust, "This is not the movies, this is the Rocío!"

SIGN SYSTEMS COLLIDE: REFLECTIONS ON THE JOURNEY HOME

Sophisticated urbanites who have recently been arriving at El Rocío in large numbers are drawn to the rite for several reasons. For some, it forms part of their search for knowable communities in a world characterized by constant change. For these individuals El Rocío constitutes a stable reference point on their calendar, an annual event where they always encounter someone they know. Many informants said they identified with this rite because it offered them the chance to be part of a community in which hospitality extends even to strangers. Although such urbanites do not participate in the rite to the degree that pilgrims do, they are occasionally invited to have a drink with pilgrims at the shrine. Thus, it is not unreasonable to argue that "spontaneous communitas" characterizes their experience of the rite (Victor Turner 1969). Somewhat paradoxically, however, it is often these very individuals who are responsible for bringing new distinctions to the fore within the context of the ritual itself. Other urbanites are drawn to the colorful and folkloric display of the pilgrims and reported their attraction to the play dimension of this celebration. They regarded it as a ludic space in which licentious behavior can be flaunted and everyday conventions subverted. But this sense of community is in conflict with the one espoused by many people of Marisol.

Through their participation in this rite, Marisoleños assert their collective identity to themselves and vis-à-vis a larger world (compare Christian 1972). The local parameters that define village identity posit a ritual community in the restrictive sense, one whose boundaries, while permeable, do not extend to include spectators whose involvement is limited to their yearly appearance at the shrine. Villagers claim that this portion of the romería is now part of a tourist and media circuit, and many lament the commodification that has overtaken the festivities. The two days spent at the shrine, which formerly provided them with a sense of community, are now the subject of contention, and there is nostalgia regarding the Rocío of bygone years.

When trying to describe their new predicament, Marisoleños often have recourse to the terms "we insiders" as distinct from the *forasteros* (the outsiders), with the latter often glossed as the "yupeez" (yuppies) or the "tourists." In this context, "insiders" refers to individuals from the brotherhood of Marisol as well as to members of the other brotherhoods.[7] The primary distinction sustained is between "rocieros," the pilgrims who undertake the camino, and the "outsiders," spectators present at the shrine who do not. But as Kelly's analysis (1990) of Ōgi festivity demonstrates, distinctions between "insiders" and "outsiders," between members of a rural periphery and denizens of an incorporating metropolitan center, can be deceptive, for the boundaries between these categories are constantly shifting.

In the case of El Rocío, in the three different instances that follow, "outsiders" are also *inside,* just as the center is also *in* the periphery. The first instance is related to the fact that local communities such as Marisol now surpass any fixed sociospatial coordinates within the Andalusian terrain. As participants in what Roger Rouse (1991) refers to as a "transnational migrant circuit," many Marisoleños migrated to northern Spain or to central Europe during the 1940s and subsequently in search of jobs. Therefore, some members of the brotherhood, although born in Marisol, now reside in distant metropolitan centers outside Andalusia. In the second instance, membership in the brotherhood has expanded in recent years to include a small number

of "outsiders" who demonstrate a willingness to "do the camino."
Individuals falling into this category in 1989 included three persons
from Bilbao and Barcelona as well as a pair of emigrants who had
recently returned to Marisol. During the course of the camino, as the
behavior of these individuals came to approximate that of the cosmopolitan spectators at the shrine, "the locals" began to refer to this
group as yupeez. Finally, analysis of the pilgrimage within an international frame also blurs the insider/outsider opposition, because certain powerful insiders have been complicit in the marketing of the
pilgrimage to metropolitan concerns. As a result of the cooperation of
these insiders, during the decade of the 1980s the surveying eye of the
camera operator's gaze was increasingly focused on the pilgrimage, as
state television from Madrid as well as international film crews became
the new protagonists in the making of this cultural production (Comelles 1991; compare Pratt 1986). The landscape surrounding the
shrine was also prized open by transnational firms during this conjuncture, and local producers and residents were displaced, as agricultural commodities, such as strawberries and carnations, were exported
to central European markets and nearby beaches were developed for a
growing national and foreign tourist market (Crain 1996).

How do Marisol pilgrims deflect these processes of change that are
transforming ritual life as they know it? What form can resistance take
to the monopoly of the code? As an extreme reaction to the transformation, several pilgrims refused to participate in any of the shrine-
related activities and remained inside the brotherhood's building during the entire time, whereas others argued for the lengthening of the
camino portion of the romería. Feeling unable to confront the agencies of change at El Rocío, by and large, Marisol pilgrims accommodate to this transformed event at the shrine itself. While the Virgin, the
figure of their devotion, remains there, the pilgrims' energies have
been primarily divested and directed elsewhere, away from the sanctuary toward a concern for everyday practices associated with their participation in the camino, in which they carry their emblem of the
Virgin along the dusty trails.

The people of Marisol have taken their religion away from the "official church," out of the hands of the travel agents and back to the land
that harbors its own forms of spirituality. Through their pilgrimages
across the years, Marisoleños link their identity with a particular place,
the marismas, and aim to redeem a past as well as a present through
the emblem of the Virgin. They retrace those paths that mark the

entire marismas as a sacred space by remembering the names of the places and the acts associated with those places — for example, the baptisms at the Quema River and the midnight masses held in the pine groves at Colinas. They await the embrace of those worn but smiling faces of elderly villagers who gather to meet them at hamlets along their route. Such actions contrast with "the placelessness" accorded to "the tourist," those spectators in need of maps. Following the equivalence characteristic of a logic of capitalist exchange, the latter will move on in search of the next Rocío-like event to attend, convinced that "the past" can be recaptured in such sacred sites.

Unlike the new audience at the shrine, the Marisoleños harbor a religious discourse of interiority that values signs of "the invisible" as well as those of an exterior, "visible world." As one pilgrim explained, "We carry our religion inside us, it is in our hearts, in our homes and in the relationships we form with one another, both while on the trail and off it." Just as Julie Taylor (1982:305) has argued that traditional *sambistas* of Rio de Janeiro's *favelas* "live the samba" and that their social identity is shaped by the forms of communal association that the dance engenders, in Marisol the cult of the Virgin provides the self with a matrix of perceptions that orient everyday life. The vows which Marisoleños make to the Virgin and which prompt their journey are invisible and unmediated pacts. According to the logic of a discourse of interiority, one's outward appearance becomes partially disengaged from those dominant codes that flaunt fashion and "style," for the pilgrim's body is often caked with dust, with sweat trickling down during the hot afternoons on the trail. In this context, "the visual" is only one aspect of a multidimensional experience in which dialogue and touch often gain priority. Here, pilgrims' bodies become sites of religiosity — men and women sacrifice their bodies by undergoing hardships on the trail. This body is not a floating image or a product of a surface culture of appearance but is materially grounded in specific gendered practices. Women often walk arm in arm behind the icon of the Virgin, and they speak to her with affection. They continue dialogues begun in the interior of their homes, where they commonly discuss their problems with her. Men are said to pray with their muscles, and physical strength, an attribute deemed characteristic of the male body, is required to maneuver the enormous oxen that propel the icon of the Virgin across the landscape.

Marisol pilgrims en route to El Rocío are positioned as "decentered subjects" and are reminded on numerous occasions that the individual self is a construct determined by a larger collectivity. People are bound together by the mutual responsibility of the trail in which all must move together and none can be left behind. During the camino pilgrims can more readily engage those practices characteristic of "outsiders" that have penetrated even this portion of the romería. Although yelling at TV camera operators seems unlikely to produce positive results, in a small face-to-face community, such as the camino, there are greater possibilities for overruling a new behavior. On the return trip to Marisol, the pilgrims crack jokes that mock "the look" and the airs put on by those self-styled "senoritos" of the 1980s, the yupeez with their individualistic ways and their peculiar eating disorders, as those who dine on nouvelle cuisine are said to eat skimpily and pathetically, like "crickets."

Those individuals who were deemed yupeez by Marisoleños during the camino of 1989 were a mixed group. They consisted of several sophisticated urbanites, such as a lawyer from Bilbao and two designers from Barcelona. Having never lived in Marisol, these individuals were along on the camino thanks to the goodwill of certain Marisol families who agreed to bring them. Although urbanites may persist in their attempts to "undertake the camino" in the future and thereby relish their experience of an "authentic Rocío," at present there are built-in constraints that limit their involvement, given that bringing another person along poses a burden for the Marisoleños (compare Urry 1990). The latter must carry more supplies, cook for, and attend to the needs of these "guests." Most Marisol families do not want to be bothered with this responsibility. Another prosperous married couple, also labeled "yupeez," reside in Seville. In contrast to the preceding individuals, these two people are actually members of the brotherhood and own property in Marisol. Finally, yet another married couple, both of whom were born in Marisol, were characterized as "yupeez." They left the community for ten years to make their fortunes in the north. Consciously emulating urban ways, they returned two years ago to reestablish residence in Marisol. Still regarded by "the locals" as "outsiders," this couple has attempted via such strategies as recent membership in the brotherhood to accrue symbolic capital on which they can draw when jockeying for power in numerous social contexts. As the only individuals within the yupeez category who are both native sons and daughters of Marisol and who maintain a daily presence in the community, this couple posed the greatest challenge to local power relations, both in the brotherhood and beyond. Consequently, pilgrims were more antagonized by their behavior than by that of the other yupeez.

During the journey all the preceding yupeez tended to wear clothing that was much more opulent than the attire sported by Marisoleños. They were also more concerned with personal cleanliness and with the "comforts of civilization." For example, the returned migrants became the butt of several jokes when they brought along a portable shower as well as a color television that could be plugged in at the shrine. Individuals classified as yupeez who jeopardize the camino with their selfishness often suffer playful retaliation. In the campsites along the route, where the covered wagons are placed in a circle, wagon doors face the center and everyone is under scrutiny. At night, it is customary to visit from wagon to wagon and then sit around the campfire while someone sings fandangos and everybody else claps. At this point, it is easy to notice if someone closes their wagon door early or fails to be neighborly, especially someone who has the means but fails to share. Those who "close up" are liable to be sabotaged, to have their wagons shaken or painted with graffiti during the night. The following day it is apparent to all that these individuals have been made the victims of a prank. Most of these practices constituted traditional responses to new challenges arising during the camino of 1989. Innovative strategies of resistance did emerge, however, from one subset of the brotherhood that confronted these new forms of domination head-on.

MINOR UTTERANCES AND STYLE WARS WITHIN A VISUAL FIELD

Positioned at the margins of the camino but nevertheless a necessary component of the brotherhood of Marisol, the young rebels in wagon 22 have established special tactics for putting the upstart yupeez in their place. These young men of working-class origins, who are employed in the olive groves and manual trades in Marisol, move along the trail in gangs. Although frequently intoxicated, they always manage to stay upright on their horses. Rather than fetishizing dress and the commodity form as signs of distinction, these young toughs are the *bricoleurs* of Marisol who "pry open the dominant signs by . . . exposing their fissures" (Hal Foster 1985:170). They call attention to themselves by creating a counterspectacle, one that makes a burlesque of elite decorum. Shirtless and with their clothes often soiled and torn, by means of their own dress code they impose an alternative visual regime that parodies "the look" so valued by the yupeez. They do their best to perform transgressive acts that provoke the elders of the brotherhood and scare the yupeez to death.

Just as the media industries and the yupeez deterritorialize the cultural sign of the Virgin and recode it both as media symbol and as a distinctive style, the lads of wagon 22 imitated this logic by appropriating signs from the transnational media culture of the West.[8] They adopted the New World category of "los Indios" (the Indians) to refer to themselves and thereby invented a cultural self against the rest. What did it mean for these subaltern youths to lay claim to the name "Indians" as part of selfhood and a politics of identity? First, in naming themselves, they also named "the other," the yupeez, as Anglo cowboys. By drawing an analogy between television recodings of the cultural practices of America's autochthonous peoples and their own self-designation, they identified metaphorically with the vanquished in other social contexts (compare Appadurai 1992).[9] In their reinscription of the frontier narrative, history reared its head, because the lads called attention to their forefathers' presence, to those who dwelt earlier in what is now contested territory, encroached on by the others, such as the yupeez and various categories of "developers" who would further commercialize this area (compare Crain 1996; Ordaz 1990; *El País* 1990). The Indian/Cowboy opposition evoked the experiences of other traditions of village and regional autonomy eventually repressed by Castilian hegemony, such as the socialist and anarchist movements established in Andalusian communities before the civil war, and it also embodied Marisoleños' apprehensions regarding further incorporation into a global system, such as the European Economic Community (compare Crain 1995; and Maddox this volume).

Yupeez who now participate in the camino in small numbers often dress in the latest fashions and ride in fancy Land Rovers instead of walking. Enclosed in their vehicles, they keep a measured distance by establishing a private space that separates them from the rest. Attempting in vain to hide from the wind and dust in a terrain in which these elements are its trademark, the yupeez have become an ideal target for the lads who strategically mar their surface appearance. When, during a brief moment, they catch the yupeez off their guard and on foot, these minors ride their horses up close and encircle them, stirring up a cloud of dust, thereby throwing a pristine image into total disarray. Similarly, during the baptism at the Quema River, a rite of purification where each "first-time pilgrims" has his or her head doused by "the old-timers," the lads, who by now are themselves old-timers, step into the river and proceed to soak the yupeez, ruining their expensive outfits.

All this leaves the yupeez confused and fearful of wagon 22 and they spread rumors to the effect that the lads carry knives and are thieves. Although the elders of the brotherhood cannot publicly approve of the lads' defiance, they often wink at one another in private asides. Meanwhile, they make a passing nod at the yupeez' assessment of the situation and make it appear as though moral authority is lacking and that the lads cannot be controlled. By letting the yupeez go on believing that the lads are dangerous, the lads' actions come to police the behavior of the yupeez. If the elders are forced to choose whom to include in "this community" — the yupeez or the rebellious lads — they side with the lads, declaring: "Sometimes we get infuriated with what the lads do and we say that enough is enough. But then they show up at mass, or lend a helping hand. These boys are our own blood. They are just like us, only with extra brute force, that's all." The elders hasten to add that unlike the yupeez, who are so concerned with their own sense of self-importance that they cannot be bothered to come to the aid of another, the lads often come to the rescue when emergencies arise. With their brute force, four of them can easily turn a wagon upright or lift a pair of oxen out of sinking sand.

On our arrival in Marisol after six days on the road, all the pilgrims eagerly awaited the limelight as they celebrated their annual return. On the outskirts of Marisol, where a crowd of onlookers, members of the press, and town officials always gather to welcome the pilgrims home, the lads of wagon 22 maneuvered their wagon out of sequence, backtracked, and inserted themselves right next to a spotless yupeez jeep. The yupeez' intentions to make a spectacle and offer themselves as the object of the public gaze were shattered when the lads proceeded to set their own wagon on fire. As the lads' wagon went up in smoke, a cloudy haze encircled the yupeez' vehicle as well. At that point the yupeez could no longer be "seen" but only "heard," crying out for help and bad-mouthing the lads. On that day at the close of the camino, it was the lads who had the last laugh and stole the show.

In this essay I have traced the progressive intervention of the mass media, tourist agencies, and municipal authorities in the transformation of the pilgrimage tradition of El Rocío. The representations of the pilgrimage produced by these institutions frequently establish meaning through a hierarchical ordering of the senses in which vision has been proclaimed the master sense. In the wake of this intervention, two new social groups, both characterized by secular orientations, have emerged at the shrine. The first group consists of individuals drawn from across Andalusia who, although not members of the Rocío brotherhoods, now arrive to celebrate the Pentecost. The motives underlying their attendance must be sought in the new cultural politics of the democratic transition in Spain in which El Rocío has become a key regional identity sign, thus condensing much of what it means to be Andalusian. Drawn from all over Spain and abroad, the second group of "newcomers" at the shrine are upwardly mobile urbanites who have been seduced by glossy media images in which the signifying complex of El Rocío has been refashioned as a pastiche of *lo Español* (the Spanish). They pursue both the "difference" that is presently attributed to this rite as well as the timeless tradition that it is said to encapsulate. But, as Fredric Jameson (1984) has argued in another context, the sense of the past that is conveyed through this pursuit is a sense of history reduced to changing styles. The recent transformations in popular religious culture effected by the media attempt to establish a highly programmed and passive event that often depends on a staging of culture in which media images may precede "the real" or stand in for reality's absence. Thus the pilgrimage can now be purchased in the form of a commercial videotape available for home consumption.

This refashioning of the rite into the spectacular is an emergent tendency, however, an incomplete project that predominates at the shrine. The unevenness of this transformation is conveyed by those Marisoleños who continue to assign meaning to this cult and whose practices do not always reproduce the dominant codes. By placing emphasis on the camino, these pilgrims have partially abandoned the "official church" at the shrine and its complicity with a media-based mode of constructing reality. They counter the distance of a highly visual cultural order with dialogue, emotion, and the proximity of touch. For these villagers, the world of the sacred is increasingly produced through everyday practices in which they prepare for the camino and reinscribe the landscape with religious significance.

Analysis of the pilgrimage demonstrates that the dominant tendency to produce one authoritative visual regime is fractured by the multiple visual regimes characteristic of the Marisol pilgrims. The yupeez' arbitrary fetishization of a pristine bodily image and fashionable dress is juxtaposed alongside the visual regime of the Marisol pilgrims, whose outer appearances are often laden with dirt but whose inner selves are held to be clean and pure. The lads of wagon 22 constitute the most extreme example of visual alterity, however. They respond with tactics that subvert the urbanites' desire for publicity and the production of a unique self. The lads create a counterspectacle that parodies "the look" of the sophisticated urbanites. While effective as a subaltern style which exposes the artificiality of the dominant codes and which seems to resist recuperation, the lad's defiance, insomuch as it defines itself against the dominant codes, is also ultimately tied to those codes.

Finally, "the local community" in all this appears not as an archaic traditional form gradually eroding in the face of a commodified, mass media–driven modernity but as a shifting reality that takes on new meanings as it is dynamically reconfigured through its encounter with the sign economy of consumer capitalism. For villagers no less than for tourists who come to sample their authenticity, ideas of locality and community must find meaning in mass-mediated relation to a modern, urban "other." For some, a new basis for local community is being sought in a deepening commitment to that which lies deeper than "the look" and is thus less subject to commodifying appropriation: spirituality, the felt qualities of the body, direct experience with the land. For others, the "Indians," locality is reinvented on the very media-saturated ground that seems to undermine it, as Hollywood images of insiders and outsiders, autochthons and invaders, are harnessed to a novel purpose. In both cases, it is instructive that mass media, consumer capitalism, and the regime of spectacular visual representation do not simply erode or weaken the old basis of local community but simultaneously provide the ground on which new, transformed conceptions of locality and community are made and fought over.

NOTES

Earlier drafts of this article were presented at the panel "Transformers: The Cultural Politics of Bricolage" at the 88th Annual Meeting of the American Anthropological Association in Washington, D.C., November 1989, and at the panel "The Revival of Public Celebrations in Europe" at the first European Association of Social Anthropology (EASA) conference held in Coimbra, Portugal, in September

1990. This article is based on fieldwork undertaken in Barcelona and in the Andalusian communities of Marisol (pseudonym), Seville, and El Rocío from 1988 to 1992. Funding was provided by two fellowships from the Wenner-Gren Foundation. My thanks go to the Wenner-Gren Foundation and to Jeremy Boissevain, James Ferguson, Akhil Gupta, Kristin Koptiuch, Roger Rouse, and, especially, Josep Maria Comelles, Universitat de Rovira i Virgili, Tarragona (Catalonia), for their critical comments and suggestions regarding revisions of this publication.

1 Sharing certain similarities with Luce Irigaray (1985), feminist film theorists intent on discerning the relationship between the field of vision, modes of domination, and sexual difference have asked whether the gaze is male (Mulvey 1975; Kuhn 1985; de Lauretis 1987). Examining the positioning of the film spectator within phallocratic signifying systems, they argue that, to some extent, we all gaze through masculine eyes. See Doane 1982 for an attempt to elaborate an alternative theory of the female spectator. For efforts to theorize diverse features of touristic as well as colonialist-voyeuristic gazes, see the respective volumes by John Urry (1990) and Malek Alloula (1986).

2 One apt illustration of Fredric Jameson's reading (1991) of contemporary culture as a "surface" that is characterized by "a new deathlessness" can be encountered in the work of the late pop artist Andy Warhol. An Italian retrospective of Warhol's work provides the artist's general commentary both on his image production and on a particular painting of his featuring both S & H Greenstamps and dollar bills. Warhol notes, "I see everything that way, the surface of things, a kind of mental Braille, I just pass my hands over the surface of things." Andy Warhol Retrospective, Palazzo Grassi, Venice, Italy, February–May 1990.

3 See Comelles 1984 and 1991 for a more comprehensive historical account of the growth of these brotherhoods over the course of the past five centuries, and see Moreno 1974.

4 A rite of modernity, Seville's fair, or EXPO 1992, coincided with the controversial celebration of the five-hundred-year anniversary of "the discovery" of the Americas by Christopher Columbus. EXPO 1992 was also targeted as a site of armed intervention by the militant Basque-nationalist group ETA. The group announced that insofar as the fair constituted a major financial project of the state and ETA was opposed to the realization of the state's goals, it intended to proceed with actions designed to obstruct the completion of the EXPO (see El Correo de Andalucía 1990:1, 12).

5 Tired of the relentless questioning from the press regarding which famous people would be accompanying them during their pilgrimage to El Rocío, members of the highly theatrical brotherhood of Triana, a neighborhood of Seville, retorted that the "only" famous person participating in their procession was "the Virgin."

6 One of Spain's largest wild game reserves, the National Park of Doñana, borders the shrine of El Rocío. Drawing visitors from all over Europe, the protection of this reserve has recently been the subject of debate between "developers" and environmental groups. This debate pivots around the desire of the

ruling municipal council of Almonte, within whose jurisdiction the park lies, to construct a large touristic complex bordering the park that would provide jobs for local workers and the plea of Spanish as well as international scientific organizations which argue that the proposed "urbanization" endangers the fragile ecosystem of the park and its wildlife (Crain 1996; Ordaz 1990; Suarez 1990).

7 Historically, members of the Andalusian landed elite have played a major role in the organization of some of the older filial brotherhoods, such as Triana. These aristocratic elites must be distinguished from the new social groups considered here.

8 During the camino of 1989 the lads briefly attempted to appropriate another visible sign of difference and of the West — myself, the anthropologist. While further discussion of their actions will be treated in a future publication, suffice it to say that the lads were quite cognizant that at some future point, their voices would constitute one of the many discursive strands included in my written account on the romería. I interpreted their act of appropriation as constituting part of their broader efforts to exercise a degree of control over the representations of their social world and of Marisol that I, as chronicler of these events, was constructing.

9 Arjun Appadurai's work (1992) on "global ethnoscapes" is particularly relevant to this portion of my analysis. He claims that as a range of transnational flows of information, capital, labor, and commodities increasingly characterizes everyday life experiences in the late twentieth century, face-to-face relations in local communities play a more limited role in accounting for the construction of contemporary selves, identities, and localities. Appadurai encourages ethnographers to pay greater attention to both individual as well as group exposure to global media (through such cultural forms as movies, videos, VCRs, and novels) as discursive fields that assume a new primacy in the imagining of both possible selves and possible communities under conditions of late capitalism. In the case here, it is evident that the lads of wagon 22 are members of a "local" Andalusian community, such as Marisol, in which many villagers actually know one another. At the same time, however, the lads increasingly conceptualize this community through a mass-mediated lens in which they rewrite their life trajectories and their oppositional identity politics by drawing on scenarios from Hollywood mediascapes.

WORKS CITED

Aall Cato. 1967. "Refugee Problems in Southern Africa." In *Refugee Problems in Africa*, ed. Sven Hamrell. Uppsala, Sweden: Scandinavian Institute of African Studies.

Abdallah, Stephanie. 1995. "Palestinian Women in the Camps of Jordan: Interviews." *Journal of Palestine Studies* 24 (4): 62–72.

Abu-Amr, Zia. 1994. *Islamic Fundamentalism in the West Bank and Gaza*. Bloomington: Indiana University Press.

Abu-Lughod, Janet. 1971. "The Demographic Transformation of Palestine." In *The Transformation of Palestine*, ed. Ibrahim Abu-Lughod. Evanston: Northwestern University Press.

———. 1983. "The Demographic Consequences of Occupation." In *Occupation: Israel over Palestine*, ed. Naseer Aruri. Belmont, Mass.: Association of Arab-American University Graduates Press.

Abu-Lughod, Lila. 1990. "The Romance of Resistance: Tracing Transformations of Power through Bedouin Women." *American Ethnologist* 17 (1): 41–55.

Aflaq, Michel. 1968. "The Socialist Ideology of the Ba'th." In *Political and Social Thought in the Contemporary Middle East*, ed. Kemal Karpat. New York: Praeger.

African Rights. 1994. *Rwanda: Death, Despair, and Defiance*. London: African Rights.

Ahmad, Aijaz. 1987. "Jameson's Rhetoric of Otherness and the National Allegory." *Social Text*, no. 17:3–25.

al-Bazzaz, Abd al-Rahman. 1962. "Summary of the Characteristics of Arab Nationalism." In *Arab Nationalism*, ed. Sylvia Haim. Berkeley: University of California Press.

Alexander, Elizabeth. 1994. " 'Can You Be BLACK and Look at This?': Reading the Rodney King Video(s)." *Public Culture* 7:77–96.

Allen, Katheryn Martin. 1945. "Hindoos in the Valley." *Westways* 37:8–9.

Alloula, Malek. 1986. *The Colonial Harem*. Trans. Glad Godzich and Myrna Godzich. Minneapolis: University of Minnesota Press.

Althusser, Louis. 1971. "Ideology and Ideological State Apparatuses." In *Lenin and Philosophy and Other Essays*, trans. Ben Brewster, 121–73. New York: Monthly Review.

Alvarez, Robert R., Jr. 1987. *Familia: Migration and Adaptation in Baja and Alta California, 1800–1975*. Berkeley: University of California Press.

Aly, Götz. 1995. *Endlösung: Völkerverschiebung und der Mord an den europäischen Juden*. Frankfurt am Main: Fischer.

Anagnost, Ann. 1989. "Prosperity and Counterprosperity: The Moral Discourse on

Wealth in Post-Mao China." In *Marxism and the Chinese Experience,* ed. Arif Dirlik and Maurice Meisner, 210–34. Armonk, N.Y.: M. E. Sharpe.

———. 1997. *National Past-Times: Narrative, Representation, and Power in Modern China.* Durham: Duke University Press.

Anderson, Benedict. 1983. *Imagined Communities: Reflections on the Origin and Spread of Nationalism.* London: Verso.

———. 1990. *Imagined Communities: Reflections on the Origin and Spread of Nationalism.* Rev. ed. London: Verso.

Andert, Reinhold. 1989. "Mein Trabbi." Song lyrics.

Ang, Ien. 1994. "On Not Speaking Chinese." *New Formations* 24 (Winter): 1–18.

Anzaldúa, Gloria. 1987. *Borderlands/La Frontera: The New Mestiza.* San Francisco: Spinsters/Aunt Lute.

Appadurai, Arjun. 1986. "Theory in Anthropology: Center and Periphery." *Comparative Studies in Society and History* 28 (1): 356–61.

———. 1988a. "Introduction: Place and Voice in Anthropological Theory." *Cultural Anthropology* 3 (1): 16–20.

———. 1988b "Putting Hierarchy in Its Place." *Cultural Anthropology* 3 (1): 36–49.

———. 1990. "Disjuncture and Difference in the Global Cultural Economy." *Public Culture* 2 (2): 1–24.

———. 1992. "Global Ethnoscapes: Notes and Queries for a Transnational Anthropology." In *Recapturing Anthropology: Working in the Present,* ed. Richard Fox, 191–210. Santa Fe, N.M.: School of American Research.

———. ed. 1986. *The Social Life of Things: Commodities in Cultural Perspective.* Cambridge: Cambridge University Press.

Appadurai, Arjun, and Carol Breckenridge. 1986. "Asian Indians in the United States: A Transnational Culture in the Making." Paper presented at Asia Society, New York, April.

———. 1988a. "Editors' Comments." *Public Culture.* 1 (1): 1–4.

———. 1988b. "Why Public Culture?" *Public Culture* 1 (1): 5–9.

Arafat, Saba. 1989. "Formal Education in UNRWA." *Journal of Refugee Studies* 2 (1): 108–12.

Archives of the Hermandad Matríz of Almonte. Almonte, Andalucía.

Arendt, Hannah. 1973. *The Origins of Totalitarianism.* New York: Harcourt Brace Jovanovich.

Aruri, Naseer, and Ghareeb, Edmond, eds. 1970. *Enemy of the Sun: Poetry of the Palestinian Resistance.* Washington, D.C.: Drum and Spear.

Asad, Talal. 1986. "The Concept of Cultural Translation in British Social Anthropology." In *Writing Culture: The Poetics and Politics of Ethnography,* ed. James Clifford and George E. Marcus, 141–64. Berkeley: University of California Press.

Atran, Scott. 1989. "The Surrogate Colonization of Palestine, 1917–1939." *American Ethnologist* 16 (4): 719–44.

———. 1990. "Stones against the Iron Fist, Terror within the Nation: Alternating Structures of Violence and Cultural Identity in the Israeli-Palestinian Conflicts." *Politics and Society* 18 (4): 481–526.

Ault, James M., Jr. 1981. Review of *Rural Responses to Industrialization: A Study of Village Zambia*, by Robert Bates. *African Social Research*, no. 32 (December).

Axen, Hermann. 1973. *Zur Entwicklung der sozialistischen Nation in der DDDR*. Berlin: Dietz.

Badran, Nabil. 1980. "The Means of Survival: Education and the Palestinian Community." *Journal of Palestine Studies* 9 (4): 44–74.

Balibar, Etienne. 1990. "Paradoxes of Universality." In *Anatomy of Racism*, ed. David T. Goldberg, 283–94. Minneapolis: University of Minnesota Press.

———. 1991a. *"Es Gibt Keinen Staat in Europa*: Racism and Politics in Europe Today." *New Left Review*, no. 186:5–19.

———. 1991b. "The Nation Form: History and Ideology." In *Race, Nation, Class: Ambiguous Identities*, Etienne Balibar and Immanuel Wallerstein, 622–33. New York: Routledge.

Balibar, Etienne, and Immanuel Wallerstein. 1991. *Race, Nation, Class: Ambiguous Identities*. New York: Verso.

Bantu, Joseph. 1989. *A Straw in the Eye*. Lusaka, Zambia: Kenneth Kaunda Foundation.

Barakat, Halim, and Peter Dodd. 1969. *River without Bridges: A Study of the Exodus of the 1967 Palestinian Arab Refugees*. Beirut: Institute of Palestine Studies.

Barlow, Tani. 1991. "Zhishifenzi [Chinese Intellectuals] and Power." *Dialectical Anthropology* 16 (3–4): 209–32.

Barnet, Richard, and John Cavanagh. 1994. *Global Dreams: Imperial Corporations and the New World Order*. New York: Simon and Schuster.

Bates, Robert. 1971. *Unions, Parties, and Political Development: A Study of Mineworkers in Zambia*. New Haven: Yale University Press.

Baudrillard, Jean. 1975. *The Mirror of Production*. Trans. Mark Poster. St. Louis: Telos.

———. 1981. *For a Critique of the Political Economy of the Sign*. St. Louis: Telos.

———. 1983a. *In the Shadow of Silent Majorities*. Trans. Paul Foss, Paul Patton, and John Johnston. New York: Semiotext(e).

———. 1983b. *Simulations*. Trans. Paul Foss, Paul Patton, and Philip Beitchman. Foreign Agent Series. New York: Semiotext(e).

———. 1988a. *America*. Trans. Chris Turner. New York: Verso.

———. 1988b. *On Seduction*. In *Jean Baudrillard: Selected Writings*, ed. Mark Poster. Stanford: Stanford University Press.

———. 1988c. *Jean Baudrillard: Selected Writings*, ed. Mark Poster. Stanford, California: Stanford University Press.

Baumann, Melissa. 1988. "When the Rest Is Quiet, There Is a Revolution in Dheisheh." *Middle East Report*, no. 152 (May–June).

Beach, Walter G. 1971. *Oriental Crime in California*. 1932. Reprint, New York: AMS Press.

Beaumont, Heather. 1992. "The X Factor." *Metro Word*, 8 November–9 December.

Becker, Franziska. 1994. *Gewalt und Gedächtnis: Erinnerungen an die nationalsozialistische Verfolgung einer jüdischen Landgemeinde*. Göttingen: Volker Schmerse.

Benedict, Ruth. 1934. *Patterns of Culture*. Boston: Houghton Mifflin.

Benjamin, Walter. 1968a. "The Storyteller" (1936). In *Illuminations: Essays and Reflections,* ed. Hannah Arendt, trans. Harry Zohn, 83–109. New York: Schocken.

———. 1968b. "The Work of Art in the Age of Mechanical Reproduction" (1936). In *Illuminations: Essays and Reflections,* ed. Hannah Arendt, trans. Harry Zohn, 217–51. New York: Schocken.

Ben Porath, Yoram, and Emanuel Marx. 1971. *Some Sociological and Economic Aspects of Refugee Camps in the West Bank.* Santa Monica, Calif.: Rand Corporation.

Benvenisti, Meron. 1984. *The West Bank Data Project Report.* Washington, D.C.: American Enterprise Institute.

———. 1987. *1987 Report: Demographic, Economic, Legal, Social, and Political Developments in the West Bank.* Jerusalem: Jerusalem Post.

Berman, Marshall. 1988. *All That Is Solid Melts into Air: The Experience of Modernity.* New York: Penguin.

Bhabha, Homi K. 1989. "Location, Intervention, Incommensurability: A Conversation with Homi Bhabha." *Emergences* 1 (1): 63–88.

———. 1990. "Introduction: Narrating the Nation." In *Nation and Narration,* ed. Homi K. Bhabha, 1–7. New York: Routledge.

———. 1994. *The Location of Culture.* London: Routledge.

Bird, Jon, Barry Curtis, Tim Putnam, George Robertson, and Lisa Tickner, eds. 1993. *Mapping the Futures: Local Cultures, Global Change.* New York: Routledge.

Bisharat, George Emile. 1989. *Palestinian Lawyers and Israeli Rule: Law and Disorder in the West Bank.* Austin: University of Texas Press.

———. 1994. "Land, Law, and Legitimacy in Israel and the Occupied Territories." *American University Law Review* 43, no. 2 (Winter):467–561.

Bishop, Dale. 1988. "Mosque and Church in the Uprising." *Middle East Report,* no. 152 (May–June).

Bloch, Maurice. 1985. *Marxism and Anthropology: The History of a Relationship.* Oxford: Oxford University Press.

Bock, Gesela. 1986. *Zwangssterilisation im Nationalsozialismus: Studien zur Rassen- und Frauen-politik.* Opladen, Germany: Leske u. Budrich.

Borges, Jorge Luis. 1964. "Pierre Menard, Author of the Quixote." In *Labyrinths: Selected Stories and Other Writings,* ed. Donald A. Yates and James E. Irby, 36–44. New York: New Directions.

Borneman, John. 1986. "Emigres as Bullets/Immigration as Penetration; Perceptions of the Marielitos." *Journal of Popular Culture* 20 (3): 73–92.

———. 1991. *After the Wall: East Meets West in the New Berlin.* New York: Basic.

———. 1992. *Belonging in the Two Berlins: Kin, State, Nation.* Cambridge: Cambridge University Press.

———. 1993a. "Time-Space Compression and the Continental Divide in German Subjectivity." *New Formations* 3 (1): 102–18.

———. 1993b. "Trouble in the Kitchen: Totalitarianism, Love, and Resistance to Authority." In *Moralizing States and the Ethnography of the Present,* ed. Sally F. Moore, 93–118. Monograph Series no. 5. Washington, D.C.: American Anthropological Association.

——. 1993c. "Uniting the German Nation: Law, Narrative, and Historicity." *American Ethnologist* 20 (2): 288–311.

——. 1994. "Towards a Theory of Ethnic Cleansing: Territorial Sovereignty, Heterosexuality, and Europe." Working Papers on Transitions from State Socialism, no. 94.4, 1–45. Cornell Project on Comparative Institutional Analysis. Ithaca: Center for International Studies, Cornell University.

——. 1995. "Education after the Cold War: Remembrance, Repetition, and Right-wing Violence." In *Cultural Authority in Contemporary Germany*, ed. Michael Geyer and Robert von Hallberg. Chicago: University of Chicago Press.

Bourdieu, Pierre. 1977. *Outline of a Theory of Practice*. Trans. Richard Nice. Cambridge: Cambridge University Press.

——. 1984. *Distinction: A Social Critique of the Judgement of Taste*. Trans. Richard Nice. Cambridge: Harvard University Press.

——. 1988. *Homo Academicus*. Trans. Peter Collier. Stanford: Stanford University Press.

Bowman, Glenn. 1990. "Religion and Political Identity in Beit Sahour." *Middle East Report*, nos. 164–65 (May–June/July–August).

Boyarin, Jonathan, ed. 1994. *Remapping Memory: The Politics of TimeSpace*. Minneapolis: University of Minnesota Press.

Brand, Laurie. 1995. "Palestinians and Jordanians: A Crisis of Identity." *Journal of Palestine Studies* 2 (4): 46–61.

Braverman, Harry. 1974. *Labor and Monopoly Capital*. New York: Monthly Review Press.

Braverman, Kate. 1989. "Nostalgia for the Empire." *Enclitic* 11 (1): 31–40.

Breckenridge, Carol, and Arjun Appadurai. 1989. "On Moving Targets." *Public Culture* 2 (1): i–iv.

Brunner, Edmund de Schweinitz. 1929. *Immigrant Farmers and Their Children*. New York: Doubleday, Doran.

Brunvand, Jan Harold. 1984. *The Choking Doberman and Other "New" Urban Legends*. New York: W. W. Norton.

——. 1986. *The Mexican Pet: More "New" Urban Legends and Some Old Favorites*. New York: W. W. Norton.

Brynen, Rex. 1990. "The Politics of Exile: The Palestinians in Lebanon." *Journal of Refugee Studies* 3 (3): 204–27.

——. 1995. "The Dynamics of Palestinian Elite Formations." *Journal of Palestine Studies* 24 (3): 31–43.

Bude, Heinz. 1987. *Lebenskonstruktionen sozialer Aufsteiger aus der Flakhelfer-Generation*. Frankfurt am Main: Suhrkamp.

Budeiri, Musa. 1995. "The Nationalist Dimension of Islamic Movements in Palestinian Politics." *Journal of Palestine Studies* 24 (3): 89–95.

Buehrig, Edward. 1971. *The UN and the Palestinian Refugees*. Bloomington: Indiana University Press.

Burawoy, Michael. 1972. "Another Look at the Mineworker." *African Social Research*, no. 14 (December): 239–87.

Burdette, Marcia M. 1988. *Zambia: Between Two Worlds*. Boulder, Colo.: Westview.

Bustamente, Jorge. 1987. "Mexican Immigration: A Domestic Issue or an Interna-
tional Reality." In *Hispanic Migration and the United States: A Study in Politics,* ed.
Gaston Fernandez, Beverly Nagel, and Leon Narvaez. Bristol, Ind.: Wyndham
Hall.

Butler, Judith, and Joan W. Scott, eds. 1992. *Feminists Theorize the Political.* New York:
Routledge.

California, State Board of Control. 1920. *California and the Oriental.* Sacramento:
State Printing Office.

California Legislature, Senate. 1953. *Seventh Report of the Senate Fact-Finding Committee on Un-American Activities.* Sacramento: California Senate Printing Office.

California State Commission of Immigration and Housing. 1918. *Report on Fresno's
Immigration Problem.* Sacramento: State Printing Office.

Carey, James W. 1989. *Communication as Culture: Essays on Media and Society.* Boston:
Unwin Hyman.

Caro Baroja, Julio. 1957. *Razas, pueblos, linajes.* Madrid: Revista de occidente.

Carvajal, Doreen. 1989. "Making North Philadelphia Their Home as Well as Mission." *Philadelphia Inquirer,* 25 June.

Center for Contemporary Cultural Studies (CCCS). 1982. *The Empire Strikes Back:
Race and Racism in 70s Britain.* London: Hutchinson in association with CCCS,
University of Birmingham.

Chakrabarty, Dipesh. 1989. *Rethinking Working-Class History: Bengal, 1890–1940.*
Princeton: Princeton University Press.

Chan, Sucheng. 1991. *Asian Americans: An Interpretive History.* Boston: GIC Hall.

Chang, K. C. 1977. *The Archaeology of Ancient China.* New Haven: Yale University
Press.

Chatterjee, Partha. 1986. *Nationalist Thought and the Colonial World: A Derivative
Discourse?* London: Zed.

———. 1990. "A Response to Taylor's 'Modes of Civil Society.' " *Public Culture* 3 (1):
119–32.

Chavez, Leo. 1991. "Outside the Imagined Community: Undocumented Settlers
and Experiences of Incorporation. *American Ethnologist* 18 (2): 257–78.

Cheal, Beryl. 1988. "Refugees in the Gaza Strip, December 1948–May 1950."
Journal of Palestine Studies 17 (3): 60–75.

Cheng, Chung-ying. 1986. "The Concept of Face and Its Confucian Roots." *Journal
of Chinese Philosophy* 13 (3): 329–48.

Christian, William A. 1972. *Person and God in a Spanish Valley.* New York: Seminar
Press.

Cirtautas, Claudius Kazys. 1957. *The Refugee: A Psychological Study.* Boston: Meador.

Clark, John, and Caroline Allison. 1989. *Zambia: Debt and Poverty.* Oxford: Oxfam.

Clifford, James. 1986a. "Introduction: Partial Truths." In *Writing Culture: The Poetics
and Politics of Ethnography,* ed. James Clifford and George E. Marcus, 1–26.
Berkeley: University of California Press.

———. 1986b. "On Ethnographic Allegory." In *Writing Culture: The Poetics and Politics of Ethnography,* ed. James Clifford and George E. Marcus, 98–121. Berkeley:
University of California Press.

——. 1988. *The Predicament of Culture: Twentieth-Century Ethnography, Literature, and Art.* Cambridge: Harvard University Press.

——. 1994. "Diasporas." *Cultural Anthropology* 9 (3): 302–38.

Clifford, James, and George E. Marcus, eds. 1986. *Writing Culture: The Poetics and Politics of Ethnography.* Berkeley: University of California Press.

Closa, Carlos. 1992. "The Concept of Citizenship in the Treaty on European Union." *Common Market Law Review* 29 (6): 1137–69.

Cobban, Helena. 1984. *The Palestine Liberation Organization: People, Politics, and Power.* Cambridge: Cambridge University Press.

Cohen, Amnon. 1982. *Political Parties in the West Bank under the Jordanian Regime, 1949–1967.* Ithaca: Cornell University Press.

Cohen, Anthony. 1985. *The Symbolic Construction of Community.* New York: Tavistock.

Collier, Jane, and Sylvia Yanagisako, eds. 1987. *Gender and Kinship: Essays Toward a Unified Analysis.* Stanford: Stanford University Press.

Comaroff, John L. 1987. "Of Totemism and Ethnicity: Consciousness, Practice, and the Signs of Inequality." *Ethnos* 52 (3–4): 301–23.

Comaroff, Jean, and John Comaroff, eds. 1993. *Modernity and Its Malcontents.* Chicago: University of Chicago Press.

Comaroff, John L., and Jean Comaroff. 1987. "The Madman and the Migrant: Work and Labor in the Historical Consciousness of a South African People." *American Ethnologist* 14 (2): 191–209.

Comelles, Josep Maria. 1984. "Los Caminos del Rocío." In *Antropologia Cultural de Andalucía,* ed. Salvador Bercerra Rodriguez, 425–45. Seville: Instituto de Cultura Andaluza.

——. 1991. "Rocío." In *Antropología Social de los Pueblos de España,* ed. Jesus Contreras, Ubaldo Martínez Veiga, Isidoro Moreno, and Joan Prat. Madrid: Taurus.

Coombe, Rosemary J. 1991a. "Beyond Modernity's Meanings: Engaging the Postmodern in Cultural Anthropology." *Culture* 11:111–24.

——. 1991b. "Objects of Property and Subjects of Politics: Intellectual Property Laws and Democratic Dialogue." *Texas Law Review* 69: 1853–80.

——. 1993. "Tactics of Appropriation and the Politics of Recognition in Late Modern Democracies." *Political Theory* 21:411–33.

——. 1996. "Embodied Trademarks: Mimesis and Alterity on American Commercial Frontiers." *Cultural Anthropology* 11 (2): 202–24.

——. 1997. *Cultural Appropriations: Authorship, Alterity, and the Law.* New York: Routledge.

Coombe, Rosemary J., and Paul Stoller. 1995. "X Marks the Spot: The Ambiguities of African Trading in the Commerce of the Black Public Sphere." In *The Black Public Sphere,* ed. Public Sphere Collective, 253–78. Chicago: University of Chicago Press.

Cossali, Paul, and Clive Robinson. 1986. *Stateless in Gaza.* London: Zed.

Crain, Mary M. 1990. "The Social Construction of National Identity in Highland Ecuador." *Anthropological Quarterly* 63 (1): 43–59.

——. 1995. "Introducing the Photography of Cristina García Rodero." In *España*

Oculta: Public Celebrations in Spain, 1974–1989, 1–6. Washington, D.C.: Smithsonian Institution Press.

———. 1996. "Contested Territory: The Politics of Touristic Development at the Shrine of El Rocío in Southwestern Andalusia." In *Coping with Tourists,* ed. Jeremy Boissevain. Europa Series. Oxford: Berghahn.

———. In press. "Negotiating Identities in Quito's Cultural Borderlands: Native Womens' Performances for the Ecuadorean Tourist Market." In *Commodities and Cultural Borders,* ed. David Howes. New York: Routledge.

Crapanzano, Vincent. 1980. *Tuhami, Portrait of a Moroccan.* Chicago: University of Chicago Press.

Dahlburg, John-Thor. 1990. "Hate Survives a Holocaust: Anti-Semitism Resurfaces." *Los Angeles Times,* 12 June, H1, H7.

Dale, Reginald. 1988. "Seville: Languishing Andalusia Sees 1992 as Year of Hope and Glory." *International Herald Tribune,* 18 May, Paris edition, 1, 17.

Daniels, Stephen. 1988. "The Political Iconography of Woodland in Later Georgian England." In *The Iconography of Landscape,* ed. Denis Cosgrove and Stephen Daniels. Cambridge: Cambridge University Press.

Davis, Lennard. 1983. *Factual Fictions.* New York: Columbia University Press.

Davis, Mike. 1986. "The Political Economy of Late-Imperial America." In *Prisoners of the American Dream: Politics and Economy in the History of the US Working Class.* New York: Verso.

———. 1988. "Los Angeles: Civil Liberties between the Hammer and the Rock." *New Left Review,* no. 170 (July/August): 37–60.

———. 1989. "Homeowners and Homeboys: Urban Restructuring in LA." *Enclitic* 11 (3): 8–16.

———. 1990. *City of Quartz: Excavating the Future in Los Angeles.* London: Verso.

Dawson, Michael. 1994. "A Black Counterpublic? Economic Earthquakes, Racial Agendas, and Black Politics." *Public Culture* 7:195–224.

Debord, Guy. 1973. *Society of the Spectacle.* Detroit: Black and Red.

de Certeau, Michel. 1984. *The Practice of Everyday Life.* Trans. Steven F. Rendall. Berkeley: University of California Press.

de Lauretis, Teresa. 1987. *Technologies of Gender: Essays on Theory, Film, and Fiction.* Bloomington: Indiana University Press.

Deleuze, Gilles, and Felix Guattari. 1983. *Anti-Oedipus: Capitalism and Schizophrenia.* Trans. Robert Hurley, Mark Seem, and Helen R. Lane. Minneapolis: University of Minnesota Press. Original French publication 1972.

———. 1987. *A Thousand Plateaus: Capitalism and Schizophrenia.* Minneapolis: University of Minnesota Press.

Derrida, Jacques. 1974. *Of Grammatology.* Trans. Gayatri Chakravorty Spivak. Baltimore: Johns Hopkins University Press.

Destexhe, Alain. 1994. *Rwanda: Essai sur le genocide.* Brussels: Editions Complexe.

Dhillon, Mahinder Singh. 1981. *A History Book of the Sikhs in Canada and California.* Vancouver: Shormani Akali Dal Association of Canada.

Diawara, Manthia. 1994. "Malcolm X and the Black Public Sphere: Conversionists versus Culturalists." *Public Culture* 7:35–48.

Di Leonardo, Micaela. 1990. "Who's Really Getting Paid?" *Nation,* 14 May.

Diprose, Rosalyn, and Robyn Ferrell, eds. 1991. *Cartographies: Poststructuralism and the Mapping of Bodies and Spaces.* Sydney: Allen Unwin.

Dirks, Nicholas B. 1990. "History as a Sign of the Modern." *Public Culture* 2 (2): 25–32.

Dirlik, Arif, and Maurice Meisner. 1989. "Politics, Scholarship, and Chinese Socialism." In *Marxism and the Chinese Experience,* ed. Arif Dirlik and Maurice Meisner, 3–26. Armonk, N.Y.: M. E. Sharpe.

Doane, Mary Ann. 1982. "Film and the Masquerade: Theorising the Female Spectator." *Screen* 23 (3–4): 74–87.

Donham, Donald. 1990. *History, Power, Ideology: Central Issues in Marxism and Anthropology.* New York: Cambridge University Press.

Dorst, John. 1989. *The Written Suburb: An American Site, an Ethnographic Dilemma.* Philadelphia: University of Pennsylvania Press.

Douglas, Mary. 1966. *Purity and Danger: An Analysis of the Concepts of Pollution and Taboo.* London: Routledge, Kegan Paul.

Douglas, Mary, and Aaron Wildavsky. 1982. *Risk and Culture: An Essay on the Selection of Technological and Environmental Dangers.* Berkeley: University of California Press.

Drescher, Thomas. 1992. "The Transformation and Evolution of Trademarks — from Signals to Symbols to Myth." *Trademark Reporter* 82:301.

Dreyfus, Hubert L., and Paul Rabinow. 1982. *Michel Foucault: Beyond Structuralism and Hermeneutics.* Chicago: University of Chicago Press.

Driessen, Henk. 1989. "Elite versus Popular Religion? The Politics of Religion in Rural Andalusia, an Anthrohistorical Perspective." In *La religiosidad popular,* vol. 1, *Antropología e Historia,* ed. Carlos Alvarez Santals, Marma Jeszs Buxs i Rey, and Salvador Rodrmguez Becerra, 1:82–104. Barcelona: Editorial Anthropos.

Duara, Prasenjit. 1988. *Culture, Power, and the State: Rural North China, 1900–1942.* Stanford: Stanford University Press.

———. 1995. *Rescuing History from the Nation.* Chicago: University of Chicago Press.

Dubisch, Jill. 1988. "Golden Oranges and Silver Ships: An Interpretive Approach to a Greek Holy Shrine." *Journal of Modern Greek Studies* 6:117–34.

Dux, Heinz. 1988. "Härtefalle: Erfahrungen eines Richters mit der 'Wiedergutmachung.'" In *Von der Gnade der Geschenkten Nation,* ed. Hajo Funke, 174–86. Berlin: Rotbuch.

El Correo de Andalucía. 1990. "ETA Advierte que su Proximo Atentado en Sevilla no Fallara." 23 April, 1, 12.

Elmessiri, Abdel Wahhab. 1982. *The Palestinian Wedding.* Washington, D.C.: Three Continents Press.

El País. 1990. "Denuncia por la Construccion de un Nuevo Hotel en el Rocío." 12 May, Andalusian edition, 3.

Emerson, Rupert. 1960. *From Empire to Nation: The Rise to Self-Assertion of Asian and African Peoples.* Cambridge: Harvard University Press.

Epstein, A. L. 1958. *Politics in an Urban African Community.* Manchester: Manchester University Press.

——. 1981. *Urbanization and Kinship: The Domestic Domain on the Copperbelt of Zambia, 1950–1956*. New York: Academic Press.

Ernst, Friedholm. 1989. "Problems of UNRWA School Education and Vocational Training." *Journal of Refugee Studies* 2 (1): 88–97.

Escobar, Arturo. 1988. "Power and Visibility: Development and the Invention and Management of the Third World." *Cultural Anthropology* 3 (4): 428–43.

Everest, Hari Singh. 1972. "Letter to the editor." *Sikh Sansar* 1 (1): 31.

Everling, Ulrich. 1992. "Reflections on the Structure of the European Union." *Common Market Law Review* 29 (6): 1053–77.

Fabian, Johannes. 1983. *Time and the Other: How Anthropology Makes Its Object*. New York: Columbia University Press.

——. 1990. "Presence and Representation: The Other and Anthropological Writing." *Critical Inquiry* 16 (4): 753–72.

Fanon, Frantz. 1968. *The Wretched of the Earth*. New York: Grove.

Farred, Grant. 1995. "Untitled Contribution to Race and Racism: A Symposium." *Social Text* 42: 21–26.

Ferguson, James. 1990. "Mobile Workers, Modernist Narratives: A Critique of the Historiography of Transition on the Zambian Copperbelt." Parts 1 and 2. *Journal of Southern African Studies* 16 (3): 385–412; 16 (4): 603–21.

——. 1994. *The Anti-Politics Machine: "Development," Depoliticization, and Bureaucratic Power in Lesotho*. Minneapolis: University of Minnesota Press.

——. 1995. "From African Socialism to Scientific Capitalism: Reflections on the Legitimation Crisis in IMF-Ruled Africa." In *Debating Development Discourse*, ed. David Moore and Gerald Schmitz. New York: St. Martin's.

——. Forthcoming. *Expectations of Modernity: Myths and Meanings of Urban Life on the Zambian Copperbelt*.

Fernandez, James. 1986. *Persuasions and Performances*. Bloomington: Indiana University Press.

Ferrick, Thomas, Jr. 1989. "The Progress on Illegal Billboards? Not Much." *Philadelphia Inquirer*, 26 March.

Ferrick, Thomas, Jr., and Doreen Carvajal. 1989. "The 25-Year-Old Scars of a Riot." *Philadelphia Inquirer*, 27 August.

Fine, Gary Alan. 1985. "The Goliath Effect: Corporate Dominance and Mercantile Legends." *Journal of American Folklore* 98 (387): 63–84.

——. 1990. "Among Those Dark Satanic Mills: Rumors of Kooks, Cults, and Corporations." *Southern Folklore* 47 (2): 133–46.

Finkelstein, Norman. 1991. "Myths, Old and New." *Journal of Palestine Studies* 21 (1): 66–89.

Fischer, Michael M. J. 1986. "Ethnicity and the Post-Modern Arts of Memory." In *Writing Culture: The Poetics and Politics of Ethnography*, ed. James Clifford and George E. Marcus, 194–233. Berkeley: University of California Press.

Flandrin, Jean-Louis. 1979. *Families in Former Times*. Cambridge: Cambridge University Press.

Flapan, Simha. 1987. *The Birth of Israel: Myths and Realities*. New York: Pantheon.

Forsythe, Diane. 1989. "German Identity and the Problem of History." In *History and Ethnicity*, ed. Elizabeth Tonkin, Maryon McDonald, and Malcolm Chapman, 137–56. New York: Routledge.

Foster, Hal. 1985. *Recodings: Art, Spectacle, Cultural Politics*. Port Townsend, Wash.: Bay Press.

———. 1988. Preface to *Vision and Visuality*, ed. Hal Foster, ix–xiv. Seattle, Wash.: Bay Press.

———, ed. 1983. *The Anti-Aesthetic: Essays on Postmodern Culture*. Port Townsend, Wash.: Bay Press.

Foster, Robert. 1991. "Making National Cultures in the Global Ecumene." *Annual Review of Anthropology* 20:235–60.

Foucault, Michel. 1961. "Introduction a l'anthropologie de Kant." Doctoral thesis, University of Paris.

———. 1973. *The Order of Things*. New York: Vintage.

———. 1975. *The Birth of the Clinic*. Trans. A. M. Sheridan Smith. New York: Vintage.

———. 1978. *The History of Sexuality*. Vol. 1, *An Introduction*. Trans. Robert Hurley. New York: Random House.

———. 1979. *Discipline and Punish: The Birth of the Prison*. Trans. Alan Sheridan. 1975. Reprint, New York: Vintage.

———. 1980. *Power/Knowledge: Selected Interviews and Other Writings, 1972–1977*. Ed. Colin Gordon. New York: Pantheon.

———. 1983a. "Afterword: The Subject and Power." In *Michel Foucault: Beyond Structuralism and Hermeneutics*, 2d ed., ed. Hubert L. Dreyfus and Paul Rabinow, 208–26. Chicago: University of Chicago Press.

———. 1983b. "On the Genealogy of Ethics: An Overview of Work in Progress." In *Michel Foucault: Beyond Structuralism and Hermeneutics*, 2d ed., ed. Hubert L. Dreyfus and Paul Rabinow, 229–52. Chicago: University of Chicago Press.

———. 1991. *Remarks on Marx: Conversations with Duccio Trombadori*. Trans. R. James Goldstein and James Cascaito. New York: Semiotext(e).

Franco, Jean. 1985. "New York Is a Third World City." *Tabloid*, no. 9:12–19.

Friedhelm, Ernst. 1989. "Problems of UNRWA School Education and Vocational Training." *Journal of Refugee Studies* 2 (1): 88–97.

Friedland, Roger, and Deirdre Boden, eds. 1994. *NowHere: Space, Time, and Modernity*. Berkeley: University of California Press.

Friedman, Jonathan. 1990. "Being in the World: Localization and Globalization." In *Global Culture: Nationalism, Globalization, and Modernity*, ed. Mike Featherstone, 311–28. London: Sage.

Fujioka, Shiro. 1957. *Traces of a Journey*. Trans. Mabel Saito Hall for Sucheng Chan. Los Angeles: Kanko Koenkai. Typescript. Original Japanese title: *Ayumi No Ato*.

Fustel de Coulanges, Numa Denis. 1980. *The Ancient City: A Study on the Religion, Laws, and Institutions of Greece and Rome*. Baltimore: Johns Hopkins University Press.

Garcia, Alejandro V. 1988. "Devoción en la Aldea." *El País*, 24 May, 23.

Gates, Henry Louis, Jr. 1988. *The Signifying Monkey: A Theory of African-American Literary Criticism*. Oxford: Oxford University Press.

Gee, Emma. 1976. "Issei Women." In *Counterpoint: Perspectives on Asian America*, ed.

Emma Gee, 359–64. Los Angeles: Asian American Studies Center, University of California, Los Angeles.

Geertz, Clifford. 1973. *The Interpretation of Cultures*. New York: Basic.

———. 1983. *Local Knowledge: Further Essays in Interpretive Anthropology*. New York: Basic.

Gellner, Ernest. 1983. *Nations and Nationalism*. Ithaca: Cornell University Press.

Geyer, Michael. 1992. "The Stigma of Violence, Nationalism, and War in Twentieth-Century Germany." *German Studies Review* (Special Issue, Winter): 75–110.

Ghosh, Amitav. 1989. *The Shadow Lines*. New York: Viking.

Giacaman, Rita. 1989. "Palestinian Women in the Uprising: From Followers to Leaders." *Journal of Refugee Studies* 2 (1): 139–45.

German Information Center (GIC). 1995. *German Unification, Five Years On*, 1–6. New York: GIC, September.

Giddens, Anthony. 1984. *The Constitution of Society*. Oxford: Oxford University Press.

———. 1987. *The Nation-State and Violence*. Berkeley: University of California Press.

Gilroy, Paul. 1990. "Nationalism, History, and Ethnic Absolutism." *History Workshop Journal* 30:114–20.

———. 1992. "Cultural Studies and Ethnic Absolutism." In *Cultural Studies*, ed. Lawrence Grossberg, Cary Nelson, and Paula A. Treichler. New York: Routledge.

———. 1993. *The Black Atlantic: Modernity and Double Consciousness*. Cambridge: Harvard University Press.

Glass, Ruth. 1989. *Cliches of Urban Doom and Other Essays*. Oxford: Basil Blackwell.

Glendon, Mary Ann. 1989. *The Transformation of Family Law: State, Law, and Family in the United States and Western Europe*. Chicago: University of Chicago Press.

Globe and Mail. 1982. "Procter and Gamble Lifts Veil a Little." 15 March, B1.

———. 1985. "P & G Loses Campaign for the Moon and Stars." 26 April, B6.

Godkin, Michael A. 1980. "Identity and Place: Clinical Applications Based on Notions of Rootedness and Uprootedness." In *The Human Experience of Space and Place*, ed. Anne Buttimer and David Deamon, 73–85. New York: St. Martin's.

Goode, Judith, and Jo Anne Schneider. 1994. *Reshaping Ethnic and Racial Relations in Philadelphia: Immigrants in a Divided City*. Philadelphia: Temple University Press.

Goodwin-Gil, Guy. 1983. *The Refugee in International Law*. Oxford: Clarendon.

Goytisolo, Juan. 1987. *Landscapes after the Battle*. New York: Seaver.

Graham, Julie. 1991. "Fordism/Post-Fordism, Marxism/Post-Marxism: The Second Cultural Divide." *Rethinking Marxism* 4 (1): 39–58.

Graham-Brown, Sarah. 1983. "The Economic Consequences of Occupation." In *Occupation: Israel over Palestine*, ed. Naseer Aruri. Belmont, Mass.: Association of Arab-American University Graduates Press.

Gramsci, Antonio. 1971. *Selectons from the Prison Notebooks*. Ed. and trans. Quintin Hoare and Geoffrey Nowell Smith. New York: International Publishers.

Graves, Robert. 1966. *The White Goddess*. New York: Farrar, Straus and Giroux.

Gregory, Steven. 1994. "Race, Identity, and Political Activism: The Shifting Contours of the African American Public Sphere." *Public Culture* 7:147–64.

Grieder, Jerome. 1981. *Intellectuals and the State in Modern China*. New York: Free Press.

Grossberg, Lawrence, Cary Nelson, and Paula A. Treichler, eds. 1992. *Cultural Studies*. New York: Routledge.

Guha, Ranajit, and Gayatri Chakravorty Spivak, eds. 1988. *Selected Subaltern Studies*. New York: Oxford University Press.

Guichaoua, Andre. 1995. *Les crises politiques au Burundi et au Rwanda (1993–1994)*. Paris: Karthala.

Guillaumin, Colette. 1995. *Racism, Sexism, Power, and Ideology*. New York: Routledge.

Gunder Frank, Andre. 1967. *Capitalism and Underdevelopment in Latin America: Historical Studies of Chile and Brazil*. New York: Monthly Review Press.

Gupta, Akhil. 1988. "Space and Time in the Politics of Culture." Paper presented at the 87th Annual Meeting of the American Anthropological Association, 16–20 November, Phoenix, Arizona.

———. 1992. "The Song of the Nonaligned World: Transnational Identities and the Reinscription of Space in Late Capitalism." *Cultural Anthropology* 7 (1): 63–79.

Gupta, Akhil, and James Ferguson. 1992. "Beyond 'Culture': Space, Identity, and the Politics of Difference." *Cultural Anthropology* 7 (1): 1–23.

———, eds. In press. *Anthropological Locations: Boundaries and Grounds of a Field Science*. Berkeley: University of California Press.

Gutting, Gary. 1994. Introduction to *The Cambridge Companion to Foucault*, ed. Gutting. New York: Cambridge University Press.

Habermas, Jürgen. 1987. *The Philosophical Discourse of Modernity*. Oxford: Oxford University Press.

———. 1989. *Structural Transformation of the Public Sphere*. Trans. Thomas Burger, with the assistance of Frederick Lawrence. 1962. Reprint, Cambridge: MIT Press.

Hacker, Jens. 1974. "Das neue Dilemma der DDR: Über bürgerliche und sozialistische Nationen." *Die politische Meinung* 19:48–60.

Hajjar, Lisa. 1993. "The Islamist Movements in the Occupied Territories: An Interview with Iyad Barghouti." *Middle East Report*, no. 183 (July–August): 9–12.

Hall, Stuart. 1980. "Cultural Studies: Two Paradigms." *Media, Culture, and Society* 2:57–72.

———. 1981. "Notes on Deconstructing 'the Popular.'" In *People's History and Socialist Theory*, ed. Raphael Samuel, 227–39. London: Routledge and Kegan Paul.

———. 1986. "Gramsci's Relevance for the Study of Race and Ethnicity." *Journal of Communication Inquiry* 10 (2): 5–27.

———. 1990. "Cultural Identity and Diaspora." In *Identity: Community, Culture, Difference*, ed. Jonathan Rutherford, 222–37. London: Lawrence and Wishart.

———. 1992. "The Question of Cultural Identity." In *Modernity and Its Futures*, ed. Stuart Hall, David Held and Tony McGrew. London: Polity Press, Open University.

———. 1993. "New Ethnicities" [1988]. In *Black Film British Cinema*, ed. Kobena Mercer et al. London: Institute of Contemporary Arts, 27–31.

———. 1994. "Cultural Identity and Diaspora." In *Colonial Discourse and Post-*

Colonial Theory, ed. Patrick Williams and Laura Chrisman. New York: Columbia University Press.

Hammami, Rema. 1990. "Women, the Hijab, and the Intifada." *Middle East Report*, nos. 164–65 (May–June/July–August).

Handler, Richard. 1988. *Nationalism and the Politics of Culture in Quebec.* Madison: University of Wisconsin Press.

Hangzhou Silk Institute. 1984. *Silk Industry Techniques.* Hangzhou: Hangzhou Silk Institute.

Hannerz, Ulf. 1986. "Small Is Beautiful?" *Comparative Studies in Society and History* 28 (1).

——. 1987. "The World in Creolisation." *Africa* 57 (4): 546–59.

——. 1989. "Notes on the Global Ecumene." *Public Culture* 1 (2): 66–75.

Hansen, Karen Tranberg. 1984. "Negotiating Sex and Gender in Urban Zambia." *Journal of Southern African Studies* 10 (2): 219–38.

Haraway, Donna J. 1985. "A Manifesto for Cyborgs: Science, Technology, and Socialist Feminism in the 1980s." *Socialist Review* 15 (80): 65–107.

——. 1986. "The Heart of Africa: Nations, Dreams, and Apes." *Inscriptions*, no. 2: 9–16.

——. 1991a. "A Manifesto for Cyborgs." In *Simians, Cyborgs, and Women.* New York: Routledge.

——. 1991b. "Situated Knowledges." In *Simians, Cyborgs, and Women.* New York: Routledge.

Harrell-Bond, Barbara. 1986. *Imposing Aid: Emergency Assistance to Refugees.* Oxford: Oxford University Press.

——. 1989. "Repatriation: Under What Conditions Is It the Most Desirable Solution for Refugees?" *African Studies Review* 32 (1): 41–69.

Harry, Margot. 1987. "*Attention, MOVE! This Is America!*" Chicago: Banner.

Harvey, David. 1985a. "The Geopolitics of Capitalism." In *Social Relations and Spatial Structures*, ed. Derek Gregory and John Urry, 128–63. New York: St. Martin's.

——. 1985b. *The Urban Experience.* Baltimore: Johns Hopkins University Press.

——. 1989. *The Condition of Postmodernity: An Enquiry into the Origins of Cultural Change.* New York: Blackwell.

——. 1993. "From Space to Place and Back Again: Reflections on the Condition of Postmodernity." In *Mapping the Futures: Local Cultures, Global Change*, ed. Jon Bird et al., 3–29. New York: Routledge.

Hastrup, Kirstin, and Karen Fog Olwig, eds. 1997. *Siting Culture.* New York: Routledge.

Hebdige, Dick. 1987. *Cut'n'Mix: Culture, Identity, and Caribbean Music.* London: Methuen.

——. 1994. "After the Masses." Reprinted in *Culture/Power/History: A Reader in Contemporary Social Theory*, ed. Nicholas Dirks, Geoff Eley, and Sherry Ortner, 222–35. Princeton: Princeton University Press.

Hegel, G. W. F. 1953. *Reason in History.* Trans. Robert S. Hartman. New York: Macmillan.

Heiberg, Marianne. 1989. *The Making of the Basque Nation.* Cambridge: Cambridge University Press.

Heller, Agnes, and Ferenc Feher. 1988. *The Postmodern Political Condition.* New York: Columbia University Press.

Herzfeld, Michael. 1986. "Within and Without: The Category of the Female in the Ethnography of Modern Greece." In *Gender and Power in Rural Greece,* ed. Jill Dubisch, 215–34. Princeton: Princeton University Press.

———. 1987. *Anthropology through the Looking-Glass: Critical Ethnography in the Margins of Europe.* New York: Cambridge University Press.

Hicks, Neil. 1992. *Lawyers and the Military Justice System in the Occupied Territories.* New York: Lawyers Committee for Human Rights.

Higgs, Peter Lawrence. 1979. "Culture and Value Changes in Zambian School Literature." Ph.D. diss., School of Education, University of California, Los Angeles.

Hijazi, Hussein. 1995. "Hamas: Waiting for Secular Nationalism to Self-Destruct (Interview with Mahmud Zahhar)." *Journal of Palestine Studies* 24 (3): 81–88.

Hobsbawm, Eric. 1983. "Introduction: Inventing Traditions." In *The Invention of Tradition,* ed. Eric Hobsbawm and Terence Ranger. New York: Cambridge University Press.

———. 1990. *Nations and Nationalism since 1780: Programme, Myths, Reality.* New York: Cambridge University Press.

Hobsbawm, Eric, and Terence Ranger, eds. 1983. *The Invention of Tradition.* New York: Cambridge University Press.

Holston, James. 1989. *The Modernist City: An Anthropological Critique of Brasilia.* Chicago: University of Chicago Press.

Honig, Emily. 1986. *Sisters and Strangers: Women in the Shanghai Cotton Mills, 1919–1949.* Stanford: Stanford University Press.

hooks, bell. 1992. "The Oppositional Gaze." In *Black Looks: Race and Representation.* Boston: South End.

Horn, David G. 1988. "Welfare, the Social, and the Individual in Interwar Italy." *Cultural Anthropology* 3 (4): 395–407.

Hsu, Immanuel. 1990. *The Rise of Modern China.* 4th ed. Oxford: Oxford University Press.

Hu, Hsien-chin. 1944. "The Chinese Concept of 'Face.' " *American Anthropologist* 46 (1): 45–64.

Human Rights Watch. 1994. *Torture and Ill-Treatment: Israel's Interrogation of Palestinians from the Occupied Territories.* New York: Human Rights Watch.

Hurewitz, J. C. 1968. *The Struggle for Palestine.* New York: Greenwood.

Huyssens, Andreas. 1984. "Mapping the Post-Modern." *New German Critique* 33:5–52.

Ichihashi, Yamato. 1932. *Japanese in the United States: A Critical Study of the Problems of the Japanese Immigrants and Their Children.* Stanford: Stanford University Press.

Ichioka, Yuji. 1988. *The Issei: The World of the First Generation Japanese Immigrants, 1885–1924.* New York: Free Press.

India-West. 1988. "Sikh Temple Announces Ninth Annual Parade." 21 October, 18.

International Herald Tribune. 1989. "Seville's Flamenco Popular in Madrid." 8 September, Paris edition, Travel section, p. 11, col. 3.

Irigaray, Luce. 1985. *This Sex Which Is Not One.* Trans. Catherine Porter. Ithaca: Cornell University Press.

Ivy, Marilyn. 1988. "Tradition and Difference in the Japanese Mass Media." *Public Culture* 1 (1): 21–30.

Iwata, Masakazu. 1962. "The Japanese Immigrants in California Agriculture." *Agricultural History* 36 (1): 25–37.

Jabr, Hisham. 1989. "Housing Conditions in the Refugee Camps of the West Bank." *Journal of Refugee Studies* 2 (1): 75–87.

Jacoby, Harold S. 1958. "More Sinned Against Than Sinning." *Pacific Historian* 11 (4): 1–2, 8.

———. 1982. "Administrative Restriction of Asian Indian Immigration into the United States, 1907–1917." *Population Review* 25:35–40.

Jamal, Vali, and John Weeks. 1993. *Africa Misunderstood: Or Whatever Happened to the Rural-Urban Gap?* Basingstoke: Macmillan.

Jameson, Fredric. 1983. "Postmodernism and Consumer Society." In *The Anti-Aesthetic: Essays on Postmodern Culture,* ed. Hal Foster, 111–25. Port Townsend, Wash.: Bay Press.

———. 1984. "Postmodernism, or the Cultural Logic of Late Capitalism." *New Left Review,* no. 146:53–92.

———. 1986. "Third-World Literature in the Era of Multinational Capitalism." *Social Text,* no. 15:65–88.

———. 1991. *Postmodernism, or, The Cultural Logic of Late Capitalism.* Durham: Duke University Press.

Jarbawi, Ali. 1990. "Palestinian Elites in the Occupied Territories." In *Intifada: Palestine at the Crossroads,* ed. Jamal R. Nassar and Roger Heacock. New York: Praeger.

Jefremovas, Villia. n.d. "The Rwandan State and Local Level Response: Class and Region in the Rwandan Genocide, the Refugee Crisis, Repatriation, and the 'New Rwanda.' "

Jensen, Joan M. 1988. *Passage from India: Asian Indian Immigrants in North America.* New Haven: Yale University Press.

Jiryis, Sabri. 1973. "The Legal Structure for the Expropriation and Absorption of Arab Lands in Israel." *Journal of Palestine Studies* 2 (4).

Johnson, Annette Thackwell. 1922. "The 'Rag Heads' — A Picture of America's East Indians." *Independent* 109 (3828): 234–35.

Jordan, Terry. 1982. *Texas Graveyards: A Cultural Legacy.* Austin: University of Texas Press.

Kafka, Franz. 1971. "The Great Wall of China." In *The Complete Stories,* ed. Nahun N. Glazer, 235–49. New York: Schocken.

———. 1974. *The Castle.* Trans. Willa and Edwin Muir. 1926. Reprint, New York: Shocken.

Kanafani, Noman. 1995. "Homecomings." *Middle East Report,* nos. 194–95 (May–June/July–August): 40–42.

Kapferer, Bruce. 1988. *Legends of People, Myths of State: Violence, Intolerance, and*

Political Culture in Sri Lanka and Australia. Washington, D.C.: Smithsonian Institution Press.

Kaplan, Caren. 1987. "Deterritorializations: The Rewriting of Home and Exile in Western Feminist Discourse." *Cultural Critique* 6:187–98.

Kaplan, E. Ann, ed. 1988. *Postmodernism and Its Discontents.* New York: Verso.

Kaplan, Martha, and John Kelly. 1994. "Rethinking Resistance: Dialogics of Disaffection in Colonial Fiji." *American Ethnologist* 21 (1): 123–51.

Katz, Cindi. 1990. "You Can't Drive a Chevy through a Post-Fordist Landscape: Everyday Cultural Practices of Resistance and Reproduction among Youth in New York City." Revised manuscript of paper presented at Marxism Now Conference, Amherst, Mass., 1989.

Kaufmann, Franz-Xaver. 1988. "Sozialpolitik und Familie." *Politik und Zeitgeschichte* B13 (88): 34–43.

Kaunda, Kenneth. 1966. *Zambia, Independence and Beyond: The Speeches of Kenneth Kaunda,* ed. Colin Legum. London: Nelson.

Kaviraj, Sudipta. 1992. "The Imaginary Institution of India." In *Subaltern Studies VII,* ed. Partha Chatterjee and Gyanendra Pandey, 1–39. New Delhi: Oxford University Press.

Kearney, Michael. 1986. "From the Invisible Hand to Visible Feet: Anthropological Studies of Migration and Development." *Annual Review of Anthropology* 15:331–61.

———. 1991. "Borders and Boundaries of State and Self at the End of Empire." *Journal of Historical Sociology* 4 (1): 52–74.

Kearney, Michael, and Carol Nagengast. 1989. "Anthropological Perspectives on Transnational Communities in Rural California." Working Paper no. 3, Working Group on Farm Labor and Rural Poverty. Davis, Calif.: California Institute for Rural Studies.

Keith, Michael, and Steve Pile, eds. 1993. *Place and the Politics of Identity.* New York: Routledge.

Kellner, Doug. 1989. *Jean Baudrillard: From Marxism to Postmodernism and Beyond.* Stanford: Stanford University Press.

Kelly, William. 1990. "Japanese No-Noh: The Crosstalk of Public Culture in a Rural Festivity." *Public Culture* 2 (2): 65–81.

Kerr, David, and Garikayi Shoniwa. 1978. *Matteo Sakala.* Lusaka, Zambia: Multimedia Publications.

Kester, Grant. 1993. "Out of Sight Is Out of Mind: The Imaginary Space of Postindustrial Culture." *Social Text* 35:72–92.

Khalidi, Muhammad A. 1995. "A First Visit to Palestine." *Journal of Palestine Studies* 24 (3): 74–80.

Khalidi, Rashid. 1987. "The Palestinians after Twenty Years." *Middle East Report,* no. 146 (May–June).

———. 1988. "The PLO and the Uprising." *Middle East Report,* no. 154 (September–October).

Kikumura, Akemi. 1981. *Through Harsh Winters: The Life of a Japanese Immigrant Woman.* Novato, Calif.: Chandler and Sharp.

Kismaric, Carole. 1989. *Forced Out: The Agony of the Refugee in Our Time*. New York: Random House.

Kondonassis, A. J., and A. G. Malliaris. 1994. "Toward Monetary Union of the European Community." *American Journal of Economics and Sociology* 53 (3): 291–301.

Koonz, Claudia. 1993. "Ethical Dilemmas and Nazi Eugenics: Single-Issue Dissent in Religious Contexts." *Journal of Modern History* 64:S8–S31.

Koopmans, Tjalling Charles. 1992. "Federalism: The Wrong Debate." *Common Market Law Review* 29 (6): 1047–52.

Koptiuch, Kristin, and Frances Negron. 1991. "Third World U.S.A.: First Stop, Philadelphia." Experimental radio production. New York: New American Radio.

Korte, Hermann. 1985. "Bevölkerungsstruktur und -entwicklung." In *Die Bundesrepublik Deutschland*, vol. 2, ed. Wolfgang Benz, 13–34. Frankfurt am Main: Fischer.

Koselleck, Reinhart. 1985. *Futures Past: On the Semantics of Historical Time*. Cambridge: MIT Press.

Kristeva, Julia. 1980. *Desire in Language: A Semiotic Approach to Literature and Art*. Ed. Leon S. Roudiez. Trans. Thomas Gorz, Alice Jardine, and Leon S. Roudiez. New York: Columbia University Press.

——. 1991. *Strangers to Ourselves*. New York: Columbia University Press.

Kroker, Arthur, and David Cook. 1986. *The Postmodern Scene: Excremental Culture and Hyper-Aesthetics*. New York: St. Martin's.

Kruger, Loren. 1987. " 'Our National House': The Ideology of the National Theatre of Great Britain." *Theatre Journal* 39 (1): 35–50.

Kuhn, Annette. 1985. *The Power of the Image: Essays on Representation and Sexuality*. London: Routledge.

Kulkarni, Diane. 1984. "Immigrant a Strength and Inspiration" [about Sunder Amer Dhutt Singh]. *Ogden Standard Examiner*, 30 April.

La Brack, Bruce. 1988. *The Sikhs of Northern California, 1905–1975: A Socio-historical Study*. New York: S. M. S. Press.

Lacan, Jacques. 1985. "The Meaning of the Phallus." In *Feminine Sexuality: Jacques Lacan and the Ecole Freudienne,* ed. Juliet Mitchell and Jacqueline Rose. New York: Norton.

Latour, Bruno. 1993. *We Have Never Been Modern*. Trans. Catherine Porter. Cambridge: Harvard University Press.

Layoun, Mary. 1990. "Narrating Nationalism: Who Speaks and How? Who Listens and How? Or, Whose Story Is This Anyway?" Paper presented at Workshop of the Joint Committee on the Near and Middle East of the SSRC and ACLS, Hanover, New Hampshire, 24–25 March.

Lazarus, Neil. 1991. "Doubting the New World Order: Marxism, Realism, and the Claims of Postmodernist Social Theory." *Differences* 3 (3): 94–138.

Leed, Eric. 1980. "Voice and Print: Master Symbols in the History of Communication." In *The Myths of Information: Technology and Postindustrial Culture,* ed. Kathleen Woodward, 41–61. Madison, Wis.: Coda.

Legrain, Jean François. 1990. "The Islamic Movement and the Intifada." In *Inti-*

fada: Palestine at the Crossroads, ed. Jamal R. Nassar and Roger Heacock. New York: Praeger.

Lemarchand, Rene. 1994. *Burundi: Ethnocide as Discourse and Practice.* Cambridge: Cambridge University Press.

Lemarchand, Rene, and David Martin. 1974. *Selective Genocide in Burundi.* Report no. 20. London: Minority Rights Group.

Leonard, Karen. 1985. "Punjabi Farmers and California's Alien Land Law." *Agricultural History* 59 (4): 549–62.

———. 1989. "Pioneer Voices from California: Reflections on Race, Religion, and Ethnicity." In *The Sikh Diaspora,* ed. N. Gerald Barrier and Verne A. Dusenbery, 120–39. Columbia, Mo.: South Asia Books.

———. 1992. *Making Ethnic Choices: California's Punjabi Mexican Americans.* Philadelphia: Temple University Press.

———. 1993. "Intermarriage and Ethnicity: Punjabi Mexican Americans, Mexican Japanese, and Filipino Americans." *Explorations in Ethnic Studies* 16:2, 147–63.

———. 1994. "The Punjabi Pioneer Experience in America: Recognition or Denial?: *International Journal of Punjab Studies* 1 (2): 271–94.

———. Forthcoming. "Punjabi-Mexican Experiences of Multiethnicity." In *We Are a People: Narrative in the Construction and Deconstruction of Ethnic Identity,* ed. Paul Spickard and Jeff Burroughs. Philadelphia: Temple University Press.

Lévi-Strauss, Claude. 1966. *The Savage Mind.* 1962. Reprint, Chicago: University of Chicago Press.

Liebes, Tamar, and Elihu Katz. 1990. *The Export of Meaning: Cross-Cultural Readings of Dallas.* New York: Oxford University Press.

Limón, Jose E. 1989. " '*Carne,*' '*Carnales,*' and the Carnivalesque: Bakhtinian '*Batos,*' Disorder, and Narrative Discourses." *American Ethnologist* 16 (3): 471–86.

Lipietz, Alain. 1987. *Mirages and Miracles: The Crises of Global Fordism.* Trans. David Macey. London: Verso.

Livingstone, Sonia M. 1994. *Talk on Television: Audience Participation and Public Debate.* London: Routledge.

Löfgren, Orvar. 1989. "The Nationalization of Culture." *Ethnologia Europaea* 19 (1): 5–24.

Ludes, Peter. 1992. "Visualisierung als Teilprozess der Modernisierung der Moderne." In *Institution, Technik, und Programrn: Rahmaspekte der Programmgeschichte des Fernsehens,* ed. Knut Hickethier, 353–70. Munich: Wilhelm Fink.

Lüdke, Alf. 1993. "The Appeal of Exterminating 'Others': German Workers and the Limits of Resistance." *Journal of Modern History* 64:S46–S67.

Ludz, Peter Christian. 1973. "Deutsche Nation in der Sicht der SED." *Deutschland Archiv* 6:9–24.

Lustick, Ian. 1980. *Arabs in a Jewish State.* Austin: University of Texas Press.

Lutfiyya, Abdulla. 1969. *Baytin: A Jordanian Village.* The Hague: Mouton.

Lyotard, Jean-François. 1984. *The Postmodern Condition.* Minneapolis: University of Minnesota Press.

Maase, Kaspar. 1985. "Freizeit." In *Die Bundesrepublik Deutschland,* vol. 2, ed. Wolfgang Benz, 209–33. Frankfurt am Main: Fischer.

Malkki, Liisa. 1985. "The Origin of a Device of Power: The Refugee Camp in Post-War Europe." "Special Paper" submitted to the Department of Anthropology, Harvard University, Cambridge.

———. 1989. "Purity and Exile: Transformations in Historical-National Consciousness among Hutu Refugees in Tanzania." Ph.D. diss., Department of Anthropology, Harvard University.

———. 1990. "Context and Consciousness: Local Conditions for the Production of Historical and National Thought among Hutu Refugees in Tanzania." In *Nationalist Ideologies and the Production of National Cultures,* ed. Richard G. Fox, 32–62. American Ethnological Society Monograph Series, no. 2. Washington, D.C.: American Anthropological Association.

———. 1992. "National Geographic: The Rooting of Peoples and the Territorialization of National Identity among Scholars and Refugees." *Cultural Anthropology* 7 (1): 24–44.

———. 1994. "Citizens of Humanity: Internationalism and the Imagined Community of Nations." *Diaspora* 3 (1): 41–68.

———. 1995a. *Purity and Exile: Violence, Memory, and National Cosmology among Hutu Refugees in Tanzania.* Chicago: University of Chicago Press.

———. 1995b. "Refugees and Exile: From 'Refugee Studies' to the National Order of Things." *Annual Review of Anthropology* 24:495–523.

Mandel, Ernest. 1975. *Late Capitalism.* Trans. Joris de Bres. New York: Verso.

Mani, Lata. 1989. "Multiple Mediations: Feminist Scholarship in the Age of Multinational Reception." *Inscriptions* 5:1–23.

Mankekar, D. R. 1978a. *One-Way Free Flow: Neo-colonialism via News Media.* New Delhi: Clarion.

———. 1978b. "Three Kinds of Gaps." In *Proceedings of the Seminar on Non-aligned News Pool,* ed. Jag Parvesh Chandra, 12–21. New Delhi: All-India Newspaper Editors' Conference.

———. 1978c. "Why News Pool." In *Proceedings of the Seminar on Non-aligned News Pool,* ed. Jag Parvesh Chandra, 85–93. New Delhi: All-India Newspaper Editors' Conference.

———. 1981. *Whose Freedom? Whose Order?* New Delhi: Clarion.

Mankekar, Purnima. 1993. "National Texts and Gendered Lives: An Ethnography of Television Viewers in a North Indian City." *American Ethnologist* 20:543–63.

Ma'oz, Moshe. 1984. *Palestinian Leadership in the West Bank.* London: Frank Cass.

Mapes, Glynn. 1990. "Polyglot Students Are Weaned Early off Mother Tongue." *Wall Street Journal,* 6 March.

Marcus, Amy Docker. 1995. "Big Palestinian Clans Enjoy a Resurgence That May Hurt Arafat." *Wall Street Journal,* 12 September, A1.

Marcus, George E. 1986. "Contemporary Problems of Ethnography in the Modern World System." In *Writing Culture: The Poetics and Politics of Ethnography,* ed. James Clifford and George E. Marcus, 165–93. Berkeley: University of California Press.

———. 1989a. "Imagining the Whole: Ethnography's Contemporary Efforts to Situate Itself." *Critique of Anthropology* 9 (3): 7–30.

———. 1989b. "Requirements for Ethnographies of Late Modernity: Local and Global Perspectives." Paper presented at the conference "Writing the Social Text," University of Maryland, 18 November.

Marcus, George E., and Michael M. J. Fischer. 1986. *Anthropology as Cultural Critique: An Experimental Moment in the Human Sciences.* Chicago: University of Chicago Press.

Marrus, Michael. 1985. *The Unwanted: European Refugees in the Twentieth Century.* New York: Oxford University Press.

Martin, Biddy, and Chandra Talpade Mohanty. 1986. "Feminist Politics: What's Home Got to Do with It?" In *Feminist Studies/Critical Studies,* ed. Teresa de Lauretis, 191–212. Bloomington: Indiana University Press.

Martin, Emily. 1987. *The Woman in the Body: A Cultural Analysis of Reproduction.* Boston: Beacon.

Masalha, Nur. 1991. "A Critique of Benny Morris." *Journal of Palestine Studies* 21 (1): 90–97.

Massey, Doreen. 1992. "A Place Called Home?" *New Formations* 17:3–15.

———. 1994. *Space, Place, and Gender.* Minneapolis: University of Minnesota Press.

Mauss, Marcel. 1969. *La nation et l'internationalisme.* Oeuvres 3, *Cohesion sociale et divisions de la sociologie,* 573–639. Paris: Minuit.

Mayer, Philip. 1971. *Townsmen or Tribesmen: Conservatism and the Process of Urbanization in a South African City.* New York: Oxford University Press.

Maykuth, Andrew. 1990. "Doctors Find a Bit of the Third World in Harlem." *Philadelphia Inquirer,* January 22.

Mbonimpa, Melchior. 1993. *Hutu, Tutsi, Twa: Pour une Societe sans Castes au Burundi.* Paris: L'Harmattan.

McDowall, David. 1989. "A Profile of the Population of the West Bank and Gaza Strip." *Journal of Refugee Studies* 2 (1): 20–25.

McRobbie, Angela. 1994. *Postmodernism and Popular Culture.* New York: Routledge.

Mears, Eliot Grinnell. 1978. *Resident Orientals on the American Pacific Coast.* Ca. 1928. Reprint, New York: Arno.

Meebelo, Henry S. 1986. *African Proletarians and Colonial Capitalism: The Origins, Growth, and Struggles of the Zambian Labour Movement to 1964.* Lusaka: Kenneth Kaunda Foundation.

Meinicke, Wolfgang. 1988. "Zur Integration der Umsiedler in die Gesellschaft, 1945–1952." *Zeitschrift für Geschichtswisssenschaften* 36 (10): 867–78.

Menache, Sophia. 1990. *Vox Dei: Communication in the Middle Ages.* New York: Oxford University Press.

Miles, Robert, and Dietrich Thränhardt, eds. 1995. *Migration and European Integration: The Dynamics of Inclusion and Exclusion.* London: Pinter.

Miller, James. 1993. *The Passion of Michel Foucault.* New York: Simon and Schuster.

Miller, Ylana. 1985. *Government and Society in Rural Palestine, 1920–1948.* Austin: University of Texas Press.

Milward, Alan S., Frances M. B. Lynch, Ruggero Ranieri, Federico Romero, and Vibeke Sørensen. 1993. *The Frontier of National Sovereignty: History and Theory, 1945–1992.* New York: Routledge.

Mintz, Sidney W. 1985. *Sweetness and Power: The Place of Sugar in Modern History*. New York: Penguin.

Mishal, Shaul. 1978. *West Bank/East Bank: The Palestinians in Jordan, 1949–1967*. New Haven: Yale University Press.

Mitchell, J. C. 1987. *Cities, Society, and Social Perception: A Central African Perspective*. Oxford: Clarendon.

Mitchell, Timothy. 1988. *Colonising Egypt*. Cambridge: Cambridge University Press.

——. 1989. "The Effect of the State."

——. 1990. "Everyday Metaphors of Power." *Theory and Society* 19:545–77.

Mitchell, W. J. T. 1986. *Iconology: Image, Text, Ideology*. Chicago: University of Chicago Press.

Mitterauer, Michael, and Reinhard Sieder. 1983. *The European Family*. Chicago: University of Chicago Press.

Mohanty, Chandra Talpade. 1987. "Feminist Encounters, Location, and the Politics of Experience." *Copyright* 1:30–44.

——. 1988. "Under Western Eyes: Feminist Scholarship and Colonial Discourses." *Feminist Review*, no. 30:61–88.

Molle, Willem. 1994. *The Economics of European Integration: Theory, Practice, Policy*. 2d ed. Aldershot; Brookfield, Vt.: Dartmouth Publishers.

Mommsen, Wolfgang. 1983. "Wandlungen der nationalen Identität." In *Die Identität der Deutschen*, ed. Werner Weidenfeld, 168–90. Munich: Goldmann.

Monheim, Heiner, and Rita Monheim-Dandorfer. 1991. *Straßen für alle*. Hamburg: Rasch u. Roehring.

Montreal Gazette. 1985. "Procter & Gamble Signals Move to Acquire Existing Brands." 3 October, E6.

Moodie, T. Dunbar, with Vivienne Ndatshe. 1994. *Going for Gold: Men, Mines, and Migration*. Berkeley: University of California Press.

Moore, Henrietta. 1986. *Space, Text, and Gender*. Cambridge: Cambridge University Press.

Moore, Sally Falk. 1989. "The Production of Cultural Pluralism as a Process." *Public Culture* 1 (2): 26–48.

Moreno, Isidoro. 1974. *Las Hermandades Andaluzas: Una Aproximacion Desde la Antropología*. Seville: Universidad de Sevilla.

——. 1985. "Etnicidad, Conciencia de Etnicidad y Movimientos Nacionalistas: Aproximación al Caso Andaluz." *Revista de Estudios Andaluces*, no. 5:13–38.

Morley, David. 1992. *Television, Audiences, and Cultural Studies*. London: Routledge.

Morley, David, and Kevin Robins. 1995. *Spaces of Identity: Global Media, Electronic Landscapes, and Cultural Boundaries*. New York: Routledge.

Morris, Benny. 1988. *The Birth of the Palestinian Refugee Problem, 1947–1949*. Cambridge: Cambridge University Press.

——. 1990. *1948 and After: Israel and the Palestinians*. Oxford: Clarendon.

——. 1991. "Response to Finkelstein and Masalha." *Journal of Palestine Studies* 21 (1): 98–114.

——. 1995. "Falsifying the Record: A Fresh Look at Zionist Documentation of 1948." *Journal of Palestine Studies* 24 (3): 44–62.

Morris, William. 1970. *News from Nowhere.* 1891. Reprint, London: Routledge and Kegan Paul.

Mortimer, Robert A. 1984. *The Third World Coalition in International Politics.* 2d ed. Boulder: Westview.

Mosse, George. 1985. *Nationalism and Sexuality: Respectability and Abnormal Sexuality in Modern Europe.* New York: H. Fertig.

Mühlfeld, Claus, and Friedrich Schönweiss. 1989. *Nationalsozialistische Familienpolitik.* Stuttgart: Enke.

Mulaisho, Killian. 1988. *Tragedy of Pride.* Lusaka, Zambia: Multimedia Publications.

Mulvey, Laura. 1975. "Visual Pleasure and the Narrative Cinema." *Screen* 16 (3): 6–18.

Nakhleh, Khalil. 1975. "Cultural Determinants of Palestinian Collective Identity: The Case of the Arabs in Israel." *New Outlook* 18 (7): 31–40.

Nassar, Jamal R., and Roger Heacock, eds. 1990. *Intifada: Palestine at the Crossroads.* New York: Praeger.

New York Times. 1982. "Procter & Gamble's Battles with Rumors." 22 July, D1 and D10.

Newbury, Catherine, and David Newbury. 1995. "Identity, Genocide, and Reconstruction in Rwanda."

Nicholson, Linda, ed. 1990. *Feminism/Postmodernism.* New York: Routledge.

Niethammer, Lutz. 1988. "Annäherung an den Wandel: Auf der Suche nach der volkseigenen Erfahrung in der Industrieprovinz der DDR." *Bios* 1:19–66.

Noble, David F. 1977. *America by Design.* New York: Alfred A. Knopf.

Norden, Albert, et al. 1967. *Zwei deutsche Staaten: Die nationale Politik der DDR.* Vienna.

Oberoi, Harjot S. 1988. "From Ritual to Counter-Ritual: Rethinking the Hindu Sikh Question, 1884–1915." In *Sikh History and Religion in the Twentieth Century,* ed. Joseph T. O'Connell et al., 136–58. Toronto: Toronto Centre for South Asian Studies.

———. 1994. *The Construction of Religious Boundaries: Culture, Identity, and Diversity in the Sikh Tradition.* New York: Oxford University Press.

Obertreis, Regine. 1985. *Familienpolitik in der DDR, 1945–1980.* Opladen, Germany: Leske u. Budrich.

O'Brien, Jay, and William Roseberry, eds. 1991. *Golden Ages, Dark Ages: Imagining the Past in Anthropology and History.* Berkeley: University of California Press.

O'Hanlon, Rosalind. 1988. "Recovering the Subject: Subaltern Studies and Histories of Resistance in Colonial South Asia." *Modern Asian Studies* 22 (1): 189–224.

O'Hanlon, Rosalind, and David Washbrook. 1992. "After Orientalism — Culture, Criticism, and Politics in the Third World." *Comparative Studies in Society and History* 34 (1): 141–67.

Okihiro, Gary. 1988. "The Idea of Community and a 'Particular Type of History.'" In *Reflections on Shattered Windows,* ed. Gary Y. Okihiro, Shirley Hune, Arthur A. Hansen, and John M. Liu, 175–82. Pullman: Washington State University Press.

Okihiro, Gary. 1994. *Margins and Mainstreams: Asians in American History and Culture.* Seattle: University of Washington Press.

Okihiro, Gary, Shirley Hune, Arthur A. Hansen, and John M. Liu, eds. 1988. *Reflections on Shattered Windows.* Pullman: Washington State University Press.

O'Laughlin, Bridgit. 1975. "Marxist Approaches to Anthropology." *Annual Review of Anthropology* 4:341–70.

Ong, Aihwa. 1987. *Spirits of Resistance and Capitalist Discipline.* Albany: State University of New York Press.

Onuf, Nicholas Greenwood. 1991. "Sovereignty: Outline of a Conceptual History." *Alternatives* 16 (4): 425–46.

Ordaz, Pablo. 1990. "La Comisión de Agricultura del Congreso Se Pronuncia Contra Costa Donana y Propone Su Traslado." *El País,* 4 May, Andalusian edition, 26.

Ortner, Sherry. 1984. "Theory in Anthropology since the Sixties." *Comparative Studies in Society and History* 26:126–66.

———. 1995. "Resistance and the Problem of Ethnographic Refusal." *Comparative Studies in Society and History* 2:173–93.

Ortner, Sherry, and Harriet Whitehead. 1981. *Sexual Meanings: The Cultural Construction of Gender and Sexuality.* New York: Cambridge University Press.

Orwell, George. 1968. *As I Please, 1943–1945.* Ed. Sonia Orwell and Ian Angus. New York: Harcourt Brace Jovanovich.

Owens, Craig. 1983. "The Discourse of Others: Feminists and Postmodernism." In *The Anti-Aesthetic: Essays on Postmodern Culture,* ed. Hal Foster, 57–82. Port Townsend, Wash.: Bay Press.

Parkin, David. 1969. *Neighbours and Nationals in an African City Ward.* London: Routledge and Kegan Paul.

———. 1978. *The Cultural Definition of Political Response.* London: Academic Press.

Parmenter, Barbara McKean. 1994. *Giving Voice to Stones: Place and Identity in Palestinian Literature.* Austin: University of Texas Press.

Parpart, Jane. 1986. "Class and Gender on the Copperbelt: Women in Northern Rhodesian Copper Mining Communities, 1926–1964." In *Women and Class in Africa,* ed. Clare Robertson and Iris Berger, 141–60. New York: Africana Publishing.

Pellizzi, Francesco. 1988. "To Seek Refuge: Nation and Ethnicity in Exile." In *Ethnicities and Nations,* ed. Remo Guidieri, Francesco Pellizzi, and Stanley J. Tambiah, 154–71. Austin: University of Texas Press.

Peretz, Don. 1990. *Intifada: The Palestinian Uprising.* Boulder: Westview.

Peteet, Julie. 1987. "Socio-Political Integration and Conflict Resolution in the Palestinian Camps in Lebanon." *Journal of Palestine Studies* 16 (2): 29–44.

———. 1992. "The Cultural Politics of Violence in the Occupied Territories." Manuscript presented at the Annual Meeting of the American Anthropological Association, San Francisco, Calif., December.

Peters, Thomas J. 1982. *In Search of Excellence.* New York: Warner.

Pettigrew, Joyce Robber. 1975. *Noblemen: A Study of the Political System of the Sikh Jats.* Boston: Routledge and Kegan Paul.

Piore, M. J., and C. F. Sabel. 1984. *The Second Industrial Divide: Possibilities for Prosperity.* New York: Basic Books.

Pitt-Rivers, Julian. 1969. *The People of the Sierra.* Chicago: University of Chicago Press.

———. 1974. *The People of the Sierra.* 2d ed. Chicago: University of Chicago Press.

Plascov, Avi. 1981. *The Palestinian Refugees in Jordan, 1948–1957.* London: Frank Cass.

Plenel, Edwy. 1990. " 'Words Are Weapons' and Le Pen's Army Knows How to Pull the Trigger." *Manchester Guardian Weekly,* 27 May, 16.

Ploetz, Alfred. 1895. *Grundlinien einer Rassenhygiene.* Part 1, *Die Tüchtigkeit unserer Rasse und der Schutz der Schwachen: Ein Versuch über Rassenhygiene und ihr Verhältnis zu den humanen Idealen, besonders zum Sozialismus.* Berlin: Deutschen Gesellschaft für Rassenhygiene.

Pollock, Griselda. 1988. *Vision and Difference: Femininity, Feminism, and the Histories of Art.* London: Routledge.

Pommerin, Reiner. 1979. *Sterilisierung der Rheinlandbastarde: Das Schicksal einer farbigen deutschen Minderheit, 1918–1937.* Düsseldorf: Droste.

Poster, Mark. 1988. Introduction to *Jean Baudrillard: Selected Writings,* ed. Poster. Stanford: Stanford University Press.

Potts, Deborah. 1995. "Shall We Go Home? Increasing Urban Poverty in African Cities and Migration Processes." *Geographical Journal* 161 (3): 245–64.

Powdermaker, Hortense. 1962. *Copper Town: Changing Africa, the Human Situation on the Rhodesian Copperbelt.* New York: Harper and Row.

Prakash, Gyan. 1990. "Writing Post-Orientalist Histories of the Third World: Perspectives from Indian Historiography." *Comparative Studies in Society and History* 32 (2): 383–408.

———. 1992. "Can the Subaltern Ride? — a Reply." *Comparative Studies in Society and History* 34 (1): 168–84.

———. 1994. "Subaltern Studies as Postcolonial Criticism." *American Historical Review* 99 (5): 1475–90.

Pratt, Mary Louise. 1985. "Scratches on the Face of the Country, or, What Mr. Barrow Saw in the Land of the Bushmen." *Critical Inquiry* 12 (1): 119–43.

———. 1986a. "Fieldwork in Common Places." In *Writing Culture: The Poetics and Politics of Ethnography,* ed. James Clifford and George E. Marcus, 27–50. Berkeley: University of California Press.

———. 1986b. "Scratches on the Face of the Coventry, or, What Mr Barrow Saw in the Land of the Bushmen." In *Race, Writing, and Difference,* ed. Henry Louis Gates, 138–62. Chicago: University of Chicago Press.

———. 1990. "Women, Literature, and National Brotherhood."

Pratt, Minnie Bruce. 1984. "Identity: Skin, Blood, Heart." In *Yours in Struggle: Three Feminist Perspectives on Anti-Semitism and Racism,* 11–63. Brooklyn: Long Haul.

Pred, Allan Richard, and Michael John Watts. 1992. *Reworking Modernity: Capitalism and Symbolic Discontent.* New Brunswick, N.J.: Rutgers University Press.

Probyn, Elspeth. 1990. "Travels in the Postmodern: Making Sense of the Local." In *Feminism/Postmodernism,* ed. Linda J. Nicholson, 176–89. New York: Routledge.

Proudfoot, Malcolm. 1957. *European Refugees, 1939–1952*. London: Faber and Faber.

Pruitt, Ida. 1979. *Madame Yin: A Memoir of Peking Life*. Stanford: Stanford University Press.

Prunier, Gerard. 1995. *The Rwanda Crisis: History of a Genocide*. New York: Columbia University Press.

Public Enemy. 1988. *It Takes a Nation of Millions to Hold Us Back*. Def Jam Recordings, CBS Records. New York: Columbia Records.

———. 1990. *Fear of a Black Planet*. Def Jam Recordings, CBS Records. New York: Columbia Records.

Rabinow, Paul. 1988. "Beyond Ethnography: Anthropology as Nominalism." *Cultural Anthropology* 3 (4): 355–63.

———. 1989. *French Modern*. Cambridge: MIT Press.

Radhakrishnan, Rajagopalan. 1987. "Ethnic Identity and Post-Structuralist Differance. *Cultural Critique* 6:199–220.

Rashad, Ahmad. 1993. *Hamas: Palestinian Politics with an Islamic Hue*. Occasional Papers Series, no. 2. Annandale, Va.: United Association for Studies and Research.

Rée, Jonathan. 1992. "Internationality." *Radical Philosophy* 60:3–11.

Reed, John. 1984. "Zambian Fiction." In *The Writing of East and Central Africa*, ed. G. D. Killam. London: Heinemann.

"Refugee Interviews." 1988. *Journal of Palestine Studies* 18 (1): 158–71.

Rehse, Helga. 1969. "Euthanasie! Vernichtung unwerten Lebens und Rassenhygiene in Programmschriften vor dem Ersten Weltkrieg." M.D. diss., University of Heidelberg.

Renan, Ernest. 1990. "What Is a Nation?" In *Nation and Narration*, ed. Homi K. Bhabha, 8–22. New York: Routledge.

Reyntjens, Filip. 1994. *L'Afrique des Grands Lacs en arise: Rwanda, Burundi, 1988–1994*. Paris: Karthala.

Roberts, Adam. 1989. "The Palestinians, the Uprising, and International Law." *Journal of Refugee Studies* 2 (1): 26–39.

Roberts, Diane. 1994. *The Myth of Aunt Jemima: Representations of Race and Region*. New York: Routledge.

Roberts, Moss, ed. and trans. 1991. *Three Kingdoms: A Historical Novel*, by Lo, Kuanchung. Berkeley: University of California Press.

Roberts. Sam. 1990. "Low Test Scores Disturb Blacks in South Africa and U.S." *New York Times,* 12 February.

Robertson, Jennifer. 1988. "Furusato Japan: The Culture and Politics of Nostalgia." *Politics, Culture, and Society* 1 (4): 494–518.

———. 1991. *Native and Newcomer: Making and Remaking a Japanese City*. Berkeley: University of California Press.

Rofel, Lisa. 1989. "Hegemony and Productivity: Workers in Post-Mao China." In *Marxism and the Chinese Experience*, ed. Arif Dirlik and Maurice Meisner, 235–52. Armonk, N.Y.: M. E. Sharpe.

Romero, Justo. 1989. "Rocío, Guapa! En Pentecostes, Todos los Caminos Conducen a la Aldea del Rocío." *El País*, 15 May, Barcelona edition, Travel section, 27–30.

Rosaldo, Michelle, and Louise Lamphere, eds. 1974. *Woman, Culture, and Society.* Stanford: Stanford University Press.

Rosaldo, Renato. 1987. "Politics, Patriarchs, and Laughter." *Cultural Critique* 6:65–86.

———. 1988. "Ideology, Place, and People without Culture." *Cultural Anthropology* 3 (1): 77–87.

———. 1989a. *Culture and Truth: The Remaking of Social Analysis.* Boston: Beacon.

———. 1989b. "Imperialist Nostalgia." *Representations* 26:107–22.

Roseberry, William. 1989. *Anthropologies and Histories: Essays in Culture, History, and Political Economy.* New Brunswick, N.J.: Rutgers University Press.

Rothenbuhler, Eric W. 1990. "Communication Is Community (and It Happens All Over the Place)." Iowa City: Department of Communication Studies, University of Iowa.

Rouse, Roger. 1991. "Mexican Migration and the Social Space of Postmodernism." *Diaspora* 1 (1): 8–23.

———. 1994. "Questions of Identity: Reflections on the Cultural Politics of Personhood and Collectivity in Transnational Migration to the United States." Paper presented at Columbia and New York University conference.

Roy, Sara. 1989. "Changing Political Attitudes among Gaza Refugees." *Journal of Palestine Studies* 19 (1): 83–91.

Ruedy, John. 1971. "Dynamics of Land Alienation." In *The Transformation of Palestine,* ed. Ibrahim Abu-Lughod. Chicago: Northwestern University Press.

Ruggie, John Gerard. 1993. "Territoriality and Beyond: Problematizing Modernity in International Relations." *International Organization* 47 (1): 139–74.

Rushdie, Salman. 1989. *The Satanic Verses.* New York: Viking.

———. 1991. *Imaginary Homelands: Essays and Criticism, 1981–1991.* New York: Viking Penguin.

Russell, Margaret. 1992. "Entering Great America: Reflections on Race and the Convergence of Progressive Legal Theory and Practice." *Hastings Law Journal* 43:749–67.

Rutherford, Dorothy Angell. 1984. "Bengalis in America: Relationship, Affect, Person, and Self." Ph.D. diss., Department of Anthropology, American University.

Sabean, David. 1990. *Poverty, Production, and Family in Neckerhausen, 1700–1870.* Cambridge: Cambridge University Press.

Sahliyeh, Emile. 1988. *In Search of Leadership: West Bank Politics since 1967.* Washington, D.C.: Brookings Institution.

———. 1992. "Ethnicity and State-Building: The Case of the Palestinians in the Middle East." In *Ethnicity and the State,* ed. Judith Toland, 177–200. New Brunswick: Transaction.

Said, Edward W. 1978. *Orientalism.* New York: Pantheon.

———. 1979. "Zionism from the Standpoint of Its Victims." *Social Text* 1:7–58.

———. 1983. "Traveling Theory." In *The World, the Text, and the Critic,* 226–47. Cambridge: Harvard University Press.

———. 1986. *After the Last Sky: Palestinian Lives.* New York: Pantheon.

Sale, Kirkpatrick. 1990. "How Paradise Was Lost: What Columbus Discovered." *Nation,* 22 October, 444–46.

Saleh, Samir Abdalla. 1990. "The Effects of Israeli Occupation on the Economy of the West Bank and Gaza Strip." In *Intifada: Palestine at the Crossroads,* ed. Jamal R. Nassar and Roger Heacock, 37–52. New York: Praeger.

San Francisco Chronicle. 1989. "Klan Rumor Helped Ruin Sport Clothing Firm." 22 July.

Saussure, Ferdinand de. 1986. *Course in General Linguistics.* Ed. Charles Bally and Albert Sechehaye. Trans. Roy Harris. La Salle, Ill.: Open Court.

Sayigh, Rosemary. 1977a. "The Palestinian Identity among Camp Residents." *Journal of Palestine Studies* 6 (3): 3–22.

———. 1977b. "Sources of Palestinian Nationalism: A Study of a Palestinian Camp in Lebanon." *Journal of Palestine Studies* 6 (4): 17–40.

———. 1979. *The Palestinians: From Peasants to Revolutionaries.* London: Zed.

Schiff, Benjamin. 1989. "Between Occupier and Occupied: UNRWA in the West Bank and Gaza Strip." *Journal of Palestine Studies* 17 (3): 60–75.

Schiller, Nina Glick. 1994. "Introducing Identities: Global Studies in Culture and Power." *Identities* 1 (1): 1–6.

Schiller, Nina Glick, Linda Basch, and Cristina Blanc-Szanton, eds. 1992. *Towards a Transnational Perspective on Migration: Race, Class, Ethnicity, and Nationalism Reconsidered.* New York: New York Academy of Sciences.

Schmida, Leslie. 1983. *Education in the Middle East.* Washington, D.C.: Amideast.

Schneider, Jo Anne, and Judith Goode. 1989. "Language: Is It Barrier or Bridge?" *Philadelphia Inquirer,* 7 November.

Schrager, Samuel. 1983. "What Is Social in Oral History?" *International Journal of Oral History* 4 (2): 76–98.

Schram, Stuart R. 1969. *The Political Thought of Mao Tse-tung.* New York: Praeger.

Schudson, Michael. 1978. *Discovering the News: A Social History of American Newspapers.* New York: Basic.

Schuster, Ilsa M. Glazer. 1979. *New Women of Lusaka.* Palo Alto, Calif.: Mayfield.

Scott, David. 1992. "Criticism and Culture: Theory and Post-Colonial Claims on Anthropological Disciplinarity." *Critique of Anthropology* 12 (4): 371–94.

Scott, James. 1985. *Weapons of the Weak: Everyday Forms of Peasant Resistance.* New Haven: Yale University Press.

Scott, Joan. 1992. "Multiculturalism and the Politics of Identity." *October,* no. 61 (Summer).

Segev, Tom. 1986. *1949: The First Israelis.* New York: Free Press.

Service, Elman. 1985. *A Century of Controversy: Ethnological Issues from 1860 to 1960.* New York: Academic Press.

Shamir, Shimon. 1980. "West Bank Refugees—between Camp and Society." In

Palestinian Society and Politics, ed. Joel Migdal. Princeton: Princeton University Press.

Shapiro, Michael J. 1991. "Sovereignty and Exchange in the Orders of Modernity." *Alternatives* 16 (4): 447–77.

Shawcross, William. 1989. "A Tourist in the Refugee World." In *Forced Out: The Agony of the Refugee in Our Time,* ed. Carole Kismaric, 28–30. New York: Random House.

Shehadeh, Raja. 1988. *Occupier's Law.* Washington, D.C.: Institute for Palestine Studies.

Shelley, Toby. 1989. "Palestinian Migrant Workers in Israel: From Repression to Rebellion." In *Palestine: Profile of an Occupation,* ed. Khamsin, 32–56. London: Zed.

Shostak, Marjorie. 1981. *Nisa: The Life and Works of a !Kung Woman.* Cambridge: Harvard University Press.

Shoufani, Elias. 1972. "The Fall of a Village." *Journal of Palestine Studies* 1 (4): 108–21.

Sidhu, Gurnam Singh. 1972. "Saga of the American Sikh." *Sikh Sansar* 1 (4): 99–105.

Simpson, John. 1939. *The Refugee Problem: Report of a Survey.* London: Oxford University Press.

Singh, Sardar Puna. 1972. "My Early Years in America," adapted by Jane P. Singh. *Sikh Sansar* 1 (4): 109–10.

Smith, Anthony. 1986. *The Ethnic Origins of Nations.* New York: Basil Blackwell.

Smith, Neil. 1992. "New City New Frontier: Lower East Side as Wild, Wild West." In *Variations on a Theme Park: The New American City and the End of Public Space,* ed. Michael Sorkin, 61–93. New York: Noonday.

Soja, Edward W. 1989. *Postmodern Geographies.* New York: Verso.

Sollors, Werner. 1986. *Beyond Ethnicity: Consent and Descent in American Culture.* New York: Oxford University Press.

Spence, Jonathan D. 1990. *The Search for Modern China.* New York: W. W. Norton.

Spillers, Hortense J. 1987. "Mama's Baby, Papa's Maybe: An American Grammar Book." *Diacritics* 17 (2): 77–80.

Spivak, Gayatri Chakravorty. 1985a. "The Rani of Sirmur." In *Europe and Its Others,* vol. 1, ed. Francis Barker et al., 128–51. Colchester, England: University of Essex.

——. 1985b. "Three Women's Texts and a Critique of Imperialism." *Critical Inquiry* 12 (1): 243–61.

——. 1988a. "Can the Subaltern Speak?" In *Marxism and the Interpretation of Culture,* ed. Cary Nelson and Lawrence Grossberg, 271–313. Chicago: University of Illinois Press.

——. 1988b. "Subaltern Studies: Deconstructing Historiography." In *Selected Subaltern Studies,* ed. Ranajit Guha and Gayatri Chakravorty Spivak, 3–32. New York: Oxford University Press.

Stein, Kenneth. 1984. *The Land Question in Palestine, 1917–1939.* Chapel Hill: University of North Carolina Press.

———. 1991. "The Intifada and the Uprising of 1936–1939: A Comparison of the Palestinian Arab Communities." In *The Intifada,* ed. Robert Freedman. Miami: Florida International University Press.

Stewart, Kathleen. 1988. "Nostalgia — a Polemic." *Cultural Anthropology* 3 (3): 227–41.

Stewart, Susan. 1987. "Ceci Tuera Cela: Graffiti as Crime and Art." In *Life after Postmodernism: Essays on Value and Culture,* ed. John Fekete, 161–80. New York: St. Martin's.

Stocking, George W., Jr. 1982. *Race, Culture, and Evolution: Essays in the History of Anthropology.* Chicago: University of Chicago Press.

Stoessinger, John. 1956. *The Refugee and the World Community.* Minneapolis: University of Minnesota Press.

Stolting, Edward. 1987. "Anthropologie." In *Wissenschaft in Berlin-Disziplinen,* ed. Tilmann Buddensieg, Kurt Düwell, and K. J. Fembach, 128–33. Berlin: Gebr Mann.

Stone, Alec. 1993. "Ratifying Maastricht: France Debates European Union." *French Politics and Society* 11 (1): 70–88.

Stork, Joe. 1988. "The Significance of Stones: Notes from the Seventh Month." *Middle East Report,* no. 154 (September–October).

Suarez, A. J. 1990. "El Ayuntamiento de Almonte se Manifiesta Contra los Ecologistas." *El Correo de Andalucía,* 25 April, 16.

Suleri, Sara. 1992. *The Rhetoric of English India.* Chicago: University of Chicago Press.

Süssmuth, Rita. 1988. "Wandlungen in der Struktur der Erwerbstätigkeit und ihr Einfluss auf das Familienleben." In *Wandel und Kontinuität der Familie in der bundesrepublik Deutschland,* ed. Rosemarie Nave-Herz, 222–34. Stuttgart: Enke.

Swedenburg, Ted. 1988. "The Role of the Palestinian Peasantry in the Great Revolt (1936–1939)." In *Islam, Politics, and Social Movements,* ed. Edmund Burke III and Ira M. Lapidus. Berkeley: University of California Press.

———. 1989. "Plundering the Plunderers: The Politics of Hip-hop." Paper presented at the American Anthropological Association meeting, Washington, D.C.

———. 1990. "The Palestinian Peasant as National Signifier." *Anthropological Quarterly* 18:18–30.

———. 1991. "Popular Memory and the Palestinian National Past." In *Golden Ages, Dark Ages: Imagining the Past in Anthropology and History,* ed. Jay O'Brien and William Roseberry, 152–79. Berkeley: University of California Press.

Taban Lo Liyong. 1976. *Ballads of Underdevelopment.* Nairobi: East Africa Literature Bureau.

Tabori, Paul. 1972. *The Anatomy of Exile: A Semantic and Historical Study.* London: Harrap.

Tamari, Salim. 1988. "What the Uprising Means." *Middle East Report,* no. 152 (May–June).

———. 1990a. "Eyeless in Judea." *Middle East Report,* nos. 164–65 (May–June/July–August).

——. 1990b. "The Uprising's Dilemma: Limited Rebellion and Civil Society." *Middle East Report*, nos. 164–65 (May–June/July–August).

——. 1992. "Left in Limbo: Leninist Heritage and Islamist Challenges." *Middle East Report*, no. 179 (November–December): 16–21.

——. 1994. *The Dispersal and Relocation of the Palestinian Coastal Bourgeoisie, in Population Displacement and Resettlement: Development and Conflict in the Middle East.* Ed. Seteney Shami. Staten Island: Center for Migration Studies.

——. 1995. "Fading Flags: The Crises of Palestinian Legitimacy." *Middle East Report*, nos. 194–95 (May–June/July–August): 10–12.

Tambiah, Stanley J. 1985. *Culture, Thought, and Social Action: An Anthropological Perspective.* Cambridge: Harvard University Press.

Taqqu, Rachelle. 1980. "Peasants into Workmen: Internal Labor Migration and the Arab Village Community under the Mandate." In *Palestinian Society and Politics*, ed. Joel Migdal. Princeton: Princeton University Press.

Taraki, Lisa. 1990. "The Development of Political Consciousness among Palestinians in the Occupied Territories, 1967–1987." In *Intifada: Palestine at the Crossroads*, ed. Jamal R. Nassar and Roger Heacock. New York: Praeger.

Taussig, Michael. 1980. *The Devil and Commodity Fetishism in South America.* Chapel Hill: University of North Carolina Press.

——. 1987. *Shamanism, Colonialism, and the Wild Man: A Study in Terror and Healing.* Chicago: University of Chicago Press.

——. 1993. *Mimesis and Alterity: A Peculiar History of the Senses.* New York: Routledge.

Taylor, F. W. 1911. *The Principles of Scientific Management.* New York: Harper & Bros.

Taylor, Julie. 1982. "The Politics of Aesthetic Debate: The Case of Brazilian Carnival." *Ethnology* 21 (4): 301–12.

Teague, Paul. 1993. "Between Convergence and Divergence: Possibilities for a European Community System of Labour Market Regulation." *International Labour Review* 132 (3): 391–406.

Temple Times. 1988. "Ford Foundation Funds Multi-Ethnic Study," 4 February.

Teveth, Shabtai. 1990. "The Palestine Refugee Problem and Its Origins." *Middle Eastern Studies* 26 (2): 214–48.

Thomas, Keith. 1983. *Man and the Natural World: A History of the Modern Sensibility.* New York: Pantheon.

Thompson, Dorothy. 1938. *Refugees: Anarchy or Organization?* New York: Random House.

Thornton, Robert. 1988. "The Rhetoric of Ethnographic Holism." *Cultural Anthropology* 3 (3): 285–303.

Time. 1990. "America's Changing Colors: What Will the U.S. Look Like When Whites Are No Longer the Majority?" (cover story), 9 April.

Torgovnick, Marianna. 1990. *Gone Primitive: Savage Intellects, Modern Lives.* Chicago: University of Chicago Press.

Trinh, T. Minh-ha. 1989. *Woman, Native, Other: Writing Postcoloniality and Feminism.* Bloomington: Indiana University Press.

Tsing, Anna. 1993. *In the Realm of the Diamond Queen.* Princeton: Princeton University Press.

Read

Tuan, Yi-Fu. 1977. *Space and Place: The Perspective of Experience.* Minneapolis: University of Minnesota Press.

———. 1980. "Uprootedness and Sense of Place." *Landscape* 25:3–8.

Tufte, Edward R. 1983. *The Quantitative Display of Visual Information.* Cheshire, Conn.: Graphics Press.

Turki, Fawaz. 1988. *Soul in Exile.* New York: Monthly Review.

Turner, Fredrick Jackson. 1962. *The Frontier in American History* (1893) 1920. Reprint, New York: Holt, Rinehart and Winston.

Turner, Patricia A. 1993. *I Heard It through the Grapevine: Rumor in African-American Culture.* Berkeley: University of California Press.

98–99 √ Turner, Victor. 1967. *The Forest of Symbols: Aspects of Ndembu Ritual.* Ithaca: Cornell University Press.

———. 1969. *The Ritual Process: Structure and Anti-Structure.* Ithaca: Cornell University Press.

United States Statutes at Large. 1915–1917. Vol. 39, pp. 874–98.

UNRWA. 1987. *What Is UNRWA?* Vienna: UNRWA.

Urla, Jacqueline. 1988. "Ethnic Protest and Social Planning: A Look at Basque Language Revival." *Cultural Anthropology* 3 (4): 379–94.

Urry, John. 1990. *The Tourist Gaze: Travel and Leisure in Contemporary Societies.* Sage: London.

Urwin, Derek W. 1991. *The Community of Europe: A History of European Integration since 1945.* New York: Hangman.

Usher, Graham. 1994. "The Islamic Movement and the Palestinian Authority." *Middle East Report,* no. 189 (July–August): 28–29.

van Binsbergen, Wim. 1981. "The Unit of Study and the Interpretation of Ethnicity." *Journal of Southern African Studies* 8 (1): 51–81.

van der Veer, Peter. 1994. *Religious Nationalism: Hindus and Muslims in India.* Berkeley: University of California Press.

Van Doren, Carl. 1968. *Benjamin Franklin.* 1938. Reprint, New York: Viking.

Verhelst, Thierry. 1990. *No Life without Roots: Culture and Development.* London: Zed.

Vernant, Jacques. 1953. *The Refugee in the Post-War World.* London: George Allen and Unwin.

Wagner, Roy. 1981. *The Invention of Culture.* Chicago: University of Chicago Press.

Wakeman, Frederic, Jr. 1973. *History and Will: Philosophical Perspectives of Mao Tse-tung's Thought.* Berkeley: University of California Press.

———. 1989. "All the Rage in China." *New York Review of Books,* 2 March.

Walder, Andrew. 1986. *Communist Neo-traditionalism.* Berkeley: University of California Press.

Wallace, Michelle. 1990. *Invisibility Blues: From POD to Theory.* London: Verso.

Wallerstein, Immanuel. 1974. *The Modern World-System.* New York: Academic Press.

Watts, Michael J. 1992. "Space for Everything (a Commentary)." *Cultural Anthropology* 7 (1): 115–29.

Weber, Max. 1991. *From Max Weber: Essays in Sociology.* Trans. H. H. Gerth and C. Wright Mills. New York: Routledge.

Webster's New Collegiate Dictionary. 1980. Springfield, Mass.: G. C. Merriam.

Wehler, Hans Ulrich. 1984. "Historiography in Germany Today." In *Observations on "The Spiritual Situation of the Age,"* ed. Jürgen Habermas, 221–62. Cambridge: MIT Press.

Weigall, David, and Peter Stirk, eds. 1992. *The Origins and Development of the European Community.* Leicester, England: Leicester University Press.

Weil, Simone. 1987. *The Need for Roots: Prelude to a Declaration of Duties towards Mankind.* New York: Ark.

West, Cornel. 1989. "Black Culture and Postmodernism." In *Remaking History,* ed. Barbara Kruger and Phil Mariani, 87–96. Dia Art Foundation, Discussions in Contemporary Culture, no. 4. Seattle: Bay Press.

Weston, Kathleen. 1993. "Do Clothes Make the Woman? Gender, Performance Theory, and Lesbian Eroticism." *Genders* 17:1–21.

Willetts, Peter. 1978. *The Non-aligned Movement: The Origins of a Third World Alliance.* New York: Nichols.

Williams, Allan M. 1994. *The European Community: The Contradictions of Integration.* 2d ed. Cambridge, Mass.: Blackwell.

Williams, Angela. 1989. "UNRWA and the Occupied Territories." *Journal of Refugee Studies* 2 (1): 156–62.

Williams, Brackette F. 1990. "Nationalism, Traditionalism, and the Problem of Cultural Inauthenticity." In *Nationalist Ideologies and the Production of National Cultures,* ed. Richard G. Fox, 112–29. American Ethnological Society Monograph Series, no. 2. Washington, D.C.: American Anthropological Association.

Williams, Raymond. 1961. *The Long Revolution.* New York: Columbia University Press.

———. 1973. *The Country and the City.* New York: Oxford University Press.

———. 1977. *Marxism and Literature.* Oxford: Oxford University Press.

———. 1983. *Culture and Society, 1780–1950.* 1958. Reprint, New York: Columbia University Press.

———. 1985a. *The Country and the City.* 1973. Reprint, London: Hogarth.

———. 1985b. *Keywords: Vocabulary of Culture and Society.* Rev. ed. New York: Oxford University Press.

Williamson, Judith. 1986. "Woman Is an Island: Femininity and Colonization." In *Studies in Entertainment: Critical Approaches to Mass Culture.* Bloomington: Indiana University Press.

Wilmsen, Edwin N. 1989. *Land Filled with Flies: A Political Economy of the Kalahari.* Chicago: University of Chicago Press.

Wolf, Eric. 1982. *Europe and the People without History.* Berkeley: University of California Press.

Woolley, Benjamin. 1992. *Virtual Worlds.* Oxford: Basil Blackwell.

Wright, Patrick. 1985. *On Living in an Old Country: The National Past in Contemporary Britain.* London: Verso.

Yahya, Adil. 1990. "The Role of the Refugee Camps." In *Intifada: Palestine at the Crossroads,* ed. Jamal R. Nassar and Roger Heacock. New York: Praeger.

Yanagisako, Sylvia, and Carol Delaney. 1995. *Naturalizing Power: Essays in Feminist Cultural Analysis.* New York: Routledge.

Yang, Mayfair Mei-hui. 1988. "The Modernity of Power in the Chinese Socialist Order." *Cultural Anthropology* 3 (4): 408–27.

Yoneyama, Lisa. 1994. "Taming the Memoryscape: Hiroshima's Urban Renewal." In *Remapping Memory: The Politics of TimeSpace,* ed. Jonathan Boyarin, 99–135. Minneapolis: University of Minnesota Press.

Young, Iris Marion. 1990. "The Ideal of Community and the Politics of Difference." In *Feminism/Postmodernism,* ed. Linda J. Nicholson, 300–323. New York: Routledge.

Zahlenspiegel. 1988. *Gesamtdeutsches Institut für Gesamtdeutsche Aufgaben.* Bonn: Bundesministerium für innerdeutsche Beziehuungen.

Zito, Angela. 1989. "Grand Sacrifice as Text/Performance: Ritual and Writing in Eighteenth Century China." Ph.D. diss., University of Chicago.

Zolberg, Aristide. 1983. "The Formation of New States as a Refugee-Generating Process." In *The Global Refugee Problem,* ed. Gilburt Loescher and John Scanlan. Special Issue of the Annals of the American Academy of Political and Social Science. Beverly Hills: Sage.

Zureik, Elia, Jim Graff, and Farid Ohan. 1990–91. "Two Years of the Intifada: A Statistical Profile of Palestinian Victims." *Third World Quarterly* 12 (3–4): 97–123.

INDEX

CONTRIBUTORS

GEORGE E. BISHARAT is a Professor of Law at Hastings College of the Law in San Francisco. He teaches in the areas of criminal practice and procedure, law and social anthropology, and law in Middle East societies. His study of the impact of Israeli occupation on the Palestinian legal profession of the West Bank is titled *Palestinian Lawyers and Israeli Rule: Law and Disorder in the West Bank*. Currently he is conducting research on the role of right-wing legal foundations in the United States, as part of an international and interdisciplinary study project on lawyers who work for social and political causes.

JOHN BORNEMAN is Assistant Professor of Anthropology at Cornell University, Ithaca, New York. He has published widely on German identities, including *After the Wall: East Meets West in the New Berlin* and *Belonging in the Two Berlins,* and has two forthcoming books: *Settling Accounts: Justice, Violence, and Accountability in Postsocialist States* and *Subversions of International Order: Studies in the Political Anthropology of Culture.* His current project is about the death of the great dictators/father figures of this century.

ROSEMARY J. COOMBE teaches at the Faculty of Law at the University of Toronto. She is the author of the forthcoming book *Cultural Appropriations: Authorship, Alterity, and the Law.* Recent articles on the politics of intellectual property have appeared in *Cultural Anthropology, Social Text, Public Culture,* and the *Yale Journal of Law and Humanities.* A review of the potential for "a critical studies of law" is forthcoming in *Law in the Domains of Culture,* ed. Sarat and Kearns. She serves on the Board of Directors of the Association for Political and Legal Anthropology.

MARY M. CRAIN is Visiting Professor in the Department of Anthropology and Latin American History at the University of Barcelona, Spain. She has carried out fieldwork in Spain (Catalonia and Andalusia) as well as in highland Ecuador and has written extensively on rituals, politics, the media, and social identities. She is coauthor, with Cristina García Rodero, of *España Oculta: Public Celebrations in Spain, 1974–1989* and author of "The Gendering of Ethnicity in the Ecuadorian Andes: Native Womens' Self-Fashioning in the Urban Marketplace," in *Machos, Mistresses, and Madonnas: Contesting the Power of Latin American Gender Imagery,* ed. Marit Melhuus and Kristi Anne Stolen.

JAMES FERGUSON is Associate Professor in the Department of Anthropology at the University of California, Irvine. He is the author of *The Anti-Politics Machine: "De-*

velopment,*" Depoliticization, and Bureaucratic Power in Lesotho.* He has coedited (with Akhil Gupta) the forthcoming *Anthropological Locations: Boundaries and Grounds of a Field Science.* He is currently completing a manuscript on urban-rural relations and conceptions of modernity on the Zambian Copperbelt.

AKHIL GUPTA is Assistant Professor in the Department of Anthropology at Stanford University. His forthcoming book, *Postcolonial Developments: Agriculture in the Making of Modern India,* will be published by Duke University Press. He has coedited (with James Ferguson) the forthcoming *Anthropological Locations: Boundaries and Grounds of a Field Science.* He is currently working on a manuscript in which he ethnographically investigates the state in northern India.

KRISTIN KOPTIUCH is Assistant Professor of Anthropology at Arizona State University West in Phoenix. Her forthcoming book, *A Poetics of Petty Commodity Production in Egypt,* examines the interplay between poetics and the political economy of Egyptian artisans. Another take on her third-worlding project is " 'Cultural Defense' and Criminological Displacements: Gender, Race and (Trans)Nation in the Legal Surveillance of U.S. Diaspora Asians," in *Displacement, Diaspora, and Geographies of Identity,* ed. Smadar Lavie and Ted Swedenburg. She is at work on aspects of third-worlding in the urban culture and social space of Phoenix.

KAREN LEONARD is Professor of Anthropology at the University of California, Irvine. Her most recent book is *Making Ethnic Choices: California's Punjabi Mexican Americans.* She has published extensively on the social history and anthropology of India and on Punjabi Mexican Americans and Asian Americans in California and works on caste, ethnicity, and family and life history. She is currently studying the construction of identity in the diaspora by emigrants from Hyderabad, India, who have settled in Pakistan, Britain, Canada, the United States, Australia, and the Gulf States of the Middle East.

RICHARD MADDOX is Associate Professor of Anthropology and History in the Department of History at Carnegie Mellon University. He is the author of *El Castillo: The Politics of Tradition in an Andalusian Town,* which received the President's Book Award of the Social Science History Association and the Robert E. Park Award of the American Sociological Association. He is currently working on a book titled "The Best of All Possible Islands: Expo '92 Seville and the Politics of Cosmopolitan Liberalism in the New Spain."

LISA MALKKI is Assistant Professor of Anthropology at the University of California, Irvine. She is the author of *Purity and Exile: Violence, Memory, and National Cosmology among Hutu Refugees in Tanzania.* She teaches and writes on nationalism and xenophobia, racism and violence, and internationalism and practices of humanitarianism. She is currently studying the social imagination of the future in the aftermath of genocide among exiles from Rwanda and Burundi.

JOHN DURHAM PETERS is Associate Professor in the Department of Communication Studies at the University of Iowa. His more recent essays have appeared in the *Journal of Communication; Public Culture; Media, Culture, and Society;* and *Critical Studies in Mass Communication*. During a National Endowment for the Humanities fellowship in 1995–96, he completed a book manuscript on the rise of the concept of communication in modern thought.

LISA ROFEL is Assistant Professor of Anthropology at the University of California, Santa Cruz. Her forthcoming book, *Imagining Modernity*, is on modernity and gender in post-Mao China. She is currently studying issues of sexuality, gender, and public culture in China.

Library of Congress Cataloging-in-Publication Data

Gupta, Akhil, 1959–
Culture, power, place : explorations in critical anthropology /
edited by Akhil Gupta and James Ferguson.
p.   cm.
Includes bibliographical references and index.
ISBN 0-8223-1934-9 (cloth : alk. paper). —
ISBN 0-8223-1940-3 (pbk. : alk. paper)
1. Anthropology — Philosophy.   2. Anthropology — Methodology.
3. Geographical perception.   I. Ferguson, James, 1959–   .
II. Title.
GN33.G924   1997
301'.01 — dc21
96-54809
CIP